Taxing Ourselves

Taxing Ourselves

A Citizen's Guide to the Debate over Taxes

third edition

Joel Slemrod
and
Jon Bakija

The MIT Press
Cambridge, Massachusetts
London, England

This book was set in Palatino by Interactive Composition Corporation and was printed and bound in the United States of America.

Library of Congress Cataloging-in-Publication Data

Slemrod, Joel.
  Taxing ourselves : a citizen's guide to the debate over taxes / Joel Slemrod and Jon Bakija.—3rd ed.
    p. cm.
  Subtitle on previous eds.: A citizen's guide to the great debate over tax reform.
  Includes bibliographical references and index.
  ISBN 0-262-19505-4 (hc. : alk. paper)—ISBN 0-262-69302-X (pbk. : alk. paper)
  1. Income tax—United States.   I. Bakija, Jon M.   II. Title.

  HJ4652.S528   2004
  336.2'05—dc22

2003070625

10   9   8   7   6   5   4   3   2

To Ava, who completes me
—JS

To Rebeccah
—JB

Contents

Preface

Albert Einstein is reputed to have said that "the hardest thing in the world to understand is the income tax."[1] But understand it we must because it is a critical part of how government affects the lives of Americans. Unfortunately, though, when tax reform enters the political arena, the subtleties of the key issues are usually lost in self-serving arguments and misleading simplifications. Academic treatments of the subject are of little help to the vast majority of citizens who are unfamiliar with the jargon and methods of economics.

This book is an attempt to bridge the gap between sound bites and treatises. It lays out what is known and not known about how taxes affect the economy, offers guidelines for evaluating tax systems, and provides enough information to evaluate both the current income tax system and the leading proposals to replace or reform it. We have attempted to present this information in a clear, nontechnical way and to avoid misleading the reader by oversimplifying. We do not conclude with our own pet plan for the U.S. tax system, which would require applying both our judgments on the economics of taxation and our values as well. If this book is successful, however, it will provide readers with enough background to make informed judgments about how we should tax ourselves.

We have been gratified by the positive response from readers of the first two editions of *Taxing Ourselves*, especially those who have used this book as a textbook or a supplementary reading in economics, accounting, and law courses. The positive e-mails we've received from citizens who have learned from this citizen's guide have been encouraging as well. At the MIT Press, first Terry Vaughn and then John Covell have been helpful throughout the development process and supportive of our desire to update the book with new editions. This third edition has been extensively revised and reflects the many major changes in tax law that have been enacted through May 2003. It provides new or expanded treatment of issues that have come to dominate the public agenda, including tax cuts, expansions of saving incentives, mitigation of the double taxation of corporate income, the estate tax, corporate tax shelters, and the economic and political consequences of budget deficits. The new edition also reflects the most recent research and data relevant to the debate over taxes. At the same time, it continues to provide a thorough discussion of options for fundamental tax reform.

In the course of writing the three editions of this book, we have assembled an extensive set of data on the historical development of the U.S. tax system. An earlier version of this information was included as an appendix to the second edition of *Taxing Ourselves*. An updated version can now be accessed on the Internet at <http://www.otpr.org>.

We have been fortunate to have at our disposal the resources of the Office of Tax Policy Research (OTPR) at the University of Michigan, where Joel is a professor at the Business School and in the economics department and Jon was a graduate student during the writing of the first edition. Jon has since moved on to the economics department at Williams College, where he is an assistant professor. Jon would also like to thank the Brookings Institution for hosting him during the time he was revising the third edition. We owe a special debt to those colleagues who read and made extensive comments on an early draft of the book—Gerard Brannon, Leonard Burman, Don Fullerton, Louis Kaplow, and three anonymous reviewers. We would also like to thank those who reviewed the first and second editions, especially David Bradford, for their insightful comments and suggestions, many of which we have tried to address in this new edition. Mary Ceccanese, administrative associate at OTPR, typed and reprocessed the entire manuscript (three times!) and has provided encouragement and advice from start to finish. Julie Skelton, Brent Smith, and Monica Young helped to track down information and citations, and Varsha Venkatesh at OTPR was instrumental in updating the second and third editions. Chris Lyddy of the Brookings Institution provided invaluable research assistance as well. Finally, Joel would like to thank Ava and Jonny for providing support and love at home, and Annie, for providing both from her apartment at the University of Michigan. Jon would like to thank Rebeccah, Miriam, and his parents for their love, support, and understanding as well.

Taxing Ourselves

1 Introduction

For at least the last quarter of a century, since the beginning of the presidency of Ronald Reagan, tax policy has thoroughly dominated economic policy in the United States. No other economic issue (and perhaps no issue at all) more clearly defines the differences between the two major political parties. In terms of dollar magnitude, the most significant laws enacted during each presidency since then have been tax bills. A large tax cut in 1981 was followed in 1986 by perhaps the most ambitious tax reform in history, which significantly broadened the tax base by removing many deductions and loopholes in exchange for lower tax rates. Acts in 1990 and 1993 raised rates on upper-income taxpayers in an effort to reduce budget deficits, and in 1997 new legislation introduced or expanded a wide variety of small, targeted tax cuts. By the mid-1990s, a growing chorus of politicians and experts was calling for a fundamental overhaul—even complete abolition of the income tax and the Internal Revenue Service. Proposals to replace the income tax with a "flat tax" or a national sales tax began to appear in Congress and presidential primaries and gained unprecedented public attention. Then the presidency of George W. Bush took Reagan's approach a step further by enacting large tax cuts in 2001 and again in 2003, each of which made significant changes in the design of the tax system.

Meanwhile, talk of a fundamental overhaul continued, and tax experts speculated about what the recent changes augured for the prospects of sweeping reform. Bruce Bartlett of the National Center for Policy Analysis conjectured that that the tax changes of 2001 and 2003 were part of a long-term strategy to move the tax system toward something like the "flat tax" in gradual steps.[1] Len Burman of the Urban Institute offered the less sanguine opinion that the tax changes were part of a strategy to make the income tax such a mess that it would "collapse under its own weight."[2] Others argued that a truly fundamental tax reform would involve such difficult and politically unpopular trade-offs (and inevitably create winners and losers) that it might need to be accompanied by a significant tax cut as a sweetener. By giving away the tax cut before the reform and by adding ever more special preferences to the tax code, which develop their own constituencies, the prospects for anything deserving of the label "fundamental reform" might have grown dimmer.

Why the tax system attracts all this attention is no mystery. It is the aspect of government that directly affects more people than any other. Although tax cuts and tax reform are appealing to many people, Americans also have a right to be apprehensive about big changes in the tax system. Some are concerned that tax cuts just presage big budget deficits and trade better times now for much higher taxes, or even a financial crisis, later. Others are concerned that fundamental tax reform would trade the deductions and credits they rely on for lower tax rates and that rates would soon afterward climb back up to where they were, leaving them worse off. In both cases, some people worry that big changes in the distribution of the tax burden will eventually shift more of it their way. Despite these concerns, there's plenty of frustration with the existing tax system and little doubt that we ought to be able to do better.

Complaints about the Current Tax System

The most common complaint about taxes is straightforward enough: they are too high. To some degree, this complaint just reflects self-interest; no one likes to pay taxes, just as no one enjoys paying utility bills. We all benefit in some way, however, from the government activities that those taxes finance. As U.S. Supreme Court Chief Justice Oliver Wendell Holmes, Jr., once noted, "Taxes are what we pay for civilized society." Unless the government cuts back on its expenditures, the alternative to taxes is to run large budget deficits, financed either by borrowing or by printing money. This deficit strategy runs the risk of causing high interest rates and high inflation, hurting private investment, and damaging our long-term prosperity.

Dissatisfaction with the overall level of taxes also arises from a deep-seated opposition to allowing government to play an active role in society or from a belief that the government is wasting money. Many voters want to see a smaller government, with a correspondingly smaller tax bill.[3] Such questions are naturally controversial and difficult to resolve. But even agreement on how big government should be—and therefore on how much tax money needs to be collected—would not resolve *how* those taxes should be raised. Similarly, people who disagree vehemently about the proper size of government might well find agreement on how our tax system ought to be designed. The *design* of the tax system generally gets short shrift in a political debate dominated by differences over the *level* of taxes, but it too is a crucially important issue.

Aside from the level of taxes, the major complaints about our current tax system are that it is too complicated and difficult to enforce, that it is excessively harmful to the economy, and that it is unfair. What is the basis for these concerns?

It Is Too Complicated

One of the most common grievances taxpayers have with the design of the U.S. tax system is that it is too complicated. For many, complying with our labyrinthine tax regulations is frustrating, costly, and intrusive. Literally billions of hours are spent every year in the United States on fundamentally unproductive tax-related activities such as record-keeping, wading through instructions, hunting for deductions and credits, and arranging personal financial affairs to take advantage of tax preferences.

Of course, the taxpaying process is not difficult for everyone. Millions of low-income households need not submit a return at all. Of the 130 million taxpayers who do file, 17 percent are able to use the very simple form 1040EZ, and 22 percent use the fairly straightforward 1040A.[4] All in all, survey evidence indicates that 45 percent of all taxpayers spend fewer than 10 hours per year on their taxes.[5] But for businesses and individuals with more complicated finances, the burden of compliance can be onerous indeed.

The cost of this complexity is staggering. In total, individual taxpayers spend as much as 3 *billion* hours of their own time on tax matters, or about 27 hours per taxpayer on average.[6] That is the equivalent of over one-and-a-half million full-time (but hidden and unpaid) IRS employees! Many buy books or computer software programs such as TurboTax to help them through tax season. On top of that, over half of all individual taxpayers purchase professional assistance from an accountant, a lawyer, or another adviser to help prepare their tax returns.[7] Businesses also face a heavy compliance burden, with a typical Fortune 500 firm spending $4.6 million per year on tax matters. The total cost of collecting income taxes, including the value of those billions of hours that taxpayers could have put to better use, is probably $110 billion per year or more, which amounts to about 10 cents for every dollar of revenue raised.

It Is Difficult and Sometimes Intrusive to Enforce

The IRS budget for 2002 was $9.5 billion.[8] In a single year, the IRS processes over 200 million returns, including about 130 million individual returns. It audits or "examines" about 800,000 tax returns and additionally sends 3.5 million computer-generated notices to taxpayers who are suspected of having reported incorrect tax liabilities. The IRS compares data from 1.4 billion documents—such as information reports from banks, stockbrokers, and mortgage lenders—to the numbers taxpayers report on their returns.[9]

Despite the significant expenditures on IRS enforcement, the massive compliance costs borne by the public, and the miseries suffered by those who are investigated by the IRS, a great deal of cheating on taxes still occurs. Such things are hard to measure accurately, but the most recent estimate by the IRS suggests that about 18 percent of personal and corporate income tax liability is not paid due to tax evasion, which would amount to $223 billion in 2002.[10] Other things being equal, this means higher tax rates and a heavier burden for the many people who are honest or who have few opportunities to cheat.

The flip side of tax evasion is that the IRS has sometimes used heavy-handed tactics to enforce the tax law. Televised congressional hearings in 1997 and 1998 highlighted cases where the IRS appeared to overstep its bounds and led to new legislation in 1998 that set up an oversight board for the IRS and shifted the burden of proof in a tax court case to the IRS, among other changes. Since then, the IRS has made progress in modernizing its operations, improving taxpayer service, and burnishing its public image. However, abundant evidence shows that this progress has been accompanied by a dramatic decline in the amount of auditing and enforcement activity undertaken by the IRS, raising concerns of a major adverse impact on tax compliance.[11] Recently, the pendulum of tax enforcement appears to have begun swinging in the other direction. Spurred by highly publicized tax shelter abuses by companies such as Enron and prominent executives, in 2003 the Bush administration proposed to give the IRS a budget increase (to $10.4 billion in 2004), including some funding for initiatives to improve enforcement of tax compliance for high-income taxpayers and businesses.[12]

It Is Bad for the Economy

Political debates often revolve around how taxes affect the economy. Proponents of tax reform or tax cuts almost always trumpet the economic benefits that they expect to result from their changes. Lately, in a time of recession, political rhetoric has focused on whether a tax cut will get a temporarily sluggish economy to recover more quickly. Other times, the focus is on how the design of the tax system affects long-term economic prosperity.

The sheer size of taxes—in 2002, federal taxes were $1.9 trillion, or 18.2 percent of the gross domestic product, while state and local taxes took up another 9.6 percent—suggests that they can have an important effect on the way the U.S. economy operates. But beyond the magnitude of tax collections, taxes affect the terms of almost every economic decision that an individual or a company makes. Taxes affect the rewards obtained from saving, working hard, taking a second job, and investing in education or training. The income tax changes how much it costs to contribute to charity, buy a home, or put children in daycare. Business decisions such as whether and how much to invest in a new technology or whether to locate a factory in the United States or Mexico can hinge on the tax consequences of the action. Because it alters the *incentives* associated with all these and other decisions, the tax system can affect the *actions* people and businesses take.

Some critics of the current income tax charge that high tax rates on the wealthy discourage the hard work, innovation, and entrepreneurship necessary for a vibrant economy. Others stress that the tax system inordinately penalizes saving and investment, which are essential for maintaining and improving the country's long-run standard of living, and that it is at least partly responsible for a U.S. national saving rate that is low by both international and historical standards. Another grievance is that the preferences and penalties that are littered throughout the individual and corporate tax codes can significantly distort economic choices. By capriciously changing the relative costs and benefits of various activities and investments from what they would be in the free market, goes this argument, the tax system causes us to channel our resources to the wrong places, hampering the efficiency of the economy and shackling long-term growth prospects.

It Is Unfair

Americans are understandably divided in their opinions on the fairness of the tax system. In response to a February-March 2003 poll sponsored by National Public Radio, the Kaiser Family Foundation, and Harvard's Kennedy School of Government, 4 percent said the federal tax system was "very fair," 47 percent called it "moderately fair," 32 percent said it was "not too fair," and 16 percent felt that it was "not fair at all."[13]

What is it about taxes that people think is either fair or unfair? To be sure, people disagree about how the burden should be shared across families of different levels of affluence. The current personal income tax is "progressive," meaning that higher-income people typically pay a larger percentage of their incomes in taxes than do those with lower incomes. For some, a "fair" tax system means maintaining this progressivity and perhaps increasing the burden on those with high incomes. But others dismiss this as "soaking the rich" or "class warfare" and would prefer a less progressive system. Not surprisingly, people's views about whether the tax system is fair are strongly influenced by how hard the tax system hits their own families.

Even among families at the same level of affluence, the tax burden can differ widely depending on whether family members are married, how many dependent children they have, how much they give to charity, whether they own or rent housing, and whether their income is mostly from wages or salaries or from capital gains. Whether these and other characteristics and choices should affect one's tax burden is a contentious and often divisive issue and raises fundamental questions about the role of government in favoring or penalizing particular types of people and choices.

Finally, a broadly held perception claims that those with good lobbyists, lawyers, and accountants are able to manipulate the tax code and take advantage of numerous loopholes and preferences to avoid paying their "fair share" of the tax burden. Such beliefs may lead to support for a streamlined tax system that eliminates opportunities for tax avoidance or for a more effective system of enforcement that prevents the tax burden from being shifted onto those taxpayers who do not have the opportunity or inclination to escape them.

A Different Way to Tax

One way to deal with these problems is to start over. Indeed, several congressional leaders and Republican presidential candidates, as well as some prominent economists, have advocated *abolishing* the existing personal and corporate income tax systems and replacing them with something quite different. Consider, for example, this statement from recently retired House Ways and Means Committee chair Bill Archer (R-TX): "We've got to tear the income-tax system out by its roots. We have to remove the Internal Revenue Service from the lives of Americans totally."[14] Or this from one-time Republican presidential hopeful Steve Forbes: "With a beast like this, the only thing to do is kill it."[15]

Representative Archer, Forbes, and others would like to replace the personal and corporate income taxes entirely with some form of tax on consumption—that is, on the portion of income that people spend rather than save. Most attention has focused on two forms of consumption tax, a national retail sales tax and a so-called flat tax.

The more familiar of the two is the retail sales tax, since it is already used by all but five states. Proposals for such a tax have been presented in Congress in recent years by Representatives John Linder (R-GA), Collin Peterson (D-MN), and Billy Tauzin (R-LA), among others. Another adherent of this approach is a former Republican presidential candidate, Senator Richard Lugar, who supported a plan to replace the corporate and personal income taxes with a 17 percent national retail sales tax.[16] Lugar argued that "the national sales tax would allow for the dismantling of the current IRS and the intrusive, inefficient, and costly enforcement of the current tax code" and that under it, "Americans [would] enjoy a capital formation boom [with] . . . increased productivity, higher paying jobs, and new investment from around the world attracted by a policy of no income taxes."[17]

Another alternative to the income tax is the "flat tax" developed by Robert Hall of Stanford University and Alvin Rabushka of the Hoover Institution. Steve Forbes championed a 17 percent flat tax in his runs at the Republican presidential sweepstakes in early 1996 and 2000, and similar proposals have been put forward in Congress by Senator Richard Shelby (R-AL) and former Representative and former House majority leader Richard Armey (R-TX). Under the flat tax, most individuals would still have to file a tax return, but it would differ from the current system on three key dimensions. First, the tax base would include wages, salaries, and pension benefits, but all other kinds of income, such as interest, dividends, and capital gains, would be completely excluded from taxation at the personal level. Second, the personal tax would feature an exempt level of income, based on family size, but all income above that level would be subject to a single, "flat," rate of tax. Finally, tax returns would allow no itemized deductions or other special preferences of any kind—no deductions for mortgage interest or charitable contributions, no child care or Hope Scholarship Credit. As a result of this clean tax base, proponents emphasize, the entire personal flat tax form could be made to fit on a postcard. As we explain in chapter 7, although it looks like a simpler version of our current tax system, the flat tax is not an income tax at all. Instead, it is actually a kind of consumption tax and a close relative of a retail sales tax or a European-style value added tax (VAT).

Advocates of the flat tax express great confidence in its potential benefits. Hall and Rabushka promise their flat tax "would give an enormous boost to the U.S. economy by dramatically improving incentives to work, save, invest, and take entrepreneurial risks"[18] and assert that it is "fair to ordinary Americans because it would provide a tax-free allowance."[19] Finally, they pledge that the flat tax "would save taxpayers hundreds of billions in direct and indirect compliance costs."[20] In short, they and the other supporters of the flat tax argue that it would address the major complaints made about today's tax system.

A few years ago Representatives Armey and Tauzin made a "Scrap the Code" national tax reform tour, which they kicked off by throwing pieces of the tax code into the trash, literally. Armey touted the flat tax and drew applause from the crowds when he showed his mock-up of a postcard-size tax return, but inevitably Tauzin brought down the house when he unveiled his *blank* tax return, representing the fact that a national retail sales tax would require no individual tax returns at all.

Objections to Radical Reform

Although almost everyone criticizes some aspects of the U.S. tax system, not everyone favors a complete overhaul. Back in 1984, President Reagan's Treasury Department studied the replacement of the income tax with some kind of consumption tax but ultimately rejected a consumption tax on the grounds that the American people would perceive it as unfair.[21] A survey of the members of the National Tax Association, the leading professional group of tax experts from academia, govern-ment, and business, suggests that they, too, are skeptical. Just 36 percent favored replacing "much or all" of the current income tax with a VAT, while 80 percent expressed support for retaining a personal income tax with rates that rise with income.[22] Although in 1998 the House of Repre-sentatives passed the Tax Code Termination Act to abolish the current system (without specifying what would replace it), the Senate did not, and Senate Finance Committee chair William Roth (R-DE) claimed that it would "create pandemonium in the marketplace."[23]

The most commonly expressed objection to radical reform proposals is that the average taxpayer would end up with the short end of the stick. Robert McIntyre of Citizens for Tax Justice says, "There is little or no disagreement among serious analysts that replacing the current, progressive income tax with a flat-rate tax would dramatically shift the tax burden away from the wealthy—and onto the middle class and the poor."[24] Unless a national sales tax is accompanied by some difficult-to-implement form of relief, it could shift even more of the tax burden toward low-income families.

Are we willing to accept a big change in who bears the tax burden in exchange for the promised benefits of the reforms? The public appears to be ambivalent. Surveys consistently find that solid majorities of the public want taxes on upper-income people to go up instead of down. On the other hand, polls generally find that support for a flat tax is close to that for a progressive income tax and which is favored depends on how the question is asked. A crucial factor is that most Americans ap-parently believe (incorrectly) that the current distribution of income tax burdens is not progressive, perhaps because they think loopholes for the rich are pervasive. Survey evidence also makes clear that most peo-ple know relatively little about the current tax system or proposals for reform, so in the event of a serious reform effort, public opinion may change as people learn more about the details.[25]

A second common critique of the radical reform proposals is that their promised economic and simplification benefits are overstated. Although proponents have promoted their potential for improving long-run economic growth and simplifying the taxpaying process, the degree to which they would accomplish these goals is subject to much debate among economists. To be sure, there is far less certainty about the economic consequences of tax reform than advocates usually admit.

In contrast, a flat tax is widely acknowledged to be significantly simpler than the current system. But much of the simplification that the flat tax promises comes at the cost of forgoing progressivity and the kind of personalized tax system that many Americans appear to favor. And while a national retail sales tax may appear simple on its surface, many experts are concerned that it would be impossible to administer equitably at the rates necessary to replace the income tax—rates probably in excess of 30 percent.

Finally, some skeptics are afraid that we're opening quite a can of worms. A free-for-all over tax policy, with special interests thrown into the mix, could conceivably end up producing legislation that is even more of a mess than what we have now. Veterans of the perpetual struggle over taxes remember a similar effort at reform under President Ford in the mid-1970s that ended up adding so many complications and preferences to the code that it was nicknamed "the Tax Practitioners Act of 1976." Similarly, some critics and advocates of reform are united by the concern that once we overhaul the system it will inevitably and gradually get messed up again. They argue that any one-time tax change ought to be accompanied by reforms in the policy process itself to prevent a gradual drift back to complexity, inefficiency, and unfairness.

Changes in the Context of the Current System

While opinions differ on the political likelihood of abolishing the income tax and starting over from scratch, don't hold your breath. In the meantime, big—if not radical—changes in the tax system are being debated and enacted all the time. Politicians are constantly fighting over and changing things like income tax rates, the tax treatment of capital gains, saving incentives, and special deductions and credits for all manner of politically favored items. These debates may not capture the imagination in the same way that throwing the whole system out and starting over might, but the resulting changes in the tax code can have important implications for the economy and for the fairness and complexity of the tax system. Indeed, it should be possible to significantly reform the income tax in a way that makes it considerably simpler, better for the economy, and arguably fairer without running afoul of the objections to more radical reforms raised above and without necessarily throwing the existing system out altogether.

The Need for Objective Analysis

The debate over tax policy shows no sign of letting up. Sorting out the claims and counterclaims made for reform proposals is a difficult task even for the most informed and interested citizens who must wade through a sea of self-serving arguments. Those groups that have the most to gain or lose from tax reform produce arguments that buttress their point of view. They don't trumpet the money they (or their constituencies) stand to make but emphasize growth, productivity, and achieving the American dream. The potential losers seldom say they are opposing a policy simply because it skins their own hides but couch their argument in terms of how the national interest is hurt, how many jobs will be lost, and how unfair it is.

Making an intelligent judgment about tax policy requires seeing through the self-serving arguments to a clear understanding of the issues involved. Unfortunately, judgments and policy decisions must be made without the luxury of having definitive answers to many of the critical questions. For example, whether cutting taxes by 10 percent will cause the gross domestic product to rise by 2 percent, fall by 2 percent, or have no effect at all will never be definitely known, although economists can shed light on such questions and rule out certain outlandish claims. Some issues, such as what is "fair," ultimately rely on individual value judgments.

What's Ahead

This book offers a guide to the never-ending debate over tax policy and is designed to help the concerned citizen come to informed judgments. Our goal is to cut through the academic jargon, the "Washington-speak," and the self-serving arguments to explore the fundamental choices and questions inherent in tax policymaking. We have no tax plan of our own to push.

Chapter 2 offers some historical and international perspectives on taxation in the United States and a concise description of the current federal tax system. Chapters 3 through 5 examine the basic criteria by which tax policy should be judged—how fairly it assigns tax burdens, whether it promotes or inhibits growth and prosperity, and whether it is simple and enforceable. As we lay out the basic principles underlying these criteria, we also explore the controversies and difficulties that arise. Moreover, these chapters examine evidence on crucial questions, such as how the burden of our tax system is distributed and what is known about the economic effects of taxation. Such evidence is critical for evaluating the claims of various policy proposals and for weighing the inevitable trade-offs among criteria in any tax system. Chapter 6 goes over the key elements of many proposals for fundamental tax reform—a clean base (removal of all the deductions and exceptions of the current code), a single rate, and a consumption rather than an income base. Although reform proposals often contain more than one of these elements, they are indeed separable issues; in principle, we could adopt any combination of these elements without accepting the whole package. We'll explore the importance and implications of each of these elements in detail. Chapter 7 provides a thorough examination of specific proposals to replace the income tax with a consumption tax. Chapter 8 addresses a variety of major policy changes that would stay within the general framework of the current tax system. Chapter 9 closes with a brief voter's guide to tax policy that summarizes some essential points to keep in mind when considering the debate over how we should tax ourselves.

2

An Overview of the U.S.
Tax System

Before addressing how we *should* tax ourselves, it will be useful to consider the history and basic features of the system we already have. First, we take a glance at the overall tax picture for the United States, surveying how much revenue governments at all levels take in, what kinds of taxes they use, and how our tax system compares to other countries. Next, we offer a bit of historical background on American taxation to put the current debates in perspective. Finally, we provide an overview of how the major taxes used by the federal government currently work, with a particular emphasis on income taxes.

How Governments in the United States Get Their Money

Table 2.1 lists the major taxes used by federal, state, and local governments in the United States, illustrating the relative importance of each. Altogether, governments in our country raised $2.9 *trillion* in taxes and other revenues during 2002. One way to put such a number in perspective is to compare it with the size of the economy, which is usually represented by the gross domestic product (GDP). GDP is a measure of the total dollar value of all goods and services produced within the United States in a single year. In 2002, total federal, state, and local government revenues amounted to 27.8 percent of our $10.4 trillion GDP. Federal revenues were 18.2 percent of GDP, while state and local revenues accounted for 9.6 percent of GDP.[1]

The biggest source of federal revenue is the personal income tax. It raised $838 billion in 2002, accounting for 44 percent of all federal revenues. Corporate income taxes took in another $180 billion. Together, the personal and corporate income taxes accounted for just more than half of all federal revenues in 2002. Because a vast amount of money is

Table 2.1
Source of revenue for U.S. governments, 2002

	Billions of 2002 dollars	Percentage of revenues at that level of government	Percentage of gross domestic product
Total federal revenues	1,901	100.0	18.2
Personal income tax	838	44.1	8.0
Contributions for social insurance	738	38.8	7.1
Corporate income tax	180	9.5	1.7
Excise taxes and customs duties	90	4.7	0.9
Estate and gift taxes	26	1.3	0.2
Other federal revenues	30	1.6	0.3
Total state and local revenues	1,007	100.0	9.6
Sales taxes	334	33.1	3.2
Property taxes	268	26.6	2.6
Personal income taxes	201	19.9	1.9
Corporate income taxes	34	3.3	0.3
Contributions for social insurance	9	0.9	0.1
Estate and gift taxes	7	0.7	0.1
Other state and local revenues	154	15.3	1.5
Total federal, state, and local revenues	2,908	100.0	27.8

Source: U.S. Bureau of Economic Analysis (2003).

raised by these two taxes, clearly a lot is at stake if we try to replace them entirely, as some advocates of fundamental tax reform hope to do.

The other major source of federal revenue, accounting for 39 percent of the total, is "contributions for social insurance." The Social Security payroll tax, which finances retirement and health benefits (Medicare) for the elderly and disabled, accounts for 91 percent of this total. [2] Taxes for unemployment insurance and a few other smaller programs make up the rest.

A handful of other items round out the federal list. Excise taxes on commodities such as cigarettes, alcohol, and gasoline, together with customs duties on imported goods, produced 4.7 percent of federal revenues in 2002. Estate and gift taxation contributed another 1.3 percent of federal revenues.

State and local governments rely heavily on taxes not levied by the federal government—sales and property taxes. In 2001, retail sales taxes accounted for 33 percent of state and local revenues, while property taxes provided another 27 percent. Income taxation plays a smaller role for states and localities; 20 percent of their revenues came from personal income taxes, while just 3 percent came from corporate income taxes.

International Comparisons

Table 2.2 shows how our nation's tax system stacks up against those of other economically advanced countries. Relative to the size of our economy, the United States has lower taxes than most comparable countries. In 1999, before the recent round of major tax cuts, the United States already had the fourth-lowest tax-to-GDP ratio of the 30 countries in the Organisation for Economic Co-operation and Development (OECD), a group of industrialized nations from North America, Europe, and the Pacific. On average, OECD countries raised taxes equal to 37.1 percent of their GDPs in 1999, compared to 28.9 percent for the United States (the definition of "taxes" used by the OECD is slightly less inclusive than the definition of "revenues" discussed above).[3] At the low end, Japan was just slightly below the U.S. level, with taxes equal to 26.1 percent of GDP. At the high end, Sweden had taxes amounting to a whopping 52.0 percent of GDP.

What sets the United States apart from most other advanced nations is not how much we raise through either income taxes or social insurance taxes; for these two types of tax, our tax-to-GDP ratio is close to the OECD mean. The big difference is in consumption taxes; we collect just 4.2 percent of GDP in consumption taxes compared to an 11.1 percent OECD average. Moreover, the United States is unusual in the kinds of consumption taxes it uses. Retail sales taxes are rare outside the United States. The value added tax (VAT), a close cousin of both the flat tax and retail sales tax discussed at length in chapter 7, is the most common variety of consumption tax in the rest of the world. By 1999, all OECD nations except the United States had adopted VATs, which on average raised 6.4 percent of GDP.

Completely replacing personal and corporate income taxation with a consumption tax, as some hope to do in the United States, would be an unprecedented move among major industrialized nations. All of the OECD countries have significant income taxes *in addition to* their consumption taxes. However, the amount of revenue relative to GDP that

Table 2.2
International comparison of taxes as a percentage of gross domestic product, 1999

	United States	OECD average[a]	Japan	United Kingdom	Canada	Germany	Sweden
Total taxes	**28.9**	**37.1**	**26.1**	**36.4**	**35.9**	**37.8**	**52.0**
Income taxes	14.2	13.3	8.2	14.1	17.7	11.3	21.6
Personal income taxes	11.8	10.1	4.8	10.4	13.7	9.5	18.5
Corporate income taxes	2.4	3.3	3.4	3.7	3.6	1.8	3.1
Consumption taxes[b]	4.2	11.1	4.7	11.1	8.8	10.2	10.9
Value-added taxes	—	6.4	2.5	6.8	2.6	7.0	7.1
Sales taxes	2.2	0.3	—	—	2.6	—	—
Social insurance taxes	6.9	9.4	9.7	6.3	4.9	14.9	13.2
Other taxes	3.6	3.3	3.5	4.8	4.5	1.5	6.3

Source: OECD (2001, 2003).
Notes: Dash indicates a tax is not used by the country in question. Includes taxes at all levels of government.
a. Unweighted average of all 30 nations in the Organisation for Economic Co-operation and Development.
b. Includes value added taxes, sales taxes, excise taxes, import and customs duties, and other consumption taxes.

would be required to replace income taxation in the United States would not be that much larger than what is raised by value added taxes already used in some other countries. Retail sales taxes of that size, though, have never been attempted in any of these nations; we discuss why in chapter 7.

Historical Perspectives on the U.S. Tax System

The Overall Level of Taxes

Figure 2.1 illustrates how government revenues have changed relative to the size of the economy in the United States since 1900. Perhaps the most striking feature is the tremendous growth in the role of the federal government in the first half of the twentieth century. Federal taxes rose from 3.1 percent of GDP in 1900 to 19.7 percent by 1943. World War II was clearly the critical juncture, although the New Deal years of the 1930s were also important. Not only did federal revenues grow significantly relative to GDP during the 1930s, but also many programs that

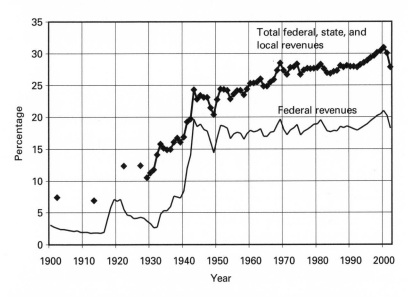

Figure 2.1
Government revenues in the United States as a percentage of GDP, 1900–2002
Sources: U.S. Bureau of the Census (1975); U.S. Bureau of Economic Analysis (2003).
Note: Before 1929, data on state and local revenues are available only for selected years.

would require high taxes in later years, such as the Social Security system, were born in this period.

Equally striking, however, is the fairly flat level of federal taxes relative to GDP in the second half of the twentieth century. Since 1950, federal taxes have averaged 18.6 percent of GDP and seldom strayed far from that level. For all the talk of the expanding federal government and attempts to downsize it, taxes have not changed greatly as a share of the economy for half a century. In the 1990s, though, something of an upward revenue trend did reemerge. This was due primarily to an unexpected, and apparently temporary, surge in federal income tax revenues that began in the late 1990s, which had more to do with economic conditions than any changes in tax law. We explore this further below when we look at the income tax. By 2002, due to tax cuts and a recession, federal taxes were back down to 18.2 percent of GDP.

State and local revenues have followed a somewhat more complicated pattern. In the early part of the twentieth century, state and local governments raised and spent more money than the federal government. At their peak in 1932, they were raising taxes equal to 11.4 percent of GDP, compared to only 2.7 percent at the federal level. As the federal role expanded, state and local revenues shrank dramatically relative to GDP, hitting a low of just 4.3 percent by 1944. They then grew back toward their former prominence throughout the 1950s and 1960s and reached 9.3 percent of GDP by 1970. Since then, they have consistently remained in the 9 to 10 percent range.

Putting federal, state, and local government revenues together, the story is as follows. Revenues grew enormously from 7 percent of GDP at the beginning of the twentieth century to 24 percent by the middle of World War II and then continued growing at a slower pace to 28.5 percent of GDP by 1969. They experienced relatively little net change throughout the 1970s and 1980s, increased a bit during the 1990s, and then came back down in the early 2000s. This left taxes at 27.8 percent of GDP by 2002. The bottom line is that despite a massive increase in taxes over the last century as a whole, there's been relatively little net change in the share of national income that goes to taxes at all levels of government for about the last 35 years. Of course, a fixed share of GDP can buy a great deal more in real terms today than it could three or five decades ago, due to the growth of the economy. Nevertheless, the total tax burden has been fairly stable relative to our incomes for a long time.

History of the U.S. Personal Income Tax

Our nation's first income tax was a temporary emergency measure used during the Civil War; it was enacted in 1861 and expired in 1871. In the late 1800s and early 1900s, popular opposition began to mount against what were then the major sources of federal revenues: tariffs, excise taxes, and property taxes. Some viewed a personal income tax as an appealing alternative because it could be made progressive, imposing a heavier proportional burden on the rich than on the poor. Congress first enacted income taxation on a permanent basis in 1894, but the Supreme Court declared it unconstitutional one year later.[4] This obstacle to an income tax was eliminated by the Sixteenth Amendment to the U.S. Constitution, which was ratified in February 1913. President Woodrow Wilson signed the modern personal income tax into law shortly thereafter in October 1913.[5]

The basic structure of the 1913 personal income tax was similar to today's, with some important differences. It had graduated rates, like the current system, but they ranged only from 1 to 7 percent. Many of today's most important deductions and exclusions were already there in 1913, including the deductions for home mortgage interest, the deduction for tax payments to state and local governments, and the exclusion of interest on state and local bonds. Deductions for charitable contributions were added just four years later in 1917.[6] The biggest difference from today was that personal exemptions were so large relative to typical incomes of the day that only those with extremely high incomes had to pay any income tax at all. In 1914, the total number of personal tax returns filed amounted to less than 0.5 percent of the total U.S. population;[7] these days the figure is about 47 percent.

Figure 2.2 illustrates how two aspects of the U.S. personal income tax—revenues as a percentage of GDP and the tax rate in the top bracket—have changed since 1913. The historical revenue pattern for the personal income tax is similar to that for the overall federal government. Until World War II, receipts were quite small, staying well below 2 percent of GDP. This was true even when top rates were very high, sometimes exceeding 70 percent, because these rates continued to apply to only a very small number of high-income people. The number of returns filed never exceeded 7 percent of the total population between 1913 and 1939.

Because of the need for a lot of revenue fast, personal income taxation was expanded dramatically during World War II. The exempt level of

(a) Personal income tax revenues as a percentage of GDP

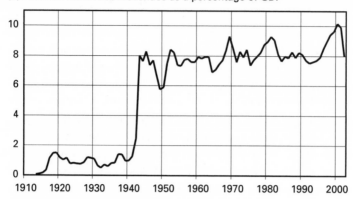

(b) Marginal tax rate in top bracket (percentage)

Figure 2.2
The U.S. personal income tax: Revenues and top rate, 1913–2002
Sources: U.S. Bureau of the Census (1975); U.S. Bureau of Economic Analysis (2003); IRS, *Statistics of Income Bulletin* (Winter 2002–2003, 224–225).

income was reduced greatly, transforming what had been a "class tax" into a "mass tax." In the five years between 1939 and 1944 alone, personal income tax revenues surged from 1 percent to 8 percent of GDP, and the number of returns filed rose sharply from 6 percent of the population to 34 percent. To facilitate the collection of taxes from so many people, employer withholding and remitting of income taxes on wages and salaries were introduced in 1943.

Ever since rising to 8 percent of GDP during World War II, the personal income tax has generally stayed close to that level. There was something of a surge in income tax revenues during the 1990s, and they peaked at 10.2 percent of GDP in 2000 before beginning to fall again. Legislated hikes in federal income tax rates on high-income taxpayers, which became effective in 1991 and 1993, played some role in this recent increase. But for the most part, the surge was driven by the booming economy and stock market and especially by a tremendous jump in the incomes of the most affluent families. When the share of the nation's income that goes to people who are already in high-income tax brackets experiences a big increase, tax revenues relative to GDP rise automatically. We examine this phenomenon in more detail in chapters 3 and 4. But it seems clear at this juncture that this revenue spike was only temporary. The Congressional Budget Office and the Joint Committee on Taxation have projected that, because of the tax cuts enacted in 2001 and 2003 and to some extent the recession and the bursting of the stock market bubble, personal income taxes would fall to 7.2 percent of GDP in fiscal year 2004, the lowest percentage since 1965.[8]

One striking feature of figure 2.2 is that while personal income tax revenues as a fraction of GDP have been fairly stable since World War II, the top tax rate has fallen dramatically. The top rate hit a peak of 94 percent in 1944–1945, stayed at 91 percent or higher from 1950 until the Kennedy-Johnson tax cut of 1964, and remained as high as 70 percent until 1981. Due to tax cuts enacted in 1981 and 1986, though, by 1988 the top rate had fallen all the way to 28 percent and in 2003 was still at a rate, 35 percent, that is low by historical standards.

This top tax rate has played a central role in the public debate over taxes, especially in recent years. But note that the top rate by itself can give a misleading impression of the personal income tax as a whole. During the years when the top rate was very high, it typically affected only a small fraction of 1 percent of the population; almost everyone else was in a significantly lower tax bracket. And even among those who did face the top rate, it applied only to the portion of their incomes that exceeded the top bracket amount; all income below that fell into lower tax brackets and hence was taxed at lower rates. Moreover, historically dramatic changes have been made not only in tax *rates* but also in the tax *base*—that is, the portion of income that is taxable after subtracting out all the deductions, exemptions, and other preferences allowed by the tax code. Both tax rates and the tax base are critical determinants of the level of revenues. Despite these caveats, the decline in the top rate has been a truly important part of the story of income taxes over the past few decades.

History of the U.S. Corporate Income Tax

As with the personal income tax, the first special tax on corporations in the United States was a temporary emergency levy enacted during the Civil War. Corporate income taxation was first adopted on a permanent basis in 1909. As with the personal income tax, its support arose from opposition to the prevailing taxes of the day and a belief that its burden would fall disproportionately on the wealthy. In addition, many thought it would facilitate the regulation of corporations in an era of loose financial reporting.[9] Unlike the personal tax, however, the corporate tax was able to escape constitutional problems because Congress packaged it as an "excise" tax.[10]

Federal corporate income tax revenues followed a pattern similar to that of the personal income tax up through World War II (see figure 2.3). Revenues increased sharply from 1.4 percent of GDP in 1939 to a peak of 6.9 percent in 1943. From 1950 to the early 1980s, however, corporate tax revenues experienced a major decline relative to GDP, falling to just 1.5 percent of GDP by 1982. Since then, corporate tax revenues have followed the business cycle, reaching 2.4 percent in 1997 as the economy boomed and then dipping back to 1.7 percent during the recession of 2002.

Precisely identifying the driving factors behind the large decline since 1950 in corporate tax revenues relative to GDP is difficult. The decline certainly is not due primarily to cuts in the basic tax rate imposed on the vast majority of corporate income (shown in figure 2.3), which hardly changed at all between 1950 and 1986 while revenues dropped sharply. Rather, most of the decline mirrors a drop in pretax corporate profits, which fell from 14.3 percent of GDP in 1950 to just 5.2 percent by 2002.[11] Some of this reflects statutory changes in the tax base, as features such as allowances for depreciation and investment tax credits (which will be explained in more detail later in this chapter) have been altered over time. Some other portion of the decline is probably not directly related to specific changes in the tax law. For example, corporations over this period increased the share of their incomes paid out as interest, which has always been deductible from the corporate tax base, as opposed to dividends and capital gains, which are not deductible. Net interest payments by corporations rose from −0.1 percent of GDP in 1950 to 2.4 percent in 2002.[12] Over the last few years, an acrimonious debate has been conducted about whether the proliferation of tax shelters has significantly eroded corporate tax revenues. In part because tax shelters are difficult to detect (or indeed to define precisely), this debate is unresolved.[13]

(a) Corporate income tax revenues as a percentage of GDP

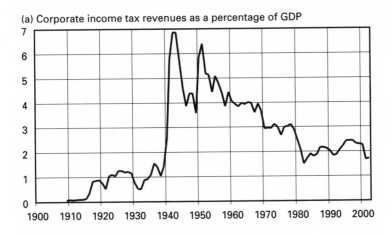

(b) Tax rate on large corporations (percentage)

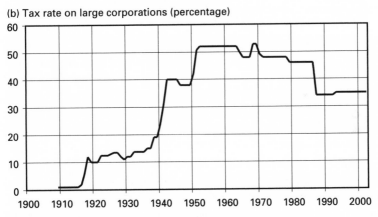

Figure 2.3
The U.S. corporate income tax: Revenues and top rate, 1909–2002
Sources: Internal Revenue Service Form 1120 Instructions (various years); Pechman (1987);
U.S. Bureau of the Census (1975); U.S. Bureau of Economic Analysis (2003).

Recent Changes

Dissatisfaction with the income tax is by no means a new phenomenon.
Throughout its existence, both its level and its structure have generated
great controversies, and the income tax has often been "reformed" in an
attempt to reassign the tax burden or to ameliorate its impact on the
economy.

Two of the most dramatic changes in the U.S. income tax system
occurred in the 1980s. Although both happened during the Reagan

administration, their underlying philosophies were vastly different, and in some ways contradictory. The impact of these changes and their implications for current and future efforts to alter tax policy remain controversial and vital questions to this day.

In 1981, President Reagan and Congress collaborated to produce the Economic Recovery Tax Act (ERTA). Reagan had just won the presidency on a campaign that emphasized what he believed to be the negative economic effects of high tax rates, and he had promised an across-the-board cut in personal rates of 30 percent. As of 1980, the top personal income tax rate was 70 percent, but even people who did not have large incomes had recently begun to face unusually high rates because inflation was gradually pushing people into higher and higher tax brackets—*bracket creep*. Unchecked bracket creep from 1976 through 1981 had caused an upward blip in revenues that is clear from figure 2.2; by 1981 the ratio of federal personal income tax to GDP was at a then unprecedented 9.3 percent.

The defining feature of ERTA was tax rate cuts. At the personal level, ERTA reduced the top rate from 70 percent to 50 percent by 1982, and it cut rates in all other brackets by approximately 23 percent of their former levels over a three-year period.[14] It also provided for automatic adjustments of tax brackets for inflation beginning in 1984 to prevent further bracket creep. In addition, several deductions in the personal and corporate income taxes were expanded or newly introduced. No sooner had the ink dried on ERTA than projections of large federal deficits grabbed public attention. As a result, in 1982 and 1984, Congress enacted some modest measures to offset a small portion of the revenue losses from ERTA. Nonetheless, revenues did decline relative to GDP following the tax cuts adopted in 1981, falling from levels that were historically high to levels close to the average to that point for the postwar era. Between 1981 and 1984, the personal income tax dropped from 9.3 percent of GDP back to 7.7 percent (see figure 2.2), while overall federal revenues fell from 19.6 percent of GDP down to 17.6 percent (see figure 2.1).

By the mid-1980s, another debate about taxes had begun, this time centered not solely on lowering tax rates but instead on simplifying the tax system, making it fairer, and reducing its harmful effects on the economy. A tax reform plan introduced in 1983 by Democrats Bill Bradley and Richard Gephardt, which broadened the tax base and further lowered tax rates, had attracted attention, and in the election year of 1984 President Reagan instructed the Treasury Department to produce its own plan to improve the tax system. This idea eventually worked its way through Congress and, in October 1986, was signed by Ronald Reagan as the Tax Reform Act of 1986 (TRA). This reform resulted from the unusual coalition of a Republican president determined to lower the top rate yet further and a Democratic Congress committed to improving the fairness of the system by curbing apparent loopholes in the law such as tax shelters. It represented a surprising departure for tax legislation in the United States. Traditionally, changes in tax law—especially those in 1981—had always added more and more special preferences and exceptions to the tax code. TRA took the opposite tack, opting to clean up the tax base.

Unlike the 1981 changes, the 1986 act was explicitly designed to maintain the existing level of revenues and the existing distribution of the tax burden across annual income classes. The top personal income tax rate was reduced from 50 percent to 28 percent when fully phased in by 1988. But while the rate reductions in TRA primarily benefited upper-income people, the act also curtailed several deductions and exclusions that were used most heavily by those same people. Deductions for state and local sales taxes, two-earner couples, and consumer interest were eliminated. Limitations were placed on deductions for certain tax-favored saving accounts, medical expenses, business meals and entertainment, and certain business losses. Moreover, tax rates on "long-term" capital gains, received largely by high-income taxpayers, were increased so that they would now match rates on other income. At the same time, features that benefit low- and moderate-income people, such as personal exemptions and the standard deduction, were increased.

At the corporate level, TRA broadened the tax base considerably by limiting depreciation deductions, eliminating an "investment tax credit," and expanding an "alternative minimum tax" provision. In exchange, the top corporate rate was reduced from 46 percent to 34 percent.

In the early 1990s, two less dramatic acts were aimed at reducing the large budget deficits that had persisted since 1981. The 1990 act, which was famous for the first President Bush's abandonment of his "Read my lips: No new taxes" pledge, raised the top personal rate from 28 percent to 31 percent. In the deficit reduction act passed in 1993 under President Clinton, the top personal rate was increased again to 39.6 percent, the top corporate rate edged up one point to 35 percent, and an "earned income tax credit" that benefits the working poor was expanded. Both the 1990 and 1993 acts affected mainly taxpayers at the top and the bottom of the income distribution: the vast majority of taxpayers in the middle were almost entirely unaffected.

Following the election of a Republican Congress in 1994, ideas for fundamental reform of the tax system began to garner much more attention. Among other things, these reform ideas promised to dramatically clean up the tax base and simplify the taxpaying process. But the next major tax law enacted, the Taxpayer Relief Act of 1997 (TRA97), was decidedly incremental and added a host of complex new provisions to the code. Among the larger changes were the introduction of multiple new tax-favored saving plans and expansion of existing ones, a couple of new tax credits for higher-education expenditures, and a new tax credit for dependent children. A proliferation of new forms and instructions, including numerous worksheets to calculate "phase-outs" of benefits for upper-income taxpayers, accompanied these provisions. The tax rate on long-term capital gains was reduced, and most capital gains from sales of homes were excluded from taxation altogether. The exemption level for the estate tax was also increased. The irony of this period is that rhetoric about "cleaning up" the tax system heated up at the same time that the tax system was loaded up with many more credits and other complicating features.

By the year 2000, the fleeting emergence of a budget surplus, in conjunction with George W. Bush's ascent to the presidency, set the stage for a large tax cut that in many ways revisited the 1981 approach to tax policy. The Economic Growth and Tax Relief Reconciliation Act (EGTRRA), a slightly modified version of the tax cut that had formed the centerpiece of Bush's campaign, was enacted in May 2001, by which time a recession was looming.[15] By far the largest provision, in terms of revenues, was a substantial reduction in marginal income tax rates. As a "down payment" on the tax cut, designed partly to stimulate the sluggish economy, tax rebate checks of up to $300 for single taxpayers and $600 for married taxpayers were mailed out to taxpayers in the summer and fall of 2001.[16] Standard deductions and tax brackets for married couples were changed to reduce "marriage penalties." Tax credits for dependent children and for child-care expenses were increased. Contribution limits for various tax-favored savings vehicles were increased, and a deduction for higher-education expenses was introduced. The exemption levels for the estate and gift taxes were set to increase over time, and their tax rates were set to slowly decline until 2010, when the estate tax would be eliminated altogether. Each of the provisions above was to be phased in gradually over time spans ranging up to 10 years.

Strangely, all of the provisions of EGTRRA were scheduled to "sunset" (expire) in 2011, at which time the tax law would revert to what it had been prior to the 2001 enactment of the new law. The technical reason for this was that budget rules in the Senate would have made it more difficult to pass a measure that increased budget deficits beyond 10 years after enactment. But the gradual phase-in and sunset provisions also had the effect of reducing the reported 10-year revenue cost of the bill, which is what typically appeared in newspaper headlines, to $1.35 trillion. Including the impact of increased interest on the federal debt, the cost was projected to be $1.73 trillion over 10 years, or about 1.2 percent of total GDP over the whole period.[17] Given the likelihood that the tax cuts would eventually be extended or made permanent at their fully phased-in levels, this meant that the "headline" cost represented a misleadingly low estimate of the true ultimate impact of the tax bill on the budget.[18]

At the beginning of 2003, in the face of new projections of budget deficits and continuing sluggishness in the economy, President Bush proposed yet another round of dramatic changes in the tax code. The major components included (1) accelerating the "phase-in" of most elements of the 2001 tax cut so that they would take effect in 2003, (2) eliminating taxes on dividends and capital gains under the personal income tax if taxes had already been paid on that income through the corporate income tax, (3) making the 2001 tax cut permanent rather than letting it expire in 2011, and (4) substantially expanding and redesigning tax-sheltered retirement saving plans. The Bush administration focused initially on getting the first two of these proposals through Congress and put off discussion of the latter two to some unspecified future date.

In May 2003, Congress enacted and the president signed the Jobs and Growth Tax Relief Reconciliation Act of 2003 (JGTRRA), which was a modified version of the first two components of the Bush proposals mentioned above. Under this new law, the reductions in tax rates and increases in standard deductions, child credits, and tax bracket sizes that were to be gradually phased in under the 2001 act fully took effect immediately in 2003. In addition, the top personal income tax rates on dividends and capital gains were reduced to 15 percent. To hold the official 10-year revenue cost of the bill to $350 billion, the act made unprecedented use of sunsets. Among other things, the capital gains and dividends provisions were scheduled to expire in 2009, and the changes to the child credit, standard deduction, and tax brackets (but not tax rates) were scheduled to expire in 2005, after which they would revert to the levels specified by the gradual phase-in of the 2001 tax act. The Urban-Brookings Tax Policy Center estimated that if all of the temporary provisions in the 2003 act are not allowed to expire as JGTRRA specifies, the revenue cost from 2003 through 2013 would be $1.1 trillion rather than $350 billion. If all of the expiring provisions from both the 2001 and 2003 acts were made permanent and the added interest on the national debt is taken into account, the annual cost would be 3 percent of GDP by 2013, or 15 percent of overall federal revenues.[19]

Now that this brief history of American taxation has brought us to the present, the rest of the chapter is devoted to explaining the basics of how most of the major components of the federal tax system currently work. We begin with the largest of federal taxes, the personal income tax, and then discuss the corporate income tax. We close with brief synopses of the Social Security payroll tax and the estate and gift taxes.

Personal Income Taxation

What Is Income? The Economist's Definition

On the road to understanding what an income tax is and how it works, a necessary first step is to understand precisely what is meant by "income." This may, at first glance, seem easy, and certainly for some taxpayers calculating taxable income is in fact easy. But in many situations determining income turns out to be rather tricky. Ideally, what we're after is a measure of anything that is received in a given period of time, from all sources, that can be used, either now or later, to purchase goods and services. This reasoning leads to the economist's definition of income—"the increase in an individual's ability to consume during a given period of time."[20] In other words, your annual income is the value of the goods and services you consume during a year, plus the net change in your wealth (saving) that occurs in that year. The latter reflects that part of annual income that you choose not to spend this year but that increases your ability to consume goods and services in the future.

Clearly, cash wages and salaries increase one's ability to consume and are part of income. A noncash benefit that your employer provides to you, such as health insurance, is also a part of income. Most people probably don't think of employer-provided health insurance as income, but it certainly does increase their ability to consume services—in this case, services provided by doctors and hospitals. Someone whose health insurance is provided by an employer is clearly better off than someone with equal cash income but no insurance. Similarly, benefits provided by the government, such as Social Security, Medicare, or unemployment insurance benefits, also increase a person's ability to consume and are considered part of the economist's definition of income.

Returns to the ownership of capital (wealth), or *capital income*, add to your ability to consume as well and thus count as income. Common examples of capital income would be interest and dividends that you accumulate on your savings or rent received on a building you own. Another example is a capital gain, which is the increase in value of an asset you own, such as a house or shares in a corporation. Symmetrically, capital losses would be subtracted from income. Whether you sell the asset does not matter because an increase in the value of assets you own increases your purchasing *power*. Ideally, only *real* capital income and losses, as opposed to those due to inflation, would be counted. For example, if you earn interest of 4 percent this year but inflation is also 4 percent, the interest you've received overstates the increase in your purchasing power because it has just compensated for the decline in purchasing power of your wealth.

The costs of earning income reduce the ability to consume and so would be subtracted from the idealized definition of income. For example, if a farmer earns $50,000 from selling crops but pays $20,000 for seeds, fertilizer, and so forth, then net income is only $30,000. On the other hand, the cost of purchasing durable business inputs, such as a tractor or a barn, would not be deducted in full right away. Durable goods still have value at the end of the year, so subtracting their full purchase price immediately would not accurately capture the change in the ability to consume. Rather, the idealized definition of income would each year subtract out only a measure of how much *depreciation* had occurred—the amount by which goods or equipment had declined in value because they had worn out or become obsolete. Finally, if you had to borrow money to purchase the materials and equipment necessary to earn your income, the interest payments on that borrowing would be counted as a deductible expense.

Most durable goods, such as a home or a car, provide consumption services to their owners over multiple years, and the value of these services is part of income according to the economist's definition. For example, buying a home is an investment, and a major part of the return on that investment is the shelter it provides to its owner every year, a service equal in value to the amount of rent that could be charged on that home. Just as dividends are a form of capital income that represent the return to investing in corporate stocks, so is the rental value of a home a form of capital income representing the return to investing in a house. So according to the economist's conception, this rental value counts as income: owning the house certainly reflects a greater ability to consume housing services. As with durable productive goods, depreciation and interest payments on durable consumption goods would be subtracted to obtain the net income associated with owning the house.

The idealized definition of income refers to individuals, so that all net income earned by businesses must be assigned in some way to individuals. This net income can either be paid out to owners of the firm or can be reinvested back into the company. In the former case, it is fairly clear that the money paid out is income to the earners. What is less clear but equally true is that the earnings retained in the firm also represent income for the owners of the firm to the extent that they increase the value of the firm.

By elaborating on a "correct" definition of income, we do not mean to imply that income is necessarily the "correct" basis for taxation. Indeed, later in the book we carefully examine the case for replacing the income tax with a tax based on consumption rather than income. Moreover, some of the things that count as economic income may seem hopelessly esoteric. But as long as we are operating an income tax, it is important to understand how the tax system's definition of income compares to the "true" measure of income. A system that taxes some forms of income and does not tax others creates incentives for taxpayers to alter their actions so that they earn (or appear to earn) less of the kind of income that gets counted and more of the kind that does not. It may also create arbitrary differences in tax burdens across otherwise similar taxpayers. Many of the problems with the income tax—including complexity, distortions of economic decision making, and arguably some unfairness—arise from differences between true economic income and the tax system's measure of income.

In some cases, differences between economic and taxable income arise because income is difficult to measure in the ideal fashion, so our tax system settles for an approximation. In many cases, special treatment has been intentionally granted to income that comes from certain sources or that is used for certain purposes in an effort to achieve policy or political goals. Whether each of these exceptions is justified must be evaluated on a case-by-case basis, and we explore many of them in more detail in later chapters. But as we show below, our current tax system is far from a *comprehensive income tax* that taxes all economic income once. Some would respond to this by arguing that we should try to move closer to a comprehensive income tax. As we show, taxable income is considerably smaller than economic income, so there is room to broaden the tax base significantly, which would enable us to lower tax rates a great deal and still raise the same revenue. But part of the divergence between taxable income and economic income is an inevitable consequence of the difficulty of measuring income (as opposed to consumption), and part is an indication of our reluctance to fully tax the return to saving. Some view these as arguments for why we should give up entirely on taxing income and switch to a consumption tax. Either way, understanding how our income tax diverges from a tax on economic income, a question we turn to next, is a crucial step in thinking about how we should tax ourselves.

The Tax System's Definition of Income

To begin, consider the items that are included in the U.S. tax system's definition of income. The process of paying personal income taxes begins with the computation of *adjusted gross income* (AGI). Of all the items that are included in AGI, wages and salaries are by far the largest, accounting for 70 percent of all AGI reported to the IRS in 2000.[21] Most other items in AGI represent returns to the ownership of capital (dividends, interest, capital gains, rents, royalties) or a combination of labor and capital income (such as profits from farms and small businesses). Some types of income, such as most wages and salaries, are included in AGI in a straightforward fashion and require little elaboration. But others involve special complications, which deserve some mention here.

One major divergence from the idealized measure of income is that our tax system counts all interest, dividends, and capital gains or losses at their *nominal* values rather than at their *real* (inflation-adjusted) values. This is true both for income received and for deductions, such as those for capital losses and interest paid on durable productive goods and homes. Ideally, the portion representing compensation for inflation would be subtracted from all of these items, but this could make the taxpaying process considerably more complicated.

For capital gains in particular, failure to adjust for the effects of inflation is only one among a multitude of ways in which what is counted as income by the tax code differs from economic income. Counting capital gains according to the economist's ideal notion of income would require measuring and reporting the increase (or decrease) in value of all assets, including corporate stocks, houses, real estate, and the like, every year. The current treatment of capital gains differs substantially from this ideal. Partly because of the difficulty of measuring accrued capital gains on an annual basis, gains are counted in AGI only when they are *realized*, generally when the asset is sold. Capital gains on assets that are held until the owner's death, moreover, are completely absolved from taxation. In 2003, the top statutory tax rate on "long-term" capital gains realizations was limited to 15 percent, while regular income could be taxed at a rate as high as 35 percent.[22] Capital gains on sales of owner-occupied housing are not taxed as long as they are below $500,000 for a married couple (or $250,000 for a single person). Deductions for capital losses (on any type of asset) are limited to just $3,000 beyond the amount of realized capital gains in any one year, although the unused portion may be carried forward into future years. A vast amount of capital gains accrue tax-free for several decades in pensions and other tax-favored saving accounts. On the other hand, if a capital gain on a corporate stock arose because that corporation reinvested some of its profits, then taxes may have already been paid on that income under the separate corporate income tax (the same issue applies to dividends on corporate stock as well, although as of 2003 these too are taxed at a personal rate no higher than 15 percent). All in all, a capital gain might never get counted as taxable income, it might get counted as income twice (under both the personal and corporate income taxes), or it could be anywhere in between, depending on the circumstances.

Some of the most difficult problems in defining income in the personal code arise from the taxation of business income. The income earned by most small businesses, amounting to about 92 percent of all firms in the United States, is taxed directly by the personal income tax.[23] Examples include sole proprietorships (small businesses with only one owner), partnerships, and S corporations (a kind of corporation that is limited to 75 or fewer shareholders). For these types of firms, all net income is allocated directly to owners and included in their adjusted gross incomes. Net income is computed by beginning with receipts and subtracting the costs of doing business, including wages and salaries paid to employees and allowances for the depreciation of capital goods and interest payments. Large businesses with many shareholders typically must pay tax under the separate corporate system described later in this chapter. Many of the issues involved in defining taxable business income, such as determining appropriate allowances for depreciation, are common to all businesses. We deal with these issues later when we describe the corporation income tax.

Table 2.3
Exclusions, deductions, exemptions, and sources of income in the
personal income tax, in billions of dollars, 2000

A. Selected exclusions	**2,403**
Excluded capital income	
Interest	843
Dividends	96
Imputed rent on owner-occupied housing	405
Other exclusions	
Excluded insurance premium payments	364
Unreported AGI and AGI of nonfilers	792
B. Reported adjusted gross income	**6,365**
Wages and salaries	4,456
Capital gains less losses	574
Business income	427
Pension, annuity, and IRA distributions	425
Interest	261
Dividends	102
Other income	121
C. Itemized deductions	**822**
Interest paid	323
Taxes paid	295
Charitable contributions	141
Medical and dental expense	39
Other	63
Itemized deductions lost to limitation	−38
D. Standard deductions and personal exemptions **(less unused deductions and exemptions)**	**999**
E. Taxable income (B − C − D)	**4,544**

Source: Authors' calculations based on data from Park (2002),
Campbell and Parisi (2002), Gale (2002), and U.S. Bureau of Economic
Analysis (2003).

Table 2.3 lists both the major sources of income that are counted in
AGI, as well as some of the main exclusions, deductions, and exemptions that constitute the gap between income and taxable income. An
estimate of the dollar value of each item as of the year 2000 is provided
to give some sense of their relative magnitudes and illustrate just how
far we are from a comprehensive tax on economic income. Going step
by step through the list of items that are left out or subtracted before
reaching taxable income will provide a good overview of the most basic
features of our personal income tax code.

Much Capital Income Is Excluded from the Personal Income Tax

By the time we get to AGI on the tax form, we've already left out a very large amount of income for a number of different reasons, which are grouped under the heading of *exclusions*. Section A of table 2.3 lists some of the largest sources of excluded income in 2000, totaling $2.4 trillion, and this list is far from exhaustive. Much of the excluded income is capital income of various forms. Section B of the table lists the portions of capital income that are included in AGI. Note at the outset that the data in table 2.3 make no corrections for inflation. So a portion of both the excluded and included items of capital income shown here represents compensation for inflation, which would not be counted as economic income. Inflation was fairly low (3.3 percent) in 2000, but it's worth keeping in mind.[24]

Excluded interest income totaled $843 billion in 2000, dwarfing the $261 billion of interest income that actually did get counted as part of AGI.[25] About two-thirds of the excluded interest figure represented interest earned on assets held within various tax-favored savings plans and pensions, life insurance policies, and tax-exempt state and local government bonds. Most of the remaining one-third reflects the difference between the market interest rate and the interest rate that financial institutions actually pay to depositors and savers. This is technically an implicit form of economic income that is used to purchase financial services (such as the convenience and security provided by a checking account), but it would probably be impractical to attempt to tax this. A small part ($28 billion) of the excluded interest total represents interest going to nonprofit institutions, which are untaxed for some of the same reasons that we allow deductions for charitable contributions.

Next on the exclusions list in table 2.3 is dividend income from corporate stocks, of which about $96 billion was excluded from AGI in 2000, accounting for almost half of all dividend payments on corporate stock in that year.[26] Of this, $86 billion represented dividends paid into tax-preferred saving vehicles like pensions, and the other $10 billion was paid to nonprofit institutions. Unlike interest, corporate dividend income has usually already been taxed under the corporate income tax.

As discussed above, the rental value of owner-occupied housing is a form of income from capital, and it amounted to an estimated $405 billion exclusion in 2000.[27] This is completely excluded from the income tax base, in part because it would be difficult to measure but also because the subsidy it provides to owner-occupied housing is strongly politically entrenched.

The other big source of excluded capital income is capital gains. This is not reported in table 2.3 because the amount of accrued capital gains fluctuates wildly from year to year primarily because of the ups and downs of the stock market, so an estimate of gains that are excluded in any particular year would not be very informative. To take a longer-term perspective, we estimate that capital gains realizations that were fully taxed by the personal income tax between 1985 and 2001 amounted to only about 16 percent of nominal capital gains accrued on all assets held by households and nonprofit institutions over that period. The average amount of excluded nominal capital gains per year was close to $1 trillion. On the other hand, profits that are taxed under the corporate income tax and then reinvested in the company are a major source of accrued capital gains, and some of the nominal capital gains accrued or realized between 1985 and 2001 represented compensation for inflation. If we adjust for both of those factors appropriately, the amount of capital-gains-related income that was included in personal or corporate taxable income over the 1985 to 2001 period as a whole was actually slightly *larger* than what would have been taxable under a comprehensive tax on economic income.[28] This does not imply that on balance the taxation of capital gains is about right. Rather, it is the net result of massive errors (relative to economic income) in both directions, as much income in the form of capital gains ends up facing little or no tax at all while a significant amount ends up being taxed more than once. Moreover, none of this takes into account the fact that the personal income taxes that were paid on capital gains were often delayed for many years after the gain was accrued. This effectively provides a substantial tax cut, as the wealth that otherwise would have been used to pay the tax could accumulate tax-free returns over that whole time.

What this discussion of excluded capital income points out most of all is that our existing income tax is in fact an awkward hybrid between an imperfect income tax and a piecemeal kind of consumption tax (which would exempt the return to saving from tax). A policy choice that contributes greatly to this hybrid status is the decision to exclude from taxation the capital income accruing in pensions and several other types of saving plans. We turn to these next.

Tax-Favored Saving Plans

Taxpayers now face a bewildering array of methods for exempting the returns to saving from income taxation, and these account for much of the excluded capital income discussed above. The options have been expanded considerably in recent years, and in 2003 the Bush administration proposed further expansion and considerable restructuring of these plans. For now, we provide a brief overview of how some major examples of these plans worked as of 2003 and save evaluation and discussion of reform options for chapter 8.

Most tax-sheltered saving for retirement takes place in two basic types of employer-provided pension plans—*defined-benefit* plans and *defined-contribution* plans. In defined-benefit plans, employees are promised a fixed level of benefits in retirement that may, for example, be set at some percentage of the average wage and salary income he or she received from the firm in some period of years preceding retirement. The employer makes regular contributions to a pooled fund for the whole firm, which are invested in financial assets to accumulate enough to pay out the benefits. In defined-contribution plans, by contrast, the employer and usually also the employee make regular contributions to a specific account for that particular employee. The worker generally has some choice of how the funds are invested, and the amount of money that is available upon retirement depends on the value of the worker's particular accounts by the time he or she retires. Some examples of defined-contribution pensions are 401(k) plans (used in the for-profit sector) and 403(b) plans (used in nonprofit and public sectors).

Generally, income used to make contributions to pension plans is deductible in the calculation of the employer's business taxable income in the same way as wages and salary payments are, but is not included in the adjusted gross income of the employees. Limits have been placed on the amount of income that can receive this favorable tax treatment, however. For defined-contribution plans, there is an annual limit (adjusted for inflation every year) on the combined employer and employee contribution that can be made to any particular individual's account, which was set at $40,000 in 2003. For a defined-benefit plan, the amount of tax saving is effectively limited by setting a maximum annual *benefit* that may be paid out in retirement (also adjusted for inflation), set at $160,000 in 2003. In either type of plan, when benefits are finally paid out in retirement, any portion that was not subject to income tax previously is then included in AGI and taxed under the personal income tax. If the marginal tax rate that applies to the disbursements from the plan was about the same as the marginal tax rate that applied when the contributions were made, taxing the payments that pension plans make to retirees would roughly offset the benefits of excluding the labor compensation that was used to make the contributions into the pension plans in the first place. But on average, the marginal tax rate is probably lower during retirement than during the working years. Moreover, the interest, dividends, and capital gains that accumulate in the pension plans are excluded from taxation while they accumulate. For these reasons, the current tax treatment of pensions roughly replicates the treatment that would be accorded by a consumption tax, at least for the portion of income that can be sheltered in this way.

Individual retirement accounts (IRAs) provide another method of sheltering capital income from taxation. As of 2003, each individual can contribute up to $3,000 (or $3,500 for those age 50 or over) to an IRA. These contribution limits are scheduled to increase to $5,000 and $6,000, respectively, by 2008. There are now three general classes of IRAs. In all three cases, interest, dividends, and capital gains that accumulate in the account are excluded from taxation from the time of contribution until the time of withdrawal. The three approaches differ with regard to the tax treatment of contributions and withdrawals from the IRA. In a "traditional" IRA, the income used to make the contribution to the account is excluded from tax, and withdrawals from the account are subject to tax. If an individual or his or her spouse is covered by an employer-provided pension, eligibility for traditional IRAs is phased out above certain levels of income. In a "Roth" IRA, the income used to make the contribution is *not* excluded from tax, but withdrawals are not subject to tax. Eligibility for these is also phased out at higher levels of income. Those who are ineligible for either of the other two types of IRAs can contribute to "nondeductible" IRAs, where the income used for the contribution cannot be excluded from tax, and the withdrawals of any funds above and beyond what was contributed are also subject to tax. In all cases, penalties are imposed if withdrawals are made before age 59½, unless the funds are used for certain approved purposes such as first-time home purchases and certain education and medical expenditures.

The above discussion only scratches the surface in terms of the array of tax-favored savings options available and their complex rules. For example, recent years have seen the introduction of a number of tax-favored savings plans for education, including education IRAs. The salient point for now is simply that these plans are a major reason that our "income tax" is in some ways not quite a tax on income after all.

Other Exclusions

Section A of table 2.3 lists two other major examples of excluded income that are worth mentioning here. First, $364 billion of income that was used to pay insurance premiums was excluded from AGI in 2000. Contributions to employer-provided health insurance plans accounted for $306 billion of this, and the rest consisted of contributions to employer-provided group life insurance and worker's compensation plans, as well as excludable health insurance premiums for the self-employed. Tax preferences for health insurance are evaluated in chapter 6.

An estimated $792 billion of unreported AGI and AGI of nonfilers also is calculated for 2000. A small portion of this represents people whose incomes are too low to be required to file a tax return. However, most low-income people do file tax returns, even though they do not owe positive tax, because they are eligible to claim various tax credits that are discussed below. Rather, the vast majority of this $792 billion figure represents an estimate of income that should be reported as AGI but was not, mainly due to tax evasion. This issue is explored in chapter 5.

A variety of other, mostly small, exclusions are not included in the table or mentioned above. Some of these are deducted from gross income on the tax form before we get to AGI and are known as *above-the-line deductions*. One example is moving expenses, which totaled $2.1 billion in 2000. Another is interest on student loans, which excluded $2.6 billion from AGI in 2000. Eligibility for that deduction is gradually phased out at higher levels of AGI ($100,000 to $130,000 for a married couple in 2003), and the maximum deduction is $2,500. A measure of economic income would indeed subtract off some portion of each of these—moving expenses to the extent they represent costs of earning income and interest to the extent that it does not represent compensation for inflation. The 2001 tax act introduced a new deduction for tuition and fees for higher education. The maximum allowable deduction is $3,000 in 2003 (scheduled to rise to $4,000 by 2004) and is available only to those with incomes below certain levels ($130,000 for married couples in 2003).

Deductions and Exemptions

Once we get through with all the various ways that income is excluded from AGI, we are left with about $6.4 trillion of AGI reported on tax forms to the IRS in 2000 (see section B in table 2.3). Another $1.8 trillion is subtracted out of AGI before we get to taxable income due to deductions and exemptions.

First of all, taxpayers have the choice of claiming the larger of *itemized deductions* or a *standard deduction*. The higher their income, the more likely taxpayers are to accumulate enough itemized deductions to make the total larger than the standard deduction. Only 23 percent of those with AGI below $75,000 chose to itemize, compared to 86 percent of those with AGI above $75,000.[29] Altogether, itemized deductions reduced the tax base by $822 billion in 2000 (see section C of table 2.3).

The largest itemized deduction, for interest payments, totaled $323 billion in 2000, $300 billion of which was home mortgage interest. A taxpayer can deduct interest on up to two homes with a total value of up to $1 million. One can also deduct up to $100,000 in interest on home equity loans (second mortgages), the money from which can be used for any purpose. Interest payments on credit cards and other consumer debt, such as automobile loans, however, are not deductible. Interest used to finance investments can be deducted, but only to the extent that it offsets investment income.

The next largest itemized deduction, for state and local taxes, amounted to $295 billion in 2000. State and local income taxes and property taxes are deductible, but sales taxes are not. Charitable contribution deductions are the next largest, amounting to $141 billion in 2000. Medical and dental expenses are deductible to the extent that they exceed 7.5 percent of AGI. The deductible portion amounted to $39 billion in 2000. An array of minor itemized deductions added up to another $63 billion, including among other things unreimbursed employee expenses (such as travel costs), casualty and theft losses, gambling losses, and tax-preparation fees. For upper-income taxpayers, some itemized deductions are subject to a limitation provision, which in 2000 effectively took back $38 billion of the deductions mentioned above. Due to the 2001 tax act, this limitation is scheduled to be gradually eliminated between 2006 and 2010.

Not all itemized deductions necessarily cause taxable income to deviate from economic income. For example, (real) interest payments are regarded as negative income in the economic conception of income (although as we discuss later, allowing interest to be deducted when so much capital income is excluded is problematic). Whether each of the other deductions would be necessary to appropriately measure economic income is less clear. What is clear is that many taxpayers have grown quite attached to their itemized deductions, so that they would undoubtedly be a major sticking point in any fundamental reform proposal that would eliminate them. We take a closer look at itemized deductions in chapter 6.

The remaining items that may be deducted before reaching taxable income are standard deductions (for those who do not itemize) and personal exemptions (see section D of table 2.3). Their 2003 values are shown in table 2.4. The standard deduction for tax year 2002 is $9,500 for married taxpayers filing joint returns, $7,000 for a single-parent head of household, and $4,750 for a single person. These deduction levels are somewhat higher if the taxpayer is elderly or blind. In addition, a personal exemption—equal to $3,050 in 2003—is allowed for each member of the taxpayer's family. Personal exemptions and standard deductions can be thought of as creating an extra tax bracket at the bottom of the income scale, within which the tax rate is zero. For example, for a married couple with two children, the first $21,700 (the standard deduction of $9,500 plus four exemptions of $3,050 each) of income was exempted from income taxation in this way. This effectively eliminates any positive income tax liability for low-income families and also contributes to the graduated nature of tax rates for those who do pay taxes, which we discuss next. The benefits of personal exemptions are currently phased out for upper-income taxpayers, but the phase-out provision is scheduled to be eliminated between 2006 and 2010.

Table 2.4
Personal exemptions and standard deductions, 2003

	Single person	Head of household with two children	Married couple with two children
Personal exemption (per family member)	3,050	3,050	3,050
Standard deduction (per return)	4,750	7,000	9,500
Sum of personal exemptions and standard deduction	7,800	16,150	21,700

Rate Structure

Once you've gone through all the hoops to get to *taxable income*, the next step of calculating your tax liability (before the tax credits) is usually pretty straightforward. Most people just look up how much they owe using a table in the back of the instruction booklet. Implicit in that table is a graduated tax rate structure that is illustrated in table 2.5. The separate rate structures depend on the taxpayer's filing, or marital, status. In most cases, a married couple will pay less tax on the same taxable income than a single taxpayer. We discuss why this is so and whether it is a good idea in chapter 3.

In 2003, the five official tax brackets for each marital status had rates that ranged from 10 percent at the low end all the way up to 35 percent. The dollar amounts that form the dividing point between each tax bracket are increased each year by the rate of inflation to prevent inflation from pushing people into higher tax brackets over time (bracket creep).

To illustrate how the tax calculation works, consider the example of a married couple that takes the standard deduction, has two children, and has an AGI of $80,000 in 2003. First, $21,700 of personal exemptions and standard deductions is subtracted off (see table 2.4), leaving a taxable income of $58,300. Although, as table 2.5 shows, this family is "in" the 25 percent bracket, their tax liability is much less than 25 percent of their income. Rather, they pay no tax at all on their first $21,700 of income, 10 percent on their next $14,000 of income (which is the first $14,000 of *taxable* income), 15 percent on taxable income between

Table 2.5
Brackets and statutory marginal rates in the personal income tax, 2003

Taxable income range, by filing status			
Single	Head of household	Married couple, joint return	Marginal tax rate
0–7,000	0–10,000	0–14,000	10%
6,000–28,400	10,000–38,050	14,000–56,800	15%
28,400–68,800	38,050–98,250	56,800–114,650	25%
68,800–143,500	98,250–159,100	114,650–174,700	28%
143,500–311,950	159,100–311,950	174,700–311,950	33%
above 311,950	above 311,950	above 311,950	35%

$14,000 and $56,800, and 25 percent on the remaining $1,500, for a total tax bill of $8,195.

This calculation illustrates a critically important conceptual issue, the distinction between an *average* tax rate and a *marginal* tax rate. The *marginal* tax rate is defined as the tax rate that would apply to the next dollar of income you could earn, given the income you already have. In the case of the family in this example, it is 25 percent. The *average* tax rate is defined as total tax liability expressed as a percentage of total income. As a share of AGI, this family's average tax rate is (8,195/80,000), or 10.2 percent, significantly lower than the 25 percent marginal tax rate. The graduated rate structure, together with the personal exemptions and standard deductions, make our income tax *progressive*, meaning that average tax rates are higher for those with higher incomes. For example, repeating the above example for the same family with $160,000 of AGI would yield a tax liability of $28,905. This is considerably more than twice the tax liability on $80,000 of AGI and amounts to an average tax rate of 18.1 percent.[30]

One common fallacy about the tax schedule is that moving to the next higher bracket can actually increase tax so much that after-tax income is reduced. This is untrue because the marginal tax rates apply only to the income within that bracket. For example, a married couple with $56,800 of taxable income is at the top end of the 15 percent bracket. Earning one more dollar pushes that couple into the 25 percent bracket but increases tax liability by only 25 cents; earning that extra dollar thus *increases* after-tax income by 75 cents.

The true structure of marginal tax rates is actually a bit more complicated than is implied by the "statutory" rates shown in table 2.5. This is because myriad provisions "phase out" the benefits of various exemptions, deductions, exclusions, and credits over certain ranges of income. In most cases, the impact of these phase-outs is more or less identical to what would happen if we just increased marginal tax rates by a bit over those same income ranges. For example, in 2003, phase-outs of personal exemptions and itemized deductions typically raised the effective marginal tax rate on a family of four with $250,000 of AGI from 33 percent to 37.2 percent.[31] These two particular phase-outs are scheduled to be eliminated when the 2001 tax cut is fully implemented, but a large number of other such provisions remain for things like IRAs, student loan interest deductions, as well as various credits discussed below.

The personal income tax's graduated rate structure contrasts to other important U.S. taxes that levy the same percentage rate regardless of one's income level. Some, like the Social Security tax, even charge a *lower* average rate for those with higher incomes because only the Medicare portion of the tax is charged on wages and salaries above a certain level.[32] Indeed, the progressive rate structure might be regarded as the reason for the existence of the income tax. As we discuss later in the book, if we didn't care about progressivity, we could find simpler ways than an income tax to raise revenue.

Credits

For many people, the process of computing what is owed does not end with the initial tax liability calculation described immediately above. A next step is to reduce tax liability by any available *credits*. Exemptions, deductions, and exclusions all reduce your taxable income, which reduces your tax bill only by the amount of the reduction in taxable income times the marginal tax rate. A tax credit, by contrast, directly reduces your tax *bill* dollar for dollar, so its value does not depend on the marginal tax rate. Credits have proliferated dramatically in the tax code in recent years.

The largest of all credits is the *earned income tax credit* (EITC), which is a program intended to improve work incentives and well-being for the working poor. The basic idea of the EITC is to subsidize earnings from work by offering a credit for every dollar earned up to a certain level. Unlike almost all of the other credits in the personal tax system, the EITC is refundable, meaning that if it is larger than your total tax bill, you get a check for the difference. In 2000, the total dollar value of the EITC was \$32 billion, with \$28 billion of that representing the refundable portion.[33] The EITC is now one of the most important federal antipoverty programs. EITC spending and revenue reductions together are larger than federal spending on welfare and similar in size to federal spending on food stamps and other nutrition assistance for the poor.[34]

In 2003, a family with two children receives 40 cents of EITC for every dollar earned from work over the range of annual work income between \$1 and \$10,510. Between \$10,510 and \$14,730 of work income, the family receives the maximum available credit of \$4,204. The credit is then phased out gradually at a rate of 21 cents per additional dollar earned between \$14,730 and \$34,692. In the phase-in range of up to \$10,510 of income, the EITC amounts to a 40 percent subsidy to working. But in the phase-out range, the EITC adds 21 percent to the actual *marginal* tax rate on working. Thus, some taxpayers in the 10 percent statutory tax bracket actually face a 31 percent marginal tax rate because every additional dollar earned generates both an additional 10 cents of tax liability and also a cutback of 21 cents in the EITC.[35] Because the credit is always positive, it always makes working more attractive relative to not working at all, but it can have positive or negative effects on incentives regarding how much to work. Note that the credit and phase-out rates are both lower for individuals and smaller families.

Another important credit is the *child tax credit*, which was introduced in 1997. As of 2003, this credit reduced a family's tax liability by $1,000 for each dependent child under age 17. Child credits are gradually phased out at higher income levels (starting at $110,000 for married couples). For those with incomes too low to face any tax liability, the child credits are refundable to the extent of 10 percent of the amount by which earned income exceeds $10,500, up to a maximum of $600 per child (as of 2003).

The EITC and child credit, together with personal exemptions and the standard deduction, contribute greatly to the progressivity of the tax system. Considering all four of these provisions together, a married couple with two children does not have a positive income tax liability until family income reaches $38,150. Largely because of the EITC, many of the lowest-income families effectively face *negative* income tax rates: they receive money rather than pay tax.

The long and growing list of other tax credits includes a credit for a portion of certain expenditures on care for a child or other dependent, such as payments to a daycare center. This applies to children under age 13 and sometimes to other family members who are unable to care for themselves. The Hope Scholarship Credit and Lifetime Learning Credit for certain higher-education expenditures were added by the 1997 act. The 2001 tax act introduced a new low- and moderate-income savers' credit, in effect from 2002 through 2006, that provides up to 50 cents of tax credit for every dollar contributed to an IRA. This credit is gradually phased out between $30,000 and $50,000 of AGI for a married couple. These and many other credits reflect a significant expansion of the implementation of social policy through the tax code in recent years. Unfortunately, the credits have been designed in a way that adds considerable complexity to the taxpaying process, requiring taxpayers to deal with confusing forms, worksheets, and instructions. These tax credits have particularly complicated the tax-liability-computation process for low-income people, who until recently had fairly simple tax returns and often did not have to file at all.

The Alternative Minimum Tax: An Obscure Provision Becomes a Big Problem

The alternative minimum tax (AMT) is a part of the personal income tax code that few people have ever heard of but that is poised to become an enormously important issue. Congress originally established the AMT to guarantee that a small number of high-income taxpayers with unusually large exclusions and deductions would not be able to escape taxation entirely. But it threatens to affect tens of millions of mostly middle-class taxpayers over the next few years.

The AMT is a parallel income tax system that requires its own computation of an alternative definition of taxable income, subtracts its own exemption, applies its own tax rates, and then requires recalculation of eligibility for certain credits. AMT taxable income disallows all personal exemptions, the standard deduction, and itemized deductions for state and local taxes, medical and dental expenses, and miscellaneous deductions. It also requires recalculating business income using different rules for things like depreciation and treats income from the exercise of stock options differently than the regular tax system, among other things. The AMT tax bracket structure provides an exemption ($58,000 for a joint return in 2003) and then imposes a tax rate of 26 percent on the first $175,000 of AMT taxable income above the exemption and 28 percent on amounts beyond that.[36] If the AMT tax liability thus calculated is larger than a taxpayer's "ordinary" tax liability (calculated before credits), the difference is added to the tax bill; effectively, each taxpayer must pay the greater of either the tax liability under the AMT or the regular income tax.

In 2000, about 1.3 million taxpayers had to pay the AMT, which represented just 1 percent of all returns filed. In terms of complicating the taxpaying process, the impact was somewhat larger: the IRS estimates that in recent years, for every person who actually owed any AMT, more than five others had to read the AMT forms and make the calculations that were needed to determine whether they were affected.[37] Unless the tax law is changed, the AMT will apply to a rapidly growing number of taxpayers because, unlike other features of the tax code, the exemptions and brackets for the AMT are not indexed for inflation, so inflation will gradually push more and more people onto the AMT. In addition, the AMT exemption is actually scheduled to *drop* in 2005 and thereafter (from $58,000 to $45,000 for a married couple) due to a sunset provision in the 2003 tax act. Finally, because the 2001 and

2003 tax acts cut marginal tax rates under the ordinary tax but not for the AMT, more and more peoples' "ordinary" tax liabilities will be pushed below their AMT liabilities.

A study by the Urban-Brookings Tax Policy Center estimates that, in 2010, by the time the 2001 tax cut is fully phased in, the AMT will affect the tax bills of *one-third* of all taxpayers (compared to 1 percent in 2000), including the majority of those with AGI between $50,000 and $100,000 and 93 percent of those with AGI between $100,000 and $500,000.[38] In contrast, only 27 percent of millionaires would be affected by the AMT, largely because their tax rates will still be high enough that their ordinary tax liability will exceed AMT liability.

Thus, as the law now stands, most middle- and upper-middle-class taxpayers will soon be subject to this complicated parallel tax system.[39] For this reason, Congress is likely to change the AMT to reduce its impact. But note that all of the projections for the revenue costs of the tax cuts enacted in 2001 and 2003 assumed that the AMT would *not* be fixed in the long run. Although the AMT raised only $9.6 billion in 2000, repealing it starting in 2003 would reduce revenues by $660 billion between 2003 and 2013 or $990 billion if the 2001 tax cut were to be made permanent as was proposed in 2003 by the Bush administration.[40]

Basic Features of the U.S. Corporate Income Tax

The majority of businesses in the United States are relatively small, and their incomes are taxed directly under the personal tax code. But if owners of a business want both the full protection from legal liability that a corporation offers and the ability to raise funds by selling stock in the company to an unlimited number of shareholders, then they must form a traditional *C corporation* (so named because they are governed by subchapter C of the Internal Revenue Code) and become subject to the corporate income tax. In 1999, C corporations accounted for only 8 percent of the total number of businesses in the United States but 58 percent of all business income.[41]

Corporate Rate Structure

The U.S. corporate income tax applies a graduated rate structure to a measure of "taxable income" to determine tax liability. Rates start at 15 percent and reach a maximum of 35 percent for net income above $10 million.

Most corporate income ends up getting taxed at the 35 percent rate even though the income of most corporations is not high enough to be subject to the 35 percent rate.[42]

Defining the Tax Base

A corporation's net income for tax purposes is, in the most general sense, the proceeds from the firm's sales less the costs of doing business. The costs of many inputs to production are deductible in the year of purchase or when the items they produce are sold. These include wages, salaries, and benefits for employees; the costs of material inputs; taxes paid to state and local governments; employer contributions to Social Security; costs of repairs; advertising costs; and many other miscellaneous expenses. The tax treatment of the costs of investment in durable equipment and buildings, however, is a bit more complicated.

Depreciation Allowances

The costs of investing in capital assets, such as productive machinery and buildings, are *not* deducted in full at the time of purchase. Instead, in accordance with the economist's concept of income described earlier, a depreciation deduction is allowed. Recall that depreciation is the decline in value of an asset, such as a factory or a machine that occurs as the asset wears out or becomes obsolete. A firm can deduct a portion of the capital asset's purchase price every year for several years until eventually the full purchase price is deducted. Spreading the deduction out over time is generally less favorable to the firm than allowing a full deduction at the time of purchase because the tax savings from an immediate deduction can be invested and accumulate interest: it's better to have the tax saving sooner rather than later.

Accurately measuring the depreciation of a capital good is difficult and would be feasible only in cases where active markets for used capital goods exist. In this case, a business would deduct the difference in the market price between, say, a two-year-old combine and a three-year-old one.[43] The depreciation allowances provided in the tax code are rough approximations of average changes in value for broad categories of capital equipment and structures. For instance, all equipment is assigned to one of six categories of useful life: 3, 5, 7, 10, 15, or 20 years.

In addition, Congress periodically enacts provisions that intentionally accelerate depreciation schedules to encourage investment.

As an example of how the depreciation rules currently work, consider a $20,000 expenditure made in 2003 on a piece of equipment assigned a five-year life, such as a "light or general-purpose truck." First of all, a provision enacted in 2002 (and expanded effective May 2003) allows 50 percent of the cost of an investment to be deducted immediately if it is made before January 1, 2005. The remaining $10,000 of the cost of the truck would be depreciated under the standard rules for a five-year asset. Using a convention that the asset is placed in service in the middle of the first year, 20 percent of the $10,000 is deductible in the first year (2003), and in each subsequent year the percentage of the $7,000 that is deductible is 32, 19.2, 11.52, 11.52, and 5.76.[44] In addition, from 2003 through 2005, up to $100,000 of investment can be "expensed" (that is, deducted immediately) by a small business (defined in this case as a business that undertakes less than $400,000 of investment in a year).

The Tax Reform Act of 1986 adjusted tax depreciation allowances so that they would be closer to true economic depreciation than they had been in the early 1980s, when "accelerated depreciation" had been instituted to spur investment. Recent years have seen a return toward accelerated depreciation, at least temporarily. But even under the 1986 rules, the allowances still only loosely resembled true depreciation. In some cases, especially generous depreciation rules have been enacted for certain industries, such as oil, gas, and mineral-extracting operations.

Deductibility of Interest and Double Taxation

If a corporation raises money by borrowing, the interest payments it pays are generally deductible from the corporate tax base in the year they are made. So business proceeds that are paid out in the form of interest escape taxation at the corporate level and are at most taxed once at the personal level (although much interest income escapes taxation at the personal level as well). On the other hand, when a C corporation raises money by issuing shares, returns to the shareholders—in the form of dividends and capital gains—are *not* deductible from the corporate tax base. So corporate income that is distributed as dividends or produces capital gains may be taxed *twice*—once at the corporate level and then again at the personal level when distributed to shareholders or realized in the form of a capital gain.

Recall, though, that only a small portion of capital gains is taxed by the personal income tax. And, as noted above, only about half of dividends are taxed at the personal level; the rest are excluded mainly due to pensions and other tax-favored saving accounts. To the extent that it occurs, double taxation of corporate income represents a troublesome and potentially costly divergence from the principles of economic income. It can produce a very high combined tax rate and creates an incentive to finance investment through debt (the selling of bonds) rather than equity (the selling of shares) because it applies only to the returns to the latter. Because it is also one of the most important differences between the tax treatment of C corporations and other businesses, it therefore affects which form of organization businesses adopt. Most of the rules regarding the definition of the tax base, depreciation, credits, and deductibility of interest apply to all businesses. But firms taxed solely at the personal level—such as partnerships, S corporations, and sole proprietorships—avoid double taxation altogether.

In 2003, the Bush administration proposed to completely eliminate personal taxes on dividends and some corporate capital gains if corporate tax had already been paid on that income. After much debate, the 2003 tax act instead reduced the maximum personal tax rates on dividends and capital gains to 15 percent, although only until 2009. Both approaches reduce the double taxation of corporate profits but also lose considerable revenue and change the distribution of tax burdens across income groups, which made them particularly controversial. In chapter 8, we examine this issue and other proposed reforms in more detail.

Treatment of International Income

The U.S. corporate income tax allows U.S. corporations a limited credit for taxes paid to foreign governments.[45] The principle here is that a corporation based in the United States should pay the U.S. tax rate on all of its income, regardless of where in the world it earns its income. The chief economic advantage of adhering to this principle, were it actually followed by the United States and other countries, is that a company's decisions about where to invest would not be distorted by tax considerations. If a firm faced the same tax rate regardless of where it invested, it would choose to invest where the pretax return was greatest, which tends to allocate resources where the social return is highest.

The mechanics of the foreign tax credit are as follows. If a corporation based in the United States invests in foreign countries, it pays corporate tax on the profits earned abroad directly to the foreign governments. If the sum of all these tax payments is less than the U.S. tax liability that would have been owed on those profits, the corporation pays the difference to the United States. In effect, the company pays the total U.S. tax due on the income earned abroad and then subtracts the credit for foreign taxes already paid on that income. If, on the other hand, the sum of tax payments to foreign governments is greater than what the U.S. tax liability would have been on those profits, the corporation's foreign tax credit is capped at what the U.S. tax liability would have been. So if a firm invested mostly in low-tax countries, it would pay (in total to foreign countries and the United States combined) the U.S. tax rate, but if it invested mostly in high-tax countries, it could pay more than the U.S. rate.

Things are actually more complicated than this because it turns out that U.S. corporations can reduce their tax burdens by investing in low-tax countries after all. First, if a company based in the United States owns a subsidiary in a foreign country, no U.S. tax is paid on the subsidiary's profits until those profits are sent back to the U.S. parent company as dividend payments. So the parent company can defer paying the difference between the U.S. rate and a low-tax country's rate indefinitely by having the subsidiary keep reinvesting its profits within the foreign country. Moreover, accounting tricks can be used to make the profits of the subsidiary in the low-tax country look larger than they really are and make the profits of the U.S. parent company look smaller. For example, the subsidiary located in a low-tax country could sell items to the parent company at an inflated price. The IRS has rules designed to minimize such practices, but they are difficult to enforce, especially when the transactions between related corporations involve difficult-to-value intangible commodities, such as patents.

Other Credits

A tax credit is currently allowed for certain expenditures on research and experimentation. It reduces a corporation's tax bill by 20 percent of the amount by which qualified research expenditures exceed an average base level for that firm. This is technically a temporary provision, but it has been extended repeatedly.[46] Investment tax credits have been in effect numerous times since 1962, although the latest version was repealed in 1986. These credits reduced tax liability by a certain percentage for every dollar of new investment spending on capital equipment.

Corporate Alternative Minimum Tax and Treatment of Losses

Like the personal tax code, the corporate tax system has its own alternative minimum tax (AMT), which is intended to prevent apparently profitable corporations from reducing their taxes "too much." The AMT applies a lower tax rate (20 percent) to a broader definition of net income, involving less generous depreciation and accounting rules. Firms then pay the larger of the AMT or the regular tax. This provision affects a sizable minority of corporations and requires many firms to do a good deal of extra accounting.

If, after subtracting out all the deductions and allowances, a corporation has a net loss, the company does not receive a refund check from the IRS. Instead, it can carry that loss either forward or backward to a limited number of other years to offset positive taxable income earned in those years. Losses from particular investments are also deductible against taxable income, although with some restrictions.[47]

The Social Security Payroll Tax

Although income taxation raises most of the federal government's revenues, about two-thirds of families pay more in Social Security payroll taxes than they do in personal income taxes.[48] In 2003, the Social Security tax, including both employee and employer portions, was 15.3 percent on individual wages and salaries below $87,000 and 2.9 percent on wages and salaries above that. The unique characteristic of Social Security payroll taxes is that the cash benefits that people eventually receive upon retirement are related by an explicit formula to the amount of taxes, or contributions, paid (or more precisely, to the amount of earnings on which such taxes were levied). People who pay large amounts of taxes into Social Security over their lifetimes typically receive larger retirement benefits from the system than those who contribute less, although the relationship is far from proportional.

A lively debate about reforming the Social Security system is ongoing, but the subject is outside the focus of this book. The Social Security payroll tax, however, often is intertwined with debates over the income tax system. For instance, some Democrats responded to Republican income tax proposals in 2001 and 2003 by advocating temporary cuts in the Social Security payroll tax instead. Because cutting income tax rates delivers little or no benefit to low-income people, since they usually face no income tax liability, Social Security tax cuts would be a way to deliver tax relief to them.

Some important interactions also occur between income taxes and the Social Security payroll tax. For instance, the portion of the Social Security tax paid by employers is excluded from income taxation, but the portion paid by employees is subject to personal income tax. In addition, a portion of Social Security benefit payments is taxable for people with incomes above a certain threshold. Some tax reform proposals would change the way these interactions work, which could have important revenue and distributional effects. Other particularly ambitious reform proposals—for instance, some national retail sales tax plans—would aim to replace both the federal income tax and the payroll tax.

Estate and Gift Taxes

The modern federal estate tax was adopted in 1916, and for much of its history it was a little-noticed part of federal tax policy. But it recently became a central issue in the public debate over taxes. The tax cut enacted in 2001 included a provision that would gradually phase out the estate tax, with full elimination coming in 2010. Because of the sunset provision of that tax act, however, the estate tax is then scheduled to come back in its 2001 form in 2011, which creates some potentially disturbing incentives regarding the timing of death. In 2003, the Bush administration proposed making the estate tax repeal permanent.

The estate tax is a tax on the assets that wealthy individuals leave at death to their heirs. As of 2003, the first $1 million of an estate is effectively exempted from tax, but above that amount, graduated rates ranging from 41 percent to 49 percent are imposed. Bequests to a spouse or to a charity are completely exempt from the tax. In 1999, only the richest 2.3 percent of decedents in the United States paid any federal estate tax.[49] The exemption level has increased significantly since then and is scheduled to continue rising, so this percentage can be expected to fall a great deal.

To limit opportunities for tax avoidance, the estate tax is integrated with a tax on lifetime gifts. In 2003, each individual is allowed to give each of any number of recipients up to $11,000 (adjusted for inflation in subsequent years), plus any gifts for educational or medical purposes, completely tax-free. The portion of any gifts beyond that begin to count against the $1 million exemption mentioned above. If the total of these gifts in excess of the $11,000 annual exemption reaches $1 million, the donor is required to start paying gift taxes while still alive. Otherwise, the excess gifts just reduce the amount of the exemption that is available to the estate at death.

The 2001 tax act will increase the estate tax exemption in stages until it reaches $3.5 million in 2009. Tax rates are also scheduled to decline until there is a single rate of 45 percent in 2009. In 2010, the estate tax is eliminated, but a gift tax with a lifetime exclusion of $1 million and a tax rate of 35 percent on gifts beyond that is retained. The rationale for maintaining the gift tax was to limit the ability of wealthy individuals to reduce their income tax burdens by nominally transferring assets to relatives in lower tax brackets.

In exchange for elimination of the estate tax, the exclusion of capital gains income held until death will be modified for very rich individuals starting in 2010. Currently, any capital gains held until death are completely absolved from income taxation forever. The decedent pays no income tax on them at death, and the heirs are treated as if they had bought the inherited assets at the price prevailing at the time of the donor's death. Starting in 2010, the amount of capital gains that can escape income taxation via this method will be limited to $1.3 million per estate, plus an extra $3 million for assets bequeathed to a spouse. For any capital gains beyond those exemptions, no tax will be due immediately. But if the heir ever sells the asset, he or she will pay income tax on a capital gain that equals the proceeds from the sale, minus the sum of the original purchase price and the amount of exemption allocated to that asset. So under this plan, records on the purchase price of assets will need to be kept across generations, which may be problematic.[50]

Conclusion

The basic background information presented in these first two chapters should be helpful as an introduction to the debate over taxes. Chapter 1 looked at the complaints about the current system, outlined the suggested replacements, and laid out some of the key issues in the debate over the future of the income tax. Chapter 2 explained the essentials of how the major federal taxes work and placed them in their historical and international contexts. Along the way, we've addressed many of the aspects of the system that bother would-be reformers. The next three chapters explore what principles ought to guide any tax system and address to what extent our current system adheres to these principles.

3   Fairness

The worst riots seen in London for decades occurred on March 31, 1990. More than 400 demonstrators and police officers were injured, and 341 people were arrested for assault, looting, and arson. Rioters set fire to parked Porsches and Jaguars, smashed restaurant and store windows, and demolished a Renault showroom. The reason? A new tax proposed by the Thatcher government was scheduled to take effect the next day. The new tax, called a community charge or poll tax, was to be a flat charge on all adults living in a jurisdiction, the same amount for rich and poor alike, and it was to replace a system of real estate taxes based on property value. The public outcry, which included not only civil unrest but also widespread nonviolent protest and noncompliance, is widely credited as the principal reason for the challenge to Margaret Thatcher's Conservative Party leadership and her eventual replacement as party leader. The government soon after abandoned the poll tax.[1]

Although the political repercussions were enormous, the public reaction to the poll tax was exceedingly mild compared to the previous time such a tax was attempted by a British government in—1381. In that year, mobs roamed from town to town, beheading several prominent citizens and tax officials and sacking their houses. One unfortunate soul dispatched to collect taxes was not only "tortured and wounded so that he was half killed, [but] the miscreants then turned to his horse, cut off its tail and ears and affixed them to the pillory there to be subjected to public opprobrium and derision."[2]

Why all the uproar over the 1990 poll tax? The government made mistakes in implementing it, to be sure, but the overriding reason for the outcry was that people thought it was unfair. The poll tax was to replace a property tax that resulted in tax payments that varied with the value of the property. Under the poll tax, every adult in a given local jurisdiction paid the same annual tax, *period*. The duke with his estate paid the same tax as the butcher in his three-room flat. That the affluent should pay more tax than everyone else struck many as a first principle of fair taxation, one that was violated by the community charge.

Although in the United States it has been a long time since controversy over fair taxation has erupted into such violence, our nation's very origin has roots in colonial indignation over the taxes imposed by England. Indeed, the Boston Tea Party was a protest of British tax policies. An excise tax on distilled spirits spurred the Whiskey Rebellion of 1794, which caused several deaths and much property damage; to quell the rebellion, President Washington nationalized 13,000 militiamen, an army three times as large as the one he commanded at Valley Forge during the Revolution.[3]

While violence over the fairness of taxation has largely subsided, the oratorical skirmishing certainly continues. These days the rhetorical weapon of choice is the term "class warfare." When in 2003 the Bush administration proposed tax cuts that would disproportionately benefit high-income families, many Democrats objected that this was unfair. President Bush responded that "You hear a lot of talk in Washington, of course, that this benefits so-and-so or this benefits this, the kind of the class warfare of politics. . . . All people who pay taxes should get tax relief. . . . This is a fair plan."[4] Democrats took up the battle. House Minority Leader Richard A. Gephardt of Missouri countered that the "president's economic policies are class warfare against all classes." Representative Charles B. Rangel of New York, the senior Democrat on the House Ways and Means Committee, went further, saying, "It is class warfare, and they've declared it. Here the president kicks the hell out of the poor and tells us we're guilty of class warfare." Moreover, the *New York Times* reported, "Mr. Rangel noted that class warfare was a phrase that 'seems vaguely un-American,' and he compared its use in the tax debate to the way people in the civil rights movement had once been called communist sympathizers."[5]

Usually the first question anyone asks about a proposed new tax is "Who pays?" and about a tax cut is "Who benefits?" For tax bills discussed in Congress, government agencies and independent organizations will publish *distributional tables* that purport to show how the burden or benefits of the proposed tax change will be distributed, or shared, among various income groups. In recent years, the distributional tables have themselves become political footballs. The economic assumptions underlying the assignment of tax burden to income classes have been challenged. Moreover, in recent years, depending on which party is in power, the distributional tables produced by government agencies have selectively excluded certain information to make it harder for members of the other party to make their points.

Sometimes the group that objects to a tax proposal is defined by something other than income or wealth. It could be defined by region, as when residents of the Northeast complain about a tax increase on heating oil or when westerners object if a gasoline tax increase is considered. The aggrieved group could be defined by age (as would be the case for a tax on Social Security benefits) or by some other characteristic (such as being a smoker, if cigarette taxes are the issue).

The prominence of fairness in tax policy debates makes it essential that the issues it raises are clearly understood. Fairness also deserves close scrutiny because of the costs that achieving it may exact. Much of the bewildering complexity of the tax law is justified in the name of fairness. Recall that it is because of its evident unfairness that what is arguably the simplest tax system of all—the poll tax—is rejected by most everyone. Slightly more complicated systems—but still much simpler than our current system—such as the flat tax, do not allow the tax burden to be fine-tuned for personal circumstances and also permit limited flexibility in assigning the tax burden across income groups. Before we resign ourselves to the bewildering complexity of taxation for the sake of fairness, it behooves us to think carefully about what we mean by fairness and how much we are willing to sacrifice to achieve it. Finally, the attempt to achieve vertical equity (discussed below) inevitably generates disincentives to earn income, which may stunt economic growth. How much of this economic cost we tolerate depends on how much we value the fairness of the assignment of the tax burden.

Vertical Equity

There are two distinct aspects to the fairness of a tax system. The first, called *vertical equity* by economists, concerns the appropriate tax burden on households of different levels of well-being. If for now we measure well-being by income, vertical equity is about how much tax should be paid by a family with $200,000 of income, a family with $50,000 of income, and a family with $10,000 of income.

A tax system can be evaluated against another standard of fairness— to what extent families of the *same* level of well-being end up bearing the same tax burden. Or to put it another way, what are justifiable grounds for assigning different tax liabilities to two equally well-off households? This issue, called *horizontal equity* by economists, is dealt with later. First we deal with the divisive issue of vertical equity or, in other words, the appropriate degree of *tax progressivity*.

Recall that a tax structure is called progressive if a family's total tax liability, as a fraction of income, rises with income.[6] If, for example, total taxes for a family with an income of $50,000 are 20 percent of income, taxes for a family with an income of $100,000 are 30 percent of income, and so on, then the tax structure is progressive. Loosely speaking, one tax structure is more progressive than another if the average tax rate rises more rapidly with income.[7] If, on the other hand, everyone pays the same percentage of income in tax, regardless of income, then the tax is called *proportional*. Finally, a tax that takes a smaller percentage of income from those with higher incomes is called *regressive*. Using this terminology, the question of vertical equity usually boils down to whether the tax burden ought to be distributed in a progressive fashion and, if so, how progressive it should be.

Before plunging in, we must make a frank admission: fairness is not in the end a question of economics. Neither an A+ in Economics 101, a Ph.D. in mathematical economics, nor a lifetime of study of the theory of political economy will reveal the one true answer. Fairness in taxation, like fairness of just about anything, is an ethical issue that involves value judgments.

The elusiveness of the concept of fairness has not stopped people from simply asserting, with absolute confidence, what is fair and what is not. In his 1992 presidential campaign, Bill Clinton advocated making an already progressive U.S. income tax system more progressive so as to achieve "an America in which the wealthiest, those making over $200,000 a year, are asked to pay their fair share."[8] Once in office, he joined with Congress to raise income tax rates on those very people. Columnist William Safire, a well-known stickler for precise language, expresses a not dissimilar view of the meaning of tax fairness when he says "most of us accept as 'fair' this principle: The poor should pay nothing, the middlers something, and the rich the highest percentage."[9]

In contrast, others argue that fairness would require us to impose the same percentage tax rate on everyone's income, perhaps above an exempt amount. Robert Hall and Alvin Rabushka, inventors of the flat tax, take this stand, saying "the meanings of *even, just,* and *equal,* in keeping with rules and logic, better fit a flat rate of taxation than any multiple-rate system that discriminates among different classes of taxpayers."[10]

A few people express more extreme interpretations of the meaning of tax fairness. A letter to the editors of the *Wall Street Journal* asserted that a fair tax would feature "the same amount charged to each citizen— much as each member pays a fixed dues to a club, irrespective of assets," which is essentially a poll tax.[11] The *Parade* magazine columnist Marilyn vos Savant, who has been listed in the *Guiness Book of World Records* under "Highest IQ," agrees, saying that it is "clearly unfair" to require some persons to pay more taxes than others, just as it is unfair to ask one person to pay more for a hamburger than another.[12] (Apparently the British, at least, do not agree.) Another letter to the editor of the *Wall Street Journal* contends that a fair tax "is never possible, any more than anyone can ever commit a fair murder or a fair rape; for taxation is, without an exception, theft."[13]

Our point is that you can *say* anything about what constitutes a fair tax system, but that doesn't make it true. Careful economic analysis can clarify the issues involved and can identify the trade-offs that arise when tax fairness questions are at issue. Economic reasoning, however, cannot be decisive in the choice about replacing one tax system with another, whenever there are winners and losers from the switch.

In spite of this, economists often proclaim, at congressional hearings and in the press, that one tax system is superior to another. To make such a judgment, the economist is implicitly introducing his or her own values into the choice, values that Congress or the majority of Americans may not share. For this reason, in principle any panel of economists offering their opinions on the best tax system should be followed by a panel of philosophers or ethicists who offer their views on tax equity. In practice, of course, we do not convene such a panel every time an adjustment in the pattern of tax liabilities is considered, and we rely on the political system to make these kinds of choices.

The Benefit Principle versus the Ability-to-Pay Principle

Economists have proposed two principles for determining the fair distribution of tax burden across income classes. Although neither of these principles provides a definitive answer to the question of exactly how we should distribute the burden of taxes, they do offer a helpful conceptual basis for thinking clearly about tax fairness. The first is the *benefit principle*, which states that each individual's tax burden ought to be commensurate to the benefits he or she receives from the government. The second is the *ability-to-pay principle,* which states that the tax burden ought to be related to the taxpayer's level of economic well-being.

When we buy ordinary goods and services in the free market, we generally consider it fair to "get what we pay for."[14] The benefit principle of taxation would apply this same reasoning to the financing of government goods and services. In some cases, this is easy. For example, postage is charged on U.S. mail, and local governments charge households for their use of water and sewage facilities. These *user charges* can be an effective policy when the government is providing what is essentially a private good; not only does the levy depend on how much a particular citizen "uses the good," but it also induces people to economize on their usage.

This may work for water, but for many important government services, such as national defense or the justice system, determining exactly how much each citizen benefits is difficult and often impossible. In these cases, implementing the benefit principle would require charging a tax based on a rough estimate of the benefits each person receives.

This is the first place where the benefit principle runs into trouble. You certainly can't just ask people what government activities like national defense are worth to them. Imagine how you would respond if you received a survey from the IRS in the mail, asking you to estimate how much the Department of Defense is worth to you. If you even suspected that your tax bill would depend on your answer, you would have a strong temptation to understate your estimate. (It's not as if the government could threaten not to defend those who claimed not to value the armed forces.) Those who answered honestly would be caught holding the bill. If the government could credibly promise not to assess taxes based on your survey response, claiming to use the information only to get a sense of the average benefit by income class, then people might respond more honestly. But even with no incentive to lie, many households would undoubtedly find it difficult to provide a sensible answer to such a question. So the benefit principle fails to offer practical guidelines about how the tax burden should be distributed.

Practical matters aside, the benefit principle may suggest that because households with higher income and wealth have more to lose from the anarchy that would prevail if the government withdrew from providing defense, a justice system, police, and so on, those households should therefore carry a higher tax burden. Still, the benefit principle doesn't tell us *how much* higher that tax bill should be. In 1776, Adam Smith, the father of free-market economics, argued on these grounds in favor of proportional taxation (the same percentage tax rate on everyone), which would indeed put a larger tax burden in absolute terms on people with higher incomes.[15] More recently, William Gates, Sr. (father of Microsoft's Bill Gates) has undertaken a campaign to defend progressive taxation (particularly the estate tax) in which he emphasizes a similar argument. He contends that rich people in the United States owe a great deal to their country, because they would not have been able to achieve such wealth in the many other countries of the world that are poorly or corruptly governed, lack effective institutions and infrastructure, and underfund scientific research, technological innovation, and education.[16] Given these disparate considerations, it is by no means obvious what the benefit principle implies about the appropriate distribution of tax burdens.

Thus, if the benefit principle supports a progressive tax system, it does not do so to redistribute income but to "charge" correctly for the progressive benefits of government programs. For example, imagine for a moment that somehow each household's true benefit from government could be determined and that their tax liability was set at exactly that value so that, on net, everyone comes out "even." There would be no way to go easy on low-income people by assigning them low or no taxes; everyone would have to pay their bill representing their individual benefit from national defense, police protection, roads, and so on. Nor would there be any scope to supplement the incomes of the very poor by providing benefits such as food stamps because the value of the food stamps would have to be exactly offset by a corresponding tax liability. Children who grew up in disadvantaged families could not be provided education free of charge. Social Security could not guarantee that virtually all participants receive at least some minimal survival level of retirement support, as it does now; retirees would get only exactly what they had paid for during their lifetimes, even if it meant that many elderly people would be impoverished. Thus, a strict application of the benefit principle has radical implications for both how the government raises money and how it spends it.

Some would argue that restricting the government in this way would be just, based on the premise that as long as the process that led to the distribution of (pretax) incomes in society was just (for example, it did not result from theft), then the outcomes are just: people deserve to keep what they earn. This might be termed a *libertarian* view of justice, which has been espoused (with varying degrees of flexibility) by philosopher Robert Nozick, economists Milton Friedman and Friedrich Hayek, and many others.[17] In this view, the government should be limited to a minimal role, providing only services, such as criminal justice and national defense, that are necessary to prevent people from violating each others' rights and to avoid chaos and anarchy, which would impoverish everyone. In a strict version of this view, income, or more broadly, ability to pay taxes no matter how measured, should play no independent role in determining tax liability. Imposing higher taxes on the rich for the purpose of redistributing some of it to the poor, without the consent of the rich, would be unjust because the rich had earned that income and had a right to decide how to use it. Taxes would still be necessary to finance even a minimal state that is in everyone's interest: a system of purely voluntary contributions would suffer from the problem that no one could be excluded from benefiting from the general lack of anarchy if they don't pay, creating a powerful incentive not to pay. All in all, this theory of justice provides little guidance about how the burden of taxes *should* be distributed (as opposed to how it should *not*), although it might be viewed as consistent with a strict application of some version of the benefit principle.

Most people, though certainly not all, would reject strict adherence to such a limitation on the appropriate role of government. Many would allow that level of well-being—perhaps measured by some observable indicator such as income, consumption, or wealth—should be taken into account to some extent in determining what people pay to government and receive from it (rather than requiring a strict relationship between the two). One might say that affluent people can more easily *afford* to pay taxes and that this should influence how the burden of taxes is shared. In the context of taxes, this may be termed the *ability-to-pay principle.*

According to the ability-to-pay principle, tax burdens should be related not to what a family receives from government but rather to its ability to bear the tax burden or, in other words, to tolerate a sacrifice. Reasoning from the plausible idea that relinquishing a dollar is a lesser sacrifice for a well-to-do family than for a poor family, an equal sacrifice requires higher tax payments from a well-to-do family. After all, $100 more in taxes may require an affluent family to cut back on magazine subscriptions, but it may force a poor family to eat less. It makes sense that a rich family would need to forgo a whole lot of magazine subscriptions before its sacrifice is as great as the one undergone by the poor family.

Although this is a sensible and even compelling proposition, it is also one that is impossible to prove. We have no way to quantitatively compare across individuals the sacrifice caused by having less money, just as it is impossible to compare the pain caused to two people by a pinprick.

Still, the idea that people place a relatively high value on increments to income when their income is relatively low is consistent with how people behave. For instance, people voluntarily buy insurance, which pays off when they would otherwise be impoverished by some unlucky event such as a health crisis or a house fire. People willingly enter into such arrangements (before the fact) even though on average they will lose money on the deal (due to the need to pay for the administrative costs and profits of the insurance company). This implicitly means that they assign a higher value to money they might receive when they are impoverished by an unlucky event than they do to the even larger total of money they pay when they are not impoverished. In other words, they have revealed by their risk-avoiding behavior that they value a dollar more when they are poor than when they are rich. Some have argued that this provides an additional rationale for redistribution through the tax system: it provides a kind of insurance that people might value but for which no private market exists.[18]

Just accepting that a dollar of tax payment is a greater sacrifice for a poor family than for a rich family, without knowing how much greater, does not indicate exactly what the relationship between income and tax burden should be. A proportionate tax, whereby everyone pays the same percentage of income, would take more dollars from a rich family than from a poor family. Indeed, even a regressive tax, with everyone paying 25 percent on the first $20,000 of income and 10 percent on all additional income, would take more dollars from a rich family than from a poor family. Whether one of these two schedules, or some other, assigns an equal amount of sacrifice across families is impossible to say.

Furthermore, why should everyone make an equal sacrifice? Why not demand greater sacrifice from the affluent than from the poor? Accepting this premise implies that two separate layers of indeterminacy are involved in implementing the ability-to-pay principle—how to measure the amount of sacrifice associated with taking one dollar away from someone and how to relate the level of sacrifice to the level of well-being. Neither of these questions is the sort that can be answered analytically.

We conclude that the ability-to-pay principle is nothing more than an intuitively appealing defense of linking tax liability to some measure of well-being rather than to an estimate of the benefits from government activities. On the compelling questions of the day, however—such as whether millionaires ought to pay 70 percent, 50 percent, or 30 percent of their income in tax or whether poor families should pay anything at all—the ability-to-pay principle has nothing concrete to offer.

Progressivity and Economic Incentives

Most economists have given up on seeking operational guidance regarding the "right" degree of progressivity from first principles of fair taxation. Instead, they have concentrated on understanding the economic consequences, or *costs*, of different levels of tax progressivity. The costs arise because of the disincentive effects of taxation. If all taxes were raised by a poll tax, so that tax liability is the same amount for rich and poor alike, the tax system would place no penalty whatsoever on all the efforts people undertake to better themselves—working hard, getting an education, starting a new business, and so on. In contrast, a proportional income tax system levied at a constant 20 percent rate levies a 20 percent penalty on the reward from all such efforts. Tax systems that are progressive place an even higher penalty on getting ahead. As Paul Krugman put it so succinctly in his book *Fuzzy Math*, "When your goal is to increase the incentive to *become* rich, it's very hard to avoid also giving benefits to those who already *are* rich."[19]

If the tax penalty on getting ahead causes some people to shy away from working hard, getting an education, and so on, there is a hidden economic cost to the taxation that is not reflected directly in the amount of tax paid. This extra cost arises because some activities for which the benefits otherwise exceeded the costs were forgone purely for tax reasons. Measuring this cost allows us to pose the critical trade-off that must be faced in resolving the vertical equity question—how to balance the potential social benefits of a more equal distribution of after-tax income against the economic damage imposed by highly progressive taxes. As Henry Simons of the University of Chicago stated so elegantly in his influential 1938 book *Personal Income Taxation*, "Both progress and justice are costly luxuries—costly, above all, in terms of each other."[20] How that trade-off is resolved depends in part on the value society places on a more equal distribution of income and in part on the bread-and-butter concern of economists—how people and businesses respond to incentives. The magnitude of the behavioral response determines the economic cost of progressive tax systems. We address this issue in the next chapter.

Just How Unequal Is the Distribution of Incomes?

If everyone in our society were equally well off, we would have little reason to worry about tax progressivity. In the United States, however, there is clearly an enormous gap between the best off and the worst off, as well as a big difference between the best off and the middle class. Moreover, government statistics provide abundant evidence that during the 1980s and 1990s the degree of income inequality grew sharply.

Figure 3.1 illustrates the degree of inequality in pretax incomes in the United States and its growth in recent years, as calculated by the Congressional Budget Office.[21] In 2000, 55 percent of all income in the United States went to the quintile (the fifth, or 20 percent) of the population with the highest incomes, compared to 46 percent in 1979. Panel B of figure 3.1 shows that average real (inflation-adjusted) incomes actually declined between 1979 and 1997 for people in the bottom fifth of the income distribution. Incomes grew sluggishly in the middle and surged at the top. Between 1979 and 2000, average real income among people in the top 1 percent of the distribution rose by a staggering 184 percent! Panel A of figure 3.1 shows that the share of overall income going to the top 1 percent jumped from 9 percent to 18 percent over this period. The top 1 percent is an exclusive group; a family of four needed at least $514,200 of income to qualify in 2000 in the CBO analysis, and the average income (adjusted for household size) in this group was just over $1.29 million.[22] Factors such as the bursting of the stock market bubble and the recent recession appear to have had a negative impact on incomes at the top since 2000. For instance, preliminary data from the IRS suggest that adjusted gross income of the top 1 percent of households dropped by 18 percent between 2000 and 2001. However, the 2001 average income in the top 1 percent was still above its 1998 level, and the drop in 2001 makes only a small dent in the longer-term increase depicted in figure 3.1.[23]

Wealth is distributed in an even more unequal fashion, and it too appears to have grown most dramatically at the very top in recent years. A study by Arthur Kennickell of the Federal Reserve Board of Governors finds that in 2001, the richest 1 percent of households held 33 percent of all net worth in the United States and the richest 10 percent held

(a) Share of total pretax income (percentage), 1979 and 2000

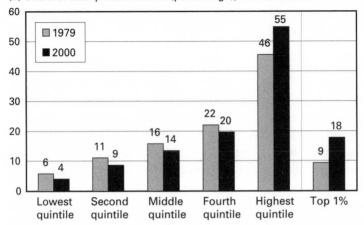

(b) Percentage growth in real income, 1979 to 2000

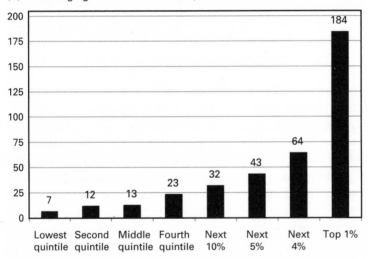

Figure 3.1
Growing income inequality in the United States, 1979–2000
Source: Authors' calculations based on CBO (2001, table B-1c).

70 percent of net worth. Annual reports in *Forbes* magazine suggest that between 1989 and 2002, the number of billionaires in the United States increased from 97 to 205, and the average wealth of the 400 richest Americans increased from $921 million to $2,148 billion (in constant 2001 dollars), a 133 percent increase. By contrast, data from Kennickell's study suggest that for households in the bottom 90 percent of the wealth distribution, average real net worth increased by just 42 percent between 1989 and 2001.[24]

When we view the distribution of incomes in a single-year snapshot and compare that snapshot with earlier years, as we do in figure 3.1, incomes are without doubt very unequal and are becoming more so. But the people in each income quintile in any given year are not necessarily the same people who were there twenty or even five years earlier. These single-year snapshots fail to capture income *mobility*—people moving among the different income classes. Some of the apparent inequality in a single-year snapshot represents temporary fluctuations, such as a family realizing a large capital gain in one year or a young person who is still in school but will one day earn a high income. If we could look at *lifetime* incomes, the distribution would not appear quite as unequal as it does in figure 3.1.

Nonetheless, the best evidence available on this subject suggests that a great deal of inequality exists even in lifetime incomes and that this too has been growing. For example, a study by economist Peter Gottschalk of Boston College followed the same group of people over twenty-three years (1968 to 1991) and found that about 47 percent of all people who were in the lowest income quintile and about 42 percent of all people who were in the highest income quintile in the beginning of that period were still in that same category by the end. The fraction of people who moved over a decade from one quintile to another was 58 percent in the 1970s and 57 percent in the 1980s. Since the degree of income mobility did not increase from one decade to the next, if "snapshot" income inequality was increasing over this period, then so too was lifetime income inequality.[25] Furthermore, income is no less concentrated among taxpayers within many age groups than it is for all taxpayers.[26] If most of the observed inequality at a point in time was due to the life-cycle pattern of earnings, we would expect to see much less inequality of incomes among people of the same age.

Another important area of controversy is the question of exactly why inequality has been increasing. The numbers shown in figure 3.1

are for before-tax income, so changes in the tax system cannot be directly responsible for the trend toward greater inequality. Some economists, however, have argued that reductions in tax rates may be indirectly responsible for some of the surge in reported incomes at the very top of the income distribution because lower marginal rates increased the incentive for the well-to-do to work harder and to invest more and reduced their incentive to hide income from the IRS. But many other factors could account for this surge, such as increased demand for the services of a small number of highly skilled lawyers, doctors, investment bankers, and entertainers, which bids up their compensation. Some of this increased demand is probably due to the growing ease of marketing these skills to global markets rather than simply to the U.S. market. The role of taxes in the recent surge of income inequality has become a key issue in the current debate over the economic effects of taxation, one that is discussed in greater detail in the next chapter.

What does this large and growing income inequality imply for how progressive the tax system ought to be? Nothing, if you don't believe in the ability-to-pay principle. But if you do accept this principle, more income inequality may suggest a need for greater tax progressivity, depending on why it happened. If the rich got richer because of good fortune and market forces that were beyond their control, while the incomes of the poor and middle class stagnated for similar reasons, then you could make a case that some of the increased inequality ought to be offset by a more progressive tax system and certainly should not be exacerbated by *reducing* the progressivity of the income tax.[27] This is not because higher incomes for the rich are bad per se. Rather, the argument is that when the incomes of the rich skyrocket, we should use the opportunity to rearrange tax burdens in such a way that makes many people better off without making the rich much worse off in terms of "happiness sacrificed."

On the other hand, if the rich got richer because lower tax rates unleashed a torrent of entrepreneurial effort, you might increase your estimate of the economic benefits of reducing tax progressivity. In that case, you might desire a less progressive tax system. In either case, the degree of progressivity that people prefer must depend partly on value judgments. But if we hold constant the ethical value that we put on having a progressive distribution of tax burdens, the optimal degree of progressivity is lower if the economic cost of achieving it is higher.

What Americans Think Is Fair

Any first principles of fairness leave plenty of room for disagreement over the appropriate distribution of the tax burden. Why not forget about first principles, and just ask people what they think is fair, based on their own values and principles? Numerous polls and academic studies have done just that. Public opinion surveys generally suggest strong support for progressivity in taxation. But the results sometimes appear inconsistent or are difficult to interpret, can differ greatly depending on how the question is framed, and in some cases seem to indicate considerable public confusion about how the U.S. tax system works.

An April 2003 Gallup, CNN, and *USA Today* poll found that 63 percent of people feel that "upper-income people" pay "too little" in taxes. The same poll has consistently shown strong support for this proposition, but support has also declined steadily from 77 percent in 1992.[28] In the 2003 National Survey of Americans' Views on Taxes, cosponsored by National Public Radio, the Kaiser Family Foundation, and Harvard's Kennedy School of Government, 57 percent of respondents said that high-income families pay "less than their fair share" in taxes. In addition, 51 percent said that the thing that bothered them most about taxes was "the feeling that some wealthy people get away not paying their fair share," easily beating out "the complexity of the tax system" (32 percent) and "the large amount you pay in taxes" (14 percent).[29]

Because the federal tax system is already quite progressive, on the surface these polls seem to suggest public support for a substantial degree of progressivity. It is not clear, however, whether Americans believe that the existing tax system actually is progressive. For instance, in the 2003 NPR, Kaiser, and Harvard poll, 51 percent said that "middle-income people" pay "the highest percentage of their income in federal income taxes," while only 26 percent said that "high-income people" do.[30] As we demonstrate later in this chapter, this impression is in fact way off, as higher-income people actually do pay a much higher share of their incomes in income taxes. A stark illustration of this apparently pervasive misperception comes from a 1989 survey that found, on average, people believed that 45 percent of millionaires paid *no income tax at all*; IRS statistics showed the actual figure was less than 2 percent.[31]

Misperceptions about who bears the burden of the current tax system may help explain why surveys find somewhat surprising levels of

support for flat-rate taxes, given that people also express strong support for increasing taxes on the rich. An April 1999 Associated Press
poll found that 51 percent of respondents agreed that "a flat tax with
the same rate for everyone" was fairer than "the system we have now,
with higher tax rates for people with higher incomes."[32] In the 2003
NPR, Kaiser, and Harvard poll respondents split almost evenly regarding whether a graduated income tax system or a flat-rate income tax
system is fairer. But strikingly, in the latter poll, 41 percent of people answered that under a flat-rate system high-income people would pay
more income tax than now (35 percent said they'd pay less, and 18 percent said they'd pay about the same amount; 6 percent didn't know).
Thus, misperception undoubtedly accounts for some of the support
for the flat-rate tax, and support might weaken if people were better
informed.

Other recent developments create further doubts about whether
most Americans want more or less progressivity in the tax system. One
is that recent surveys find solid majorities favoring elimination of the
estate tax, which as of 2003 applied only to estates over $1 million, a
level of wealth attained by only the richest 1 or 2 percent of the population.[33] The vast majority of the population, objectively speaking, has an
exceedingly small chance of ever getting rich enough to have to pay
this tax. The fact that a majority of people oppose it anyway seems
on the surface to be strong evidence that people are concerned about
more than just their own personal tax burdens when they think about
tax fairness and that they oppose a very progressive tax. But the lessons
to take from this episode are not obvious, given the unique nature of
the tax, the public's apparent lack of understanding about how it works
or about their likelihood of becoming subject to it, and the aggressive
and highly effective public-relations campaign mounted recently by
the tax's opponents. Meanwhile, as of early 2003, significant majorities
of respondents to several different polls agreed that George W. Bush's
tax policies "mostly benefited the rich."[34] Although it's not clear how
many people thought that this was a good thing or a bad thing, many
were apparently not too bothered by this issue relative to other pressing
issues of the day, given Bush's high overall approval ratings at that
time.

A 1991 study by Peggy Hite of Indiana University and Michael
Roberts of the University of Alabama provides some of the most
detailed information available about public opinion on progressivity.
Hite and Roberts asked a random sample of 593 Americans what they

Table 3.1
Personal income tax rates at various income levels desired by survey respondents

Income in 1987 dollars	Income in 2001 dollars	Mean desired average tax rate	Mean desired tax dollars converted into an average tax rate
5,000	7,800	2.4	2.7
10,000	15,600	4.7	4.2
15,000	23,400	8.3	6.6
20,000	31,200	11.7	8.9
25,000	39,000	13.9	10.4
30,000	46,800	16.1	11.8
40,000	62,400	19.1	13.3
50,000	78,000	22.7	15.6
100,000	155,900	29.2	20.1

Source: Hite and Roberts (1991).
Note: The survey asked respondents to assign average personal tax rates and tax dollars to married couples with no children at various income levels.

thought the average rate of personal income tax should be at nine different levels of income. The average responses, displayed in the third column of table 3.1, show a strong degree of progressivity, with the average rate increasing uniformly with income. The fourth column is interesting as well. When the respondents were separately asked to give the appropriate tax liability in dollars rather than in average tax rates, the mean responses converted into average tax rates were almost uniformly lower, although still quite progressive. It's almost as if the sacrifice of paying taxes became more palpable when the responses were measured in dollars rather than in the more abstract concept of average tax rates and that people therefore shied away from higher taxes. Another possibility is that some people may have trouble distinguishing between *marginal* and *average* tax rates, which could cause upward bias in the average tax rates respondents said they desired on upper-income people.[35]

When forced to choose among five alternative tax schedules, 34 percent of the respondents chose one that featured a flat rate of 20 percent on all income above $5,000 a year. But two-thirds preferred a more progressive, graduated rate structure. Twenty-eight percent chose graduated rates that were about as progressive as the current system, and 38 percent chose rates that were more progressive than the current system. Not surprisingly, people could not exactly put aside their own self-interest in choosing their preferred tax systems. Lower-income people tended to favor relatively low rates on low incomes, while higher-income people favored relatively low rates on high incomes.

Fairness in taxation is an elusive concept about which reasonable people with different values may disagree. How progressive the tax burden should be depends on values, on the extent to which progressive taxation discourages productive economic behavior, and on the cost in terms of simplicity in achieving finer and finer degrees of fairness. All things considered, the evidence on public opinion suggests that most Americans prefer a progressive tax system, but it is less clear whether they want it to be more or less progressive than it is now because by and large they don't know how progressive it is now. Some would apparently be satisfied with a system that achieves its progressivity by exempting a certain level of income and then applying a flat rate to all income above that level. Many others seem to prefer an even more progressive system that applies increasingly higher tax rates on successive increments of income. Whether in asserting these preferences people are considering the trade-off with economic performance or with simplicity is an open and intriguing question.

Tax Incidence: Who Bears the Burden of a Tax?

How is the burden of taxation distributed in the United States, and how does this compare to Americans' views about the proper distribution of the tax burden? Answering these questions is a much more difficult task than it might first appear. The most straightforward approach—adding up how much money people send to the IRS each year and tabulating these figures by income group—is inappropriate because the burden often is shifted off of the person who sends the check to the IRS onto someone else via changes in market prices. For example, if the owner of a business can respond to a particular tax levy by raising prices, then even though he or she is the one sending a check to the IRS, the firm's customers are bearing part of the burden of the tax. To understand where the burden of taxes lies and whether that burden is shared fairly, it is necessary to look beyond who writes the checks.

If "paying" taxes means writing checks to the IRS, most wage and salary earners would be surprised to learn that they have no right to complain about income taxes because they pay no tax at all! Of course, all this means is that taxes on wages and salaries are withheld from paychecks by the employer and forwarded by the employer to the IRS.

By April 15 (or the extended deadline), employees must send the IRS the difference between their tax liability and what has already been withheld from their earnings—the amount paid on their behalf by their employers.[36] Because about three-quarters of taxpayers get a refund, most Americans never "pay" any income taxes, if *paying* means writing a check to the IRS. Most Americans are familiar enough with employer withholding to know instinctively that you can bear the burden of taxes without ever writing a check to the government.

Neither is the key to who bears the burden of taxes to be found in where the legal liability to remit taxes resides. Imagine if all taxes levied on wages and salaries became the legal liability of the business employing the labor and were simply renamed labor *usage* taxes rather than labor *income* taxes. There would be no change in who really bears the burden of the taxation: only the wording on the pay stubs would change. A weekly stub that used to show $600 in wages, $200 in federal taxes withheld, and $400 in take-home pay would instead show simply $400 in wages because the employer would pay the $200 "labor usage tax" separately. The bottom line is that the worker takes home $400 either way. Changing the name of the tax won't suddenly make an employer more generous; firms will still try to pay as little as they can to maintain a workforce of the size and quality they desire. Whether the legal liability to pay taxes resides with the buyer of labor services (the firm) or the seller of labor services (the worker), the same result is attained in the end. This is a critically important but often misunderstood concept that recurs in much of the analysis that follows.

As always, some exceptions can be found to the general rule that where the legal responsibility for remitting taxes lies doesn't affect who bears the burden of those taxes. For example, who must remit taxes would matter in the transition to a new tax regime if salaries are not immediately flexible. If a worker's salary is fixed as part of a long-term collective-bargaining agreement, then changing the legal responsibility for remitting income taxes from employee to employer would certainly make the worker better off, at least until the employment contract could be renegotiated. Similarly, someone receiving the minimum wage would be better off because the wage could not be reduced below that level to make up for the change. The employer would either have to accept a higher cost of employing the worker or let the worker go.

Despite these exceptions, in most cases over a reasonable length of time wages and prices are flexible, so it doesn't ultimately matter on which side of the transaction the legal responsibility for taxes lies.

Although our example features a tax on labor income, the same conclusion applies to any kind of tax: in the long run, it is irrelevant whether the seller or buyer owes or remits the tax.

So far, we have explained how *not* to measure the burden of taxes—by calculating who remits taxes or is legally responsible for remitting money to the IRS—but we have yet to explain how to do it right. Does a tax on labor income make workers worse off by lowering their take-home pay, or does it make employers worse off by increasing the cost of labor? Do taxes on cigarettes burden smokers, the owners of cigarette companies, the people who work for these companies, or tobacco farmers?

The phenomenon that taxes that are ostensibly levied on one group of people may end up being borne by others is known as *tax shifting*, and who ultimately ends up bearing the burden is called by economists *tax incidence*. For any given tax, these are difficult questions to answer precisely, and for some taxes there is still considerable disagreement among economists about what the truth is.

The burden of a tax can be shifted when the tax changes the pretax prices of the goods and services that people buy and sell. What determines whether shifting occurs? A good rule of thumb is that the better one's alternatives to what is taxed, the less likely one is to bear a burden.[37] Some examples may help to illustrate this idea. Will a tax of 5 cents per can of Coca-Cola cause its price to rise and thus be borne by Coke consumers, or not? The answer is no if most consumers can't tell the difference between Coke and Pepsi—that is, if they have good alternatives to the taxed good.[38] If one is as good as the other, the market simply will not support Coke selling for 55 cents a can, tax included, while Pepsi sells for 50 cents: no one would buy Coke at those prices. In that case, Coke would sell for 50 cents, and Coke's producers would bear the burden of the tax; if their net-of-tax receipts no longer covered their costs, they might have to shut down production entirely. If, on the other hand, neither Pepsi nor any other drink is viewed as a good substitute for Coke, the market price of Coke is likely to rise toward 55 cents, so that the burden of the tax is borne by consumers of Coke.

The alternatives to supplying the taxed good are equally important. Consider the incidence of a surprise tax of 10 cents per tomato imposed on farmers as they arrive at the farmers' market. Because the tomatoes will soon start to rot, the farmers have no alternative but to sell them that day. In that case, the likely scenario is that the market price will be not much more than what would have prevailed in the absence of the tax, and the farmers will lose out by receiving a lower net-of-tax price than otherwise. If, however, the tomato tax had been announced months in advance, the farmers would have had the option of growing other crops or taking their tomatoes to be sold elsewhere. With fewer tomatoes to be sold, the price at the farmers' market would be bid up, causing the tax burden to shift away from the farmers toward the people who shop at that market, who will find that tomatoes cost more than otherwise. Lovers of fresh tomatoes bear a burden yet remit no money to the tax authority.

The same logic applies to taxes on labor income. A tax on wages and salaries will be shifted off workers to the extent that the tax causes wage rates to rise. It will be completely shifted if wages rise enough so that after-tax wages are no lower than they would have been absent taxes. How does the rule of thumb about shifting apply to this case? It says that shifting will tend to occur if workers have better alternatives to working than employers have to hiring workers. For workers, the alternative to paid work is leisure or unpaid work at home; for employers, the alternative to hiring labor is to economize on workers by moving to more capital-intensive, or automated, modes of production.

As shown in chapter 4, most evidence suggests that labor supply is not highly responsive to the after-tax wage, suggesting that on average people do not perceive they have any alternative but to work. On average, firms are more flexible in their ability to find alternatives to labor. The relative flexibility of firms compared to workers implies that very little of the income tax is shifted off workers by forcing up wage payments and that the tax is borne largely by the workers themselves.

In some cases, a tax will cause a change in the price of *untaxed* goods or services that are related in some way to the taxed good. For example, if a tax on butter causes people to substitute margarine on their toast and in their cooking, this will drive up the price of margarine. In this way, part of the tax burden is shifted onto margarine consumers. Another important example applies to state and local government bonds. Interest on these bonds is excluded from federal taxation, while the returns on federal and corporate bonds are fully taxable. Because of this tax advantage, there is greater demand for state and local bonds. This bids up their price or, in other words, lowers the interest rate they offer. Because of the tax on other investments, holders of state and local bonds—who remit no tax at all—pay an *implicit tax* equal to the difference between the interest rate they receive and the higher rate they would receive on a taxed bond of similar maturity and riskiness.

Corporations Don't Pay Taxes, People Do

The controversial slogan of the National Rifle Association—"Guns don't kill, people do"—may seem like a semantic fine point, but at first blush the tax version seems just plain wrong. Corporations certainly do remit a great deal of taxes; federal, state, and local corporate profits taxes amounted to $214 billion in 2002.[39] Many people favor higher taxes on corporations in the hope that this means that they or their constituents will avoid bearing any burden.

Nevertheless, in an important sense, corporations do not pay tax. The fact that General Electric Company's treasurer signs checks made out to the IRS tells us nothing about which Americans bear the burden of taxation. Certainly the treasurer does not bear the burden of his employer's corporation income taxes, but who exactly does bear it? Is it GE's stockholders, its employees, or perhaps its customers? It is simply not meaningful to say that the legal entity that is General Electric will be worse off because of the corporation income tax. Rather, we need to identify precisely which *people* end up bearing the burden of a tax.

Who bears the burden of the corporate income tax? To answer this question, imagine imposing a corporate tax in an economy that previously has no such tax and that contains many businesses that are corporations and many that are not. In the short run, it is holders of corporate stock—the owners of the corporation—who suffer as a result of imposing this tax, as share prices will tumble in anticipation of lower after-tax earnings. This is not the end of the story, though, because further investment in corporations is now less attractive compared to investment in noncorporate firms such as partnerships, sole proprietorships, most farms, and real estate. Corporate investment dries up, while noncorporate investment expands. But more people seeking noncorporate investments will inevitably drive down the return in these sectors, as the most profitable opportunities are used up and less profitable ones are pursued. The reduced profitability of noncorporate business, due to more competition, shifts some of the burden of the tax to the owners of these other forms of wealth. In the long run, the after-tax, risk-adjusted return on investment will be the same for corporate investments as it is for noncorporate investments, and the burden will be shared among all owners of business capital.

Because this is a difficult bit of economic reasoning, the following analogy may be helpful. Imagine there are two highways leading from a suburb to the central city. The two highways get commuters to work in about the same amount of time, and almost everyone has settled into the habit of regularly taking one road or the other. Now imagine that a toll-booth is constructed on one of the roads. Who will be worse off? At first, the losers will be those who are accustomed to taking the newly taxed route to work. Over time, though, more and more commuters will switch to the untaxed alternate highway, making it more congested and increasing the commuting time. In this way, the burden of the toll im-posed on taking one road is shifted to those people who usually had taken the other. Once the dust has settled, all commuters will probably be about equally burdened by the toll. (If not, people will continue to change their commuting habits.) By analogy, a tax on the income from corporations will be spread to the recipients of all types of capital income as funds that otherwise would have been invested in corporations flow into the noncorporate sector.

Do Workers Bear Taxes on Capital?

Some economists argue that the shifting story does not end here and that the burden of a corporation income tax, or of any tax levied on the return to capital investment, will be shifted from wealth owners to wage earn-ers. Their argument goes as follows. Taxes on capital income (including, but not restricted to, corporation income taxes) reduce the rate of return to saving, which in turn reduces how much people save. Because saving finances capital investment, a decline in saving over time means that the economy is less capital-intensive and therefore labor is less produc-tive. By this reasoning, workers ultimately bear some of the burden of taxes on capital income because their wages are reduced when they are less productive.

This argument is highly controversial because it depends on a couple of hotly debated presumptions about how the U.S. economy works. First, it requires that individual saving behavior be responsive to changes in the after-tax return they receive. The experience of the 1980s and 1990s, when the after-tax rates of return to saving surged but the savings rate gradually declined, has cast doubt on that proposition.

Second, the argument requires that domestic investment must de-cline if U.S. saving declines. The global economy reduces the impact of a decline in domestic saving on domestic investment because that in-vestment need not be financed entirely by U.S. residents' savings. If a tax on the capital income of U.S. citizens, a budget deficit, or anything else is causing a reduction in our nation's saving, foreign savers have proven only too happy to pick up some of the slack and finance some of our investment.[40] In this case, the link between the future productivity of American workers and the return to our own investments is weakened, and more of the burden of taxes on the return to saving will be borne by American savers—that is, American wealth owners. Evidence that rates of domestic saving across countries are highly correlated with rates of domestic investment suggests, however, that declines in domestic saving are probably only partly offset by inflows of saving from abroad.[41]

We have argued that the possibility that foreigners will invest in the United States makes it less likely that a tax on U.S. residents' savings will be shifted onto U.S. workers. The possibility that U.S. citizens will invest abroad, though, makes it more likely that taxing U.S. domestic *investment* will in fact be somewhat shifted onto American workers. Investment abroad is an alternative to domestic investment, which limits the degree to which investors will accept a lower return to investing in the United States. Thus, an attempt to tax U.S.-located investment to some extent drives investment offshore, leaving U.S. workers with less productive work opportunities and downward pressure on their wages. As noted in chapter 2, the U.S. income tax includes provisions intended to make the tax rate on income from investment done by U.S. corporations the same regardless of where in the world that investment is done. This mitigates the extent to which the corporation income tax drives investment offshore. But for a variety of technical reasons, it is difficult to achieve this ideal, so incentives to move investment to low-tax countries remain.

The lesson of the global marketplace is that any one country finds it difficult to impose a tax burden on individuals whose income-earning opportunities are mobile across borders. Capital currently is more mobile than labor, implying that taxes on the income from capital in a particular location will tend to be shifted onto those workers who reside in that location. Evidence suggests, however, that capital is still far from perfectly mobile across borders for a large country such as the United States, so even in this case capital owners are likely to bear a substantial part of the tax burden.[42]

The nineteenth-century French pamphleteer and leader of the free-trade movement, Frédéric Bastiat, wrote that there is only one difference between a bad economist and a good economist: the latter considers both policy effects that can be seen and those that cannot be seen.[43] Because individuals and businesses can respond to taxes by changing their behavior, the true burden of taxes can be shifted in ways unanticipated and unintended by policymakers. Taxes on capital income can, in principle, be shifted to workers. Taxes on the profits from innovation can, in principle, be shifted to those consumers who would have enjoyed the innovative products that the tax discouraged from reaching market. It is impossible to know for sure how much tax shifting occurs, however. Good economists provide answers based on reasonable and explicit assumptions about the critical factors, and, ideally, they provide a range of possible consequences based on alternative sets of reasonable assumptions. Even if their answers to these questions differ, all economists recognize the four principles of tax incidence analysis that we have discussed:

- The entire burden of taxes must be traced to individuals.

- The ultimate distribution of the tax burden usually differs from the statutory liability.

- The long-run effect of taxes does not depend on which side of the market taxes are imposed.

- The better the alternatives that someone has to the taxed good or activity, the less likely that person is to bear the burden of the tax.

Who Does Pay?

So who does bear the burden of federal taxes in the United States? For federal taxes as a whole, the most recent and thorough analysis available was conducted by the Treasury Department's Office of Tax Analysis in 1999, based on tax law effective in the year 2000. In table 3.2 we present their findings, plus the results of an analysis of the distribution of federal income tax burdens alone that was done in 2003 by the Brookings-Urban Tax Policy Center, which reflects the impact of tax laws passed in both 2001 and 2003.

Both studies assume that the entire burden of the individual income tax falls on those families that have the legal liability, with no shifting at all of tax levied on either labor or capital income. This assumption would be consistent with a situation where neither labor supply nor saving is responsive to its after-tax return. The Treasury study, which also examines other types of taxes, must make assumptions about who ultimately bears these taxes. The study assigns corporate income tax burdens to families on the basis of their total capital (not just corporate-source) income; this is consistent with perfect mobility of investment across the

Table 3.2
Recent estimates of the distribution of federal taxes

Families ranked by income	Treasury Department[a] Average tax rates as a percentage of family economic income 2000 tax law			Urban-Brookings Tax Policy Center[b] Average tax rates as a percentage of AGI Personal income tax		Size of income tax cut, 2000–2003	
	All federal taxes	Corporate income tax	Personal income tax	2000 tax law	2003 tax law	Percentage point cut in average tax rate	Average dollar amount of tax cut
	(1)	(2)	(3)	(4)	(5)	(6)	(7)
Overall	21.5	2.3	10.1	14.4	11.8	2.6	1,217
Lowest quintile	5.9	0.9	−2.4	−10.0	−10.2	0.2	3
Second quintile	11.7	1.4	0.8	−3.5	−5.2	1.7	235
Middle quintile	17.4	1.6	5.6	6.1	3.6	2.5	676
Fourth quintile	20.1	1.6	7.8	10.1	7.9	2.2	1,074
Next 10 percent	21.9	1.6	9.5	12.5	9.8	2.7	2,121
Next 5 percent	23.3	2.0	11.4	15.2	12.3	2.9	3,212
Next 4 percent	24.1	3.0	13.6	19.4	16.9	2.6	4,571
Top 1 percent	29.1	4.6	20.2	28.5	25.2	3.3	26,335

Sources:
[a]Cronin (1999).
[b]Urban-Brookings Tax Policy Center (2003b, table 5.18, May 23).
Notes: Numbers for 2003 include effects of both 2001 and May 2003 tax cuts (EGTRRA and JGTRRA).

corporate and noncorporate sectors. Payroll taxes are attributed to families (according to their income from wages or self-employment) paying those taxes directly or indirectly through their employers, so that the assignment of legal liability between firm and individual is, as it should be, ignored. Estate and gift taxes are assumed to be borne by decedents.[44]

For purposes of illustrating average tax rates (tax burden divided by income), the Department of the Treasury uses *family economic income*, a broad definition that is close to the economic income concept discussed in chapter 2. The Urban-Brookings study uses *adjusted gross income* (AGI) as its measure of income. In aggregate, AGI was just 67 percent of family economic income in 2000, which explains why the average income tax rates look considerably smaller according to the Treasury analysis.[45]

Column 1 of table 3.2 indicates that distribution of federal taxes as a whole is quite progressive, with average tax rates rising from 5.9 percent for people in the lowest fifth of the income distribution, to 17.4 percent in the middle fifth, and then to 29.1 percent in the top percentile. This is true despite the fact that the Treasury uses a comprehensive measure of income that attempts to capture just about every possible form of income, including estimates of income underreported due to tax evasion. According to this analysis, the notion that by taking advantage of loopholes, tax shelters, and the like, upper-income people are typically able to pay a smaller share of their incomes in tax than everyone else is far from the truth.

The Treasury's estimate of the distribution of corporate taxes is shown in column 2 of table 3.2. Under the assumption that the tax is borne in proportion to capital income, its burden is distributed progressively. The Congressional Budget Office has done calculations that assume that half or all of the burden of the corporate tax falls on labor rather than on capital owners. This makes the overall distribution look a bit less progressive, but the corporate tax represents a small enough share of overall federal taxes that it doesn't make a big difference to the overall pattern shown in column 1.[46] If we made the extreme assumption that the burden of *all* taxes on capital income falls on labor (which would be consistent with a situation where saving was extremely responsive to incentives), this could be expected to further reduce but certainly not eliminate the progressive pattern of tax burdens in the overall federal tax system.

The third and fourth columns of table 3.2 show the Treasury and Urban-Brookings estimates of the personal income tax distribution in 2000. In both cases, the tax burden is found to be highly progressive. According to the Treasury analysis, average income tax rates as a percentage of family economic income range from –2.4 in the bottom quintile, to 5.6 percent in the middle, to 20.2 in the top percentile. According to the Urban-Brookings study, average tax rates as a percentage of AGI range from –10 to 28.5. Negative income tax rates at the bottom are due to the refundable portion of the earned income tax credit. The largest differences between the Treasury and Urban-Brookings analysis are at the top of the income distribution (due to forms of capital income not appearing in AGI) and at the bottom (due to government cash transfers and in-kind benefits that are not counted in AGI), which makes the Treasury denominator higher. Comparing the Treasury estimates for overall federal taxes (in column 1) and income taxes (in column 3) makes clear that income taxation accounts for nearly all of the progressivity of the federal tax system; most other federal taxes are either proportional or regressive in their distribution.

Columns 4 through 7 show the combined impact of the 2001 and 2003 tax cuts on income tax burdens and their distribution. First, it's clear that these were big tax cuts. Comparing the top row of column 4 and 5 shows that the overall average tax rate dropped from 14.4 percent to 11.8 percent, a decline of nearly one-fifth. Second, even after 2003, the income tax undeniably remained a highly progressive tax, with average tax rates clearly rising with income. Third, the cuts in average tax rates were bigger for those with higher income. The poorest 20 percent of the population received essentially no tax cut. As a percentage of income, tax cuts were more evenly spread out above that but were higher at the top. For example, the middle quintile received a tax cut equal to 2.5 percent of their incomes, while the top 1 percent had their average income tax rates decline by 3.3 percent. Note, though, that this analysis does not include the effects of phasing out the estate tax (included in the 2001 act), which would eventually be roughly equivalent to an annual average tax rate cut of another couple of percentage points of AGI for the top percentile.[47]

When expressed in dollar terms, as in column 7, the differences in the benefits of the tax cut appear more stark. For instance, the average tax cut per return in the middle fifth of the income distribution was $676, while the average tax cut for a taxpayer in the top 1 percent was $26,335, nearly 40 times as large. On the other hand, President Bush emphasized that the tax cuts represented a larger percentage of income tax liability for moderate-income people than for upper-income people.[48] This was true simply because to begin with, upper-income people were paying a large amount in income tax. Moderate-income people, by contrast, paid very little (or even negative) income tax beforehand—but they do bear substantial burdens from other federal, state, and local taxes that were not cut.

Table 3.2 suggests that people in all income groups have disposable incomes that are at least as high after the 2001 and 2003 tax cuts as they were before, and a broad swath of the population did receive tax cuts. So critics' complaints that the tax cuts are unfair may seem churlish to some. But of course, the table gives an incomplete picture of the winners and losers from the tax cuts. Tax cuts do not come for free. Ultimately, either government spending will have to be lower than it otherwise would have been, future taxes will have to be higher than they otherwise would have been, or some combination of the two will have to occur. We address this point in more detail in the next chapter. Those who argue that the tax cuts are unfair believe they disproportionately benefit today's upper-income taxpayers at the expense of tomorrow's taxpayers and the people who lose out from whatever government spending cuts may occur.

For some historical perspective, figure 3.2 illustrates how average federal tax rates changed between 1979 and 2000 for people at different points in the income distribution. This is based on a CBO analysis that takes a similar approach to the Treasury study shown above but uses a less comprehensive measure of income that is closer to AGI (and hence shows higher average tax rates than Treasury).[49] One remarkable feature of this figure is that between 1979 and 2000, despite several major revisions of the tax law that engendered tremendous political controversy, the average federal tax rate imposed on the middle 60 percent of the income distribution hardly changed at all. As table 3.2 suggests, the tax cuts enacted in 2001 and 2003 push these rates down somewhat. Since 1979, significant changes occurred at the bottom and top of the income distribution. The average federal tax rate on the top 1 percent fell dramatically from 37.0 percent to 25.5 percent between 1979 and 1986 as a result of the Reagan tax cuts, recovered much of that ground by 1995, and stood at 33.2 percent in 2000. The 2001 and 2003 tax cuts have likely pushed this figure down close to its Reagan-era level again. The bottom quintile saw a gradual decline in the average tax rate from 10.2 percent in 1984 to 6.4 percent in 2000 due to increases in the earned income tax credit, personal exemption, and standard deduction.

As is often pointed out, even though tax rates on high-income people were no higher in 2000 compared to 1979, the share of total taxes they paid increased. This is true for a very simple reason: as figure 3.1 shows, the share of before-tax income received by the rich increased

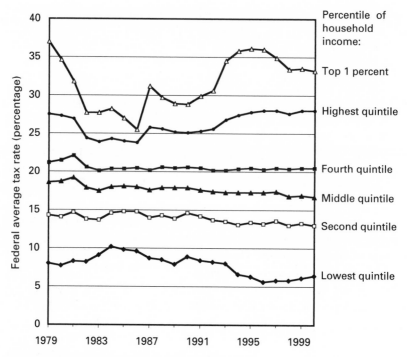

Figure 3.2
Average federal tax rates on families at various income levels, 1979–2000
Source: CBO (2003c, table B-1a).
Note: Depicts all federal taxes (except for estate and gift taxes) as a percentage of the Congressional Budget Office's measure of "adjusted pretax comprehensive household income" (see text for further details).

dramatically during this same time period. Somewhat lower average tax rates on much higher incomes brought in more tax revenue; we return to this issue in the next chapter.

How close does the distribution of the tax burden come to what, in surveys, Americans say they prefer? Figure 3.3 compares the progressivity of the personal income tax in 1991 (which is not vastly different from what it is today) with evidence on desired progressivity from the Hite-Roberts survey results from that same year (shown earlier in table 3.2). Comparing lines b and c reveals that the pattern of average rates in the current system was strikingly similar to the pattern that emerges when the "fair" tax bills assigned by survey respondents to families at each income level are converted into average tax rates. The general similarity of these two distributions suggests one or both of two things. It may mean that we have managed to get the sharing of

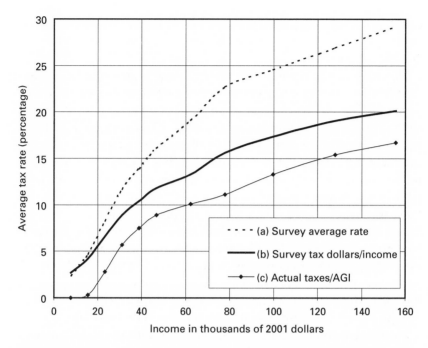

Figure 3.3
Actual progressivity of personal income taxes compared to survey evidence on desired progressivity, 1991
Source: Hite and Roberts (1991); authors' tabulations from the 1991 IRS individual tax model data files.
Notes: Each line represents average rates of federal personal income tax on married couples with no children:
(a) Means of survey respondents' desired average rates;
(b) means of survey respondents' desired tax dollars converted to average rates;
(c) actual average rates for 1991 defined as income tax after credits divided by adjusted gross income.

tax burdens about where Americans, on average, want it to be. Alternatively, it may mean that, when asked their preferences, people tend to mimic the system currently in place.

Horizontal Equity: Equal Treatment of Equals

Special Privileges for Everyone

According to Garrison Keillor, in Lake Wobegon all the children are above average. A similar paradox applies to the U.S. income tax system: everyone gets special privileges. You get a special tax break if you have children, if you are elderly, if you give money to your favorite charity, if you set up an IRA, if you receive fringe benefits from your employer, and the list goes on.

Of course, it is no more possible for everyone to get special tax breaks than it is possible for everyone to be above average. Remember, *we are taxing ourselves.* To raise a given amount of revenue, the long list of special tax privileges requires higher tax rates. Allowing large families to take additional dependent exemption allowances lowers their taxes but inescapably increases taxes on smaller families. The fact that mortgage interest payments are deductible certainly lowers taxes for those folks who have borrowed to buy their homes but inevitably raises taxes on those who rent housing. A family benefits from the whole system of tax breaks only if it receives more of them than other families at the same income level receive. Otherwise, what it saves in tax preferences is just offset by the higher-than-otherwise tax rates. But some people benefit and others lose. In fact, Alvin Rabushka of flat-tax fame has called the tax code "the most discriminatory body of law in a country that has tried to exterminate discrimination everywhere else in society."[50]

To expose the Wobegonish nature of our income tax system, allow us to reconfigure the tax system a bit. Gone is the current system of calculating your baseline gross income, subtracting off the deductions, and taking the credits that are your special privileges. The new system features a radical reduction in all tax rates, but—and there must be a but—now there are special tax *penalties* rather than special tax *privileges* for particular characteristics and activities. For example, there is a tax penalty for being under 65 years of age, for giving less than 1 percent of your income to a charity, for not setting up an IRA, and for receiving labor compensation in cash rather than in fringe benefits. If this tax redesign were done carefully enough, it could come pretty close to replicating the current pattern of tax liabilities, so that everyone would be right back to where they are now. The charitable would pay less tax than the uncharitable, the elderly would pay less than the non-elderly, and so on.

We're not suggesting that we go through the hassle of converting our tax system with special privileges for all to one with special penalties for all. The point is that we are all in the tax game together and that what is a privilege to one group of people ends up being a penalty to everyone else through higher tax rates.

Is there any justification for imposing special tax penalties—the inevitable consequences of granting privileges—on some families? Or do these penalties imply a failure to achieve what economists call *horizontal equity,* the principle that tax liability ought to be the same for any two families with the same level of well-being—equal treatment of equals?[51]

Certainly we could probably all agree it would be inappropriate to base tax liability on some characteristics—such as race or religion. Although your race or religion won't lead to higher taxes today in the United States, many other personal characteristics and choices will. Which, if any, of these are justifiable reasons to penalize someone?

Let's start with spending patterns. Would it be fair that the Hatfields pay more tax than the McCoys just because they like to go to the movies, while the McCoys prefer to watch television? Would it be fair to tax the Astors more than the Vanderbilts because the Astors prefer yachts, while the Vanderbilts favor private trains? Such distinctions based on one's "tastes" for consumption appear arbitrary and without a place in the tax system. If you agree, then tax penalties based on spending patterns are inappropriate, and taxes on particular goods and services are inappropriate because both will discriminate against families that have a penchant for those things. Taxes on movies discriminate against movie lovers, taxes on yachts discriminate against yacht lovers, and so on.[52] Note that taxing some goods but not others would not be a major problem for horizontal equity if the taxed goods represented the same share of total income for most people. If, for example, all families spent 20 percent of their income on food, then a 5 percent excise tax on food sales would be no more horizontally inequitable than a 1 percent income tax. If most, but not all, families spent 20 percent of their income on food, then the food tax would be almost as equitable but not quite.

Many aspects of the U.S. income tax system can be viewed as discriminating against certain people simply because of their tastes. For example, the home mortgage interest deduction penalizes those who prefer to rent housing rather than own housing. The charitable contribution deduction penalizes those who are not charitable. The deduction for state and local taxes penalizes people who prefer to live in places with low levels of public services. And the dependent exemption effectively penalizes families that prefer to have a small number of children.

Is there a more positive way to look at those tax features we've labeled as discriminating? If they encourage behavior that directly benefits other Americans, special tax treatments can serve a legitimate social purpose by in essence subsidizing taxpayers for the benefits they provide to others. This argument does not contradict that special tax treatments are horizontally inequitable, though; instead, the horizontal inequity is tolerated to achieve a more efficient economic system. The next chapter explores how to evaluate such arguments.

Tax preferences or penalties may also be justified on the grounds that income is an imperfect measure of a family's level of well-being and certain adjustments to income are required to make it a better measure. According to this argument, these tax features *improve* the horizontal equity of the tax system. This argument certainly applies to the existing deduction for extraordinary medical expenses. Comparing two families with the same income, one that incurs $10,000 in involuntary medical expenses is clearly not as well off as one that doesn't and may justifiably be liable for less taxes. What makes this case different than the Hatfields and McCoys is that medical expenses are mainly not a matter of taste: you don't choose to get a serious illness.[53] Allowing a deduction of medical expenses helps out families singled out by circumstance, not by taste, and thus is unlikely to be a source of horizontal inequity. Even in this case, however, some discrimination by taste creeps in: those who prefer to buy the best medical care they can find, instead of economizing, will receive an extra tax benefit.

Misleading Inequity

In some cases of potential horizontal inequity, it is tricky to tell whether circumstances or tastes are involved. Consider the deductibility of casualty losses due to earthquake damages. If earthquakes were truly a random event, not at all predictable by location, then this deduction makes sense as a way to adjust tax liability to reflect the reduced ability to pay of earthquake victims: they are victims of circumstance. In fact, earthquakes are much more likely to occur in certain areas, such as California. Living on a fault line is a choice that is to some degree compensated by lower-than-otherwise housing prices. In this situation, allowing the casualty loss deduction provides a reward to people who are willing to take the risk of an earthquake, which is certainly a matter of taste, and it penalizes everyone else. The argument gets even murkier when private earthquake insurance is available; in this case, the deduction rewards those who not only choose to live in a risky place but also choose not to insure themselves against a catastrophe.

In this example, lower housing prices were partial compensation for earthquake risk, weakening the argument for a tax break. Differences in tax payments do not reflect inequity if market prices offset the tax benefits. For example, the fact that some investors pay no tax on the interest they receive from state and local bonds does not indicate horizontal inequity to the extent that the market interest rate on these bonds is lower than taxable bonds because of their federal tax exemption. People with jobs in which a large part of their compensation is tax-exempt fringe benefits are not better off than others if their total pretax compensation is lower than otherwise. Offsetting changes in market prices are more likely to happen if the tax-preferred activity is available widely; when it is restricted to only certain people, the benefit is less likely to be offset by price changes. Tax-exempt bonds surely fall into the former category.[54] A tax privilege granted to one company, sometimes called a *rifle-shot* provision, is certainly in the latter category. Legislators who want to benefit some particular company based in their district or an important campaign contributor occasionally succeed in writing such provisions into the law, sometimes by sneaking provisions into a larger bill shortly before it is voted on, when few are paying attention to the details.

Who Are Equals: Families or Individuals?

If horizontal equity requires "equal treatment of equals," who exactly should be considered equals—individuals or families? This choice inevitably raises some tricky and controversial policy issues, ranging from the so-called marriage tax to the proper role of government in family-size decisions.

Our tax system uses the family as the unit of taxation but compromises between treating equal individuals equally and treating equal families equally. To see how this works out, consider how the number of children in a family affects tax liability. Under the current system, a family's tax bill declines with each additional child because each dependent qualifies the family for an additional exemption allowance, which amounts to a $3,050 deduction from taxable income in tax year 2003. The rationale here appears to be that in families with, say, $50,000 of gross income, each member will not be as well off if the family has six people compared to a family that has three people. So our tax system treats the larger family more generously on ability-to-pay grounds and imposes a lower tax liability.

This sounds reasonable because a dollar has to stretch further in a big family. But the other issue here is that it is not at all clear that parents are made worse off by each additional child they have. Having children is largely a voluntary choice and may even be viewed as a matter of personal consumption preference, or "taste," from the point of view of the parents. Some adults prefer to save their money and spend it on an around-the-world trip, while others prefer the joy of children with the attendant costs of food, diapers, video games, and possibly college. Is it fair to reward adults who prefer to have more children with lower taxes at the expense of adults who prefer other ways of spending their money?[55]

Undoubtedly, some people would object to lumping together child rearing and globetrotting as two comparable ways to spend money, and they would consider the former as a sacred duty rather than a choice. Whether something is a choice or a duty is not an issue that economics can resolve. Moreover, the choice of how many children will be in the family is not voluntary from the children's point of view. So a child in a six-person family may indeed be economically worse off than a child in a three-person family with the same income.

These are tough issues to resolve, but they are unavoidable in any tax system. Some tax systems, such as a retail sales tax, eliminate any tax preference based on family size. Others, such as the flat tax, would make these preferences more generous than they are now by making dependent allowances larger.

Common sense suggests that a system that rewards families with children would also reward or at least not penalize marriage. Common sense would be wrong for the U.S. tax system. Sometimes, getting married can increase a couple's total tax bill. This increase in tax is something called the *marriage penalty* or *marriage tax*. This is not actually a separate tax but a consequence of the income tax system. It arises not because any politician wants to dissuade people from getting married but because we insist on two requirements for our income tax system—that the tax system be progressive and that tax liability be based on total family income and not on how that income is divided between spouses. It turns out that these two requirements are incompatible with *marriage neutrality*, the principle that getting married should have no tax consequences.

An example illustrates how this happens. Barbie and Ken are considering tying the knot but are practical people who are worried about the tax consequences of this decision. Each now makes $30,000. For this example, assume that the average tax rate on $30,000 of income is 15 percent and the average tax rate for $60,000 income is 20 percent. Thus, Ken and Barbie now each pay $4,500 as singles. As a married couple, however, they would pay $12,000, amounting to a marriage tax of $3,000. Note that there would be no marriage tax at all if Barbie earned all the money or, for that matter, if Ken did.

In this example, the marriage tax happens not because anyone thinks it is good policy but rather as an unavoidable consequence of progressivity and family-based taxes. Some argue that a marriage tax is appropriate on ability-to-pay grounds because it reflects savings in the cost of living that marriage provides—sharing a kitchen, a telephone, and so on. These savings could, though, be achieved largely by having a roommate, and no one is suggesting that tax liability should depend on how many roommates you have.

If these are not convincing arguments for a marriage penalty, what can be done to alleviate it? One way around the problem is to have separate tax tables for single taxpayers and for married couples, as we do in the United States. Each schedule can be progressive on its own terms, so that the fraction of income owed in tax rises with income for single taxpayers and also for married taxpayers. If the tax due on the same income is lower for a married couple compared to a single taxpayer, then the marriage tax can be reduced or erased completely. Let's go back to Barbie and Ken and see how this would work. For single taxpayers, let the average tax rate still be 15 percent for $30,000 income and 20 percent for $60,000 income; this is progressive. For married taxpayers, let the tax rate be 10 percent on $30,000 and 15 percent on $60,000; this is progressive, too (at least when considering only married taxpayers). This scheme eliminates the marriage tax on Barbie and Ken because they pay $4,500 each as singles and $9,000 as a married couple.

Some important consequences arise, though, when we try to get rid of the marriage tax in this way. First of all, it imposes a penalty for being single because under this system a single taxpayer earning $60,000 pays $12,000 in tax, while a married couple with exactly the same family income owes only $9,000. This situation provides what is usually called a *marriage bonus* of $3,000, but it just as well could be called a penalty for being single.

As long as we desire a progressive tax system based on family income, there is no way to make it also marriage-neutral. Any tax schedule will feature either a marriage bonus (single penalty) or a marriage penalty (single bonus), or some combination of both depending on the tax schedules and circumstances of the people involved.

In the United States, we have opted for a compromise among the approaches. A two-earner couple has typically faced a penalty for getting married, although the penalty is not as large as it would be if all families and individuals were taxed under the same schedule. A single-earner couple has typically received a tax bonus for getting married. There is a single penalty, as well, because a single person pays more tax than a single-earner married couple with the same income. According to the Congressional Budget Office, as of 1996 this compromise meant that nearly 21 million couples incurred marriage penalties averaging $1,400, raising their taxes by a total of $29 billion. Another 25 million couple received marriage bonuses averaging $1,300 each, saving them a total of about $33 billion in taxes.[56] Provisions were included in the 2001 tax act in an effort to reduce marriage penalties for some people. For instance, for married couples filing jointly, the amounts of the standard deduction and the top limit of the 15 percent bracket would be gradually increased until they reached twice the amounts applying to singles. The 2003 act accelerated the phase-in of these provisions to begin taking full effect that year. Adam Carasso and C. Eugene Steuerle studied the impact of the 2001 tax law changes on marriage penalties and concluded that the new tax legislation would "significantly reduce marriage penalties or increase marriage subsidies for most households." They also noted, however, that many marriage penalties would remain. [57]

We could achieve marriage neutrality if tax liability was based on individual rather than family income, as is the case in several European countries and as was the case in the United States in the early days of the income tax.[58] Under this system, marriage can have no tax consequences at all. But under this system, a family's tax liability depends on who earns what; a family in which the total income is divided up fairly equally will owe less than another family with exactly the same total income but with one primary earner. It also gives rise to incentives to shift income from the highest-earning family member to lower-earning members. Couples can manipulate which spouse receives capital income and incurs deductible expenses, all of which are difficult for the IRS to monitor.[59]

Lifetime and Generational Perspectives on Equity

If the government announced a special annual tax of $1,000 on half of all taxpayers, to alternate every other year with a special $1,000 grant to the same people, everyone would understand that (ignoring interest) over a two-year horizon the net benefit comes to nothing, even though a one-year analysis would reveal apparently capricious horizontal inequity. More seriously, when comparing two tax systems that require a different timing of tax payments but that add up to the same burden over a longer horizon, it is important not to be misled by an annual analysis to conclude that there is inequity. For example, special credits to the elderly don't have significant equity consequences if everyone eventually is elderly. The fact that, over a lifetime, income taxes are levied during the working years and sales tax payments are apparently spread out more evenly over the consuming years, including retirement, is not in itself relevant for horizontal inequity, even though in any one year the tax payments of two individuals with the same income will tend to differ depending on their ages. We return to this issue in chapters 6 and 7, where we discuss replacing the income tax with a consumption tax.

Some tax policy issues require us to look beyond even a lifetime perspective to a multigenerational perspective. As the next chapter shows, this perspective is essential for discussing deficit finance of government expenditures because borrowing puts off specifying who will bear the burden of taxes and tends to impose that burden on future generations. This issue also enters the debate over whether to replace the income tax with a consumption tax because, depending on how the transition is handled, that could shift a substantial tax burden onto the elderly and decrease the tax burden on future generations.

Transitional Equity

Whenever the tax system changes, some people will lose out and others will benefit. This is true regardless of whether the change ultimately makes the tax system fairer. The losers lose in part because they have entered into some long-term commitment that made sense only because of the old tax system. They may have bought houses counting on the mortgage interest deduction and will lose out if it is abolished. They may have taken jobs far from their homes, counting on cheap gasoline for commuting, and will lose if gasoline taxes are increased. They may have invested in state and local bonds, counting on the benefit of tax-free interest, and will see the value of these bonds fall if marginal tax rates are reduced and plummet if the tax exemption is removed entirely.

Others will reap windfall benefits when the tax law changes. These are people who happen to be in the right place at the right time. For example, individuals who own stock in companies that pay or likely will in the future pay dividends will see their shares rise in value if the tax on dividends is eliminated, as President Bush proposed in early 2003, or reduced, as the 2003 tax law provides for. Of course, the political pressure against change always comes from those who stand to lose from a tax change, not those who stand to win. What should be done about them?

Some would say "tough beans" and leave it at that, arguing that there are constantly ups and downs in the economic environment and everyone has to expect to lose out from time to time. This argument is especially compelling when talk of tax changes has been in the air for a while. In that case, the possibility of windfall losses is probably already reflected in the price of the activity or asset. For example, serious congressional consideration of lower tax rates can drive down the price of tax-exempt securities, increasing their yield. The bargain price and high interest rate reflect the possibility that tax rates might go down. If that does occur, fully compensating the holders of the bonds wouldn't make sense. They took a gamble when they bought the bonds, fully aware of the possibility of a tax reduction, and they've already been partly compensated for this risk through a higher return on their investment.

In other cases, there is simply no way that the tax change could have been anticipated. A family that took out a home mortgage five years ago, counting on the interest deduction, could not have reasonably anticipated that the deduction would be eliminated. If the mortgage deduction were to be eliminated, what can be done to prevent this family from being hurt? The usual fix is to "grandfather" existing mortgages so that interest on them remains deductible, even as interest on new mortgages is no longer deductible.

This seems reasonable, but grandfathering arrangements and other transition rules can easily become quite complicated. They require two parallel sets of rules—one to apply to decisions taken under the old tax law and one to apply to decisions taken since; the dividing line requires monitoring to prevent abuse. These arrangements also cost the Treasury revenue and thus require higher tax rates than otherwise, at least for a while.

Transitional equity is an absolutely critical concern when considering replacing the income tax with a consumption-based tax. Here one important dividing line is age. If people knew from birth that they had to pay a tax equal to 20 percent of their lifetime incomes, it probably wouldn't matter to most of them whether they paid most of it by the time they retired or whether the tax was spread evenly over their working and retirement years. As long as the payment schedule was known in advance, it shouldn't be a big problem.

Changing the rules in midlife, however, can be a big problem. Imagine living and paying taxes under an income tax regime all your working life, expecting to pay few or no taxes in retirement, and then waking up on the first day of your retirement to learn that the income tax had been abolished only to be replaced by a retail sales tax! No one would blame you for being upset. But this is exactly what could happen to millions of elderly people if we were to shift to a consumption tax, depending on how that tax is implemented.

Just as with the mortgage interest deduction, there are fixes. For example, elderly people can be granted an exemption from the sales tax or at least be taxed at a lower rate. But as with the mortgage deduction, these fixes have problems. The elderly "exemption card" would be valuable indeed: imagine making sure your elderly parents buy your next car for you and give it to you as an anniversary present. Even if such a scheme were preventable, the exemption would require that the sales tax rate on everyone else would have to be much higher to make up for the lost revenue.

The point is that even if we could all agree that another tax system is fairer and simpler, getting from here to there might be unfair to many people. If, though, we try to devise rules to compensate losers, the transition can become extremely complicated. Moreover, if only those losers who are politically powerful get compensated, the transition can end up becoming both extremely complicated *and* unfair.

Conclusion

What's fair in taxation plays a crucial role in the debate about tax reform because many reform proposals effect a radical reshuffling of the tax burden. Some proposals collapse the graduated rate structure to a single rate, substantially lessening the tax system's progressivity. Other proposals cut back on the special provisions in the tax law that are justified on the grounds that they fine-tune the sharing of the tax burden or reward socially beneficial activities. Whether these changes represent steps toward or away from tax equity cannot be answered in isolation because fairness is inextricably tied to the simplicity of the tax system and how it affects economic performance. Fine-tuning tax liability and ensuring progressivity inevitably complicate the tax process, and abandoning these goals can allow significant simplification. Moreover, the effort to use the tax system to redistribute incomes and single out particular activities for reward may inhibit economic growth. How much is the subject of the next chapter.

4 Taxes and Economic Prosperity

The question of how taxes affect the economy has long been at the heart of the American political debate. At one end of the spectrum are those who argue that our tax system is a serious drag on the economy and that radical changes could unleash a new era of unbridled growth and prosperity. Ronald Reagan made this a central theme of his presidential campaigns and rode to landslide victories as he promised and delivered lower income tax rates, with dramatic reductions concentrated at the top. During the 1996 and 2000 Republican presidential primaries, candidate Steve Forbes claimed that abolishing the existing income tax and replacing it with a flat-rate consumption tax could *double* the long-term rate of economic growth.[1] During the 2000 campaign and throughout his presidency, George W. Bush argued that low taxes are critical for prosperity, stating that "countries with low taxes, limited regulation, and open trade grow faster, create more jobs, and enjoy higher standards of living than countries with bigger, more centralized governments and higher taxes."[2]

In contrast, most Democratic politicians rarely mention the economic costs of taxation except to say that their opponents are greatly exaggerating them. Instead, they stress the economic benefits of the programs that tax revenues make possible, such as Social Security. Although not all of these benefits are reflected in typical measures of prosperity, they are real nonetheless. Democrats also decry the fact that many of the Republicans' tax proposals end up benefiting the most affluent at the expense of the beneficiaries of government expenditure programs today and (in the case of tax cut proposals that increase budget deficits) at the expense of future generations.

Economists' views of the impact of taxation and the potential benefits of reform tend to be considerably more circumspect than those expressed by political advocates, but they still present a broad range of opinion.

Stanford economist Robert Hall, a designer of the flat tax, says adopting it would most likely increase incomes by a total of 6 percent over seven years.[3] Some economists would put that figure higher, but almost none would promise a sustained doubling of the growth rate. Others are less sanguine; for example, William Gale of the Brookings Institution has argued that the long-run gain in economic well-being would probably be closer to 1 percent of income.[4] Just as important as the differing estimates, however, is what economists know and agree on; this often diverges in important ways from the focal issues and claims in the public debate.

Understanding how the tax system affects the economy and how to evaluate claims about those effects is critically important to assessing what tax policy we should have. For one thing, if certain features of our tax code hinder the economy without good reason, most of us could agree that we should change those features. Often, however, changes to the tax code that could improve economic performance conflict with other valued goals. In these cases, there is a trade-off or balance to be struck, and the terms of that trade-off depend crucially on how large the economic benefits arising from the tax change would be.

The greatest and most controversial of these trade-offs is one we briefly mentioned in the previous chapter—that between progressivity and economic efficiency. Taxes reduce the incentive to engage in all of the activities people undertake to better themselves—working harder, acquiring education and training, thinking of new products and ways to do business, and so on. The more progressive the tax system, the more these incentives are blunted. As shown in the previous chapter, however, progressive taxes also play a big role in determining how the burden of paying for government is distributed among people with differing abilities and fortunes. Many view a progressive distribution of the burden as fair. Hence, there is an inescapable trade-off.

In recent years, one of the Republicans' most effective rhetorical weapons has been the parable of the pie, where the pie represents national wealth. Democrats, they claim, are obsessed with how to slice the pie and with ensuring that their natural constituencies get a good-size slice. Republicans, in contrast, say they are determined to enact policies that enlarge the size of the pie so that everyone can obtain a bigger slice. When framed in this way, the critical questions are how much bigger the pie can get and more specifically exactly how the size of the pie depends on how it is sliced. Whether most people are ultimately made better off or worse off by a change in the tax system can depend crucially on the answer to these questions.

This chapter explores how taxes affect the economy. Our main concern is how the *design* of the tax system influences the level of economic prosperity in the long run. We examine the specific ways that taxes affect economic behavior and the evidence on the magnitude of those effects. Before we begin this task, we address some important issues that are in principle separate from how the design of the tax system affects long-run prosperity but that often get mixed together with that question and often dominate the political debate.

Taxes and the Business Cycle

The economy does not proceed steadily along a long-run trend, but instead it experiences temporary ups and downs known as the business cycle. The downs, periods when the economy is sluggish and stuck significantly below its capacity, are known as recessions. Unemployment rates rise above their normal levels, and industrial plant and equipment go underutilized. Recoveries from recessions are generally periods of unusually rapid growth rates, as we make up lost ground and more fully utilize the capital and labor that are already available. This kind of growth is fundamentally different from the kind of long-run growth that involves an expansion of the economy's capacity or potential—more and better capital and technology and more and better-skilled labor.

The first thing to note about recessions and recoveries is that they generally occur for reasons that have little or nothing to do with taxes. Recessions are situations of insufficient economywide "demand": the economy temporarily operates below its capacity to produce because consumers, firms, and government are not willing to buy everything that producers in the economy are willing and able to make. A recession may be triggered, for example, by a drop in consumer or business confidence. If consumers become worried about their jobs and the state of the economy, they may reduce their purchases of cars, homes, appliances, and other goods. Normally, this need not be a problem. Lower consumption means higher saving. In the long run, some combination of price adjustments and reductions in interest rates will happen automatically until firms are willing to use the extra saving to finance investments in factories, machinery, and so forth, picking up the slack from consumers and preventing any drop in overall demand. In fact, this is the opposite of a problem, as higher saving and investment mean a more productive economy and higher incomes in the future. One difficulty, however, is that frictions in the economy may prevent the necessary adjustments in prices and interest rates from happening fast enough. In addition, when consumers reduce their spending, businesses may become more pessimistic about their ability to sell goods in the future and thus want to *reduce* their investment. As a result, economywide demand for goods and services can drop. This in turn reduces the incomes of the workers who produce those things, who in turn buy fewer goods, which produces a downward spiral. Sometimes, a drop in business confidence and investment happens first, and as a result of the aforementioned frictions and pessimism, consumers fail to pick up enough of the slack. Sluggishness in the economy in 2001 to 2003 appears to have resulted from this latter version of the story, as business investment dropped sharply when firms started to realize they had overinvested during the excessively optimistic technology bubble of the late 1990s.

The main job of the Federal Reserve ("the Fed") is to keep economywide demand stable by overcoming the frictions that cause interest rates to adjust too slowly on their own. It does this by engaging in *monetary policy*. For instance, if the Fed suspects that demand for consumption or investment is dropping, it can print money and use it to purchase bonds on the open market. The reduced supply of bonds will push down short-term interest rates (when fewer bonds are available, interest rates do not need to be as high to attract people to buy them). Lower interest rates can boost the economy by making it less expensive for businesses to borrow for investments in plant and equipment and for consumers to borrow to buy cars, homes, and the like; higher interest rates can have the opposite effect. Between December 2000 and November 2002, the Fed cut the targeted federal funds rate (a short-term interest rate often used as a signal of the Fed's overall stance on policy) 12 separate times, taking it from 6.5 percent to 1.25 percent to lean against the weakening economy.[5] Other times, when the economy is booming, the Fed takes action to push interest rates up to restrain demand and prevent inflation.

The role of taxes in moderating the business cycle is more controversial among economists. A tax cut does put more money in people's pockets, and to the extent that people go out and spend some of it, this gives a boost to demand in the economy, which could help get us out of a recession more quickly. But the same is true for an increase in government spending or transfer payments. Using tax cuts or government spending to fight a recession is known as *fiscal policy*. Note that the increased demand caused by either a tax cut or a spending increase is helpful only if the economy is operating below its capacity. If the economy is already at or near capacity, as it normally is, a big increase in spending can't be met by a big increase in output, so the result instead will be higher inflation, higher interest rates, and less investment or some combination of these.

Recent U.S. history reveals a number of episodes in which tax cuts have been explicitly used in an attempt to spur demand and jump-start a sluggish economy. The Kennedy-Johnson tax cut of 1964 is often cited as an example of a tax cut that was intentionally and successfully used for this purpose. In other cases, stimulating demand is not a stated rationale for a tax cut but may have that effect anyway. For example, some argue that the recovery from the 1981 and 1982 recession was spurred in part by increased consumer demand induced by the Reagan tax cut. Finally, income taxes may help dampen recessions even in the absence of legislated changes by acting as an *automatic stabilizer*. Income tax revenues decline automatically in recessions because incomes are shrinking and people are slipping into lower tax brackets. This may help cushion the blow to consumer demand.

Fighting recessions with deficit-increasing tax cuts or government spending no longer garners as much support among economists as it once did. This has not stopped politicians from embracing tax cuts as antirecession measures, although it did arguably influence politicians' decision to rely entirely on monetary policy to deal with the 1991 and 1992 recession. One reason for the lack of enthusiasm among many economists is neatly summarized by Paul Krugman: "Monetary policy and fiscal policy are like aspirin and morphine. Both are painkillers, but when you feel a headache coming on you reach for the aspirin first."[6] By this Krugman means that in most cases, monetary policy should be the first line of defense, whereas fiscal policy tends to be addictive (that is, hard to reverse) and should be used to fight a recession only in special circumstances when nothing else works. Enacting tax cuts or new spending programs that make sense only in a recession can cause problems later on when they stick around long after the recession is over. Among these problems would be larger long-term budget deficits, the negative economic consequences of which we discuss later. Thus, fighting a recession with larger budget deficits might mean short-term gain but long-term pain. This problem is compounded by the fact that by the time the government recognizes a recession and enacts a tax cut or spending increase, the economy has often begun to rebound on its own, making the policy unnecessary at best and inflationary at worst.

A second drawback of a tax cut as a recession-fighting measure is that the extra disposable income may be saved rather than spent, in which case it will be largely ineffective at achieving the needed boost in demand. Theoretically, this should be especially true of a temporary tax cut. If people know that their taxes are temporarily low today and will go up again in the future, they may want to save most of today's tax cut to smooth their consumption over time instead of living a "feast or famine" lifestyle.

The evidence on this question is mixed and even somewhat contradictory. On the one hand, some evidence suggests that peoples' consumption spending tends to match up closely with fluctuations in their after-tax incomes over time, so that they apparently do only a limited amount of consumption smoothing. For example, people who earn wages and salaries above the limit for Social Security payroll taxes ($87,000 in 2003) get a temporary tax cut every year: at the point in the calendar year when their accumulated earnings for the year rise above that level, the payroll tax stops being deducted from their paychecks. Jonathan Parker of Princeton University found that such workers end up spending a significant portion of these predictable, temporary tax cuts when they get them, rather than smoothing their consumption spending over the course of the year.[7] When in 1992 the first President Bush ordered a reduction in withholding of income taxes from peoples' paychecks in an effort to boost consumer spending and speed recovery from a recession, nearly half of survey respondents said they would spend the extra money from their paychecks immediately.[8] This was even weaker than a temporary tax cut. In fact, it was just a change in the timing of taxes, as it would reduce the amount of refunds received (or increase the tax balance due) the following year by an equal amount. This sort of evidence suggests that a temporary tax cut might be effective at boosting consumer demand after all.

On the other hand, evidence on the 2001 tax cut leads to the opposite conclusion. To make the tax cut more vivid to taxpayers, part of the tax cut for 2001 was converted into a tax-rebate check—usually $300 or $600—mailed to taxpayers' homes. Surveys of taxpayers taken at the time suggested that less than a quarter of those who got those checks planned to mostly spend them, even though these checks were "down payments" on a very large 10-year tax cut rather than a one-time tax reduction.[9] This is difficult to reconcile with the other evidence mentioned above but may indicate that the degree to which people spend any increase in their after-tax incomes depends heavily on their perceptions of the state of the economy at that particular point in time. In any event, these surveys cast doubt on the effectiveness of even persistent tax cuts as recession-fighting measures.

Our point here is not to pass final judgment on the wisdom of using tax cuts as a countercyclical policy. What we do want to emphasize is that this issue is completely separate from the question of how our tax system should be designed. Indeed, what might work to counter a recession (stimulating private consumption) might be exactly the opposite of a common goal of many fundamental tax reform proposals—to increase the national saving rate. This leads us naturally to the next issue.

Budget Deficits and Surpluses

The budget deficit or surplus—that is, the difference between the level of tax revenues and the level of government spending—is a second important issue that, in principle, is separate from the question of how our tax system should be designed. Just about any tax system could raise enough revenue so that there is neither a deficit nor a surplus if its rates are set at the right levels. Moreover, people on all sides of the tax reform issue tend to agree, at least publicly, that persistent large deficits should be avoided.

The debate about the appropriate level of surplus or deficit, though, does get mixed into the tax reform debate when advocates of radical reform plans argue that tax rates can safely be set much lower than what is conventionally considered *revenue neutral* on the grounds that the induced economic growth will make up the revenue shortfall. (This is one more reason that understanding the evidence on the economic impact of taxation is important.) The question of deficit levels certainly arises when a tax cut proposal is unaccompanied by any cuts in overall government spending, as was the case in 2001 and again in 2003. In either case, we need to understand the economics of deficits to know what is at risk if the extreme growth optimists are wrong (as we and most other economists believe they are) and deficits increase due to tax cuts.

Point number one is that running a deficit doesn't reduce the cost of government expenditure; it merely puts off the reckoning of who pays the cost. The massive deficits of the 1980s and early 1990s mean that one of the biggest categories of federal government expenditures continues to be interest on the federal debt, in fiscal year 2002 accounting for 8.9 percent of total outlays. This expense is unavoidable; not paying it would precipitate financial catastrophe because the government would lose credibility and have great difficulty ever borrowing again. Paying this interest requires higher taxes or lower spending on other things, and the more the debt grows, the higher these interest payments become. Repaying the debt itself would require even higher taxes or deeper spending cuts, although this could be avoided by rolling over the debt, which is sustainable as long as only the debt doesn't grow too large relative to the size of the economy.

A key way that budget deficits push the cost of today's government onto future taxpayers is by reducing the size of the future economy relative to what it would otherwise be. Budget deficits do this by eroding *national saving*—that is, private saving minus government borrowing—which reduces the funds available for private investment in such things as machinery, technology, and factories. When the government runs a budget deficit, it borrows from the public by selling bonds. This causes people to put their savings into government bonds instead of, say, corporate bonds or stocks that would be used to finance productive investments in the private sector. The reduced supply of saving available for private investment pushes up the interest rate, making borrowing more costly for firms that need to finance investments and thereby depressing the rate of investment. A decline in investment reduces the productivity and long-run growth potential of our economy because it results in less machinery, factories, and technology, and therefore less productive workers.

As noted above, running a deficit during a recession can be a good thing because the lower taxes and higher government spending it implies can boost demand and get the economy to put its existing productive capacity back to work. But what matters for the long-run prosperity of the economy is boosting *supply*—that is, increasing the productive capacity of workers and capital. Budget deficits are bad for that. While this may seem paradoxical, it is not much different than the situation faced by a household. In times of temporary financial hard times, it makes sense for you to reduce your saving or to borrow. But if you reduce your saving persistently, in good times and bad, you will be a lot worse off in the future. Similarly, the nation as a whole is made worse off in the future when the government borrows more because it means the nation saves less.

Deficits need not reduce national saving dollar for dollar. One argument is that taxpayers may correctly perceive that deficits imply higher taxes or lower government transfers for themselves or their children in the future and correspondingly increase their own saving and bequests to make up for the consequences of the deficit. In this way, private saving would increase and somewhat offset the increase in government dissaving. Another argument is that to the extent that deficits tend to raise interest rates, this could induce people to save a bit more, offsetting some of the government dissaving. If the deficit was caused by cutting tax rates on capital income, the lower tax rates would increase the incentive to save even more. But national saving will still decline unless people save *every single dollar* of the tax cut, which would require a strong responsiveness of saving to incentives. In recent U.S. history, these factors do not appear to have significantly offset the impact of deficits on national saving; as we discuss later, private saving rates *declined* considerably when the United States cut taxes and started running large budget deficits in the early 1980s. Finally, deficits might not reduce national investment if foreigners are induced to increase their holdings of U.S. government bonds and other U.S. investments. This has, in fact, occurred to some extent in the United States since the 1980s. Foreign investment is of only limited help to us, however, because foreigners will also end up reaping most of the rewards of that extra investment and interest payments will flow out of the country.

Recently, members of the Bush administration have implied that, for a number of different reasons, we shouldn't worry about long-term budget deficits and should instead focus on cutting taxes as much as possible regardless of the level of government spending. A key element of this campaign was the claim that budget deficits do not affect interest rates and thus will not reduce investment and long-run growth. For instance, in 2002, R. Glenn Hubbard, the first chair of the Council of Economic Advisers under President Bush, said, "I don't buy that there's a link between swings in the budget deficit of the size we see in the United States and interest rates. . . . There's just no evidence."[10] This is not the consensus view among economists and in fact apparently contradicts what Hubbard himself writes in an economics textbook he has authored, where he indicates that the large budget deficits of the 1980s pushed up interest rates and harmed growth, while the surpluses of the 1990s reduced interest rates and improved growth.[11]

The first thing to emphasize about this controversy is that even if budget deficits do not affect interest rates, this does not mean they have no economic cost. There is no free lunch. For instance, a budget deficit could possibly have no effect on interest rates if the decline in national saving it caused was fully offset by inflows of foreign saving to finance our investment. But this doesn't change the fact that Americans are made worse off in the future by saving less as a nation: the extra investment financed by foreigners is owned by them, and they reap most of the benefits. Similarly, a deficit-increasing tax cut might have no effect on interest rates if people saved all of it in anticipation that they or their heirs will have to pay higher taxes in the future. But in that case, the tax cut is not making anyone better off at all: the gain from lower taxes today is fully offset by having to set aside extra money to pay for future tax bills, and any positive effects of improved incentives from lower tax rates today are offset by the negative effects of worsened incentives from higher tax rates in the future.

A second important point is that there is in fact good evidence that, *other things equal*, larger budget deficits *do* cause long-term real interest rates to rise. The reason the relationship between deficits and interest rates is not immediately obvious is that both interest rates and budget deficits are strongly affected by a third factor, the business cycle. During recessions, real interest rates tend to be low, both because demand for investment is low and because the Fed pushes interest rates down in an effort to fight the recession. At the same time, budget deficits increase automatically during a recession because income tax revenues fall and spending on items like unemployment insurance increases. Therefore, during a recession, real interest rates will be low and budget deficits will be high for reasons completely unrelated to the effect of budget deficits on interest rates. The oft-cited facts that interest rates were relatively low in the United States and Japan in recent years at the same time that budget deficits were increasing dramatically tells us nothing one way or the other about how deficits affect interest rates other things equal. In both cases, the low interest rates and some of the deficits were caused by a recession.

One way to get around this problem is to look at the relationship between projected *future* budget deficits and the real interest rates being charged on *future* years of loans. Each of these tends to be based on expectations about what the budget deficit and interest rates will be in the long run, after any recession is over, so they can help separate out how deficits affect interest rates from how each are affected by the business cycle. William Gale and Peter Orszag of the Brookings Institution reviewed the economic literature on this topic as of 2002 and found that studies that take this approach overwhelmingly found that deficits increase real interest rates.[12] A more recent study by Thomas Laubach of the Board of Governors of the Federal Reserve confirmed this finding.[13]

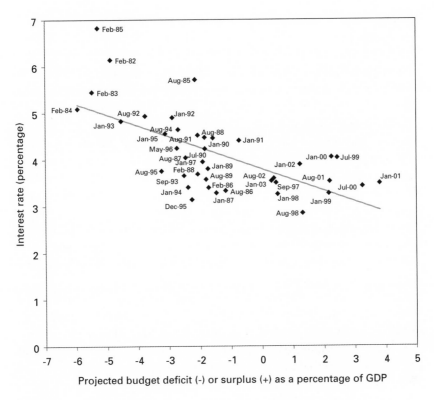

Figure 4.1
Long-term real interest rates versus projected long-term budget deficit or surplus in the
United States, 1982–2003
Source: Authors' calculations based on data provided by Thomas Laubach of the Federal
Reserve Board of Governors.
Notes: Depicts Congressional Budget Office projections of the federal budget deficit as a
percentage of gross domestic product five years in the future and the average implicit real
interest rate in years 5 through 14 on U.S. Treasury bonds at the date of the CBO
projection. Labels on data points depict the month and year the projection was made.

Figure 4.1 plots the relationship between the Congressional Budget
Office's projection of the budget deficit as a percentage of GDP five years
in the future and the real interest rate being paid in years 5 through 14
on U.S. Treasury bonds being issued at the time the projection was
made, for the years 1982 through 2003. In years when projected long-
term budget deficits were larger, long-term real interest rates were
indeed higher. The simple relationship in the graph suggests that a
persistent increase in the annual budget deficit of 1 percent of GDP
causes real interest rates to rise by about a quarter of a percentage point,
and statistical studies that control for other important influences on

interest rates typically find effects in the range of one-quarter of a percentage point to one percentage point.[14] By 2003, the Bush administration's Council of Economic Advisers had come around to this point of view, estimating that a persistent $100 billion increase in the budget deficit (which is approximately equal to 1 percent of GDP) would increase long-term interest rates by 0.3 percentage point.[15]

While economists and policymakers certainly still dispute the magnitude of the effect of budget deficits on interest rates, a more important question is whether the positive economic effects of a tax cut will be large enough to offset much of the negative effect of the resulting deficit. As we noted above, during a recession, deficit-financed tax cuts or spending increases could provide a short-run stimulus. But monetary policy alone could be equally effective at getting us out of a recession, while avoiding the negative side effects of budget deficits. A deficit-financed tax cut could also have a positive long-run effect on the economy to the extent that it improves incentives to work, save, invest, and so on, and these behavioral responses will partly offset the negative effects of the deficit itself. But if tax cuts are not accompanied by cuts in government spending programs, then today's borrowing means that future taxes eventually must be *higher* than they otherwise would have been. When that time comes, the higher taxes will harm incentives and depress the economy. If low taxes now are accepted as a boon to the economy, then the higher taxes that must come in the future must be accepted as a large liability. This discussion raises two crucial questions that are explored later in this chapter: how responsive is economic behavior to incentives, and do deficit-financed tax cuts change the behavior of politicians toward the level of government spending?

In February 2003, Federal Reserve Board chair Alan Greenspan bluntly challenged the Bush administration's contention that big budget deficits pose little danger or that the government can largely offset them through faster economic growth. Greenspan told the Senate Banking Committee that "faster economic growth, doubtless, would make deficits easier to contain" but added that "faster economic growth alone is not likely to be the full solution to the currently projected long-term deficits." Greenspan also took issue with the Bush administration's arguments that budget deficits have little effect on interest rates, saying, "Contrary to what some have said, it does affect long-term interest rates and it does have an impact on the economy."[16]

For these reasons, increasing the deficit (or reducing the surplus) is likely to make us worse off in the long run.[17] Although modest deficits are likely to have modest costs, they do have a cost. Many analyses of the economic impact of taxation conveniently ignore this fact of life. They predict that a general reduction in taxes will have a beneficial impact on economic activity because it unleashes demand and reduces the disincentives that taxes create. This prediction may be true to a degree, but it ignores the very real negative consequences that the increased deficit has.

How Much Should Government Do?

Another issue that is often confounded with tax reform is the question of how big the government should be. Many of the proponents of radical tax reform plans and big tax cuts are also strong advocates of sharply reduced federal government spending. Still, people who disagree on the proper size of government needn't necessarily disagree on what's the best way to finance whatever level of government services we choose.

This is not a book about how big the government should be. Rather, it is about how the tax system ought to be designed, given whatever level of government spending is chosen. We limit the scope in this way not because we believe that the level and composition of government expenditures are exactly right, but because otherwise reasonably comparing the impact of two different tax policies is too difficult. Many arguments have been made about why government should or should not undertake certain tasks. Each government function needs to be evaluated on its merits, and this is not the place to do that. For example, whether an additional aircraft carrier should be purchased is in the end a question of whether the benefits it provides by increasing national security exceed its cost; as in many cases, the benefits are difficult to quantify, and the ultimate resolution must come through the political system.

With that said, some important connections can be drawn between the economic impact of taxation and the appropriate size of government. Most important, how big the government should be depends in part on how costly raising taxes is to the economy. The cost of raising one dollar in taxes is more than one dollar: it also involves some cost due to the disincentives it causes as well as some cost of collection (a point addressed in the next chapter). So when the government decides to spend a dollar on something—whether for an aircraft carrier or for redistribution to a low-income family—it had better produce social benefits worth more than a dollar. If you believe the economic and collection costs of taxes are very large, you may be less willing to accept a high level of government spending.

Second, the distinction between "taxes" and "spending" is sometimes not as clear-cut as it appears. Much of the federal government is a check-writing operation. In particular, many of these checks are written to pay for retirement benefits and health care for the elderly, a point we illustrate below. Whether these payments are called "spending," "transfers," "negative taxes," or "entitlements earned through contributions made earlier in life" is somewhat arbitrary. The justifications for such payments are often no different than those offered in chapter 3 for tax progressivity: they derive from a desire for a "fair" distribution of economic well-being.

For this reason, the debate over tax increases versus spending cuts often boils down to the trade-off between fairness and economic efficiency. A cutback in Medicare benefits makes elderly Americans worse off in the same way that a tax increase on upper-income Americans makes that group worse off—so it is a question of whose ox will be gored. Since the beneficiaries of government spending tend to be less well off than the people who pay the bulk of taxes, the spending cuts on average come at the expense of that segment of society. On the other hand, increasing taxes rather than cutting spending exacerbates the penalty on achieving affluence, blunting the incentive to get ahead.

Even this distinction is not always clear-cut. Certain ways of limiting government spending can have exactly the same kind of negative economic consequences that high marginal income tax rates have. For example, suppose we were to cut spending by "phasing out" 50 cents of Medicare benefits for every dollar of income or savings that an elderly person has. For those people, the result would be similar to a 50 percent marginal tax rate on the rewards to working and saving, and it would be a big disincentive to do either. We can find many examples of this in our current government spending programs. For example, "phase-outs" of welfare and Medicaid benefits, when combined with other tax rates, can produce marginal tax rates near 100 percent for some low-income people.

Some people believe that there is another important connection between spending and taxes because certain approaches to taxation lead to higher levels of government spending than others do. In particular, they argue that taxes should be as "visible" as possible so that people will know exactly how much they are paying for government. Otherwise, they contend, government will tend to expand beyond what the citizens would prefer if they were better informed. In this sense, visibility might help reduce the economic costs of government. The argument may have some merit, although it depends on the empirical question of whether citizens are more likely to get the government they want when taxes are more visible—an unsettled proposition. Some take the argument one step further, arguing that the taxpaying process should be made particularly painful precisely to restrain growth in government.[18] We see little justification for this view, and this book adopts a diametrically opposed perspective. This book seeks to find ways to streamline the tax system and to make it as efficient and unintrusive as possible. If institutional flaws bias the political system toward overspending, these flaws should be addressed but not by shackling American taxpayers with a needlessly costly and obtrusive tax system.

Tax Cuts to Force Spending Cuts versus Surpluses to Prepare for an Aging Population

Some who favor tax cuts do so in part because they hope it will put pressure on Congress to restrain its spending in the future. R. Glenn Hubbard, the first chair of the Council of Economic Advisers under George W. Bush, publicly embraced this idea.[19] Milton Friedman, the Nobel Prize–winning economist, is explicit about this, saying that "deficits will be an effective—I would go so far as to say, the only effective—restraint on the spending propensities of the executive branch and the legislature."[20]

Creating large budget deficits could plausibly change the terms of the political debate, eventually making it more difficult to propose new spending programs and creating pressures to slash existing ones. If the strategy turns out to be effective, then whether it is also a good idea depends in part on the costs of running large budget deficits until the goal of reduced spending is met and in part on whether you think the forgone spending was more or less valuable than the benefits provided by lower taxes. There's no guarantee that the most wasteful kinds of spending will be cut. For instance, if there is any kind of spending that economists agree is wasteful, it is farm subsidies. Milton Friedman would most definitely agree with that statement. Yet in 2002, at the same time that the Bush administration was implementing its strategy of large tax cuts, a law was enacted to increase farm subsidies by $83 billion over 10 years.[21]

Whether tax cuts will actually effectively restrain government spending later is ultimately an empirical question.[22] There are reasons to believe that it may not succeed, so that the results will instead be

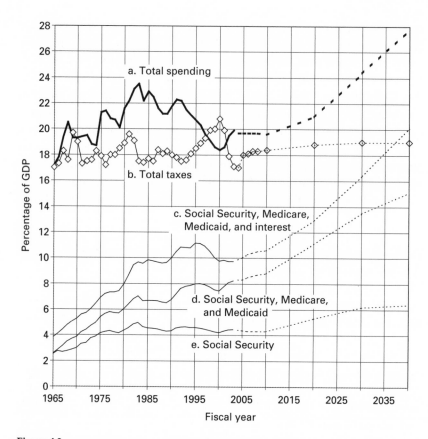

Figure 4.2
U.S. federal government spending and taxes as a percentage of gross domestic product, 1965–2040
Source: OMB (2003, Historical Tables, Analytical Perspectives).
Note: Data after 2002 are projections and are indicated by dashed lines.

persistently large budget deficits that will eventually lead to higher taxes. Figure 4.2 depicts federal government spending and taxes as a percentage of gross domestic product since 1965, including projections of future spending and taxes through 2040 that were made in the budget released by the Bush administration in early 2003. The first thing to note is that the last major tax cut, in 1981, was not obviously successful, at least in the short run, at restraining government spending and that large budget deficits ensued. For instance, between 1980 and 1985, taxes were cut from 18.9 percent of GDP to 17.7 percent, yet spending increased from 21.6 percent of GDP to 22.9 percent. Still, spending did start to come down eventually, and it's possible that this might not have happened without the pressure created by the deficits of the 1980s. But the big decline in spending relative to GDP actually occurred in the 1990s at the same time that tax revenues were increasing. Between 1990 and 2000, taxes rose from 18.0 percent of GDP to 20.8 percent, yet spending still fell from 21.8 percent of GDP to 18.4 percent. This suggests that politicians are not necessarily helpless to resist government spending when faced with rising revenues. If politicians and voters make reducing the deficit or accumulating a surplus a high priority, as they did in the 1990s, the budget balance will improve; if they don't, it won't. Moreover, there's nothing about tax cuts that automatically leads to spending cuts: the politically painful decision to cut spending still must be made. Note that the projected future spending in figure 4.2 reflects the Bush administration's own estimate of the impact of the proposals it made in 2003 and that there is no evidence of any future decline in spending in these projections.

The second essential fact illustrated by figure 4.2 is that a large portion of federal government spending is for health care and retirement benefits for the elderly. Social Security, Medicare, and Medicaid alone accounted for 41 percent of federal spending in 2003. Social Security and Medicare go entirely to the elderly and disabled. Approximately 70 percent of Medicaid spending goes to the elderly and disabled as well, much of it to cover long-term care such as nursing homes, which are not covered by Medicare.[23] All of this spending will automatically increase by a great deal in the future as the elderly become a much larger share of our population and health-care costs continue to climb. As the chart indicates, by 2040, Social Security, Medicare, Medicaid, and interest on the debt alone are projected to be 20 percent of GDP, as large as *all* federal government spending is today.

This sort of spending is very difficult to cut. The elderly understandably receive public sympathy, and they have great political power in their own right that will probably grow over time. In the case of Social Security and Medicare, in particular, people have been promised benefits on the basis of having paid payroll taxes, or *contributions*, all their lives to support previous generations' benefits. Polls consistently show overwhelming opposition to cutting these programs. For instance, a 2003 poll sponsored by NPR, the Kaiser Family Foundation, and Harvard's Kennedy School of Government found that 80 percent of respondents said that "maintaining spending levels on domestic programs such as education, health care, and Social Security" was more important to them than "lowering your taxes."[24] And these are by no means the only kinds of spending that are either popular and therefore difficult to cut or unavoidable. If, for example, we add national defense, veterans' benefits, administration of justice, and interest on the national debt to Social Security, Medicare, and Medicaid, we are already up to 71 percent of 2003 federal outlays.

For these reasons, a large increase in future government spending may be inevitable. If that is so, then a case can be made that we should be running budget *surpluses* today to increase national saving and investment in preparation for a known future need. More investment would mean a richer economy in the future, which would make it easier to deal with the largely unavoidable expense of an aging population. Opponents of this strategy, on the other hand, argue that budget surpluses are politically unsustainable and will ultimately lead the government to adopt more wasteful spending programs that wipe out the surplus anyway, so surpluses should be avoided. Given the dramatic impact of an aging population and rising health-care costs illustrated in figure 4.2, the economic stakes in this debate are large.

How Taxes Affect Long-Run Economic Prosperity: A First Cut at the Evidence

Now that we've put to one side such issues as business-cycle management, the surplus or deficit, and the appropriate level of government spending, we can address the impact of taxes on long-run economic prosperity. To what extent does our income tax system reduce our well-being, and could a better-designed tax system avoid some of these costs? Before getting into the details, we'll take a look at the big picture—the relationship between the level of taxation and economic performance from historical and international perspectives.

Economic Growth, Tax Levels, and Tax Rates in Recent U.S. History

Table 4.1 depicts the historical record of U.S. economic growth since 1950. The first column of data shows real per capita growth rates for gross domestic product (GDP), a measure of the total output of our economy and a standard indicator of economic performance. GDP per capita, however, has the drawback that part of its growth over this time period is due to rising labor-force participation rates, particularly among women. As such, it overstates the degree to which Americans have become better off because some of the growth has come at the

Table 4.1
U.S. economic growth since 1950

| Years | Average annual rate of real growth (percentage) | |
	GDP per capita	Productivity
1950–1973	2.5	3.1
1973–2002	1.8	1.8
1950–1960	1.7	2.8
1960–1970	2.9	3.2
1970–1980	2.1	1.8
1980–1990	2.2	1.7
1990–2000	2.0	2.1

Sources: U.S. Bureau of Economic Analysis (2003); U.S. Bureau of Labor Statistics (2003).
Note: Productivity is measured here as gross domestic product produced in the private business sector per hour worked in that sector; GDP data are based on chained 1996 dollars.

expense of leisure, the value of which is not captured in GDP. For this reason, we show in the second column growth in "productivity," defined as GDP produced in the private business sector divided by the total number of hours worked in that sector. This is a valuable indicator of changes in living standards because it is closely connected to growth in hourly wages and compensation. Note, though, that neither of these measures accounts for changes in aspects of well-being unrelated to output, wages, or consumption, such as the quality of the environment. Nevertheless, these are the most reliable measures of prosperity and its underlying determinants that are available.

Based on growth of productivity, our economy grew at a much faster rate in the 1950s and 1960s than it has since. Most noticeably, productivity grew at an annual rate of 3.1 percent between 1950 and 1973 but at only 1.8 percent per year from 1973 to 2002. When this diminished growth is combined with the increasing income inequality discussed in chapter 3, it implies that the economic well-being of many low- and middle-income people has stagnated for the past three decades. The growth rate of the 1980s as a whole was almost identical to that of the 1970s, and both were much lower than the "golden era" of the 1950s and 1960s. Productivity growth in the 1990s was slightly higher than in the 1970s or the 1980s.

Advocates of tax cuts often give the impression that our taxes were much lower during the "golden age" of economic growth in the 1950s and 1960s and that many of our current economic problems, including the slowdown of productivity growth since 1973, are caused by the strangling influence of big government and high taxes. By implication, all we need to do to return to the halcyon days of yesteryear is to lift this burden.

One problem with this argument is that, as chapter 2 details, overall federal taxes were not that different during the period of fast growth than they are today. Federal taxes averaged 18.5 percent of GDP from 1950 to 1973, 19.4 percent of GDP from 1974 to 2002, and stood at 18.2 percent in 2002. The composition of federal taxes has, though, changed greatly since then. For example, Social Security taxes were only 10.9 percent of federal revenues in 1950 compared to 35.3 percent in 2002, while corporate income taxes declined from 35.3 percent of revenues to 9.5 percent over the same span. Looking only at personal income and Social Security taxes gives the impression of a substantial increase in taxes, but that is misleading because the higher corporate tax payments of the 1950s were inevitably passed on to individuals either in the form of lower wages, lower returns to investment, or higher consumer prices. Substituting taxes on corporations for taxes on individuals does not make the burden of taxes go away.

Total taxes, including those of state and local governments, also have risen somewhat. They averaged 26.4 percent of GDP from 1950 to 1973 and 29.3 percent from 1974 to 2002 and were at 27.8 percent in 2002. But few economists believe that this increase is responsible for much of the slowdown in growth, and the culprit is almost certainly not federal income taxes.

What is detrimental to a vibrant economy may be not the overall level of taxes but rather particular aspects of the tax system. Some argue that steep marginal tax rates on high-income people are particularly destructive as they discourage the most highly talented and innovative members of society from pursuing the activities they do best. The emphasis on taxation of high-income households has been dubbed by its detractors as *trickle-down economics*. We discuss this idea in more detail later, but for now, take a look at figure 4.3, which shows the top tax rate on individuals and the rate of productivity growth for certain periods. Rather than telling a trickle-down story, the graph suggests the opposite. The strong growth periods were the periods when the top tax rates were the *highest*.

We're certainly not arguing that levying high marginal tax rates on the rich *causes* faster economic growth. On the contrary, most economists agree that marginal rates in the vicinity of 90 percent are too high to do much good for anyone. Our point is that no simple relationship

(a) Marginal income tax rate in top bracket, average over period (percentage)

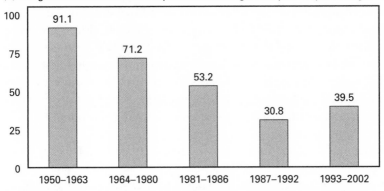

(b) Productivity growth (average annual percentage rate over period)

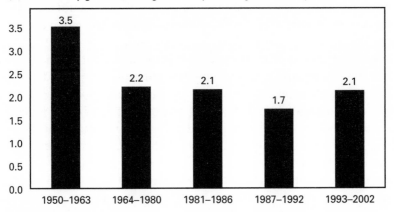

Figure 4.3
Top marginal income tax rate and productivity growth in the United States, 1950–2002
Source: U.S. Bureau of Labor Statistics (2003).
Notes: The bottom panel shows annual percentage growth in real gross domestic product produced in the private business sector per hour worked in that sector, fourth quarter over fourth quarter of the end of the previous period.

or single graph can establish how the tax system affects economic prosperity or growth. The many dimensions of the tax system—rates on individuals, the corporation income tax rate, the tax rate on capital gains, the definition of the tax base, and so on—all matter. Furthermore, many factors unrelated to taxation probably have a much more profound influence on the economy. For example, the unusually fast growth of the 1950s and 1960s may have resulted from the adoption of many important technological advances that had been developed over previous decades but that had not yet been fully utilized to the benefit of consumers because of the Great Depression and World War II. After 1973, the huge jump in the price of oil caused major economic disruption and probably contributed, at least temporarily, to slower growth in the United States and throughout the world. Identifying precisely what role a slightly increasing overall tax burden and changing features of the tax system have played in the slowdown is impossible. A more promising approach is to look at the evidence across countries. Have low-tax countries flourished and high-tax countries floundered?

International Evidence on Economic Prosperity and the Level of Taxes

Figure 4.4 plots for the 30 industrialized OECD countries the relationship between GDP per capita and the ratio of total tax to income. If a high level of taxes is the kiss of death for prosperity, we would expect to see the points on figure 4.4 clustering along a line with a negative slope. But no such pattern emerges from figure 4.4. Some of the world's most prosperous countries, such as the United States and Japan, do have relatively low tax ratios. But other countries, particularly in Scandinavia, have done quite well, thank you, with far higher tax ratios. That Sweden could maintain a 2000 GDP per capita of $24,779—6 percent above the OECD average, in the face of a whopping 54.2 percent tax-to-income ratio—challenges the hypothesis that high taxes are a sure cause of economic decline.

Our disclaimer about figure 4.3 also applies to figure 4.4: no simple diagram could possibly settle such a complicated issue as this one. The Scandinavian nations could possibly be even better off than they are now if they lowered their tax burdens. Figure 4.4 might simply be telling us that history, nature, culture, and demography have enabled some countries to be more prosperous than others and that those countries so favored have chosen to spend relatively more of their bounty on the services provided by government and to tax themselves more to provide these services. Alternatively, because richer countries also tend to have a higher literacy rate and to be more urbanized, they might be more suited to take advantage of modern ways to raise revenue, such as income taxes. In either of these cases, comparing the relative levels of prosperity to total tax burdens will not reveal the economic impact of taxation, positive or negative.

One might also look to see whether any relationship exists between tax ratios and the *growth rate* of economies. Analyzing the rate of growth over a given time period frees us from having to explain why some

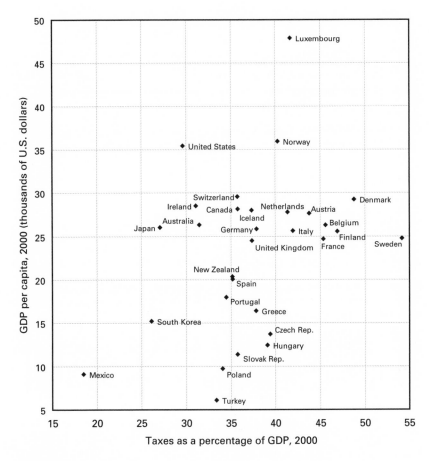

Figure 4.4
Economic prosperity and the level of taxes in 30 OECD countries, 2000
Sources: OECD (2001, 2002).
Note: Gross domestic product per capita is converted to 2000 U.S. dollars using OECD estimates of purchasing-power parity.

countries were more prosperous than others at the start of the period and allows us to focus on what has caused them to better themselves.

Figure 4.5 does just this. For the period 1970 to 2000, it plots the average tax ratio of 26 of the OECD countries against their real growth rate. Yes, some low-tax countries such as South Korea did exceptionally well over this period, and high-tax countries such as Sweden did relatively poorly. But some high-tax countries did well, and some low-tax countries (like the United States) performed below average. Again, no clear relationship emerges. More sophisticated statistical analyses of the

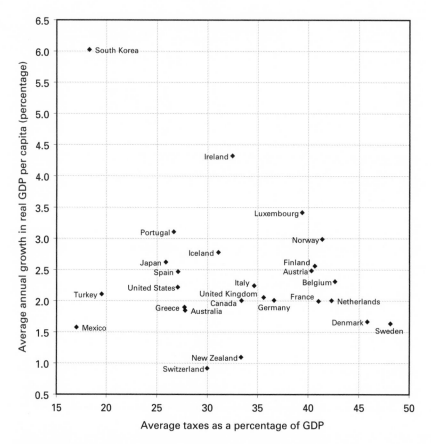

Figure 4.5
Economic growth rates and tax levels in OECD countries, 1970–2000
Source: Authors' calculations based on OECD (2003) data.

relationship between economic growth and the level of taxation, which attempt to hold constant the impact of other determinants of growth to isolate the tax effect, have come to no consensus.[25]

Our point is not that taxes do not affect the economy. On the contrary, in certain situations taxes have a telling impact. The effect of taxes on economic performance, however, is subtle and cannot be established by any one simple graph—not by the figures presented here and not by other ones that purport to demonstrate the damaging effects of high taxes. Understanding how taxes affect the economy requires looking behind data on overall economic performance and instead examining the kinds of choices that taxes affect and the ways that taxes influence these choices.

How Taxes Affect Economic Prosperity: The Specifics

It goes without saying that having to pay taxes means having to change your behavior. For every dollar paid to the government, taxpayers have one less dollar to spend or save. Belts must be tightened. This is as true for a poll tax (also called a lump-sum tax) as it is for an income tax or a sales tax. But a lump-sum tax is different in one important way from all other taxes—there is nothing you can do to change your tax liability. That sounds ominous for the family whose income barely exceeds the lump-sum tax amount: nothing can be done to reduce this burden. But reversing the emphasis reveals the unique characteristic of the lump-sum tax: nothing you do *increases* your tax bill. In particular, nothing you do to better your lot—getting a second job, buying a new house or car, even winning the lottery—increases your taxes. Under a lump-sum tax, any decision you can think of can be made without a moment's consideration to the tax consequences.

This is quite a contrast to the current situation where taxes change the terms of just about any decision that a taxpayer faces. A spouse contemplating returning to work must consider that taxes (federal and state income plus payroll) will possibly take 50 percent of any earnings, while many expenses incurred will not be deductible. A wealthy alumna contemplating a gift of $1 million in stock to her alma mater will be gently reminded that, compared to selling the stock, donating it could save her and her heirs more than $600,000 in taxes. The CEO of Hewlett-Packard may be tempted to open another research lab by the knowledge that, because of the research and experimentation tax credit, 20 percent of its cost may be creditable against tax liability.

The belt tightening that accompanies taxation is an inevitable cost of taxation, but raising taxes does more than force people to tighten their belts. It also changes the cost and reward of most economic decisions, and it distorts these choices away from what would otherwise be chosen. What is the cost to the economy when the tax system changes the terms of economic choices?

Economists agree that, in most situations, the baseline for measuring these costs is how the economy would operate in the absence of any taxes other than lump-sum taxes.[26] The idea is that firms and individuals, guided by the signals given by market prices, are generally the best judges of what goods and services they value and make spending decisions to maximize their well-being according to their own preferences. In the interest of maximizing profits, firms will seek out those investments and opportunities that offer the highest reward and pursue them using the most cost-effective techniques. The result, as Adam Smith observed more than 225 years ago, is that an unfettered free-market economy, whatever its other faults, tends to organize itself (as with an "invisible hand," in Smith's words) to make efficient use of the country's physical and human resources. Taxes interfere with that efficiency because they induce firms and individuals to shun taxed activities in favor of relatively untaxed ones, keeping us from making the best use of our resources.

There are exceptions to this story, referred to as cases of *market failure*. When the difficulty of obtaining necessary information, the presence of activities with spillover effects, or monopoly leads markets to function inefficiently—when the invisible hand fails—taxes do not necessarily detract from efficiency. On the contrary, they may correct an inefficiency. For example, a tax on pollution might correct a market failure rather than cause a misallocation of resources.

The problem of market failure figures prominently in our subsequent discussion of a number of key tax policy issues. For now, though, we leave market failures aside and examine several specific areas of economic behavior where taxes do have a distorting effect. Because one of the goals of most tax reform plans is to mitigate these distortions, understanding these issues is crucial for evaluating the potential benefits of reform.

Labor Supply

Labor income in the form of wages, salaries, and benefits constitutes nearly three-quarters of national income.[27] Therefore, any story about how taxes affect the economy must come to terms with how they affect the incentive to work. If the tax system makes it unattractive to work hard or work at all, then it cannot be contributing to a vibrant economy. Many tax reform plans seek to change the tax system so that work is rewarded more generously.

Taxes have two countervailing influences on the decision to work. First of all, most taxes, including income and consumption taxes, reduce the marginal reward for working. Work becomes less attractive because working that extra hour or taking on a second job buys fewer consumption goods and services. Put differently, leisure and other nonmarket activities become more attractive because the alternative of working becomes less remunerative. The reduced return to working provides an incentive to substitute more leisure and nonmarket endeavors for less work and less consumption of goods and services. This impact of taxes is called the *substitution effect*, or sometimes the *incentive effect*, by economists.

Besides changing the marginal reward to working, *any* kind of tax makes you poorer, so you need to work harder to achieve a given level of consumption. When people are poorer, they tend to cut back some on all the things they value, including leisure. This is known as the *income effect*. In other words, the income effect of taxes causes people to work *more*. Because of the countervailing effects of the substitution and income effects, it is not clear whether taxes make people work more than they otherwise would or less.

Note that the decision whether to work a few extra hours or to choose a harder job that pays a little better is affected only by one's marginal tax rate—that is, the tax rate on the next few dollars of income. What is relevant for the "income effect," however, is the total tax burden or, expressed as a fraction of income, the average tax rate.

The relationship between total taxes collected and marginal tax rates is a crucial characteristic of any tax system and is inextricably linked to how progressive the tax burden is. A lump-sum tax system could, in principle, raise a trillion dollars a year while imposing a zero tax at the margin for everyone's work decisions. Under a purely proportional tax system, in which tax liability is the same fraction of income for everyone, the marginal tax rate equals the average tax rate. The more progressive the distribution of the tax burden is, the higher the marginal tax rates will be, and therefore the greater the overall marginal disincentive to work, per dollar raised will be.

Note also that the correct marginal tax rate for measuring the disincentive effect is not necessarily the statutory marginal income tax rate. For example, a 20 percent statutory marginal rate levied on labor income excluding fringe benefits is not, in terms of its incentive effect on labor supply, materially different from a 16 percent statutory marginal tax rate levied on labor income including fringe benefits, if fringe benefits constitute about one-fifth of total labor compensation for everyone.[28] In principle, such a policy change does not in itself provide a significantly increased incentive to work. This is an important point to keep in mind when we later discuss proposals that broaden the tax base and use the revenue so collected to lower marginal tax rates. Note also that a consumption tax such as a retail sales tax has the same kind of effects on the incentive to work as an income tax because it reduces the purchasing power that an additional hour of work provides. This must be kept in mind when we address moving from an income tax to a consumption tax.

An example can help illustrate the economic cost of the incentive effect. Consider the case of Roger Brown, who works 40 hours a week on construction sites. Roger is also a talented carpenter and can earn $20 an hour working at nights and on weekends; he can find 10 hours a week of such work. Roger has plenty of hobbies and enjoys spending time with his family, so it goes without saying that he won't work for nothing. In fact, he won't work those extra 10 hours unless he can earn at least $15 an hour; in economics jargon, that is the *opportunity cost* of his time—what his leisure time is worth to him.

In the absence of any taxes, Roger will clearly decide to moonlight. The $200 he earns for the 10 hours of extra work exceeds the $150 he requires as compensation for the reduced leisure time. Everyone is better off from this decision. Roger's customers are better off, or else they wouldn't have been willing to pay him the $200. Roger is better off. We can even put a dollar measure on how much everyone is better off—$50. This represents the difference between $200, which is the value put on Roger's carpentry by his customers, and $150, which is Roger's own evaluation of the next best use of this time.

Alas, there is taxation, and on an extra $200 per week of income Roger's tax bill turns out to be $60, or 30 percent. He is a dutiful citizen, so he does not consider simply not reporting his outside income to the IRS. Given his 30 percent rate of tax, he concludes that his after-tax compensation for carpentry, $14 per hour ($20 minus 30 percent of $20), is not high enough to justify giving up the extra leisure. This is an example of the disincentive to work caused by the tax system; it has changed the reward to working and in this case changed the decision of how much to work.

What is the economic cost of the altered decision? You might jump to an answer of $200, Roger's forgone wages. But that is not correct because although Roger has decided to forgo the $200 in income, by so doing he has 10 more hours per week to pursue his other interests, 10 more hours he values at $150. The loss to Roger, and to the economy, is the difference between $200 and $150, or $50. Because of the tax system, a transaction that should have been made was not; Roger consumes "too much" leisure and works "too little."[29]

Per dollar of revenue raised, the cost depends on how responsive labor supply is to changes in the after-tax return to working.[30] If it is not responsive,[31] then the fact that taxes lower the return to working does not translate into significant economic costs because people are not dissuaded from working. The more responsive the decision is, the larger are the economic costs of imposing taxes that reduce the reward to working.

What does the evidence show? The responsiveness of labor supply, both in hours worked and the labor-force participation rate, has been studied extensively. Indeed, this is a rare example of a question on which there is a broad consensus among economists.[32] Nearly all research concludes that male hours worked respond hardly at all to changes in after-tax wages and therefore to marginal tax rates. Some evidence suggests that participation decisions, especially among females, are responsive to incentives, but those responses do not contribute enough to total labor supply to alter the conclusion that, overall, labor supply is not greatly affected by taxes. One sort of evidence comes from examining a large sample of individuals in a single year and comparing their hours worked with their after-tax wages. Among working men, those with higher after-tax wages do tend to work longer hours on average, but the differences in hours worked are very small compared to the differences in after-tax wages. Statistical studies distinguish income and substitution effects by looking at how hours respond to changes in nonlabor income (the more hours worked decline when nonlabor income increases, the larger is the income effect) and generally find that both the income and substitution effects are small for prime-age male workers. In the case of women, this evidence suggests a stronger labor supply response to after-tax wages, particularly in the decision of whether to work at all. But in the case of women who work, evidence suggests that the labor supply responsiveness of women is not very different than that of men.

One could also look at how hours worked have changed over time in response to large increases in real after-tax wages. In the case of men, average hours worked and labor force participation tended to decline as after-tax wages increased through the twentieth century (especially through earlier retirement). This is consistent with a situation where the income effect of higher wages outweighs the substitution effect. By contrast, women greatly increased their labor force participation over the course of the twentieth century as wages rose, which would be consistent with a strong substitution response to incentives. It is difficult, though, to distinguish this from the effects of other influences, such as changes in cultural attitudes.[33]

Yet another strategy for learning how taxes affect labor supply is to study policy changes that affect the after-tax wages of one group relative to another to see how changes in hours worked matched up with changes in incentives. The tax cuts of the 1980s arguably provided such an experiment. Nada Eissa of the University of California at Berkeley examined changes in hours worked by men with education beyond college, who typically have high incomes and received large tax cuts during the 1980s. Compared to the recent historical trend and trends for workers with less education (who did not on average receive large tax cuts), she estimates that these men increased their hours of work by only 2 percent in response to the sharply reduced marginal tax rates after 1986.[34] James Ziliak of the University of Oregon and Thomas Kniesner of Syracuse University estimated that the tax reforms of the 1980s increased male labor supply by 3 percent. Robert Moffitt of Johns Hopkins University and Mark Wilhelm of Indiana University–Purdue University at Indianapolis examined data that followed the same group of people between 1983 and 1989, and they found no evidence of a significant labor supply response to lower marginal tax rates, even among the high-income group that saw their marginal tax rate fall from 50 percent to 28 percent.[35]

These studies all come with some important caveats. The first is that economists can measure fairly accurately hours worked, but that is only one part of a broader definition of labor supply that includes work effort, occupational choice, and the acquisition of education and job-specific skills. Taxes may also affect these dimensions of labor supply; unfortunately, little quantitative evidence allows us to say much one way or the other about this issue. Second, behavioral patterns of work may be set early in life and may be hard to break once set, so that the effect of taxes on labor supply is felt only gradually as new generations reach working age. Assar Lindbeck of the Institute of International Economic Studies in Stockholm has suggested that this explanation applies to high-tax Sweden, which has experienced a gradual decline in hours worked over the past two decades.[36] Linda Bell and Richard Freeman of Harvard University argue that the lower average hours worked in Germany compared to the United States is consistent with the fact that economic inequality, due both to more dispersed pretax wages and less progressive taxes and transfer programs, has long been greater in the United States.[37] Greater inequality increases the incentive to work in the United States, since the gains from working hard are larger and the consequences of not working hard are worse. These caveats add uncertainty to the claim that labor supply effects are negligible, but they certainly do not provide any decisive evidence against that conclusion.[38]

Robert Triest of the Federal Reserve Bank of Boston has examined the policy implications of these low labor supply responsiveness estimates.[39] He calculates that increasing the two lowest tax rates at the time—15 percent and 28 percent—by 1 point to finance a larger earned income tax credit would have an efficiency cost of 16 cents per dollar raised. In other words, because of labor supply distortions, a $1 increase in the credit requires that taxpayers be made worse off by $1.16. Notably, the cost increases to 52 cents on the dollar when the increased credit is financed by increases in the 28 percent and 36 percent rates of the time. Triest cautions, however, that this latter result arises in part because his model assumes that the responsiveness of labor supply to taxes is higher for people with higher incomes, a fact that has not been decisively established and indeed is inconsistent with evidence on the effects of the 1980s tax cuts cited above. In any event, these figures provide one reasonable estimate of the trade-off between equity and efficiency. Based on these estimates, if in your judgment the increased progressivity of a larger tax-financed EITC (a more equal "slicing of the pie") is worth 16 cents on the dollar of efficiency cost per dollar raised and redistributed ("a smaller pie"), then it is worth doing. Of course, if Triest and others have underestimated the labor supply response to taxes, then the economic cost is higher than these calculations suggest.

Saving and Investment

A second critical choice affected by taxes is the one people make about how much to consume in a given year versus how much to save for future years or for bequests. Income taxes affect the terms of this choice because, by taxing interest and other returns to capital, they reduce the rate of return that can be earned on savings. Many would-be tax reformers support a switch to a consumption tax, which would effectively eliminate the negative influence of taxes on the incentive to save. Chapter 6 explains how consumption taxes accomplish this; for now, we focus on how our current system affects the incentive to save and how saving behavior is influenced by such incentives.

It's easy to see that a tax of 20 percent on interest income reduces the reward to saving that income. If the before-tax interest rate is 10 percent, you only get an 8 percent return after tax. Another feature of our tax system can exacerbate this distortion: it fails to adjust the measurement of capital income for inflation. Suppose that in the example above, inflation was 5 percent. In that case, half of the 10 percent interest you earn is just making up for the decline in the real purchasing power of your savings. So in this case, the 20 percent tax rate on nominal interest rate turns out to be a 40 percent tax on *real* interest because a 5 percent real (inflation-adjusted) return turns into a 3 percent return after tax.

Income taxes can also reduce the reward to saving indirectly by taxing the returns to business investment. Leaving aside international capital flows, savings and investment are two sides of the same coin. The saving of individuals—often funneled through a financial interme-diary such as a bank, a savings and loan, or an insurance company—eventually is used by businesses to finance the purchase of physical capital goods such as factories, equipment, and inventories and intan-gible capital such as "know-how." Through this process, individual saving adds to the productive capacity of the country and increases the productivity of the workforce.

Although the connection is not always apparent to the saver, the re-turn to saving is governed by the return to the productive investment that the saving finances. If the return to investment is taxed at the busi-ness level, then the amount that can be paid out to those who financed it, by lending money or buying shares, must fall. As explained in chap-ter 2, certain forms of corporate income, such as dividends and some capital gains, can be "double taxed"—once under the corporate tax and again at the personal level. The extent of this taxation depends not only on the rate of tax applied to net business income but also on the depre-ciation schedules, the generosity of any investment tax credits, and the preferential treatment now accorded to both capital gains and dividend income in the personal tax.

Together, taxes on the returns to saving and business investment distort the choices of individuals, inefficiently encouraging people to consume more today and save less for the future. One negative consequence is that people may end up with too little savings when they retire. In the likely event that myopia and temptation cause people to save too little for their own and their children's futures even in the absence of taxes, reductions in saving caused by taxes would be even more harmful. A progressive income tax puts the highest disincentive to save on a small group of people who account for a very large portion of national saving—the rich.

If the tax law does in fact reduce national saving and investment, our future national economic prosperity will be lower than it otherwise could be. Part of the appeal of the consumption tax reform plans—including the flat tax and the national retail sales tax—is that they would eliminate all tax on the return to saving and investment.[40] To the extent that this boosts saving and investment to more efficient levels, we would be better off.

If empirical evidence showed a strong positive relationship between saving and its after-tax rate of return, the economic costs of our income tax and the economic benefits of switching to a consumption tax could be quite large. However, the available evidence does not readily reveal any such relationship. Figure 4.6, which is derived from a study done by Jane Gravelle of the Congressional Research Service, plots the net private saving rate and a measure of the real after-tax return to saving.[41] The net private saving rate includes saving by individuals and

Figure 4.6
Percentage of income saved versus the incentive to save in the United States, 1960–2002
Sources: (a) Private saving net of depreciation as a percentage of disposable income (gross national product less depreciation and taxes), from U.S. Bureau of Economic Analysis (2003). (b) Interest rate on Baa corporate bonds plus a fixed equity premium, adjusted for expected inflation and the average marginal tax rate on personal interest income, calculated by the authors following Gravelle (1994). See note 41 for further details.

also that done by corporations in the form of retained earnings, subtracts off depreciation, and does not include the effects of government
"dissaving" through budget deficits. It is expressed as a percentage of
after-tax income. If anything, figure 4.6 suggests a *negative* relationship
between saving and the incentive to save. Saving as a fraction of disposable income was relatively high in the 1960s and 1970s, when the incentive to save was relatively low, and then declined dramatically after
about 1980, at the same time that the incentive to save went up significantly. Saving rates continued to drop through 2002 despite long-term
real after-tax interest rates that were persistently high by historical
standards.

Of course, no simple graph can decisively disprove or prove that saving is or is not responsive to incentives. One obvious problem is that the
causality runs both ways. If people decide to reduce their saving for a
reason unrelated to interest rates, this will reduce the supply of saving
and push up interest rates. A second problem is that the definition of
saving used here does not include capital gains arising from sources
other than reinvestment of corporate profits (for example, it excludes
capital gains arising from greater optimism about future profits or
greater tolerance of risk).[42] Therefore, this saving rate does not fully reflect the effect of the stock market boom of the 1990s on household
wealth. For the purposes of measuring the amount of resources that are
being set aside and made available for private investment, this is perfectly appropriate. But this third factor, the stock market boom, might
explain the decline in saving, as increased wealth led people to feel less
need to save for retirement. However, no evidence has been found of a
large surge in saving following the 2001–2002 stock market collapse, so
it is unclear how much of the saving patterns the earlier boom can
explain. Finally, many other factors could have influenced aggregate
saving behavior over time, such as business cycles, demographic
changes, or changes in cultural attitudes, and these are hard to distinguish from the effects of the after-tax return to saving. Some of these
factors, though, suggest that saving should have gone up. For instance,
the end of this period represents prime saving years for the large baby
boom cohort.

A large number of studies have attempted to address these problems
to some degree, and they generally come to the conclusion that saving is
not very responsive to incentives.[43] In contrast to the evidence on labor
supply, the evidence on how saving responds to incentives is subject to
much greater uncertainty because of the lack of good data. The research

is based on evidence that is not much better than the simple relationship shown in figure 4.6 and is subject to many of the same problems. Still, given the state of the evidence, any claim that reducing or eliminating the tax on the return to saving would lead to large increases in saving must be viewed with skepticism.

The quality of evidence on how firms' investment decisions respond to incentives is a bit better. For example, a recent study by economists Robert Chirinko, Steven Fazzari, and Andrew Meyer examines how the investment decisions of a large number of individual firms are affected by differences in the cost of investing, which varies in their sample because of differences in tax rates across firms and across time, among other reasons. They estimate that there is indeed a modest negative relationship between investment and the cost of investment.[44]

Neutrality

A major goal of tax reform is to make our tax system more "neutral" so that it exerts less influence on our economic choices. The economy almost always benefits when people make decisions based on the economic merits of the alternatives rather than on their tax consequences. Reducing the influence of taxes on the incentives to work, save, and invest is an important example of this principle.

The only tax system that is perfectly "neutral," however, is a lump-sum tax because in this case *no* decision you make has any impact on your tax bill, so taxes cause no disincentive effects at all. The kind of neutrality that tax reformers strive for is less ambitious but still important—making sure that tax rates do not differ across various types of consumption and investment. Note that even if this kind of neutrality is achieved, distortion is still introduced by the tax system because the return to working and to saving is reduced. No distortion, however, is introduced with respect to what goods and services people consume or how goods are produced.

Our current tax system is a far cry from this kind of neutrality. The many deductions, special preferences, compromises in the measurement of capital income, and idiosyncrasies mean that different types of consumption and investment are taxed at widely different rates. Cleaning up the tax base to eliminate such distorting features is a major goal of most tax reform plans.

Before discussing how our tax system diverges from this particular brand of neutrality, a couple of qualifications are in order about its economic advantages. First of all, uniform taxation of different kinds of consumption does not necessarily minimize the economic cost of raising a given amount of revenue. Other things being equal, it is desirable to tax more heavily those goods for which demand (and supply) is relatively price insensitive. Taxing these goods will change behavior less for any given amount of revenue raised compared to taxing price-sensitive goods: it effectively makes the tax system more like a lump-sum tax. Moreover, singling out for taxation recreational goods such as skis and amusement parks could offset the inevitable disincentive to labor that income and consumption taxes create. Among economists the idea that certain deviations from uniform taxation of consumption might actually reduce the economic cost of raising revenue is known as the *optimal tax principle*.

Although the optimal tax principle is correct in theory, it runs into practical problems that make it not particularly useful as a guide to policy. First, identifying which goods and services are more or less responsive to taxation (or more or less likely to be complementary to leisure) is difficult. Second, even if economists could measure such things accurately, differentiating taxes according to this approach often conflicts with both equity and simplicity. Whenever some goods are taxed at higher rates than others, taxpayers whose tastes happen to favor those goods are penalized; this is horizontally inequitable. Moreover, the goods taxed most heavily would probably be necessities (for example, the demand for food is relatively inelastic), so a disproportionate burden would be placed on the poor. It is also more costly to operate a tax system that differentially treats goods. Finally, politicians are unlikely to distinguish among goods based solely on their price sensitivity. Particularly in the face of uncertainty about which goods have relatively price-elastic demand, the pleadings of special interests would almost certainly carry the day. For all these reasons, uniform taxation—either in the form of a broad-based income tax or consumption tax—is still a very good rule of thumb. It is likely to cause much less economic distortion than any other feasible approach, and it allows lower rates of tax because of the broader base it covers.

One more qualification deserves serious consideration. In some special cases, the free market does not lead to efficient outcomes. The most important case is when an activity has a direct impact on other people in a way that is not reflected in the price paid or received for the activity. Economists refer to this as an *externality*. A classic example of a *negative* externality is pollution; businesses that pollute impose a cost on their neighbors by reducing the quality of air they breathe or the water they drink. If these costs are not reflected in the prices faced by the owners of these businesses, too much pollution will be produced. In such a case, taxes can be used to alter incentives and therefore to mitigate the problem.

In our tax system, we tend to subsidize particular activities rather than penalize them. By requiring higher tax rates, though, these subsidies cause all other activities to be penalized. But such subsidies may be justified if they encourage activities with *positive* externalities. A fairly clear-cut example is research and development (R&D). Engaging in R&D can be costly, and when it leads to a good idea, the benefits almost never accrue entirely to the researcher or to his or her employer. Although the patent system is designed to ensure that inventors are amply rewarded for their ideas, people other than the inventor inevitably will capitalize on and profit from the idea. This means that there are some R&D projects that are not worth doing from a private individual's or firm's perspective but are worth doing from society's point of view. In an attempt to alleviate this problem, our income tax system grants preferential tax treatment to R&D expenses. Unlike other types of long-lived investment, these expenses can be deducted immediately. Moreover, certain R&D expenditures qualify for a 20 percent tax credit to the extent that they exceed a base amount meant to approximate the "normal" level of expenditures for that firm. It is hard to tell whether this is the appropriate level of subsidy, but most economists would agree that at least some subsidy is justified.

The externality argument should be a high hurdle for justifying preferential treatment of particular goods or activities. That an activity is "good for the economy" is a wholly inadequate argument. Yet our tax system violates the principle of neutrality over and over again, often for no good economic reason. The Treasury Department has identified over 100 specific deviations from a uniform, comprehensive income tax base, which in the aggregate cost hundreds of billions of dollars in revenue.[45] Next we discuss some of the most important examples of nonneutrality and discuss some of the consequences.

Let's look first at the taxation of capital income and the returns to investment. Different types of investments face vastly different tax treatment under our current system. Because of double taxation at the corporate and personal levels, investments in a corporation are often taxed more heavily than noncorporate business investments. Both are taxed more heavily than investments in owner-occupied houses, whose owners can claim a mortgage interest deduction but need not report as taxable income the value of the services the house provides. Treasury Department economist James Mackie estimated in 2002 that the effective tax rate on returns to corporate investment in the United States averaged 32.2 percent, the tax rate on returns to noncorporate business investment averaged 20.0 percent, and the tax rate on returns to owner-occupied housing averaged just 3.9 percent.[46] The result of such disparities is that much more money has flowed into housing and non-corporate investments—and less to corporate investment—than would have occurred otherwise, leading to a less productive economy.[47]

Among corporate investments, those that are financed by debt are taxed less heavily than those that are financed by equity (selling shares of stock), which has no good economic rationale. Capital gains are treated more favorably than dividends or interest, so that assets whose return comes in the form of appreciation are favored over other types of assets. Depreciation schedules are only rough approximations of true economic depreciation, so they will inevitably cause some distortions. In our system, they cause various types of equipment or structures to be favored over others and cause certain industries to receive more generous treatment while others are penalized.[48] The Tax Reform Act of 1986 reduced many of these kinds of distortions, but many still remain.

There's no better example of the kind of waste that can be caused by these distortions than the commercial real estate boom of the mid-1980s. During this period, the tax advantages of real estate were so large that putting up a building—even if the expected occupancy rate was very low—made good business sense. The result: unoccupied office space in so-called "see-through" buildings that were profitable only because of the tax advantages. The tax benefits to real estate caused the invisible hand to fail: the private interest of developers was not the public interest of society. The result was a waste of resources because the bricks, mortar, steel, and time that went into building these unoccupied offices could instead have produced goods and services that had greater value.

Many features of our tax code provide special preferences for particular types of consumption spending; most of these arise from deductions, exclusions, and credits in the personal code. Some of the most important preferences are for housing, health care, and charitable contributions, all of which are addressed in chapter 6. A few of these exceptions may be justified, but there is broad agreement among economists that eliminating many of these features would provide significant benefits by rationalizing the allocation of resources. The potential economic gains from making the tax system more uniform are hard to quantify precisely, but they may well be as important as the benefits that could be derived from reducing the tax-induced disincentive to work and save.

Risk-Taking and Entrepreneurship

Some critics argue that the tax system is particularly harsh for small, risky start-up firms that embody the ideas and energies of those entrepreneurs who are an important engine of growth for the U.S. economy. Another common complaint is that our tax system is biased against risky investments in general.

What truth is there to these criticisms? First of all, treating entrepreneurial or risky activities *more* favorably than other kinds of activities, except to the extent that they embody R&D or innovation that spills over to benefit others that do not pay for it, has little economic rationale. Nor would singling out "entrepreneurial" income for favorable tax treatment be feasible, as we have no meaningful way to define it precisely. On the other hand, *penalizing* such activities relative to others has no good economic rationale, and some argue that the current tax code does in fact penalize such activities in a number of ways.

The most frequent complaint is about capital gains taxes. The prime movers behind risky ventures often receive their return in the form of large capital gains when they sell all or part of the company; however, they also risk the possibility of a capital loss. The U.S. tax code imposes a tax on the gains but allows only a small amount of net loss to be deducted against other income in a given year (although the losses can be carried over to future years). This tax treatment has a practical rationale because unlimited deductibility of losses would open up opportunities for some sophisticated and troublesome avoidance schemes. However, the loss limitation discourages risk-taking because the system taxes away some of the rewards if the venture is successful but doesn't provide symmetrical insurance against a loss.

Capital gains are also blamed for a "lock-in" effect in which individuals are deterred from selling stocks because they pay tax only at the time of sale. The fact that capital gains are taxed only on realization and are not taxed at all if held until death creates such an incentive. Critics contend that investment funds are kept locked up in the stocks of older, established firms at the expense of newer entrepreneurial ventures that might offer a higher return. Evidence on whether capital gains tax rates have an important lock-in effect has been difficult to discern.[49] Even a strong lock-in effect, moreover, probably affects mainly *who* owns particular stocks rather than which companies receive investment funds.

Although these arguments may have some merit, the conventional solution, a cut in capital gains tax rates, has many problems of its own. For one thing, it is a very blunt instrument for addressing this problem because innovative entrepreneurial ventures are the source of only a tiny fraction of the total value of capital gains.[50] Thus, only a small fraction of the revenues lost from preferential taxes on capital gains is going toward improved incentives for entrepreneurship. Many other important factors should be considered in the taxation of capital gains, which we address when discussing options for income tax reform in chapter 8.[51]

Some people point to the graduated nature of income tax rates as discouraging entrepreneurship and risk-taking. In many cases, the incentive to engage in such activities depends on a small possibility of a very large return, and progressive rates have their largest impact on just such returns. In addition, the returns to entrepreneurship represent largely the product of hard work, so this is to some extent an argument about how marginal tax rates affect labor supply. The difference is that the work effort of entrepreneurs and other small businesspeople may not be accurately captured by the data on hours worked mentioned above, so that studies of labor supply may not effectively measure how strong the labor supply response is in this sector.

Another argument points out that because of imperfections in capital markets and lack of collateral, small start-up firms often have trouble obtaining loans and have to rely heavily on equity financing provided directly by the entrepreneur and his or her family.[52] This suggests that, even in the absence of taxes, a less than efficient amount of entrepreneurial activity might occur. Highly progressive income taxes and heavy taxes on capital gains might then make the problem worse. Moreover, to the extent that these firms become C corporations, the double taxation of corporate equity would be particularly harmful to entrepreneurs, and corporate entrepreneurial ventures are penalized relative to other investments that have access to more tax-favored debt.

Some evidence suggests that decisions of the currently or potentially self-employed are influenced by taxes. One study found that changes in the incentive to invest caused by the Tax Reform Act of 1986 had an impact on investment undertaken by self-employed people.[53] Another found that people who face (1) a larger gap between the income tax rates imposed on a gain versus a loss relative to their current incomes, and thus (2) a higher tax rate on "success" relative to "failure"[54] are slightly less likely to take the risk of becoming self-employed. However, on many of the key empirical questions regarding entrepreneurship, there is little compelling evidence.

Entrepreneurship is hard to define and measure, and partly for that reason, little evidence can be found to contradict the claims that are made about the deleterious effects of the tax system in this area. Such claims should not necessarily be discounted, and the fact that tax reform might help improve incentives in this area (for example, by eliminating double taxation) should be viewed as a plus. Yet there is also no hard evidence demonstrating that the potential economic benefits in this area are large. Some have suggested that a burgeoning of entrepreneurial efforts, in response to lower marginal tax rates, was partly responsible for the surge in the incomes of the affluent during the 1980s and 1990s. This question is addressed in more detail at the end of this chapter.

International Competitiveness and International Aspects of Taxation

Another claim sometimes made about tax reform is that it would somehow improve America's "international competitiveness." We put quotation marks around that term because what it really means is unclear. Are there circumstances under which we should sacrifice expanding national income to increase something called international competitiveness? We and nearly all other economists think not.

The United States is not in competition with other countries in the same sense that the Los Angeles Lakers are in competition with the Sacramento Kings, in which one side wins and the other side loses. IBM rightly views Toshiba as a competitor in this sense, but the United States should not view Japan in this way. For at least two centuries, a broad consensus among economists has held that the opposite is true—that unfettered commercial relationships benefit all participating countries because they allow nations to concentrate their resources on what they do best.[55] In general, looking for ways to boost our standard of living *at the expense* of other countries is not a useful pursuit. Our standard of living ultimately depends on our own productivity, resources, and efficiency in using these resources, and this is where we should focus our efforts.

With that said, a number of interesting and controversial issues do arise in connection with taxation in a global economy. For instance, how should we tax foreign investment done by U.S. companies and U.S. investment done by foreign companies? Should the tax system actively discourage U.S. companies from moving operations abroad, or should it strive to be neutral toward such locational choices?

In most situations, a good rule of thumb is that the tax system should be neutral with respect to the location of investment. Applying that rule to foreign investment implies that the tax system certainly shouldn't encourage multinational corporations to invest offshore when they otherwise wouldn't, but neither should it offer tax breaks to induce firms to invest in the United States when investments abroad would be more profitable for them. From a global point of view, if all countries follow this practice, firms are induced to make investment decisions undistorted by differences in countries' tax systems, which leads to an efficient allocation of investment. This approach maximizes worldwide income.

Each individual nation, however, may be able to gain at the expense of others by lowering its tax rate to attract some extra investment away from other countries. To the extent that investment moves to particular locations for favorable tax treatment instead of for productive investment opportunities, it is inefficient and worldwide income is reduced. But the income of the country that attracts the extra investment may increase. If *all* countries try to lower tax rates to attract investment from each other, they may end up worse off than if they had agreed to refrain from competing in this manner. Investment ultimately goes where it would have gone anyway, but each country ends up with lower tax revenues.

As we discuss in chapter 2, the U.S. corporate income tax includes a foreign tax credit provision that attempts to impose the same tax rate on U.S. corporations regardless of where in the world they invest. Many other countries offer symmetric treatment. This may be regarded as an implicit agreement among countries to avoid the kind of tax competition described above. However, as we also note in chapter 2, corporations have a variety of technical ways to get around this and still effectively reduce their tax bills by investing in a low-tax country. Some are concerned that as capital becomes increasingly mobile across countries, a "race to the bottom" in taxation of capital income might be triggered as countries compete to reduce their tax rates to attract more foreign investment. This sometimes leads to proposals for *harmonization* of tax rates across countries—a mutual agreement to conform to a single tax rate, which would eliminate most of the remaining opportunities for firms to reduce their taxes by relocating, at least among the countries that are party to the agreement.[56]

This argument is similar to the one economists use to justify multilateral free-trade agreements. The two arguments are not identical, however, because most economists believe that a zero-tariff free-trade policy is beneficial for any country even if it is adopted unilaterally. In the case of international tax competition, by contrast, there is at least the possibility that a country can make itself better off at the expense of others.[57]

Opinions on whether tax competition is really a problem and whether harmonization would be a good idea vary greatly. Dani Rodrik of Harvard University contends that "it is generally accepted that integration into the world economy reduces the ability of governments to undertake redistributive taxation or implement generous social programs" because countries that attempt to do this will end up driving capital abroad.[58] Others argue that tax competition is actually beneficial—for instance, because they believe taxation of capital income is inefficient or because such competition might induce governments to provide services more efficiently to attract more capital.

While international tax competition is a legitimate issue that raises interesting and potentially important questions, some people see opportunities to use the tax code to benefit their own country at the expense of other nations where no such opportunity actually exists. The most obvious example is a tariff (a tax on imports). This is a particularly inefficient tax from the perspective of the country that imposes it because it induces the home country to buy domestically produced goods that could have been produced at a lower relative cost abroad, diverting domestic resources away from their relatively most productive uses.

Another common red herring particularly relevant to the debate over tax reform has to do with the value added tax (VAT). Some American business people and politicians look with envy at a particular feature of European VATs: the tax is levied on imports, while all tax that had been collected on goods for export is rebated to the exporters, making exports effectively tax free. Although at first glance this might seem like an ingenious export promotion scheme, it is nothing of the sort. All it does is reproduce how a retail sales tax works. States that have sales taxes levy them on goods sold to their residents, regardless of where they were produced, and don't charge sales taxes on goods exported to foreigners. This treatment doesn't give our domestically produced goods any special edge. Suppose we were to implement a 20 percent VAT and tack it on top of the price of everything we buy. Charging a 20 percent VAT on imports would simply mean they are treated equally to domestic goods, just as they are now. The same story holds true for our exports: we wouldn't charge foreigners any VAT on the goods they imported from us, but their home countries would, just as they do for any other goods sold to their residents.

More fundamentally, even if we could figure out some way to give a temporary edge to our domestically produced goods through the tax system, it would soon be dissipated by adjustments in exchange rates. Any apparent advantage to exports would be offset by a combination of a strengthening of the U.S. dollar, which makes dollar-priced exports less attractive to foreigners, and domestic price level increases, which make U.S. markets more attractive to both foreign exporters and U.S. manufacturers. If the exchange rate strengthening and domestic price increases did not occur, the trade surplus stimulated by the demand for U.S.-produced goods would drive up the value of the dollar, dissipating the temporary advantage obtained.

Jobs, Jobs, Jobs

Politicians love to promise more and better jobs for voters, and so do advocates of tax reform. Moreover, whenever any kind of tax increase or elimination of tax preference is threatened, the affected parties immediately produce and publicize a study purporting to show how many jobs it will cost. For example, during the debate over the Tax Reform Act of 1986, when eliminating the deductibility of business lunches was being considered, the restaurant industry association warned that thousands of jobs would be lost in the restaurant business. In support of the Bush administration's 2003 tax cut proposal, his economic advisers claimed it would create 2.1 million jobs over the following three years.[59]

Aside from the natural tendency of interested parties to exaggerate, do such claims about jobs have any economic content? In a word (okay, two words)—not much. Standard economic theory suggests that if the economy is functioning normally, there is nothing about taxes that would cause people who are willing to work at the going wage rate to be unable to find jobs.[60] Jobs in certain sectors may indeed be lost as a result of eliminating preferences in the tax code because the relative demand for those formerly favored items will fall. But that doesn't mean that the total quantity of jobs in the economy is reduced. Rather, demand shifts away from the formerly tax-preferred sectors toward the production of other goods and services in the economy. Extra jobs will open up in these sectors as a result. Shifting jobs from one sector to another can be a jarring process, but it happens all the time for reasons unrelated to taxes and is a key to keeping the economy running efficiently. The transitional costs should not be dismissed, but they are likely to be outweighed by the economic benefits that arise if eliminating an unwarranted preference shifts resources into a more productive area; the latter gain persists long after the transitional disruption has past.

Tax policy can certainly help the economy and generate more employment in the short term if it increases demand and if the economy is operating below capacity because of a recession. Even in this case, though, the effect is only to restore the number of jobs to their normal level more quickly, not to increase the number of jobs in long run. For this purpose, tax cuts and spending increases are about as effective as one another in stimulating the economy, and monetary policy is usually effective as well.

Not coincidentally, liberal economists tend to think that the best countercyclical policy is either tax cuts for low-income households or social spending directed to the same folks. And conservative economists generally think that the best stimulus is a tax cut designed to stimulate saving and investment and maybe just investment in the stock market. It is a troubling fact for the aspiration of economics to be a hard science that our values about equity end up being so correlated with our beliefs about what kind of fiscal, or tax, policy works best for the economy. The underlying and generally unspoken concern is that these alternative stimulus plans benefit different people and have different implications for the long-term level of government spending. These things matter, to be sure, but they have nothing to do with which is the most effective short-term economic stimulus.

The truth is that, for reasons discussed earlier, many economists of widely varying political inclinations are not very enamored of any kind of short-term fiscal policy—whether tax credits targeted to the poor, tax cuts aimed at the affluent, or expenditure increases. In spite of this, the ubiquity of such policies continues. We suspect that there are at least two reasons for this. First, when the economy is going well, governments are quick to claim credit, whether or not their policies had anything to do with the good times. Then, when bad times roll around, voters naturally look to government for another dose of the apparently effective fiscal medicine, and no administration, and especially the second Bush administration, wants to be seen as uninterested in the economy. The doctor may or may not have effective medicine, but something must be prescribed. Second, a recession provides a convenient marketing opportunity for politicians who support tax cuts to achieve other objectives, such as shrinking the size of government or improving incentives.

Another important point is that the number of jobs or the amount of employment should not be relied on as the sole indicator of economic health. To see why, consider the following sure-fire way to generate millions of new jobs—pass and enforce a law requiring that every able-bodied adult work 60 hours per week. This law would "create" millions of new jobs and cause GDP to soar. But it would not make us better off because we value our leisure time and have for the most part chosen how we will allocate our time between working for pay and using our time in other ways we value.

Although claims about the effects of tax cuts on the number of jobs are suspect, at least when the economy is operating normally, the idea that tax reform could lead to *better* jobs has some economic content. This could happen if tax reform caused a more efficient allocation of resources by shifting them from less productive, tax-preferred sectors to other, more productive areas. But for the most part, this claim depends on the idea that reduced tax rates on high-income people, combined with greater incentives for saving, will lead to a larger and higher-quality capital stock. In turn, workers would have better "tools" to work with, increasing their productivity and raising their wages. This is the essence of how tax changes that are targeted mainly at high-income people are supposed to help the rest of the population. This is essentially the same thing as saying that part of the burden of taxes on capital income is currently falling on workers. Democrats have often derided this thinking as "trickle-down economics," while Republicans have made it one of their central themes. Although the logic of the argument is sound, the crucial question is the magnitude of the effect; as discussed above, the evidence is uncertain and not extremely promising.

Human Capital: Education and Training

A more direct way to increase worker productivity and generate better, if not more, jobs is to induce people to acquire more education and skills. Economists refer to the stock of productive skills that people possess as *human capital*. Just as investing in better physical plant and equipment adds to labor productivity, so does investing in skills. Many economists contend that human capital and research and development are the most important elements of long-run economic growth. Although putting a dollar value on such things is difficult, the aggregate value of human capital is probably at least as large as that of physical capital in our country.[61]

Acquiring human capital requires an investment. Some of this investment takes the form of tuition and other direct outlays, which can be substantial, in excess of $25,000 per year at many universities. The other important cost, to the student and to society, is whatever the student could have earned but passed up while at school—their "forgone" earnings. For some college students, forgone earnings are undoubtedly lower than the cost of tuition, although they are many times higher than tuition for some MBA and law students.

How our tax system treats investments in human capital depends on the nature of the investment. The investment of time spent at school rather than at work is treated more generously than most investments in physical capital. Although you pay tax on the return to your investment in skills (higher wages), you save any taxes you would have paid on the earnings you pass up while at school. In essence, you get an immediate write-off for your lost wages. In contrast, an investment in long-lived physical capital would typically be depreciated over many years rather than immediately deducted.

Until recently, human capital investment in the form of direct costs such as tuition was treated less generously by the tax system than physical capital because it generated no tax deductions whatsoever, yet the return to the investment (in the form of higher earnings) was fully taxed. The Taxpayer Relief Act of 1997 altered this comparison by introducing the Hope Scholarship Credit and Lifetime Learning Credit, which allow nonrefundable credits for qualified tuition and related expenses, and a new limited deduction for interest on qualified education loans. Furthermore, you can deduct interest on a home equity loan used for education, the government pays the interest on some student loans while the student is in school, and scholarships used for tuition are tax-free. The 2001 tax cut introduced a limited deduction for higher-education expenses, expanded the deductibility of student loan interest, and expanded opportunities to save for education in tax-preferred accounts. It is not clear whether the tax system now favors human or physical capital investment more, but the balance seems to be tilting toward the former.

An argument can be made that human capital ought to be treated *more* generously than physical capital by the tax code. Because people can't pledge their future labor earnings as collateral for a loan, private capital markets on their own often fail to provide loans even to students who are "good investments." However, government-guaranteed loan programs already exist to address this problem. In addition, some external benefits produced by education (such as creating better citizenship and passing on knowledge) might flow to people who do not pay directly, which would suggest that some degree of subsidy would be efficient. While a case can be made for providing tax incentives for education, the hodgepodge of current provisions is unlikely to be the most efficient approach. First, the code's considerable duplication and complexity seem to suggest that some consolidation and simplification are in order. Second, low-income people, whose decisions about pursuing higher education are most likely to be influenced by financial considerations, often receive little or no benefit from these provisions because they pay no tax. Third, many of the benefits of the tax provisions serve simply as windfalls to students who decide how much education to pursue regardless of tax considerations.

Avoidance and Evasion

Our current tax code provides many opportunities for individuals and firms to reduce their taxes without making any significant changes in how much they work, save, or invest. For example, people with enough accumulated savings can often reduce their tax bills easily by transferring those assets into Individual Retirement Accounts (IRAs); such a transaction requires no actual increase in the amount of their saving. If you know tax rates are going to increase next year, you might try to make sure that any bonuses or royalty checks that are coming your way are paid to you this year. If tax rates go up too much for your tastes, you might simply fail to report some of your income.

These types of responses, called *tax avoidance* when the methods are legal and *tax evasion* when they're not,[62] are key to understanding how taxes affect the economy. First of all, they are symptoms of the economic cost of taxation in the same way that tax-induced reductions in "real" behavior (such as labor supply or investment) are. Although real behavioral responses to taxation might appear to be more important than the others, this reasoning is faulty. On all the margins of choice, taxpayers will undertake behavior that reduces tax liability up to the point that the marginal cost equals the marginal tax saving. In the real-behavior case, the cost is that people's consumption patterns or business investment plans are not what they would, absent taxes, prefer. With avoidance, the cost may be expenditures on professional assistance. With evasion, the cost may be exposure to the uncertainty of an audit and any attendant penalties for detected evasion. Most of these costs represent a deadweight loss to the economy.

The relationship among avoidance, evasion, and decisions such as labor supply is particularly subtle. The avoidance responses may mitigate the extent to which real economic decisions are affected by taxation; you'd almost always prefer to relabel your compensation as a fringe benefit than to make a real sacrifice such as earning less pay. In addition, avoidance responses can cloud the evidence about how taxes are affecting real economic decisions. For example, if the taxable incomes of the rich go down significantly when their tax rates go up, they might have cut back on their labor supply or they might be reporting less of their income and taking greater advantage of avoidance opportunities. Distinguishing among these kinds of responses is important because they can have very different policy implications. In the example just mentioned, if we care about progressivity, then the appropriate policy response might be to limit opportunities for avoidance and evasion rather than to abandon a progressive tax structure because of the apparently large disincentive effects it causes.

Past experience has shown that individuals and firms are very willing to take advantage of opportunities for tax avoidance when they present themselves. Probably the best example of this happened in 1986. The tax reform bill of that year was passed by both houses of Congress in September and signed into law by President Reagan on October 22. According to the law, the tax on long-term gains realized by a top-bracket taxpayer was scheduled to increase from 20 percent to 28 percent as of January 1, 1987. Thus the tax rate was 20 percent *for a limited time only*. Savvy taxpayers took note, and the result was an unprecedented boom in capital gains realizations. Realizations of capital gains increased from $167 billion in 1985 to $322.2 billion in 1986, only to fall back to $137.4 billion in 1987. Even more striking, long-term capital gains on corporate stock in December 1986, the last month of the tax sale, were nearly seven times their level in the same month of 1985.[63]

A second dramatic example of such a response occurred when the 1986 act reduced the top marginal tax rate in the personal income tax below that in the corporate income tax for the first time in decades. This, combined with the promise of avoiding double taxation of business income, made it much more attractive to organize a business as an S corporation or a partnership, which are taxed solely under the personal code, instead of as a traditional C corporation, which is taxed under the corporate code. The response was swift and dramatic. The number of S corporations, which had been rising at a 7.7 percent annual pace from 1965 to 1986, jumped by 17.5 percent a year from 1986 to 1990. The number of C corporations, which had been growing by an average of 3.5 percent per year from 1965 to 1986, dropped by 4.8 percent per year between 1986 and 1990; the biggest decline was among small C corporations, the ones that can more easily switch to S status.[64]

The vast amount of evidence produced by the tax changes since 1981 suggests a hierarchy of behavioral responses to taxation. At the top of the hierarchy—the most clearly responsive to tax incentives—is the timing of certain economic transactions. The pattern of capital gains realizations before and after the 1986 tax reform is the best example, but there are many others, including foreign direct investment into the United States, which was $16.3 billion in the fourth quarter of 1986, more than double the rate of adjacent quarters, as investors raced to beat the expiration of tax rules favoring mergers and acquisitions. In the second tier of the hierarchy are financial and accounting responses, best exemplified the shift from C to S corporations after 1986, and the large post-1986 shift away from newly nondeductible personal loans into still-deductible mortgage debt. On the bottom of the hierarchy, where the least response is evident, are the real economic decisions of individuals and firms concerning labor supply, savings, and investment. The consensus among economists is that the evidence shows that aggregate labor supply responds little to its after-tax return, the evidence is not clear on whether saving responds to its after-tax return, and the evidence regarding investment is decidedly mixed.

How Do Very High-Income People Respond to Tax Cuts?

The hierarchy of behavioral responses provides a useful perspective for evaluating one of the most dramatic impacts of a tax change in history. Right after the Tax Reform Act of 1986, which reduced the top marginal tax rate from 50 percent to 28 percent, the reported taxable income of affluent Americans increased strikingly. Between 1984 and 1990, the total inflation-adjusted gross income of the most affluent 1 percent of taxpayers rose by 68 percent, and their share of total AGI increased from 9.9 percent to 13.4.[65] Data that follow the same taxpayers over time reveals the same pattern: those high-income households for which the 1986 tax reform provided the biggest reductions in marginal tax rates experienced the biggest increases in reported income.[66]

Did the reduced marginal tax rates of the 1980s *cause* the large increase in reported incomes of the affluent? Or was the timing of the high-income surge just a coincidence? After all, income inequality, led by an explosion in the incomes at the top of the income distribution, had been steadily increasing since about 1970, and many explanations for this trend have nothing to do with tax changes. For example, the demand for the services of a select few highly skilled "superstars" in various fields appears to have been increasing over time, and the ability to deliver their services to a worldwide audience has increased with technological advances in telecommunications.[67] The share of income received by the highest earners undoubtedly would have increased, even without any tax changes. But the sharpness of the increase right around 1986 suggests that the tax cut was a major factor in the increase.

A closer look at the anatomy of the high-income behavioral response suggests that it had little if anything to do with increased hours worked.[68] Some of the increased income was accounted for by the shift in legal organization of firms from C corporations, whose income shows up on corporation tax returns, to S corporations, whose income shows up on individual tax returns. Such a shift does not reflect the creation of new income or an increase in total tax revenues: although income reported by individuals went up, the taxable income of C corporations showed a mirror-image decline. Another part of the explanation is that the 1986 tax reform sharply reduced the advantages of using partnerships as tax shelters. To the extent that these tax losses stopped showing up after 1987 on the tax returns of high-income taxpayers, their incomes appear to have risen, but any such increase reflects only the tightening up of the rules governing tax shelters. In sum, not all of the post-1986 increase in reported income of the affluent reflected improved incentives due to the cut in tax rates.

This issue became critical in the debate over the impact of the increases in the top marginal rate enacted in 1990 and especially in 1993. Bill Clinton was elected in 1992 on a platform that included tax increases on the affluent, and he delivered on that promise starting in tax year 1993, when the top federal tax rate increased from 31 percent to 39.6 percent. Proponents of this policy argued that it was appropriate that high-income taxpayers pay their "fair share" of the necessary increase in tax burden. Opponents cautioned that the revenue projections were overstated because they ignored the inevitable behavioral response of high-income taxpayers.

Once the initial evidence on tax year 1993 was compiled, Daniel Feenberg and Martin Feldstein of Harvard University examined tabulations of tax-return data for 1992 and 1993. They concluded that compared to previous trend growth and the income growth of other taxpayers, the reported taxable incomes of very high-income families *fell* by 7.8 percent in 1993, the year of the tax increase. If correct, then the Treasury collected only half of the revenue that it had claimed it would collect from the rate increase.[69] Feenberg and Feldstein argued that this large behavioral response indicated that the ratio of the efficiency cost due to distorted behavior to the revenue raised was high—much higher than for alternative ways to raise revenue. The policy implication: high taxes on the rich are a bad idea.[70]

There's more to this story, though. Bill Clinton was elected in early November 1992, leaving plenty of time for many high-income taxpayers to shift taxable income that would otherwise have been received in 1993 and afterward into 1992, when it would be taxed at a rate no higher than 31 percent. In December, the financial press was full of stories advising readers to do just that and full of stories about prominent citizens who already had. Walt Disney executives Michael Eisner and Frank Wells cashed in stock options worth $257 million. Several baseball players, including future (but fleeting) home-run champion Mark McGwire, made sure that their new long-term contracts had front-loaded the bonus payments into 1992 to reduce the tax bite. The New York State Bureau of the Budget's annual survey of the year-end bonuses paid to Wall Street high flyers revealed that about two-thirds was paid in December of 1992 and one-third in January of 1993, compared to the usual breakdown of one-third in December and two-thirds in January.[71] Austan Goolsbee of the University of Chicago Business School has shown that, among high-income executives, almost all of the difference between 1992 and 1993 income was due to changes in timing of the exercising of stock options.[72] The Commerce Department has estimated that, all in all, about $20 billion of income in total was shifted from 1993 into 1992.[73]

For all these reasons, the lower-than-trend 1993 incomes of the high-est income group could reflect nothing more than the fact that taxable income was shifted backward from 1993 to 1992 to escape the expected higher taxes. In fact, compared to data from 1991, which would not be contaminated by the shifting, the 1993 incomes of affluent taxpayers do not look particularly low.[74] The evidence from years surrounding announced or anticipated tax changes clearly reveals a mixture of timing responses and the more permanent responses to tax changes, and it is difficult to sort out one from the other. All in all, although affluent taxpayers surely take note of and respond to the tax system, no clear evidence shows that they altered their behavior enough to undermine the tax increases of 1990 and 1993.

Figure 4.7 puts this debate into a longer-term historical perspective, based on a study of tax-return data by Thomas Piketty of ENS-CEPREMAP, a research center in Paris, and Emmanuel Saez of the University of California at Berkeley.[75] It shows, for the years 1913 through 2000, pretax income (excluding capital gains) reported by people in the top 1 percent of the income distribution as a share of the total of such income in the United States and the marginal tax rate in the top bracket of the personal income tax.

The short-run relationship between marginal rates and the share of income earned by the top 1 percent of earners suggests that a number of features are not particularly consistent with the notion that a behavioral response to tax rates is the main factor driving the surge of incomes at the top of the distribution. While the very large surge in income following the Tax Reform Act of 1986 is readily apparent, the incomes of the top 1 percent increased nearly as fast during the 1990s as during the 1980s. Between 1990 and 2000, the share of income (excluding capital gains) reported by the top 1 percent surged from 13 percent to 16.9 percent. Capital gains also increased dramatically for this group during the 1990s, but because these gains reflect mainly the stock market boom, we exclude them from the analysis. The sharp rise in incomes at the top of the distribution occurred despite increases in the top marginal tax rate in 1990 and 1993. Thus, the soaring reported incomes of the affluent continued until 2000, nearly a decade and a half after the last tax cut and a few years after two tax increases, which casts some doubt on the hypothesis that movements in the top tax rate were the principal cause of the striking changes in the reported income of high-income households since 1980.

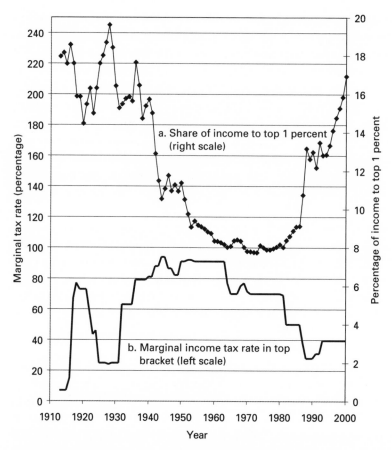

Figure 4.7
Share of total U.S. pretax income going to top 1 percent of income distribution versus marginal personal income tax rate in the top bracket, 1913–2000
Source: Piketty and Saez (2003); <http://emlab.berkeley.edu/users/saez/index.html>.
Note: Income excludes capital gains.

Other instances of patterns that do not suggest a strong response to incentives include the Kennedy-Johnson tax cut, which cut the top rate from 91 percent to 70 percent between 1963 and 1965 and was not accompanied by a surge in top reported incomes anything like what happened in the 1980s. Not reflected in figure 4.7 is the 1971 cut in the maximum tax rate on labor income from 70 percent to just over 50 percent, which produced no evidence of a surge in reported incomes in its aftermath either.[76]

Over the longer run, however, a clear negative relationship does appear between the top marginal income tax rate and the reported incomes of the top 1 percent. At the beginning and end of the century, marginal tax rates were relatively low, and incomes of the rich were very high. In the middle of the century, marginal tax rates were high and incomes were low. Thus, there is some broad support for responsiveness to incentives here. One reasonable interpretation of the data would be that very high marginal rates like those imposed in the middle of the century have a negative impact on reported income of the rich but that modest changes around the levels of the marginal rates we have today do not necessarily have a significant effect (as evidenced by the experience of the 1990s). Some of the response to changes in incentives might also take time to materialize.[77] Finally, figure 4.7 depicts income reported to the tax authorities. Thus, to the extent that the share of income reported by the top 1 percent responded to tax rates, the data reflect a combination of "real" behavioral responses (like altered labor supply) with other responses (such as avoidance and evasion). Figure 4.7 strongly suggests that in times when statutory tax rates are as high as 70 to 90 percent, affluent taxpayers report relatively less income. It does not tell us, however, whether this is due to less earnings or more avoidance and evasion.

How Do Tax Cuts Affect Revenues?

The proposition that across-the-board tax cuts would lose no revenue is now associated with the economist Arthur Laffer, who claimed in the 1970s that high tax rates might be harming the economy so much that tax cuts would provide more, rather than less, revenue. The free lunch promised by Laffer proved irresistible to politicians and was one of the ideological underpinnings of the tax cuts in the Economic Recovery Tax Act of 1981. The massive increase in the budget deficit following that tax cut weakened support for such views, but some such support still persists today. For example, on the campaign trail in 1996 and 2000, one of Steve Forbes's mantras was that tax cuts in the United States have always increased revenues.

With almost two decades of hindsight, most economists now admit that Laffer's proposition did not apply to the tax-rate cuts of 1981. This should not be surprising given all of the evidence we discussed above, such as the apparently small responsiveness of labor supply to taxes. The reduction in tax rates did not cause the economy to expand enough to recoup the revenues; revenues turned out to be significantly lower than what they would have been had there been no tax cut. All but the most ardent supply-siders now concede this point.

Certainly, individual income tax revenues fell relative to GDP after 1981. From 1981 to 1984, they dropped from 9.6 percent of GDP down to 8 percent, despite continued inflation-induced "bracket creep" that pushed taxpayers into higher tax rates. President George H. W. Bush's Treasury Department estimated that by 1990 the rate reductions of the 1981 act alone were costing the federal government $164 billion per year, assuming no departure from the normal trend of economic growth.[78] The only way such facts could be reconciled with claims that the 1981 cut caused revenues to *increase* would be if it caused the economy to grow significantly faster than it otherwise would have. As table 4.1 shows, however, the productivity growth rate of the 1980s was actually slightly below that of the 1970s, as well as below that of the 1990s. Some point to the growth rate experienced in the years immediately after 1982, but this confuses the recovery from a deep recession with sustainable long-run growth.

Dynamic Scoring

Even if we dismiss the claim that tax cuts "pay for themselves," a legitimate and important question remains: exactly how do revenues respond to changes in tax rates? Advocates of tax cuts often complain that official analyses of their proposals fail to take into account *any* possibility of induced economic growth and that they therefore make tax cut proposals appear to cost more revenue than they really would. They argue that the revenue-estimating process of the government should be made *dynamic* (assuming that economic growth will be affected) rather than *static* (assuming that growth is unaffected).[79] For example, in February 2003, House Majority Leader Tom DeLay (R-TX) argued vehemently against taking seriously the $674 billion static revenue estimate provided by the Bush administration itself. "The number 674 is meaningless," DeLay said, because it fails to account for the "dynamic" effect of tax cuts.[80]

Some background is necessary to understand this issue. The budget act of 1974 assigned to the Congressional Budget Office (CBO) the tasks of making baseline projections of revenues and outlays and of estimating the budget effects of the spending proposals reported by committees. It assigned to the Joint Committee on Taxation (JCT) of Congress the task of preparing estimates for most revenue legislation. The two groups coordinate their efforts on estimates of complex pieces of legislation that affect both revenues and outlays. This process is designed to provide Congress with the information it needs to evaluate budgetary proposals independently. *Scoring* refers to the official estimates of the revenue and spending effects of each proposal, which are used to determine whether the proposal is consistent with whatever congressional budget rules are in effect at that time. In practice, these tend to become the numbers most often cited in the media in connection with any big tax or spending proposals.

Under current practice, both the CBO and the JCT already incorporate into their revenue estimates a wide variety of behavioral changes in response to economic incentives. In his May 2002 testimony to the House Budget Committee about dynamic scoring, outgoing CBO director Dan Crippen cited two examples of the CBO methodology.[81] First, he noted that when the CBO does a revenue estimate of an increase in the capital gains tax, it accounts for the fact that this tax will accelerate the realization of gains to avoid the higher tax rate. Note that this is a timing response. He then said that when the CBO does cost estimates of a change in marginal income tax rates, it includes the effect on the tax base that comes from recharacterizing compensation from taxable wages and salaries to nontaxable fringe benefits. Note that this is a renaming effect.

What is *not* now part of revenue scoring is any macroeconomic effect of proposed legislation and the budgetary implications of those effects. In other words, gross domestic product is not allowed to be affected by tax policy in calculating a revenue estimate. The main long-run macroeconomic effects that current procedures leave out of revenue estimates are those that affect the level of production through labor supply and saving. Those responses on the lowest rung of the hierarchy of behavioral responses—the ones that the evidence suggests are likely to be the least responsive to taxes and therefore will cause the least error in revenue estimates if ignored—are left out.

The first main argument for dynamic scoring is that an imprecisely right answer that recognizes behavioral responses is better than a precisely wrong answer, the precisely wrong answer being that tax cuts or changes have absolutely *no* effect on the macro economy. Argument number two is that nondynamic, or static, scoring biases decision making toward big—indeed, bloated—government because it overestimates both the revenue cost of tax cuts and the revenue gain from tax increases. It is by no means obvious that this latter point is true, however. For instance, if the tax cut is not accompanied by a cut in government spending, and the economy is operating at capacity, the negative economic effects of the resulting budget deficit are likely to outweigh the positive economic effects of improved incentives. In that case, the tax cut will reduce economic growth and cut revenues even further, so that the static estimate would *understate* the revenue cost of the tax cut.

The principal arguments against dynamic scoring are that (1) the uncertainty about its true impact would politicize the revenue scoring process and threaten its integrity, (2) it would bias the process toward fiscally irresponsible outcomes, and (3) because it is infeasible to do for all proposals, it would force proposals to be big if only big proposals are dynamically scored and force proposals to be tax-expenditure programs rather than regular expenditure programs if only tax proposals are dynamically scored.[82]

In evaluating these claims, it is important to keep in mind that cutting taxes without cutting expenditures is not a free ride. A plan to cut taxes is not a plan to spend less of the taxpayers' money; it is instead a plan to put off assigning to our citizens the burden of that spending. One dynamic effect that is indisputable is that large, persistent budget deficits are unsustainable. Thus, a proper dynamic scoring of a tax cut that is not offset elsewhere in the budget should show it eventually having a negative effect on the economy. As we noted above, if taxes are cut and government spending is not cut, the resulting deficit is bad for the long-run economy. Moreover, taxes will eventually have to go up in the future, which harms incentives then. If it does not recognize this, dynamic scoring can obfuscate the nature of the choices we face rather than improve the accuracy of the trade-offs we face.

In March 2003, under new director Douglas Holtz-Eakin, CBO released a dynamic analysis of the Bush administration budget proposals for fiscal year 2004, which included a large tax cut as well as a number of spending increases.[83] CBO took the reasonable approach of presenting estimates from a number of different models involving different conceptions of how the economy works, including several academic models and two models used by professional business forecasters. It presented only estimates of the economic and budgetary impact for the next 10 years, assuming no changes in taxes or spending to offset the tax cuts during that time. But it also correctly noted that government borrowing must eventually be paid for with higher taxes or lower spending, and it indicated that in the simulations where the borrowing is eventually paid for outside the 10-year window with higher tax rates (rather than reduced spending), there is a "negative effect on output in the long run."[84] Moreover, in some models, the economic impact in the next 10 years depends on peoples' *expectations* about how the deficits will eventually be paid for; CBO appropriately presented how the results would change under different assumptions about those expectations. The analysis produced a range of estimates of the impact for the next 10 years, with some finding that the plan would slow economic growth, thereby exacerbating deficits, while others found modest improvements in growth that would reduce deficits. None of the dynamic analyses comes close to overturning the conclusion that tax cuts unaccompanied by spending cuts will increase government borrowing, which must eventually be paid for in the future.

The results were not surprising given the elements of the plan. The types of spending increases proposed, as well as some of the tax cuts, were not the sorts of things that would be expected to increase growth, as they did nothing to improve incentives. Had the analysis been done for a tax cut that focused mainly on improving incentives and that was paid for by an equal and explicit cut in government consumption or in the context of a revenue-neutral tax reform, it would likely have sent a much clearer and more uniform signal of positive economic effects. The fact that such an analysis is capable of pointing out important distinctions like this makes it a useful exercise. It was also, encouragingly, an honest exercise, as it recognized the wide range of uncertainty in any such exercise, and it did not focus on the aspects of the plan that produce benefits while ignoring the aspects that impose costs. But note that this was not a dynamic "score" but rather a set of dynamic estimates produced purely for informational purposes. A "score" would require picking one number and making that the official estimate that governs the budget process, which is considerably more problematic.

Conclusion

Our tax system unquestionably imposes costs on the economy, but exactly how large those costs are no one knows for sure.[85] Although a certain amount of this cost cannot be eliminated, tax reform could succeed in reducing these costs. Some tax changes that are "good for the economy" eliminate unnecessary and misguided features that are violations of neutral tax treatment of economic activities. In other cases, the economic gains are achieved by exploiting the inherent trade-off with progressivity by loosening the link between tax liability and economic success. Depending on one's views about equity, it may be reasonable to reject any economic gains that come only at the cost of penalizing the poor and middle class. For this reason, these cases must be carefully distinguished. This is a major theme of chapters 6 through 8, where we discuss options for tax reform. Before moving on, however, two other aspects of a good tax system need to be considered—simplicity and enforceability.

5   Simplicity and Enforceability

To this point, we have explored two fundamental criteria for judging a tax system—how it assigns tax burden and how it affects economic prosperity. The two other desirable features of a good tax system are that it be simple and easy to enforce. This chapter begins by examining just how complex our income tax is, what makes it so complex, and how to go about simplifying it. Then we look at the problem of evasion and enforcement in the current income tax and discuss the features of a tax system that make it easy or difficult to enforce.

How Complicated Is Our Tax System?

For several years, *Money* magazine invented a tax situation of moderate but not exceptional complexity and asked a few dozen tax professionals to calculate tax liability. The last time it did this, in 1997, it got back 46 different answers from the 46 professionals who submitted returns; the answers ranged from $34,420 to $68,192. The actual tax liability was $35,643, although some legitimate differences in interpreting the law could have changed that total a bit. Not a single preparer turned in an error-free return.[1]

Another springtime ritual of *Money* is to call the IRS help line and ask a set of common questions that people face when filling out their tax returns. In 2002, the IRS workers answered only 75 percent of the questions accurately, far short of a perfect score but a large improvement over the 55 percent correct figure reported in 1988.[2]

The fact that, in some situations, neither tax professionals nor the IRS itself can be sure of a taxpayer's tax liability is just one indicator of the tax system's complexity. Another is the sheer length of the tax code. West Publishing Company's 2002 edition of the *Internal Revenue Code* includes 9,833 sections covering 2,940 pages, while the accompanying

Federal Tax Regulations 2002 spans 9,246 pages.[3] The total number of words in these two documents probably exceeds 7 million.[4]

Although these figures are eye-catching, they are not of direct concern to most taxpayers. Does it matter whether the tax code has 5, 50, or 500 million words, as long as your own tax affairs are straightforward? In some situations, having a detailed set of rules could even make things simpler if it clears up gray areas in the tax law. Many of these rules have been adopted to stop the increasingly complicated tax-avoidance strategies that some taxpayers and their advisers are continually inventing. Clearly, more than anecdotes and page numbers are needed to get a good picture of how complex our tax system is and whether it needs to be simplified.

The Costs of Compliance

The most informative measure of tax complexity is the resource cost of collecting taxes. This cost certainly includes the budget of the IRS, which in 2002 spent $9.5 billion enforcing all varieties of federal taxation, or about 0.5 percent of the revenue it collected.[5] The IRS budget—the *administrative cost* of raising taxes—is, however, only the tip of the iceberg of the total cost of collection. It is dwarfed by the costs borne directly by taxpayers, known as *compliance costs*. Part of this cost is the money spent on accountants and other tax preparers, software, and tax guidebooks. Compliance costs also include the expense incurred by third parties to the tax-collection process, such as employers who withhold and remit tax on behalf of their employees. But the largest resource cost of compliance consists of the time that taxpayers devote to doing their taxes and keeping track of the information needed to document their tax liability. Both the monetary outlay and the time spent are resource costs because they could be used for some valuable purpose if it weren't for the tax system.

A 1989 survey of taxpayers suggested that in that year individuals spent about 3 billion hours, or an average of about 27 hours per year per taxpayer, dealing with both federal and state income taxes.[6] Of the total time, less than 20 percent was spent on preparing the return itself. The bulk of it—about 60 percent—was spent on recordkeeping. The remainder was spent in activities such as researching the tax law, meeting with an adviser, or arranging financial affairs to minimize taxes. The time burden of tax compliance is highly concentrated: more than half the total hours were incurred by just 16 percent of taxpayers.

Self-employed taxpayers were particularly hard hit, spending an average of 60 hours per year on tax matters. People with capital gains, dividends, rental income, and itemized deductions also tend to have higher-than-average compliance burdens.

In addition to the cost of taxpayers' own time, direct monetary outlays are made for professional guidance and supplies. About half of all taxpayers purchased assistance from an accountant or other professional tax adviser. Those who did spend an average of about $204 annually (in 2003 dollars).[7]

What does this all add up to in 2003? If time spent complying with personal income taxes is valued at a reasonable average of $15 per hour and adjusted to apply to federal income taxes only, the total cost of that time comes to about $50 billion for 2003.[8] Professional assistance and other monetary expenses add another $10 billion, for a total personal income tax compliance cost of $60 billion. This figure makes no effort to quantify the "psychic" costs the tax imposes in the form of anxiety suffered by taxpayers concerned about getting their taxes done on time, done right, and worrying about an audit. In addition, much of the estimate is based on data from 1989, which was the last time a thorough survey was done; the complexity of the tax code has gotten worse since then. On the other hand, some of the recordkeeping required for the personal income tax would be required anyway for purposes such as applications for mortgages, college financial aid, and government transfer programs, so it does not represent an incremental cost imposed by the tax system. All things considered, the tax-compliance cost for individuals was probably at least $60 billion in 2003.

This $60 billion figure, however, doesn't even count the compliance cost imposed on most businesses, which any business owner will tell you can be onerous, indeed. To be sure, there are many fewer corporate income tax returns than there are personal returns (5.6 million versus 130 million in 2001),[9] but the amount of time and money spent per corporate return is much greater. Consider the country's largest companies. The average Fortune 500 company spends $4.6 million per year on tax matters; many of the largest spend over $10 million.[10] The 1,700 largest companies spend a total of $3.8 billion (in 2003 dollars) in complying with federal, state, and local corporate income taxes.[11] The biggest sources of complexity for large corporations are depreciation rules, the alternative minimum tax, the lack of uniformity among states and between the federal income tax rules and those used by the states, and the rules governing income earned abroad. The latter are particularly complex, accounting for 40 percent of the total cost of compliance for these companies, although foreign operations account for less than a quarter of assets, sales, or employment for these large corporations.[12]

Even after all this expense, often neither the company nor the IRS is completely sure what the correct tax liability is. Audits, appeals, and lawsuits often drag on for years, so it is not at all uncommon for a big corporation to have its tax liability still unsettled 10 years after the return was filed.

Small and medium-size businesses also incur significant compliance costs. In fact, studies consistently find that the smaller the firm, the larger the cost of complying with the tax system per dollar of tax payment, sales, assets, or any other measure of the size of the firm.[13] The cost of compliance for some small businesses, particularly sole proprietorships, is already counted in our $60 billion estimate for the personal code; but for many small businesses it is not.[14] A recent study estimated total compliance costs of $22 billion for businesses below the biggest 1,500 but with assets in excess of $5 million.[15]

Note, though, that any survey-based estimate for business is bound to be only a rough guess because of the difficulty of separating the accounting and bookkeeping activities that were done solely for tax purposes from those that would have been done anyway for general business purposes. This is a particular problem for small businesses that do not have a separate tax department.

Taking all of these factors into account, our best estimate of the total annual cost of enforcing and complying with the federal corporate and personal income taxes in 2003 is $110 billion, or about 10 cents per dollar raised.[16] Others have argued that compliance costs are much higher than this. Writing for the Tax Foundation, Arthur P. Hall claimed that they amount to 27 percent of revenues.[17] In the popular press, even more exorbitant compliance cost estimates are routinely cited. For instance, in 1995, former House Ways and Means Committee chair Bill Archer was quoted on the front page of the *Wall Street Journal* as saying, "The current income tax system costs, by the most conservative projections, $300 billion a year just for compliance."[18] House Democratic leader Richard Gephardt repeated this figure at a press conference presenting his own tax reform proposal.[19] We think these are vast overestimates but that the costs are still substantial.

A cost of $110 billion per year is worth taking seriously. This is the dollar value of the time, goods, and services that would be freed up if it were not for the complexity of the tax system. For both cost and fairness reasons, we should take seriously proposals to simplify the tax system. To properly evaluate these proposals, however, it's important to put this cost into its proper perspective.

It's Not Complicated for Everyone

How complex the tax system is depends on who you are. For the over 50 million taxpayers who file Form 1040EZ or 1040A, it's not much of a hassle. In 2001, about 17 percent of taxpayers used Form 1040EZ.[20] Although this form is an 8.5-by-11-inch, two-sided page, it could be put on a (large) postcard. Filing a 1040EZ requires writing down wage and interest income, subtracting the personal exemption and standard deduction, and then looking up the tax owed (and in some cases the earned income tax credit) in the tax tables. If you prefer, the IRS will even do the tax liability calculation for you. Another 22 percent of taxpayers filed Form 1040A, which is not quite as simple as the 1040EZ but is still pretty straightforward.[21] Users of this form may have a few other types of income to report, such as dividends or pension disbursements, some IRA contributions to subtract, or perhaps a child-care credit to compute, but otherwise it's not much different from the 1040EZ.

Even some of those who must file the more complicated Form 1040 do not necessarily face a daunting task. Surveys suggest that 30 percent of taxpayers spend fewer than five hours on all tax matters over an entire year; 45 percent spend fewer than ten hours, and 66 percent spend fewer than twenty.[22] In any attempt to reform the tax system, we must be careful not to throw the baby out with the bath water and destroy the relative simplicity that already exists for many millions of taxpayers. The tax system is highly complex only for a minority of taxpayers with relatively complicated financial affairs.

Complexity often is and certainly should be a matter of concern, however, even for the millions of taxpayers with fairly simple tax returns. For one thing, many of these people believe that other, more sophisticated taxpayers take advantage of the complexity to find loopholes that lower their tax liability, leaving the less sophisticated taxpayers holding the revenue bag. To these people, one attraction of a flat tax is its promise to ensure that high-income people have no way to avoid paying their share. Furthermore, some of the cost imposed by complexity on businesses is undoubtedly passed on to individuals in the form of higher prices or lower wages, in just the same way as an explicit tax liability on businesses would be passed through. Although businesses directly incur these costs, the ultimate burden is borne by individuals.

Increasing numbers of taxpayers are using computers to help prepare their tax returns. Over time, improvements in technology may gradually reduce the burden imposed by any given level of tax complexity. However, University of Chicago economist Austan Goolsbee, who has studied this question carefully, cautions that the potential for technology to overcome tax complexity in the foreseeable future should not be overstated. Tax preparation software can indeed reduce the difficulty of filling out tax forms and calculating tax liability. For example, the software obviates the need for taxpayers to go through special worksheets to calculate phase-ins and phase-outs of exemptions, deductions, and credits. Goolsbee notes, though, that filling out the form is only one small component of the overall compliance burden of the tax system. Tax software does little or nothing to reduce the burden of recordkeeping or of transactions undertaken to avoid taxes. Second, he finds that 9 percent of households used tax preparation software in 2000 and 10 percent did in 2001. At that rate of growth, it will be a very long time before most taxpayers are using such software. Third, based on survey data, Goolsbee estimates that other things equal, people with more complex tax situations are no more likely than others to use tax software. Rather, it appears that by far the most important determinant of whether people use such software is how comfortable and experienced they are with computers and the Internet. The people who are not so comfortable with such things and thus do not use tax software are also likely to be the people who have the most trouble coping with tax complexity in the first place.[23]

Is Our Tax System Too Complex?

Is a cost of collection of about 10 cents on the dollar outrageously high, remarkably low, or about right? There are no comparable, reliable figures from other countries or alternative tax systems against which we can judge 10 cents.[24] Even if there were, a simple comparison of cost per dollar raised could be misleading. A lower cost could mean that the tax is being raised in an inequitable way. As an extreme example, we could simplify the taxpaying process for many people if we stopped enforcing it, making it effectively voluntary. But this would place the tax burden entirely on those who view taxpaying as a duty, allowing everyone else to escape with no obligations. Most everyone would agree this is patently unfair and not worth the cost saving of a voluntary tax system. This example illustrates the point that before we dismiss the U.S. system as unnecessarily complex and therefore too costly, we must consider what, if anything, this complexity is buying us. If it is buying us nothing or something that is not worth the cost, the tax system certainly ought to be simplified.

What Makes a Tax System Complicated?

Tax complexity arises for many reasons. The desire to achieve equity and fairness in the assignment of tax burdens is one. The attempt to encourage certain activities deemed socially or economically beneficial is another. Sometimes, purely political factors appear to be responsible. Below, we discuss these and other causes of tax complexity.[25]

Measuring Ability to Pay

One reason that paying for government is complicated, costly, and time-consuming is that we are not willing to have one price for all. The line for tickets at a movie theater moves fairly quickly where there is one basic admission price; it moves a bit less quickly when there is a separate charge for children below a certain age. It would move more slowly still if each child had to produce identification to prove his or her age; to speed things along, most theaters are willing to take the parents' or child's word for it. Paying for a meal at a restaurant is usually a simple process, but imagine what it would be like if the bill depended not only on what was ordered but also on the income, number of children, and annual medical expenditures of each member of the party.

One reason our system is complex is that we think simpler methods of assigning tax burdens are inequitable. Achieving each kind of equity discussed in chapter 3—vertical and horizontal equity—puts demands on the tax system. First, consider vertical equity, the appropriate sharing of tax burdens across families of different levels of well-being. A poll tax, under which every adult pays the same amount of tax, period, is the essence of simplicity but is unacceptable to most everyone on equity grounds.[26] Instead, we require that tax liability be tied to how well off a family is. But as soon as tax liability is tied to some indicator of well-being such as income or consumption, things start to get complicated fast.

In the income tax system, the basic indicator of well-being is constructed from adding up various sources of income, some more difficult to measure than others. Measuring labor compensation is often straightforward, although it runs into difficulties when fringe benefits are involved or when the compensation can be relabeled as capital income to receive more generous tax treatment. For example, employers can substitute benefits such as free parking in lieu of wages. Fringe benefits can be a valuable source of labor compensation, but assessing their precise value is difficult. Similarly, labor income can be repackaged as a capital gain, for instance, by spending time fixing up a home and then selling it. Much executive compensation comes in the form of a stock option, the value of which is notoriously difficult to measure accurately at the time it is granted.

Income earned from business or investments is often much more difficult to measure precisely. At the business level, it creates the need to measure the depreciation of assets, which is impossible to do precisely. Even the standardized but approximate depreciation deductions used by our tax code require considerable recordkeeping and calculation. At the personal level, including capital gains in the tax base as they accrue would be prohibitively complex in some cases, and even including them as they are realized raises nettlesome problems. Other requirements of a completely accurate measure of capital income, such as including the rental value of services from a home and adjusting capital income for inflation, are so complicated that we don't even attempt them. Despite all the compromises we make in our tax code, measuring and reporting capital income are still burdensome for many taxpayers.

The difficulty of administering and complying with taxes based on consumption rather than income depends on how it is done. Imagine the hassle if each household had to keep track of all of its expenditures over the course of the year and report the total to the tax authorities. Alternatively, we could measure each household's consumption as income minus saving, which, if done appropriately, could avoid most of the complexities of measuring income but would require keeping track of all deposits and withdrawals from savings. On the other hand, taxing consumption at the business level rather than the individual level, through either a sales tax or value added tax (VAT), could greatly simplify the taxpaying process relative to an income tax. But removing individuals from the taxpaying process would limit the degree to which tax liabilities would vary according to ability to pay or other household characteristics.

Achieving horizontal equity—the equal treatment of people with equal ability to pay—also exacts a cost of complexity. If we accept some measure of income or consumption as the basic measure of well-being, how much fine-tuning needs to be done? If two families with the same income are not equally well off because one has high unavoidable medical expenses and the other doesn't, should that be reflected in tax liabilities? Probably so, but accomplishing this and other adjustments to accurately measure ability to pay inevitably complicates the tax system. Thus there is a tax policy choice that must be made—how to trade off fine-tuning tax liability for family circumstances against the complexity required to implement that fine-tuning. Substantial simplification will require that we give up on the notion that the bill we pay to the government must be personalized in great detail and settle instead on rough justice only.

Taxing Individuals Instead of Taxing at the Business Level

As we noted in chapter 3, the *incidence* of a tax (who ultimately bears the burden) is not affected by which side of a transaction remits the tax to the IRS. How simple a tax is, however, depends on the mechanics of how tax is collected. For example, a consumption tax that required retailers to charge a fixed percentage tax on every sale and remit it to the government (a retail sales tax) would be much simpler than one that required each individual to keep records of his or her consumption. Similarly, in an income tax, it is simpler to have employers, financial institutions, and corporations remit tax on various items of income paid to individuals than to have each individual keep track of the income he or she receives.

Our income tax system is relatively simple in the areas where it follows this principle and more complex where it does not. Taxation of wage and salary income is facilitated because employers are required to withhold and remit tax to the IRS on the wages and salaries of each employee. This adds some compliance burden for the employer but saves even more for the employee. The more income we treat in this fashion, the simpler the taxpaying process can become. In Japan and the United Kingdom,[27] most taxpayers don't even have to file tax returns in most years because their systems for withholding on wages are more precise than ours and because taxes are withheld not only for wages and salaries but also on other types of income such as interest.

Graduated Tax Rates

A graduated tax-rate structure does not by itself directly contribute any significant complexity to the taxpaying process. Once taxable income is computed, looking up tax liability in the tax tables is a trivial operation that is not perceptibly simplified by having fewer brackets.

But a graduated rate structure does indirectly add to the complexity of the tax system because it implies that, due to the need to measure ability to pay family by family, the tax system must go beyond taxation at the business level to include individuals in the collection process. In conjunction with other changes, having only one tax rate could facilitate a major simplification. If everyone were subject to the same tax rate, then taxes on most types of income could be remitted at the source of the income payment rather than by the recipient, and little or no reconciliation would be required of the individual. One reason the United Kingdom's system of final withholding is able to get most people's tax liabilities right without having them file returns is because all earners except those with very high incomes are subject to a single rate.

This same principle applies to consumption taxation as well. With a single rate with no exemptions, aggregate consumption can be measured and tax remitted entirely at the business level, with no reconciliation required on the part of individuals.

A Messy Tax Base

How we deal with fundamental issues of fairness is responsible for some of the complexity of our current tax system, but a lot of the complexity arises from reasons that are not fundamental. Consider the deductions and other tax preferences that complicate and narrow the tax base. The personal code has numerous adjustments, credits, and itemized deductions for things such as home mortgage interest, state and local tax payments, child-care payments, tuition expenses, and the like. At the business level, there are various tax credits, special depreciation rules, and other preferences. Each of these features requires record-keeping and calculation. Moreover, each deduction or credit involves ambiguities about exactly what kinds of activities qualify. As but one example, the Lifetime Learning Credit is available for "qualified tuition and related expenses." The credit can be taken for fees required for enrollment and attendance but not for fees associated with meals, lodging, student activities, athletics, or insurance, or the cost of books.

Further complexity ensues as regulations are written to clarify the ambiguities and as taxpayers come up with new ways to circumvent them.

Because nearly every economic issue has a tax angle, just about any time someone comes up with a bright idea about how the government should encourage one activity or discourage another, the tax system gets the call. This is especially true because the current political environment favors tax credits rather than outright expenditures, even if they add up to essentially the same thing. As a result, our tax system is now an awkward mixture of a revenue-raising system plus scores of incentive programs, and it is much more complicated than it would be if raising revenue in the most equitable and cost-efficient way possible were its only function.

Although it is generally better to leave economic decisions to the free market, in some situations subsidizing certain activities may be legitimate—for example, when an activity generates positive externalities. Such activities may be cheaper and simpler to subsidize through the tax code rather than through a separate program. After all, the administrative machinery already exists for the government to collect and, in some cases, remit money to over 130 million individual taxpayers and 5.5 million corporations. If we as a society decide to subsidize, say, child-care expenditures, from a purely administrative point of view it doesn't make sense to set up a separate system for processing child-care credit applications and remitting checks to eligible people. Since the IRS is already set up to process tax forms and send out checks, piggybacking a child-care credit onto the taxpaying process is surely cost-effective.[28] Why not keep just one set of accounts—one-stop shopping—between the government and its citizens?

The biggest problem with piggybacking policies onto the revenue-raising system is that important economic policies that would never be enacted as stand-alone policies are often thereby hidden in the tax system. As an example, consider the political prospects of the following proposal. The federal government has decided to subsidize the activities of state and local governments. It has decided not to limit the kinds of activities it will subsidize: municipal swimming pools and golf courses will be treated the same as primary education and fire departments. The subsidy payments will not be remitted to the state and local governments but rather will be remitted directly to the resident taxpayers. The rate of subsidy, though, will not be the same for all citizens. In fact, only about one-third of households, mostly high-income ones, will receive any subsidy at all. Those who do receive subsidies will do so according to several rates of subsidy: 10, 15, 25, 28, 33, and 35 percent. And the higher the income, the higher the rate of subsidy! And one last thing: the subsidy is lost to the extent that the families' state and local governments decide to finance their expenditures with a sales tax instead of income or property taxes.

This is certainly a peculiar kind of subsidy program and one that, presumably, would never be passed by Congress. Strange as it sounds, it is essentially the same as the current deduction for state and local income and property taxes. This deduction can be claimed only by the 34 percent[29] of taxpayers who itemize their deductions, who are typically the most affluent of families. The value of the deduction depends on the household's marginal tax rate, which is higher for higher-income households.[30] Income tax and property tax are deductible, but sales tax payments are not. Similar parables could be told about the deduction for home mortgage interest, the exclusion of employer-provided health insurance, and a host of other features of the tax code. The point is that these features are enormously popular because they have been enshrined as "tax reductions," but exactly the same features probably wouldn't survive as stand-alone policies.

Eliminating all of the "bells and whistles" and starting over with a clean tax base would go a long way toward simplifying the taxpaying process. Chapter 6 examines the merits of major preferences in our tax code, considering the equity, economic efficiency, and simplicity aspects of each one. Even when all these factors are considered, many of the exceptions to a clean base are difficult to justify. Whether the political system is ready to undertake such a hardheaded analysis remains an open question.

Institutional Pressures Favoring Complexity

One of the reasons that our tax base is a mess has nothing to do with principles: strong political and institutional factors bias the U.S. tax system toward greater complexity. Under the current system, being a member of one of the tax-writing congressional committees—either the House Ways and Means Committee or the Senate Finance Committee—is a plum assignment. For example, although only 9 percent of the House's members are on the Ways and Means Committee, members of that committee received 23 percent of all political action committee (PAC) contributions given to members of the House of Representatives during the 2000 election cycle.[31] Clearly, representatives' potential influence over tax policy leads lobbyists to curry their favor. If

Congress were to bind itself to make no major changes in tax law during the next congressional session—or ever again—the contributions would start to dry up, these members' lunch and dinner invitations would taper off, and so on.[32]

Once adopted, tax preferences develop strong lobbies that fight to retain them—for instance, by making campaign contributions to like-minded politicians. In contrast, no well-organized constituency opposes the complexity that these preferences generate. Yes, business groups bemoan complexity and support simplicity. But when push comes to shove, they are quite willing to accept a provision that saves them $100 million per year in tax payments, even if it means adding a few more staffers and buying some expensive software to do tax and project planning. Yes, individual taxpayers complain about having to keep records of their charitable contributions to deduct them, but they'd be even more unhappy if this deduction were eliminated—and so would the charities themselves.

To counterbalance these institutional pressures toward greater complexity, several countries have instigated a formal mechanism for making compliance costs more visible during the policy process. Since 1985, the United Kingdom has required its officials to produce compliance cost assessments (CCAs) for all regulations affecting business, including tax regulations. The Netherlands has required qualitative CCAs for changes in tax legislation since 1985, and both New Zealand and Australia have something similar.

Starting in 1999, the United States began something like a CCA procedure. The Internal Revenue Service Restructuring and Reform Act of 1998 contains a provision requiring the Joint Committee on Taxation to provide a "tax complexity analysis" for any change in tax law being considered by Congress.[33] This analysis includes an estimate of the cost to taxpayers of complying with the provision and a statement about whether taxpayers would be required to keep additional records. As in the other countries with CCAs, this provision is designed to focus attention on complexity and offset the built-in institutional biases that perpetuate it. These reports do not appear to be attracting media attention or having any impact on policy, however.

Another approach to counterbalancing institutional pressures toward greater complexity would be to remove incentives for government officials to write complicated regulations. Lawyer Schuyler Moore notes that "there is a perverse incentive for the draftsmen of Treasury regulations to write the regulations as long and complex as possible. The draftsmen know that they will probably soon be entering private practice, where they can make a lucrative living pontificating on their own regulations."[34] An existing law prohibits former government employees from immediately representing clients on matters about the regulations they wrote, but the prohibition applies for only one year, and it does not prevent them from profiting by giving advice, making speeches, or writing books.

Phase-Outs, Phase-Ins, and Floors

In some cases, complexity creeps into the tax system because legislators desire to obfuscate their true intent. This was certainly the case in 1990, when Republicans averse to further increases in the top income tax rate settled instead for a variety of difficult-to-administer luxury taxes. Another example is the proliferation of "phase-ins" and "phase-outs" of various exemptions, deductions, and credits that now litter the tax code. In almost all cases, these features are exactly equivalent to raising the marginal tax rate a few percentage points in certain income ranges, and so they are just a way of raising tax rates without making it obvious to the public. In other cases, the goal is to limit the benefits of certain credits such as the earned income tax credit and the child- and dependent-care credits to families below a certain income range. Again, one effect of these phase-outs is to increase the effective marginal tax rate on income: losing a credit as your income rises has the same effect as paying more tax.

As a result of these features, many taxpayers must needlessly go through extra calculations that could have been avoided if the true tax rates were directly incorporated into the tax tables. In 2001, the Joint Committee on Taxation identified 20 separate provisions of the personal income tax code involving phase-ins or phase-outs and estimated that taxpayers were required to go through over 30 million worksheet calculations as a result of such provisions.[35]

Opportunities for "Tax Arbitrage": Transactional Complexity

Whenever the same transaction is taxed differently depending on how it is "packaged," complexity ensues as taxpayers seek to repackage things to their advantage and the IRS resists. Economists call this *tax arbitrage*. For example, taxing the ordinary income of top-bracket taxpayers at 35 percent while taxing realized capital gains at 15 percent offers a large reward for converting ordinary income—wages, salaries, interest, and dividends—into capital gains. This can be accomplished in a variety of ways, such as allowing executives to take qualified stock options in lieu of extra salary.

The same argument applies to the differential between the corporation tax rate and the individual rate. When the corporate rate is significantly lower than the top individual rate, as it was for high-income individuals until 1986, an incentive is created for shareholders and executives to retain income within corporations as long as possible and to get compensation in back-door, tax-preferred ways. For this reason, the border between what is corporate income and what is individual income creates a major source of complexity as taxpayers seek to recharacterize income to reduce their taxes and the IRS seeks to limit such behavior.[36]

Finally, many taxpayers are engaging in tax arbitrage in ways they may not even realize. For example, suppose you borrow $3,000 under a home equity loan and in the same year make a $3,000 contribution to your IRA. Together these two transactions produce no net increase in your saving, as they cancel each other out. But the transactions can reduce your taxes because the interest, dividends, and other returns in the account are untaxed, and you can deduct the interest on the home equity loan all the while. Such features create an incentive to engage in needless and meaningless financial transactions purely for tax reasons, resulting in added costs of compliance and administration.

One argument for replacing the income tax with a single-rate consumption tax is that the latter is much less susceptible to tax arbitrage. For example, arbitrage strategies involving changes in the timing of income would generally convey no tax advantages.

Attempts to Limit Tax Avoidance and Evasion

Taxpayers can reduce their tax liabilities in a wide variety of ways. The legal ways, such as using legitimate itemized deductions or some forms of tax arbitrage, are called *tax avoidance*. The illegal ways, such as failing to report income or overstating deductions, are called *tax evasion*. Because of the amount of money at stake, people and companies are continuously developing new and ingenious ways of achieving both. Government attempts to curb these activities often make the tax code even more complicated and burdensome, even to those who never contemplate pursuing evasion or even avoidance. Countless intricate regulations—such as the alternative minimum tax and passive-loss restrictions—are geared toward preventing tax-reduction strategies.

It follows that one way of achieving simplification would be to scale back government efforts to curb avoidance and evasion. For example, many economists advocate the elimination of the corporate alternative minimum tax, the objective of which is to put a limit on the tax savings from legitimate tax-reducing activities. But in some other cases, halting these efforts could have a major cost in terms of additional avoidance and evasion, making the tax system considerably less fair and less efficient.

Our tax system is complex for a variety of reasons, including a desire to achieve many goals other than raising revenue, strong institutional pressures to keep the system complex, and a desire to limit the ability of individuals to take advantage of "loopholes" in the system. In the past few years, tax evasion and enforcement have drawn a lot of attention. In the late 1990s, the focus was on whether the IRS had become too zealous and intrusive. In the early 2000s, the focus shifted to corporate and individual tax shelters and other forms of avoidance and evasion that were draining money from the Treasury and exacerbating the deficit. We turn next to issues of tax evasion and address the right balance between an equitable enforcement of the tax system and excessive intrusion into people's lives.

Evasion and Enforcement

Why Enforcement Is Necessary

For many taxpayers, the real problem with the taxpaying process has little to do with filing their returns per se and a lot to do with the fear and hassle of dealing with the IRS. Few words in our language are more anxiety-producing than *audit*. Dissatisfaction with the IRS has grown to the point that the centerpiece of some tax reform proposals is complete abolishment of the IRS.

As exhilarating an idea as this may sound, living without the IRS is not a real possibility. Under a radically different tax system, the tax-enforcement apparatus could be scaled down or focused entirely on businesses. But human nature being what it is, announcing a tax-base definition, setting tax rates, and then relying on taxpayers' sense of duty to collect over a trillion dollars of taxes just won't work. Some dutiful people undoubtedly would pay what they owe, but many others would not. Over time the ranks of the dutiful would shrink as they see how they are being taken advantage of by others.

We cannot rely on voluntary contributions because the benefits of citizenry do not depend on the payment of income taxes.[37] The auto mechanic who on the weekends also paints houses for cash without reporting his painting income to the IRS still has access to the national parks. The trucker who overstates his expenses on gas will still be protected by our system of national defense. Even if the mechanic, the trucker, and everyone else agree that the government should collect taxes to provide highways, defense, and everything else the government does, they still would not find it in their individual interest to contribute voluntarily to the government's coffers. Each citizen has a strong incentive to "ride free" on the contributions of others because one individual's contribution is just a drop in the bucket and doesn't materially affect what that person gets back from the government.

For this reason, paying taxes must be made a legal responsibility of citizens. In the United States, failure to pay taxes in a timely manner is a civil offense that subjects taxpayers to a variety of penalties. Fraud can expose the citizen to criminal charges and jail sentences, although this is a rare occurrence. Even in the face of those penalties, substantial evasion persists.

Tax Evasion and the Case of the 7 Million Vanishing Exemptions

Tax evasion by the wealthy tends to make the headlines. For example, in 2002, newspapers were filled with stories like that of Dennis Kozlowski, head of Tyco International, who was charged with failing to pay $1 million in sales taxes on artwork, and former tennis star Boris Becker, who was forced to pay a fine of nearly $3 million to avoid jail time for extensive tax evasion.[38] In 2002, Deputy IRS commissioner Dale Hart estimated, based on data provided by Mastercard, that 1 to 2 million Americans might have moved assets to offshore banks in places like the Cayman Islands to evade taxes and obtained credit cards from those banks so they would have easy access to the funds.[39] The General Accounting Office estimated in 2002 that the United States annually loses $20 billion to $40 billion in tax revenue due to offshore accounts.[40]

But evasion on a smaller scale is also a pervasive phenomenon. One fascinating example in the 1980s involved exemption allowances for dependents. For a long time the IRS had suspected that many taxpayers were claiming exemptions for dependents who either did not exist or did not qualify as dependents under the tax law. An IRS employee by the name of John Szilagyi thought that this overstatement was costing the Treasury—and ultimately all other taxpayers—hundreds of millions of dollars each year, and he suggested the following change in the tax return: to claim an exemption allowance for a dependent over the age of five, you must report the dependent's Social Security number.

When implemented in tax year 1987, the effect of this change was astonishing to everyone, with the possible exception of Szilagyi himself. Between tax years 1986 and 1987, the number of dependent exemption allowances claimed fell by 7 million. This simple change increased tax revenues by about $2.9 billion per year, or approximately $28 per taxpayer. Undoubtedly, a few of the 7 million cases represented legitimate dependents whose parents or guardians just hadn't gotten around to obtaining Social Security numbers for them, and a few others were children who had been improperly claimed by both parents after a divorce. But certainly the great majority represented people who were claiming their dogs as, or simply inventing, dependents.[41]

How Much Tax Evasion Is There?

Most people don't have to read such anecdotes about tax evasion to be convinced that it exists. Moreover, reciting anecdotes does not convey any sense about whether tax evasion is a big problem or a little problem. For obvious reasons—would you answer honestly survey questions about tax evasion?—it is difficult to determine just how big a problem tax evasion is. Although measuring how much tax is paid is easy enough, measuring what *should* be paid is not at all easy. The IRS has periodically estimated what it called the *tax gap*, meaning the amount of income tax that should have been paid but wasn't. The IRS came up with its estimates by combining information from a program of intensive random audits known as the Taxpayer Compliance Measurement Program (TCMP) with information from special studies about sources of income, such as tips, that are difficult to uncover even in an intensive audit. The last TCMP was undertaken in 1988; the program was cancelled in 1995 due to cuts in the IRS budget and complaints in Congress that it was excessively harsh. A "kinder, gentler" version of the TCMP, called the National Research Program, was recently implemented to examine returns from the 2001 tax year, but data are not yet available from that study.[42]

The last thorough tax gap study was for the year 1992, based on the 1988 TCMP. Noncompliance with individual and corporate income taxes was estimated to cost the Treasury about 18 percent of actual tax liability, which at 2002 levels of revenue would have amounted to $223 billion.[43] An average tax rate of 22 percent[44] implies that there is about $1 trillion of unreported income and illegitimate deductions. The procedure for estimating the tax gap is an imperfect one, and even the IRS would admit that its measures were only approximations. In addition, some types of evasion that are difficult to uncover, such as unreported income from illegal activities, are not included in the estimate.[45] Finally, the estimates are based on data that is now over fifteen years old. But these are the best numbers around.

Figure 5.1 presents estimates of the 1992 tax gap for income taxes. Of the total, 25.8 percent came from corporate evasion and 74.2 percent came from personal evasion. The most important form of evasion was underreporting of income by those who filed personal tax returns;

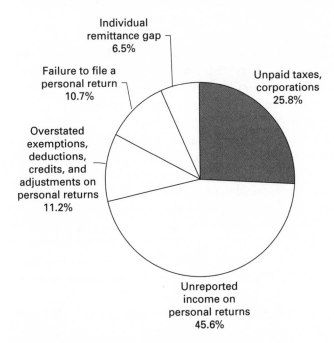

Figure 5.1
Components of the income tax gap, 1992
Source: General Accounting Office (1997).
Note: Math errors on personal returns, not shown, account for another 0.1 percent of the tax gap. Estimates exclude illegal-source income.

it accounted for 45.6 percent of the total tax gap. Overstating of exemptions, deductions, adjustments, and credits on personal returns was a significant but much smaller problem, accounting for 11.2 percent of the tax gap. People who were required to file a personal return but do not caused another 10.7 percent of the gap. The *individual remittance gap*—tax liability that is reported but not remitted with the filed tax return—was 6.5 percent.

Why Is Tax Evasion a Problem?

For the sake of argument, let's assume there's currently $223 billion of income tax evasion. Why is this a problem? One obvious answer is that if evasion vanished, then the deficit could be $223 billion lower than otherwise. Alternatively, we could spend $223 billion more per year to finance health research, job training, transportation infrastructure, a stronger military, and a host of other worthy projects. Or perhaps the revenues raised from eliminating evasion could be used to finance a cut in tax rates for everyone, thus benefiting honest taxpayers.

But there are not very satisfactory answers to the question. Decreasing the deficit or expanding government programs could be financed in a number of other ways, such as raising tax rates or broadening the income tax base. A tax reduction could be financed by cuts in overall spending. The real question is whether curbing evasion would improve the equity and efficiency of how we tax ourselves.

Consider the following hypothetical example. Imagine that all Americans were genetically predisposed to underpay their legal tax liability by 20 percent, sort of the way that most car buyers presume that the actual price of a car is considerably below the sticker price. Thus, a family that initially calculated its true tax liability to be $15,000 would as a matter of course find ways to understate its income so it appeared to owe only $12,000, 20 percent less than $15,000. Similarly, families that legally owe $50,000 would fiddle around with the numbers so that they remit $40,000, and so on. Imagine further that the IRS looked the other way.

In this imaginary world, tax evasion wouldn't matter at all. Government would simply readjust everyone's "sticker-price" tax liability upward so that the desired amount of tax would be collected, even after the 20 percent "discount" was taken. Each taxpayer might think that he or she is beating the system, but in fact no one gains compared to a world with no evasion. In this example, evasion is just a shell game that no one wins or loses, and spending money on enforcing the tax laws would be a waste.

But a lot of things are wrong with this picture as a description of real-life tax evasion, and they turn tax evasion from the benign phenomenon of this imaginary world to one that has important implications for equity and efficiency. First and foremost, not everyone evades tax by the same proportionate amount. Some people evade a great deal, while others engage in little or no evasion at all. Evasion varies because of differences in personal characteristics, such as intrinsic honesty, willingness to gamble, and attitudes toward government and the tax system. Evasion also varies because the opportunities and potential rewards for evasion vary. As long as people differ in these characteristics or opportunities, evasion can cause serious inequities and inefficiencies.

Evasion creates horizontal inequity because equally well off people end up with different tax burdens. Unlike the imaginary 20 percent "discount" example presented above, tax rates cannot be adjusted to offset the advantage gained by the free-riding evaders because we don't know which people are evading. Moreover, if opportunities or predilections for evasion were related to level of well-being (for instance, if the rich could evade more easily than the poor), then evasion would make it difficult for us to achieve whatever degree of progressivity we deem to be consistent with vertical equity.

A lot of evidence suggests that the world is divided into evaders and nonevaders. According to an IRS-sponsored study in 1979, 42 percent of all returns had some understatement of taxable income.[46] Not surprisingly, surveys that have outright asked people about their past tax compliance behavior come up with lower numbers, indicating that between 22 and 28 percent of taxpayers have failed to comply at some point in their lives and that 12 to 20 percent have failed to comply at some point within the past five years.[47] Regardless of which figures are right, it is clear that a significant fraction of taxpayers complies with the tax law and another significant fraction often does not. This pattern of tax evasion means that some people pay less tax than they ought to and everyone else pays more.

Considerable evidence also suggests that evasion depends on opportunities for successful tax evasion and that these differ widely depending on the circumstances of the taxpayer, including type of income, occupation, and other factors. The odds that a particular kind of income understatement will be uncovered by the IRS vary from practically zero for a small bit of moonlighting income to very high for wages earned at

Table 5.1
Compliance estimates for selected types of personal income, 1992

Type of personal income	Reported net income as a percentage of true net income from this source	Percentage of individual income tax gap caused by underreporting of this item
Wages and salaries	99.1	3.4
Pensions and annuities	96.0	1.9
Interest	97.7	0.9
Dividends	92.2	1.4
Capital gains	92.8	2.6
Partnerships and S corporations	92.5	3.8
Informal suppliers	18.6	12.9
Other sole proprietors	67.7	17.9

Source: General Accounting Office (1997).

a company that sends the IRS a computer-readable file of all its W-2 forms that detail—with employee Social Security numbers—who was paid what.

In part, tax evasion is a gamble like any other, with a chance of coming out ahead and a chance of coming out behind. As you would expect, the lower the chance of getting caught, the more likely people are to try to get away with tax evasion. This is borne out by the data in table 5.1, which presents information from the 1992 IRS tax gap study about what percentage of several types of income are reported by individuals. It ranges from 99.1 percent for wages and salaries (taxes on which are difficult to evade successfully because of employer reports to the IRS) down to 18.6 percent for informal suppliers (sidewalk street vendors, moonlighting craftsmen, unlicensed child-care providers, housepainters, and the like, who are notoriously difficult for the IRS to monitor). The reporting percentage for other sole proprietors is 67.7 percent. These two categories account for over 30 percent of the overall individual tax gap. Tip income, which is not shown in table 5.1, is also very hard for the IRS to find. An earlier study found the reporting rate for tip income to be just 59.8 percent. These facts suggest that significant horizontal inequities persist because of evasion, although, as we discuss below, in some cases the market mitigates these inequities.

How evasion affects vertical equity is a little less clear. Certainly, on average high-income people appear to evade more. But contrary to what many may suspect, some evidence suggests that, relative to the

Table 5.2
Voluntary compliance rates by income, 1988

Adjusted gross income range (dollars)	Voluntary compliance rate (reported income as a percentage of true income)
0–5,000	84.2
5,000–10,000	78.7
10,000–25,000	88.8
25,000–50,000	92.4
50,000–100,000	93.2
100,000–250,000	91.3
250,000–500,000	95.7
Over 500,000	97.1

Source: Christian (1994), based on 1988 Taxpayer Compliance Measurement Program.

size of their income, higher-income people actually evade *less* than those with lower incomes. Table 5.2 displays the voluntary reporting percentages for taxpayers from the 1988 Taxpayer Compliance Measurement Program study, ranked by income. According to this study, those with adjusted gross incomes (AGIs) of $500,000 and over on average reported 97.1 percent of their true incomes to the IRS, compared to just 78.7 percent for those with AGIs between $5,000 and $10,000. This pattern appears consistent with the old saying among tax professionals, "The poor evade, and the rich avoid," meaning that the rich tend to reduce their taxes through legal "avoidance" measures such as deductions, exclusions, tax arbitrage, and loopholes, while those with lower incomes attempt more outright evasion. But this table may be misleading because the TCMP audits of personal tax returns generally do not investigate business tax returns, so any evasion at the business level is not accounted for. Because high-income individuals have proportionately more business income, the relatively high rates shown in this table may overestimate the voluntary compliance of this group.

Tax evasion not only compromises the equitable sharing of tax burdens; it also imposes economic costs. Other things being equal, evasion raises tax rates, which will penalize extra work and thrift by honest taxpayers. This is partially offset by lower effective tax rates on the evaders but not enough to make up fully for the loss. More important, because tax evasion depends on opportunities that are tied to particular activities, it provides an incentive—which is inefficient from a social point of view—to engage in activities for which it is relatively easy to evade taxes.

Consider the market for house painting, in which many deals are made in cash, to facilitate tax evasion. Because the income from house painting is hard for the IRS to detect, this occupation is more attractive than otherwise. The supply of eager house painters bids down the market price of a house-painting job. Thus, the amount of taxes evaded overstates the benefit of being a tax-evading house painter, and comparing taxes actually paid may overstate the extent of horizontal inequity. The biggest loser in this game is the honest house painter, who sees his or her wages bid down by the competition but who dutifully pays taxes.

Although a supply of eager and cheap house painters undoubtedly is greeted warmly by prospective buyers of that service, in fact it is a symptom of an economic cost of tax evasion. The work of the extra people drawn to house painting or to any activity that facilitates tax evasion would have higher value in some alternative occupation. This is just an example of the principle, discussed in chapter 4, that deviations from a uniform tax system, uniformly enforced, have economic costs. Several years ago Georgia State University economist James Alm estimated that the cost of having too many resources diverted into activities (both legal and illegal) that facilitated tax evasion was as high as $100 billion per year.[48]

It's clear that widespread evasion endangers the fairness of how we tax ourselves and may have a substantial economic cost. Thus, an enforcement agency like the IRS is a necessity for any tax system. But how should it be run?

How the IRS Operates

Mention the IRS, and most people think of the dreaded tax audit. But you may be surprised to learn that the IRS now audits only about one-half of 1 percent of all individual tax returns; in 2002, the figure was 0.57 percent.[49] This fraction has declined dramatically over the last three decades; it was typically about 4 percent during the 1960s.[50]

Does this mean that if you file a tax return and omit reporting your wages or capital gains, you have only about a 1 in 200 chance of being caught in the act? Absolutely not, for several reasons.

First of all, the IRS does not just pick out of a hat which returns to audit, which would give you as good (or bad) a chance as anyone else of being audited. Instead, the probability that a return will be examined is influenced by a carefully developed secret formula, called the *discriminant index function* (DIF). This formula assigns a score to each return reflecting the estimated likelihood of noncompliance for that taxpayer, based on the amounts stated on the return for each type of income and deduction. Returns that fit the profile of those that have a significant dollar amount of evasion are the most likely to be examined. For example, in fiscal year 2002, the fraction of nonbusiness returns audited was 0.23 percent for people with incomes between $25,000 and $50,000 but 0.75 percent for those with incomes above $100,000.[51] Among very large corporations, nearly every single one is audited every year by a team of IRS examiners, although recent events make clear that these audits fail to catch all noncompliance among these firms.

Face-to-face audits are by no means the only way the IRS checks on the accuracy of tax returns. Another important tool for the IRS is *information reporting*. For example, employers are required to send information reports on wages and salaries for all their employees to the IRS. The IRS computers then match up most of these information reports against tax returns. About 72 percent of the audits that go into the 0.57 percent audit rate mentioned above refer to correspondence by tax examiners generated by computer matching of returns to information reports.[52] If the computer detects a discrepancy, a computer-generated notice is automatically sent out to the taxpayer asking him or her to pay up or provide an explanation. Most interest and dividend income and pensions are also subject to information reporting. It is therefore no accident that these types of income, together with wages and salaries, have near 100 percent compliance rates, as reported in table 5.1. In 2002, the IRS received 1.4 billion information reports, 97 percent of which were transmitted electronically or via tapes or diskettes.[53] The increased use of computer checks based on information reporting has clearly substituted for the decline in face-to-face audits.

Another major enforcement tool of the IRS is withholding of taxes on wage and salary income, a practice it has followed since 1943. All firms above a certain size are required to remit payments directly to the IRS based on an estimate of the personal income taxes owed by their employees. In 2001, 82 percent of net individual income tax collections were withheld in this manner.[54] The amount withheld for an employee is usually greater than actual tax liability over the course of the year, so the vast majority of individual taxpayers (72 percent in 1999) are eligible for a refund.[55] This creates an added incentive for taxpayers to file their returns in a timely manner. Together, information reporting and withholding are powerful enforcement mechanisms. Without them, compliance rates for wages and salaries might not be much different from the income of informal suppliers, which, as discussed earlier, has a voluntary reporting rate of only about 19 percent.

One additional way the IRS makes sure the proper tax liability gets paid is by helping taxpayers understand and comply with the tax law. A substantial number of taxpayers would ideally like to comply with the tax laws but do not either because they do not understand what is expected of them or they are frustrated with the process. For this reason, the IRS makes help available over the phone and on the Internet and undertakes education and outreach programs.

Why More Enforcement May Not Be the Answer

With an income tax gap of around $223 billion, why don't we devote more resources to enforcement? Wouldn't this make the tax system fairer and more efficient and generate money that could be used to reduce the national debt, cut tax rates, or achieve some other worthwhile purpose? The answer is that although extra enforcement may indeed bring many benefits, we must also consider the costs. Just as stationing a police officer at every corner would certainly reduce street crime, more audits and higher penalties could almost certainly make a dent in the extent of tax evasion. But as a society we choose not to have police everywhere and not to impose the death penalty for minor infractions. We tolerate some level of crime because we judge that the benefits of eliminating crime would not outweigh the costs of achieving zero crime. The same is true of the crime of tax evasion.

Would the benefits of extra enforcement by the IRS outweigh the costs? Consider that one analysis of TCMP audit data suggested that for every extra dollar the IRS spends on auditing returns, it could gain between four and seven dollars of additional revenue directly from the audited returns.[56] Such a yield could not be achieved immediately because time would be needed to train new agents, but it is plausible that eventually the gain could be realized. Indeed, this amount probably underestimates the potential revenue yield because it doesn't take into account the deterrent effect of extra enforcement. For instance, if the audit rate were increased, the greater likelihood that evasion would be detected probably would persuade some people that were not audited to become more compliant.

Although a 4-to-1 or a 7-to-1 ratio of extra revenues to spending is certainly impressive, this comparison does not correctly compare the true costs and benefits of engaging in extra enforcement. For that reason, we should not jump to the conclusion that tax enforcement ought to be vastly expanded. An apples-and-oranges fallacy is lurking here. The expenditure on expanded IRS enforcement activities certainly represents a real resource cost to the country: the people and computers doing the auditing could be employed elsewhere in the economy to produce valuable goods and services. But the increased revenue from greater enforcement does not by itself represent a gain to the economy. Seven dollars handed from a taxpayer to the IRS does not create seven new dollars worth of goods and services. This transfer from private to public hands could be achieved in any number of alternative ways, such as by raising tax rates.[57]

Increased tax enforcement does produce social benefits. These benefits, including a more efficient and equitable tax system, were discussed above and are certainly important. The benefits of reduced evasion, however, are not at all well measured by the extra revenue that more enforcement will produce and are less concrete than dollar revenue. Although the size of the tax gap and the revenue yield from extra expenditures on the IRS are informative, by themselves they do not make it obvious whether the level of enforcement is about right or whether it should be increased or decreased.

A Kinder, Gentler IRS

For every anecdote about flagrant tax evasion, there is another about heavy-handed IRS handling of a taxpayer.[58] Many taxpayers are concerned about the intrusiveness of the IRS into their lives. Balancing the rights of taxpayers against the desire for an equitably enforced tax system raises critical issues of, among other things, privacy. Many Americans do not want the IRS to get "too good" at its job and legitimately object to procedures that would facilitate enforcement of the tax law.

By the late 1990s, the balance between achieving equitable enforcement and avoiding intrusiveness started to swing toward the latter. In 1997 and 1998, Congress held highly publicized hearings that highlighted supposedly inappropriate practices by the IRS. In an October 1997 NBC/*Wall Street Journal* poll, 70 percent of respondents said they believed that "incidents in which the IRS . . . behaved unethically or treated people unfairly during audits" occurred "fairly regularly." Notably, though, only 9 percent of respondents said they themselves had ever been treated unfairly by the IRS.[59]

Spurred on by the hearings, Congress enacted and the president signed the Internal Revenue Service Restructuring and Reform Act of 1998. This act set up an oversight board for the IRS that includes six private-sector members, ordered the IRS to undertake major organizational restructuring and management changes, and included several provisions designed to improve service provided to taxpayers by the IRS and to protect taxpayers' rights. Most controversially, the new law shifted the burden of proof in civil court cases from the taxpayer to the IRS. Taxpayers will still have to keep records and cooperate with the IRS, but in questions of fact, the IRS will have to prove the taxpayer wrong rather than the other way around. This is the rule in nontax court cases and may sound reasonable, but many experts oppose it. They argue that requiring the party with the documents and the facts (that is, the taxpayer) to bear the burden of proof is less costly and intrusive and that putting the burden of proof on the government means that audits will become more invasive. In many cases, the tax liability of would-be evaders will be understated because the IRS will not be able to learn and marshal all the facts required to prove that a tax return is wrong.[60]

Since that time, improvements have been noted in several indicators of IRS public image and "customer service." A Roper poll found that the percentage of Americans with a "favorable opinion" of the IRS increased from 34 percent to 46 percent between 1997 and 2001.[61] In an April 2002 *ABC News* poll, 50 percent of respondents believed the IRS was either "not tough enough" in enforcing tax laws or "about right."[62] The General Accounting Office found evidence of reduced waiting times and improved accuracy of answers on the IRS toll-free telephone help line and noted substantial improvements in the services provided through the IRS Web site.[63]

The degree to which the IRS actually enforces the tax law, however, has declined sharply along several dimensions (which may partly explain its relatively favorable rating by taxpayers). Between 1996 and 2002, the share of nonbusiness individual returns audited dropped from 1.67 percent to 0.57 percent, and the share of corporate returns subject to face-to-face audits dropped from 2.62 percent to 0.88 percent.[64] The number of criminal tax cases recommended for prosecution by the IRS declined by 50 percent between 1992 and 2002.[65] IRS use of its three main weapons for collecting tax debts from recalcitrant tax evaders—levies (garnishing wages or seizing money from bank accounts), liens (taking ownership of the taxpayer's property until a tax debt is paid), and outright seizures of property—also declined sharply.

Between 1996 and 2002, the number of levies fell from 3.1 million to 667,000, liens fell from 750,000 to 492,000, and seizures fell from 10,449 to 364.[66] The IRS even recently fell behind substantially in its efforts to do anything about cases where it had already determined there was cheating. In 2002, then-IRS commissioner Rossotti reported that the IRS was currently failing to pursue 60 percent of people with known tax debts, 75 percent of people the IRS knew owed taxes but did not file a return, and 79 percent of taxpayers it had identified as evading taxes through offshore accounts or abusive tax shelters. He estimated that $30 billion in tax revenue had been lost in that year just from failing to pursue known tax evaders.[67]

Some of the decline in IRS enforcement is a temporary phenomenon. In response to the 1998 act, the IRS had to divert resources to its reorganization efforts. Many of the enforcement indicators mentioned above have already started to rebound a bit; they were even lower in 2000. But some of the decline is due to a longer-term trend where the resources of the IRS are not keeping up with the rising difficulty of its job. For instance, between 1992 and 2002, the number of tax returns grew by 12 percent, but the number of IRS tax auditors fell by a quarter from 16,000 to 12,000.[68] In the meantime, both the complexity of the tax law and the sophistication of abusive tax shelters and other means of evading taxes increased dramatically. The decline in enforcement poses the danger that tax evasion will increase substantially as people respond to the incentives created by a reduced probability of being caught or punished and as public confidence that other people are paying their legally required taxes declines. As a result, there does seem to be growing support in both political parties for stronger enforcement. For example, in 2003, President Bush proposed a modest increase in the IRS budget explicitly to address some of the aforementioned problems.[69]

What Facilitates Enforcement?

Congress has handed the IRS a difficult if not impossible task—to fairly and efficiently administer a tax system that is plagued with inequities and complexities. Bill collectors are never popular nor will the IRS ever be, but the enforcement process could be less painful and costly if the tax system were different. What features of a tax system facilitate enforcement?

As we discussed earlier in this chapter, some of the aspects that make a tax system simpler also facilitate enforcement. Information reporting and tax withholding at the source of payment are the best examples. The effectiveness of these measures is amply demonstrated by compliance rates that are vastly higher for income that is subject to them (such as employee wages and salaries) than for income that is not (such as income of informal suppliers), shown in table 5.1. Another feature that facilitates enforcement is limiting the number of credits, deductions, and other nonrevenue-raising aspects of the tax system that stretch IRS resources. But a number of other factors also strongly influence the effectiveness of tax enforcement. We turn to these next.

For obvious reasons, compliance with taxation is low when taxpayers have little incentive to comply. Threats of audits and penalties for noncompliance provide one kind of incentive, but there are others as well. For example, the fact that most U.S. personal income taxpayers receive a refund gives them a strong incentive to file their forms, which provides useful information to the IRS. Another example is provided by the operation of most VATs throughout the world. In the event of an audit, a business that claims a credit or deduction for an input purchased from another firm must be able to prove that the other firm paid tax on it. So each firm has some incentive to make sure other firms are complying. Whenever incentives of this sort can be worked into the tax system, enforceability is improved.

At first blush, the most direct cause of tax evasion might seem to be high tax rates. To lower evasion, therefore, why not simply lower tax rates? This is too simplistic an answer when a fixed amount of revenue must be raised. The appropriate question is whether evasion would be curtailed if marginal tax rates were reduced, holding revenues constant, either by making the system less progressive or broadening the base. In either case, the quantitative evidence is not decisive. Even on theoretical grounds, the argument that lower rates reduce evasion is not certain. If penalties for detected evasion are proportional to the understated tax, then lowering the tax rate automatically lowers the penalty, making the effect on evasion indeterminate.[70] Furthermore, for some kinds of evasion, such as nonfiling, the marginal tax rate is immaterial because the entire tax liability is at stake; it is the average tax rate that matters.

Much of the tax evasion in our country occurs on types of income that are difficult for the IRS to monitor. Self-employment income is the most important example. Some types of capital income are also relatively easy to conceal, at least when compared to wages and salaries. The tax system could become considerably easier to enforce if we simply give up on trying to tax some of these types of income. For example, a sales tax, VAT, or flat tax would no longer attempt to tax capital income; furthermore, most VAT systems exempt from tax all businesses below a certain size.

In some ways, this is similar to arguing that drug crimes could be eliminated by legalizing drugs. In this case, the crime is evading taxes on capital income, which could be eliminated by making this income tax exempt. Whether this is fair is questionable—capital income is disproportionately received by affluent families—but it would at least improve horizontal equity between honest and dishonest people who earn capital income. Keep in mind, though, that even "legalization" solutions like this have enforcement problems of their own, particularly when they are introduced in a piecemeal fashion. For example, eliminating all tax on difficult-to-enforce capital gains would greatly increase the incentive to convert ordinary income into capital gains and put more, rather than less, pressure on enforcement.

A complex tax system makes complying with the rules more difficult for taxpayers. It is also frustrating and puts people in less of a mood to comply. Moreover, if people feel that other taxpayers are taking advantage of complexity to avoid paying their "fair share," they may feel less morally obligated to pay their own taxes honestly. Evidence from surveys and laboratory experiments provides some support for this notion, although the findings are mixed.[71]

These arguments are often cited by advocates of simpler alternatives to the income tax, such as the flat tax, and they undoubtedly have some merit. Simplifying the tax code could well improve people's attitudes toward compliance. But we can't rely entirely on public goodwill. It's unclear whether moving to a streamlined tax system that is perceived to be fairer would by itself have a dramatic impact on compliance, and it certainly wouldn't eliminate the need for an enforcement authority, as some have implied.

The more taxpayers are required to document their incomes and deductions, the easier it is to enforce the tax system. The current requirement that a Social Security number be provided for each dependent exemption is one particularly effective example. But most types of deductions, such as those for charitable contributions or employee business expenses, are generally reported without any documentation. If the taxpayer is audited, he or she must provide the documentation, but audits are rare. Requiring documentation for more items would make evasion much more difficult. A potentially even more effective approach would be to have the IRS check most or all returns, requiring taxpayers to provide some justification for each item. This may seem far-fetched, but in the Netherlands, the tax authority annually audits every single personal income tax return, at least briefly.[72]

Of course, requiring more documentation from taxpayers and expanding auditing could make the taxpaying process considerably more complicated for both the taxpayer and the IRS, even as it cuts down on evasion. In this case, there is a clear trade-off among the multiple objectives of tax policy. In other situations, costs of enforcement can be transferred from the government budget to the private sector with substantial flexibility. For example, requiring more documentation of taxpayers who make some personal use of a business car may facilitate an audit, but it certainly increases the taxpayers' cost of compliance. For a given degree of enforcement effectiveness, whether this is a good idea depends on whether the sum of these costs declines. Shifting the costs off the budget onto the taxpayers does not necessarily constitute an improved process.

Conclusion

Other things equal, a tax system should be simple and enforceable. In some cases, such as requiring more taxpayer documentation, efforts to achieve one of these goals are costly in terms of the other. But many policies can foster both goals. For example, settling for rough justice and getting rid of all of the bells and whistles in the tax code would clean up the tax base, making the system simpler and easier to enforce. So would more dramatic changes, such as moving to a single rate or changing to an impersonalized consumption tax base, especially to the extent that they would allow wider use of withholding and less involvement of individuals in the taxpaying process. The simplicity and enforcement benefits of these approaches are a major reason that they are often at the heart of radical tax reform proposals. But what else is sacrificed by moving to these simpler ways to tax ourselves?

One important lesson of the past three chapters is that conflicts and trade-offs often arise among the criteria by which we evaluate tax policy. More progressivity generally is accompanied by greater disincentives to work and to otherwise seek economic advancement. More fine-tuning of the tax burden to achieve a fair sharing of the tax burden has a cost of complexity. The most radical and most simplifying tax reform options abandon or sharply reduce progressivity, and they eliminate all or nearly all personalization of the tax burden. We are now ready to consider the major proposals for tax reform and how they strike a balance among the criteria we have set out.

6   Elements of Fundamental Reform

Tax reform proposals fall into two categories: some would wipe out the current income tax structure altogether and start over from scratch, replacing it with something very different, and others would start from the existing structure and then move in a set of discrete steps, either gradually or all at once, toward a system that might be different in any number of ways. In a sense, the distinction is a bit arbitrary, as either approach could conceivably get us to the same place in the end. Historically, the second type of approach is far more common in all areas of policy, not just taxes. But regardless of the political odds of different approaches to reform, thinking about how the tax system might be designed if we could start over anew and what its effects might be is a useful exercise. It can help us evaluate possible replacements for the income tax and illuminate some of the principles and controversies involved in debates over the incremental changes that occur all the time. Chapter 7 examines some specific examples of the first approach that would replace the income tax with some type of consumption tax. Chapter 8 discusses specific examples of the second approach. These include changes to the existing system that would arguably make it a better income tax, changes that would move it more in the direction of a consumption tax, as well as changes that would affect the simplicity, efficiency, and fairness of the system in either framework.

In this chapter, we examine the common elements of many of the proposals for "fundamental reform," keeping in mind that some of these elements might show up in plans for more incremental reform as well. A useful starting point for this exercise is to examine the appeal of so-called flat taxes. Many reform proposals that differ tremendously from each other bill themselves as flat taxes. That flatness has been elevated to the highest compliment to be paid to a tax structure is a bit surprising, if only because in other contexts "flat" is not always a good thing. Just think of beer, musical notes, or tires. *Webster's Unabridged Dictionary* lists 16 major definitions for *flat* as an adjective, ranging from praiseworthy ones such as "level" and "exact" to much less attractive ones, including "shallow," "dull and stupid," "commercially inactive," and even "having no money." In the context of taxation, the word flat conjures up *Webster's* definition of "not varying." But even that is open to multiple interpretations; most of us wouldn't want a tax in which liability does not vary with circumstances such as income or wealth.

There are three distinct dimensions of flatness in a tax—a single tax rate, a consumption tax base, and a clean tax base. The single rate is what most people pick up on, but the other two dimensions would represent even more fundamental changes in the way we tax ourselves. Some proposals seek flattening in all three dimensions; other plans focus on only one or two aspects of flatness. This chapter explores each of these aspects of flatness.

A Single Rate

The most eye-catching feature of flat taxes is the flat *rate*. In place of our current system of graduated tax rates that increase with higher incomes, all or most taxpayers under a flat tax system would be subject to a single rate of tax. Although a truly flat-rate tax would apply the single rate to the entire tax base, from the first dollar to the last, in most flat-tax proposals the single rate applies only to the base in excess of some exemption level. For that reason, they really are a form of graduated tax, with an initial bracket to which a zero tax rate applies, plus an open-ended bracket subject to a single tax rate. Under such a system, the average tax rate increases gradually as the tax base increases starting from zero and topping out at the single rate. Moreover, the degree of progressivity can be varied by adjusting the level of tax-exempt income and the tax rate.

To distinguish this aspect of flatness from the others, we refer to a tax system with this characteristic as a *single-rate tax*. Abandoning the graduation of tax rates for a single rate can be accomplished independently of any and all of the changes in the tax base, to be discussed below, that are usually associated with flat taxes. A single rate can be applied to a narrow, preference-ridden base or to a broad, clean base, and it can be applied to all of income or just to the portion that is consumed. Similarly, we can certainly clean up the tax base while maintaining graduated rates and implement a consumption tax in a way that allows us to preserve graduated rates.

Simple math dictates that if we are going to raise the same level of revenue, substituting a single tax rate for the progressive features of the current personal income tax, without changing anything else, would make the distribution of tax burdens dramatically less progressive. Figure 6.1 illustrates this point. The thin line depicts how average income tax rates vary with adjusted gross income in 2003 for married couples with two children who have average deductions, dividend income, and capital gains for their income class. It takes into account the effects of the tax cut enacted in May 2003. One thing to note about current law is that income tax rates are currently *negative* for low-income families, due mainly to the earned income tax credit. A second is that the tax-exempt threshold is already quite large: a couple with two children does not face a positive income tax liability unless it has more than $38,150 of income in 2003. Third, above that tax-exempt threshold, income tax burdens are still

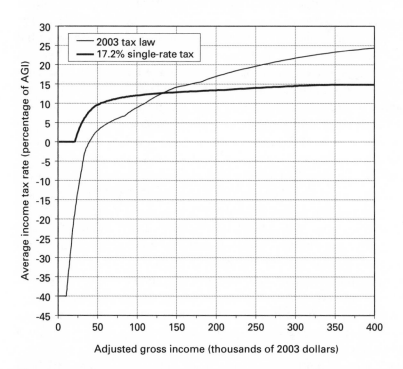

Figure 6.1
Average personal income tax rates for married couples with two children: the 2003 law versus a single-rate tax that has the same exemptions and deductions and raises the same revenue
Sources: Authors' calculations based on data from Campbell and Parisi (2002) and unpublished data provided to the authors by the Urban-Brookings Tax Policy Center.

distributed very progressively, as *marginal* rates gradually rise from 10 percent at the lowest levels of taxable income up to 35 percent above $311,950. As a result, *average* tax rates continue to rise well into the upper end of the income distribution.[1]

The thick line in figure 6.1 illustrates the effects of switching to a single rate with a large tax-exempt threshold, in the spirit of some flat tax proposals floated in recent years. To isolate the effects of switching to a single rate from the effects of other components of tax reform, we remove features (other than personal exemptions and the standard deduction) that contribute to the current system's progressivity but otherwise leave the tax base the same. Thus, the graduated rate structure, tax credits, and the alternative minimum tax are removed, but all the existing deductions, exemptions, and exclusions are retained. We calculate that to raise the same revenue as the current income tax in 2003, such a tax would require a 17.2 percent tax rate. The standard deduction and personal exemption would continue to provide a large tax-exempt threshold ($21,700) for these families. As advocates of flat taxes emphasize, as long as there is an exempt level of income, such a flat-rate tax is indeed still progressive: average tax rates do rise with income. However, such a tax is significantly less progressive than the current system. Abandoning the EITC greatly increases average tax rates for the lowest-income families, while raising the 10 percent and 15 percent rates to 17.2 percent and eliminating child credits increases tax burdens for most of the middle class. At upper income levels, average tax rates start to flatten out much earlier and settle at a level lower than under current law. For instance, a family with $350,000 of AGI gets a tax cut of $29,580, or about 8.5 percent of AGI. A family with $75,000 of AGI, by contrast, faces a tax increase of $3,882, or 5.2 percent of AGI.

It would certainly be possible to make a single-rate tax more progressive than the one in our example. In particular, retaining the EITC and child credit would restore much of the progressivity at the low end of the income scale. Alternatively, dramatically increasing personal exemptions and standard deductions would mitigate the tax increase most of all at moderate income levels. Either change, however, would require the single rate to be much higher than 17.2 percent.

This exercise points out starkly how much the appeal of a single-rate tax depends on dramatic measures to broaden the tax base. In practice, most advocates of a flat tax are also advocates of a flat, *low* tax rate, usually in the high teens or low twenties. As shown above, switching to such a rate by itself would radically shift tax burdens toward low- and middle-income families. Therefore, cutting back on exclusions and itemized deductions that disproportionately benefit upper-income families would be absolutely essential if we want to maintain a low single rate, raise the same revenue as the current tax, but at the same time mitigate the negative impact on low- and moderate-income families. In chapter 7, we consider the distributional impacts of some specific plans that combine a single rate with significant base cleaning and a consumption base. Even with substantial base broadening, however, it would be practically impossible to get a tax with a low single rate that is significantly below the current top rate of 35 percent to replicate the current tax burden on people with extremely high incomes. As a result, somebody else will have to pay more in taxes.

As we note in chapter 3, survey evidence suggests that the flat tax apparently appeals to some people because they think it will make the rich pay *more* in taxes. This is almost certainly not true. As shown in chapter 3, despite all the loopholes and deductions in the current system, on average people with very high incomes pay taxes that are a much higher percentage of their incomes than everyone else does. And recall from chapter 5 that evasion is by no means entirely an upper-class pursuit. Thus, abandoning graduated rates for a single rate will lower the tax burdens on very high-income people, even if we get rid of every loophole and every bit of evasion there is.

So why go to a single rate? Perhaps the most commonly cited reason is to improve economic incentives. A graduated rate structure means higher marginal rates, which can discourage work and saving and cause a whole host of other economic distortions and inefficiencies, which are discussed in chapter 4. Thus, a trade-off occurs between progressivity and economic prosperity. Improved economic growth could eventually compensate some of the people who initially face higher tax burdens as a result of switching to a single rate. As shown in chapter 4, however, the economic costs of progressivity are uncertain and are almost certainly not as high as they are often made out to be by many political advocates of a flat rate. Other things being equal, lower marginal rates are better for the economy, but economics reveals nothing magical about a single rate. For example, the economic cost of having two low marginal rates—say, 15 percent and 25 percent—is not likely to be significantly higher than the cost of a single 20 percent rate.

Some argue that a single-rate tax structure is "neutral" toward distributional issues and thereby avoids "class warfare." By advocating a single rate, they suggest they are transcending the controversy over "fairness" and are promoting the system that maximizes economic performance. This is a fallacious argument. The only tax system that would truly eliminate all the economic costs of taxation is a lump-sum tax (that is, a poll tax), under which tax *liability*, not the tax *rate*, is the same for everyone, rich or poor. In place of income taxes, we could have a fixed annual charge of $4,900 per adult, whether that adult is Bill Gates, a homeless person, or yourself.[2] This eliminates any tax penalty tied to work, saving, or investing. Presumably, the reason that the proponents of a single-rate tax prefer it to a lump-sum tax is that they find the latter abjectly unfair (or else they are too timid to admit the opposite.) Thus, the single-rate tax structure already reflects a balancing between equity and efficiency. A two-rate or multiple-rate structure reflects another balancing, as does a lump-sum tax. We can argue about how best to make this balancing, but no tax system avoids this trade-off.

On the other hand, when it comes to simplicity and enforceability, there is indeed something special about a single rate. As discussed in chapter 5, however, it's not what most people think. Applying the tax-rate schedule to your taxable income to calculate how much you owe is the least complicated part of the whole taxpaying process. Most people can just look it up in a table, in which case it hardly matters at all whether there are one, two, or twenty rates.

Rather, the real advantage is that accepting a single rate facilitates a potentially much simpler, business-based system of collecting taxes, such as a value added tax. Even if some taxation continues at the personal level to further adjust tax burdens for ability to pay, as under a flat tax, a single rate still makes it easier to calculate and withhold taxes at the business level, a major simplification and enforcement advantage. This is a key to having personal tax returns on postcards. Reducing the disparity of tax rates also reduces the incentives for individuals to shift taxable income from high-rate to low-rate taxable entities and from high-tax to low-tax periods; this too serves to dampen tax complexity.

Although these are important advantages, it's debatable whether they're worth the distributional consequences of a low flat rate. Moreover, adding another rate on top of the main flat rate doesn't entirely destroy the simplicity advantages. The United Kingdom greatly simplified its income tax system by moving to a single rate for most people and improving its withholding system but still retained a higher marginal rate for high-income individuals. And having the same *top* rate across individuals, businesses, and different types of income eliminates most of the opportunities for complex income shifting and avoidance schemes, even if there are graduated rates below that top rate.

A Consumption Base

The second element of many fundamental tax reform plans, a consumption-based rather than income-based tax, is not commonly associated (by noneconomists) with flatness. But to economists, a consumption tax imposes a uniform (call it flat, if you like) tax on current consumption and future consumption, in the sense that it does not alter the reward for postponing consumption (that is, saving). In contrast, an income tax, because it taxes the return to saving, makes consumption in the future more expensive than consumption now. We explain further below.

What Is a Consumption Tax?

For some readers, the word *consumption* may conjure up memories of their introductory college economics class, where they may have first encountered consumption as being something other than an old-fashioned word for tuberculosis. Consumption is just economists' language for what people do when they use up goods and services. A consumption tax simply means that the "tax base" (what triggers tax liability) is consumption, as opposed to income, wealth, or some other concept.

There are multiple ways to measure consumption. Because annual income—for a family or for the country as a whole—is equal to annual consumption plus saving, consumption can be either measured directly or, alternatively, by first measuring income and then subtracting saving. It is also true by definition that the amount of saving done by an individual or a country equals the amount of investment on which they have a claim to the returns, and total output equals total income in a closed economy. So another way of measuring consumption is output minus investment.

Varieties of Consumption Tax

To make our discussion more concrete, let's consider some examples of consumption taxes. The *retail sales tax* is the probably the one most familiar to Americans, as almost all states already operate one. Under this approach, tax liability is triggered by the final sales of goods and services at the retail level, and the tax is collected entirely from retailers (that is, firms that sell directly to consumers).

Another kind of consumption tax that is much more commonly used around the world, partly because it is easier to administer and enforce, is the *value added tax* (VAT). Instead of collecting tax only from retailers, the VAT collects some tax revenue at each stage of the production and distribution process. Each firm pays tax on its "value added," which is simply its total sales minus the costs of the goods and services—except for labor but including investment—that the firm buys to produce its output. For example, a furniture-building company would pay tax on its sales of furniture but would get to deduct immediately the full cost of wood, nails, tools, machinery, and factories that it had purchased in that year. The furniture retailer pays tax on its sales to consumers but can deduct the value of its purchases from the furniture maker, so that all business-to-business purchases ultimately cancel each other out, leaving final sales to consumers—equal to final output minus investment—as the tax base. Thus, the VAT measures consumption by taking the net contribution of each firm to the nation's output and then subtracting off its investment.

A third approach to taxing consumption is economically equivalent to a VAT—the only difference being that labor compensation is deducted from the business tax base and then taxed separately, and at the same rate, at the personal level. This method makes it easier to introduce some progressivity by incorporating a large exemption, and possibly graduated rates, in the personal tax on labor compensation. The Hall-Rabushka flat tax proposal, most recently championed by 1996 and 2000 Republican presidential candidate Steve Forbes and former House majority leader Dick Armey, is the most famous example of this type of tax.

A fourth approach to consumption taxation, called a *personal consumption tax*, attempts to measure how much each family actually consumes during the year, but not by triggering tax liability each time a purchase is made as under a retail sales tax. Instead, each year a taxpayer would calculate and report both income and net saving. Personal consumption tax liability is based on the difference between the two— that is, income minus saving. This kind of tax could easily accommodate progressive rates. The major change to the current system that would get us to this tax would be to create unlimited IRAs although, as we discuss in the next chapter, other changes would be necessary as well to avoid massive and destructive loopholes. An example of a proposal along these lines is the Unlimited Saving Allowance (USA) tax, championed in the mid-1990s by Senator Pete Domenici (R-NM) and former Senator Sam Nunn (D-GA).

The various methods of taxing consumption differ in how they *appear* to divide the tax burden up among consumers, workers, and businesses because different people write the checks. As explained in chapter 3, however, who writes the checks is essentially irrelevant to who ultimately bears the burden of the tax and to what are its economic effects, so the different approaches have more in common than it might appear on the surface. In the next chapter, we examine in more detail how each of these approaches would work, explore the differences among them, and evaluate them. In this section, we focus on the many elements that are common to all consumption taxes.

Consumption Taxes, Income Taxes, and Incentives to Save and Invest

The key distinction between an income tax and a consumption tax is that income taxes have a negative impact on the incentive to save and invest, whereas consumption taxes do not. The easiest way to see this is to consider an example. Suppose you get a $100 bonus at work and are trying to decide whether to spend it today or to put in the bank and save it for next year at a 10 percent interest rate. If there were no taxes, you'd have a choice between consuming the $100 today or saving it so you have $110 next year, a 10 percent reward for saving.

First, consider how things change when there's a 20 percent income tax. If you choose to spend your raise immediately, you'll get to consume $80—your take-home pay after the income tax. If you decide instead to save it, your $80 will earn an extra $8 in interest. An income tax, however, subjects that interest to taxation as well. After taxes, you only get $6.40 in interest—so your choice is between consuming $80 today or $86.40 next year. The income tax thus reduces your reward for saving from 10 percent to 8 percent.

Now consider what happens when there is a consumption tax of 20 percent. If you spend your $100 raise today, you pay a 20 percent tax immediately, so you get to consume $80 after taxes, just like you would under the income tax.[3] But if instead you save that income, you can put all $100 in the bank. Because it earns 10 percent interest, you'll have $110 in the bank next year: no tax is triggered by the interest earned. When you finally do spend that money, you pay a 20 percent tax, leaving you with 80 percent of $110, or $88, to spend. So under the consumption tax, your choice is between consuming $80 today and consuming $88 in a year. Thus, the reward for saving is still 10 percent, exactly what it would be in the absence of any tax at all.

This is what economists mean when they say that a consumption tax is "neutral" between current and future consumption: the terms of the choice between consumption today and consumption in the future are the same as they would be in the absence of taxes. In our example, you get the 10 percent reward under the consumption tax, just as you would if there were no taxes, while the income tax leaves you with only an 8 percent reward for saving. Our example is admittedly simplified, but complicating it in any number of ways, such as considering multiple time periods or allowing inflation, would not change the basic result. Moreover, the argument applies to any form of consumption tax, including not only retail sales taxes but also value-added taxes, the flat tax, and a personal consumption tax.

Some of these tax systems levy taxes on businesses, so to ensure that there is no reduction in the return to saving *or investing,* we need to investigate further. It turns out that there is a key difference between how business investment is treated under the two systems. An income tax allows deductions for capital goods as they *depreciate* (lose value due to wearing out or technological obsolescence), while a consump-tion tax allows the cost of capital goods to be deducted in full immedi-ately, which is known as *expensing.* Modifying our example a bit can show why expensing removes the tax system's impact on the incentive to invest in the same way that a consumption tax has no impact on the return to saving.

Suppose you're the owner of a small business that has just earned a $100 profit. You could take the portion that is left over after taxes out of the business today and use it to finance present consumption. Alterna-tively, you could invest what is left over after taxes in machinery that will next year produce goods that are worth 10 percent more than the cost of the investment. You know that immediately after producing the goods, the machinery will break down and produce nothing more.

Under either an income or a consumption type of business tax, if you pay the profit to yourself today and consume it, it will be subject to tax. If the tax rate is 20 percent, you have the option of consuming $80 after tax today. The difference is in what happens if you invest in the machinery. Under the income tax, you would still pay a 20 percent tax on your $100 profit today, even if you were to invest in the machinery;

there is no deduction yet because the machinery hasn't worn out yet. So you have $80 left over to invest, which will produce $88 in goods for you in the future. Next year, you will have $8 in taxable income—$88 in sales, minus an $80 deduction for depreciation. You would pay $.2 \times 8 =$ $1.60 in tax next year, leaving you with $86.40 to consume next year. So the business income tax leaves you with a choice of consuming $80 today or, if you invest, $86.40 next year—reducing the reward to investing from 10 percent to 8 percent, just as in the personal saving example.

In contrast, under expensing the tax has no effect on the return to investing. If you decide to spend all of your profit on the machinery, you face no tax liability today because you get to deduct the full purchase price of the machinery immediately, which makes your tax base today $0. This leaves you with $100 to invest in the machinery. Next year, you'll have $110 of output to sell but no depreciation deductions. After paying a 20 percent tax on that $110, you will have $88 dollars left. Thus, you have a choice between consuming $80 today or $88 next year. This is, of course, a 10 percent return, the same as what you would get in the absence of taxes. Although our example could be made more complicated—for instance, by allowing the machine to depreciate over several years—this would not change the basic conclusion that with expensing the rate of return to investment is the same as it would be in the absence of taxes.

Similarities and Differences between a Consumption Tax and a Wage Tax

Another way to eliminate the effect of taxes on the incentive to save and invest is to base tax liability on labor compensation, while exempting from tax all interest and other capital income. This approach is generally called a *wage tax*, although it is sometimes called a *yield-exempt tax* because the yield from saving and investment does not trigger tax liability. Extending our example to this case is straightforward. Under a 20 percent wage tax, when you earn $100, you receive $80 after tax. Saving it at a 10 percent interest rate would give you $88 next year, and there's no tax on the interest. So just like a consumption tax, the wage tax gives you a choice of consuming $80 today or $88 in a year. Not only is there no impact on the incentive to save—the rate of return remains at 10 percent—but the amount you get to consume after tax is exactly the same in both periods under either the wage tax or the consumption tax.

These two alternative methods for exempting the return to saving are reflected in the two different kinds of IRAs in the current system. A traditional IRA allows a deduction for contributions to the account, exempts capital income on the account from taxation while it accrues, and then taxes withdrawals (which are presumably made to finance consumption). A Roth IRA, on the other hand, does not allow an initial deduction, does exempt capital income on the assets in the account from tax, but does not impose tax on withdrawals. Thus, the traditional IRA is like a consumption tax, while the Roth IRA is like a wage tax. Except for some technicalities (for example, marginal tax rates may differ at the time of contribution and the time of withdrawal), the two approaches are equivalent in the same way as consumption and wage taxes are.

A crucial distinction between a wage tax and a consumption tax arises, however, in considering the transition from an income tax to one or the other. If we switch entirely to a pure consumption tax, any preexisting wealth that gets spent on consumption after the transition will be taxed as it is spent. If we switch entirely to a wage tax, on the other hand, all preexisting wealth can be spent on consumption tax-free forever. This is indeed an enormous difference, as accumulated wealth in the United States was approximately $48 trillion by the end of 2002.[4]

Not All "Capital Income" Represents the Return to Saving

So far, we've seen that a hallmark of both consumption taxes and wage taxes is that they exempt from taxation the return to saving. The return to saving can be thought of as the reward to deferring consumption. Certainly some of what we loosely call "capital income" (interest, dividends, capital gains, small business income, and so on) represents returns to deferring consumption. But some of it represents something else entirely. In what follows, we consider what the other components of capital income represent and how they are treated under different tax systems.[5]

Consumption Taxes, Income Taxes, and Inflation

As we have noted before, some portion of capital income represents compensation for the fact that inflation erodes the real purchasing power of the underlying wealth. Consumption and wage taxes automatically exempt this compensation for inflation from tax. For instance, if half of the 10 percent interest in our examples above reflected inflation, the consumption and wage taxes wouldn't tax it because they exempt the full 10 percent from tax. In our current income tax, to the extent that capital income is taxed, the inflationary component is taxed too. As we discuss in chapter 4, this can greatly increase the effective tax rate on the return to saving if inflation is high.

Compensation for inflation does not have to be taxed by an income tax. Indeed, it would be exempt under a comprehensive tax on economic income. But this is more difficult to achieve under an income tax than in a consumption or wage tax. The key difference is that in an income tax, we would need to distinguish what portion of capital income represented inflation and what portion didn't, instead of just exempting the whole thing. Accurately distinguishing the two would require not only a measure of the dollar amount of capital income, which is what we currently observe on the tax form, but also a measure of the value of the underlying wealth that generated the return, which can be administratively difficult to obtain. For example, suppose that someone receives $10 of interest income and inflation is 5 percent. If that interest was earned on $100 of wealth, we should be exempting 5 percent of $100, or $5. But if it were earned on $125 of wealth, we should be exempting 5 percent of $125, or $6.25. If we don't know whether the underlying wealth was $100 or $125, we don't know exactly how much of the $10 to exempt. It would be possible to come up with rough approximations— for example, based on average interest rates in the economy in a particular year—but these would be just that, rough approximations. A correct measure of income would also require adjusting capital gains as well as the value of depreciation deductions, interest deductions, and inventory allowances, for inflation. For similar reasons as above, this is difficult in an income tax and unnecessary in a consumption or wage tax.

Consumption Taxes, Income Taxes, and Risk

Another important component of capital income is the compensation— or premium—for bearing risk. On average, riskier opportunities for saving and investment yield higher returns because people dislike risk and need to be compensated to be willing to accept it. For example, corporate stocks have historically earned a higher return, on average, than government bonds, partly because the return on stocks is much more uncertain (the recent experience of the stock market being a perfect example of this). Therefore, there is a trade-off between risk and expected average return, and in choosing their portfolio savers need to choose some optimal balance between them. Some argue that, historically, the part of capital income that represents compensation for risk has been higher than the part that represents compensation for deferring consumption. But evidence also suggests that the return for deferring consumption has been increasing over time and the premium for bearing risk has been declining.[6]

Compensation for bearing risk is exempt from consumption taxes and wage taxes in exactly the same way as the compensation for inflation and for postponing consumption are. To illustrate, consider a risky asset that offers a 1-in-2 chance of earning a 40 percent return, and a 1-in-2 chance of losing 10 percent of its value, so the return is expected to be 15 percent on average. Suppose once again that you've got $100 before taxes available to save and there's a 20 percent tax rate, so you have the option of consuming $80 after taxes today. Under a consumption tax, if the money is saved, no tax is paid today, $100 gets saved, and it yields either $140 or $90 next year. After paying the 20 percent consumption tax, you get to consume either $112 or $72 next year. Relative to the $80 you can consume today, that still translates to a 40 percent return if you have good luck, a 10 percent loss if you have bad luck, and a 15 percent return on average. Under the wage tax, you pay tax immediately today even if you save, leaving $80 to be saved. Next year you get to consume $1.4 \times \$80 = \$112$ if you have good luck or $0.9 \times \$80 = \$72$ if you have bad luck, exactly the same outcomes as under the consumption tax. So either way, your expected return from investing in the risky asset is 15 percent, the same as it would be without any taxes, and there is no distortion to your decisions regarding how much risk to take. Comparing a consumption tax to a wage tax, the people who are lucky after the fact remit more tax, and the unlucky people remit less tax. But this distinction is in fact meaningless. What people actually get to consume either today or tomorrow, whether they have good luck or bad, is exactly the same under both taxes.

A more surprising principle is that under a proportional income tax that allows full deductions for losses, the compensation for risk is also effectively exempt from tax. The argument for why, which dates back to an article written by economists Evsey Domar and Richard Musgrave in the early 1940s, is based on the key insight that the income tax absorbs some of the risk from your portfolio. If an investment turns out well, the income tax takes away some of the resulting capital income, but if it turns out badly, the tax partly compensates you by allowing you to deduct the loss, thus reducing tax liability. Thus, the income tax reduces both the expected after-tax return *and* the variance in the after-tax return. Domar and Musgrave showed that the reduction in the expected after-tax return is the fair market price for the reduction in risk, so that even though the government collects revenue from imposing income tax on the portion of the return that represents compensation for bearing risk, that part of the tax does not place a burden on the taxpayer. In fact, by increasing the share of one's portfolio invested in risky assets, an investor can exactly replicate the risk-return possibilities that would have been available if only the risk-free portion of returns were taxed.[7] Since the income tax on the risky portion of the return leaves you with exactly the same opportunities as you would have had with no tax at all on that portion of the return, it is in a sense equivalent to not taxing that portion of the return at all.

Of course, the income tax does not treat gains and losses symmetrically. Progressive tax rates and limitations on deductibility of losses both mean that the government takes a larger share of capital income if you have good luck with your portfolio than if you have bad luck. However, this is not an inherent or unique feature of income taxes. The reasons for these features (vertical equity and the need to limit tax avoidance schemes) can apply to consumption tax plans as well.[8] A consumption tax with these features would indeed tax some of the returns to risk.

"Supernormal" Returns and Mislabeled Labor Compensation

Some of what we call "capital income" may represent a variety of things that we haven't yet addressed. These include returns to innovation, returns to entrepreneurial skill and effort, returns to establishing a monopoly in some market, returns to early units of investment that may be more productive than the last "marginal" units of investment, or simply mislabeled returns to labor effort. What all of these have in common from an economic point of view is that they are *supernormal returns*—meaning they produce income that is larger than the "normal" return that can be earned on a marginal investment in capital, which is competed down to a fairly low level. It turns out that these supernormal returns are effectively taxed by both income taxes and consumption taxes. A wage tax, on the other hand, would not tax them.

A highly visible example of a supernormal return would be Bill Gates's income, which comes mainly from his share of the profits of Microsoft. This is labeled "capital income" by our income tax. In the Hall-Rabushka flat tax, it would be labeled "business income." But only a tiny portion of that income represents a reward for postponing consumption or taking on risk. Mostly, it represents some combination of returns to Bill Gates's labor (including effort put into innovation and entrepreneurship) and returns arising from being in the right place at the right time and gaining an early lead in a particular market that happens to naturally tend toward monopoly. Under the current income tax, these returns are indeed taxed, mainly by the corporate income tax and also by the personal income tax to the extent that Gates realizes any of his capital gains by selling shares.

A *wage tax*, on the other hand, would never tax these returns as long as Microsoft continued to pay Gates only a nominal salary. Under a wage tax, relabeling your labor compensation as capital income would be an easy avenue to escape taxation altogether. The difficulty of distinguishing what is labor income and what is capital income is an important reason that a pure wage tax would end up being highly inequitable and costly to enforce.[9]

In contrast, a consumption tax does indeed tax supernormal returns and mislabeled returns to labor (like those received by Bill Gates) in the same way as an income tax does. One way to look at this is that no matter what these returns are labeled, they will eventually be taxed when the recipient, or his or her heirs, eventually consume more because of these returns. Another way of thinking about this is that at the business level, the reason the normal return to saving and investment is exempt under a consumption tax is that investments in physical capital (such as productive machinery and factories) are expensed (deducted immediately). The factors that produce supernormal returns for someone like Bill Gates lead to big increases in the taxable revenues of his company but do nothing to increase the size of the expensing deduction that the company gets to take early on: the supernormal returns did not result from larger than usual investments in physical capital. Similarly, under the Hall-Rabushka flat tax, if a firm mislabels the labor compensation of its proprietor as "dividends" or "capital gains," no tax will be paid on that income at the personal level, but tax is paid at the business level, and the mislabeling produces no expensing deduction for capital investment to offset it. Thus, as long as the tax rates on the personal and business bases in the flat tax are the same, mislabeling labor income as returns to capital and vice versa make no difference to tax liability. The same would be true of a flat-rate comprehensive income tax as well.

How Different Is the Current Income Tax from a Consumption Tax?

The bottom line of the above discussion is that an income tax taxes the return to deferring consumption (the incentive to save) and a consumption tax does not. Compensation for inflation need not be taxed under either type of tax, but it is administratively easier to exempt it from a consumption tax. Compensation for risk also need not be taxed under either approach: the features that make it partly taxable (including progressive rates and limitations on loss deductibility) might apply under either type of tax. Finally, "supernormal" returns and labor compensation mislabeled as capital income are generally taxable under either approach. Thus, much of what is generally thought of as capital income can be treated similarly by income taxes and consumption taxes. A wage tax, on the other hand, would completely exempt *all* of these forms of capital income, so its difference from an income tax is starker.

The difference between a consumption tax and the system that we have now is mitigated further by the fact that, as we detail in chapter 2, our current tax system is in many ways a hybrid between an income tax and a consumption tax. For example, revenue is collected from taxing nominal interest income. But even more revenue may be forgone due to the deduction of nominal interest payments, both because those deducting the interest tend to be in higher tax brackets than those receiving interest and because so much interest income is sheltered from tax by pensions, IRAs, and other means. Large portions of dividend and capital gains income are excluded from personal tax, and generous depreciation allowances further reduce the effective tax on capital income.

One rough metric of how different the current income tax is from a consumption tax is the amount of revenue that it would cost to switch the base from one to the other, while leaving the other features of the current system intact. Forgoing tax on *all* returns to postponing consumption, instead of just some, should cost revenue, but for reasons noted above, it's not immediately obvious whether the cost would be large. The existing income tax could be almost entirely converted to a type of consumption tax in just three steps: (1) exempt all interest, dividends, and capital gains from tax; (2) replace depreciation deductions with expensing of all new investment, while eliminating depreciation deductions for past investment; and (3) eliminate all interest deductions. One of the authors of this book, along with Roger Gordon of the University of California at San Diego and Laura Kalambokidis of the University of Minnesota at St. Paul, have estimated that taking these steps in 1995, while leaving the rest of the tax code the way it is, would have reduced revenues from personal and corporate income taxes by a total of $108 billion, or about 15 percent of revenues from those taxes.[10] Not surprisingly, the largest gains from these changes would go to people at the top of the income distribution, since they are the ones most likely to have unsheltered capital income under the current system. The average tax cut per return for those in the top 10 percent of the labor income distribution was estimated at $4,491, while the average tax cut for everyone else was $175 per return. Therefore, making this change revenue- and distributionally neutral would require *raising* tax rates on upper-income people relative to current law, which is the opposite of what flat tax proponents typically propose to do. If depreciation deductions were still allowed for prior investments, the one-year revenue loss from converting the 1995 income tax to a consumption tax would have been $246 billion, or about *one-third* of income tax revenues in that year. The revenue loss relative to the current system could then be expected to gradually shrink in subsequent years back toward 15 percent, as prior depreciation deductions ran out.

While these estimates suggest that a significant net difference exists between the current system and a consumption tax, this conclusion is sensitive to when you make the comparison. For instance, doing a similar calculation for 1983 suggested that switching to a consumption base would have slightly *increased* revenues. The difference arose because in 1983, depreciation deductions were more generous, tax sheltering opportunities were more numerous, the inflation rate was higher (making deductions more valuable), and the economy was in recession (which reduced corporate profits below normal levels). Since 1995 was an unusually good year economically and changes since 1995 have reduced taxation of capital income, the long-run cost of changing the current system to a consumption tax, holding other features of the tax code constant, would probably be somewhat less than 15 percent of revenues.

Now that we've examined how the different approaches to taxation treat capital income, let's consider how they treat the other major source of income, labor.

Consumption Taxes, Income Taxes, and the Incentive to Work

One thing that consumption taxes, wage taxes, and income taxes all share is that they reduce the reward for working (the quantity of goods and services that can be purchased per hour of work). The reward for working can be reduced in either of two ways—by lowering take-home pay and holding fixed the prices of the things you buy or by increasing the prices of everything you buy and keeping take-home pay the same. A comprehensive 20 percent tax on wages and salaries has the same effect on reducing the reward for working as a comprehensive sales tax that's 20 percent of the price inclusive of tax.[11]

It is sometimes argued that a consumption tax reduces the incentive to work *more* than an income tax does. The argument goes like this. Total consumption is smaller than the total amount of income. Therefore, the tax rates required to raise a given amount of revenue must be higher under a consumption tax than under an income tax with an equally clean base, and a higher tax rate means a greater disincentive to work. The problem with this argument is that it ignores the fact that, because a consumption tax allows you to earn higher after-tax returns on the portion of your labor income that you save, working becomes more financially attractive.[12] This helps offset the effect of the higher tax rates (on an apparently smaller base) that would be required under a consumption tax.

Is a Consumption Tax More or Less Fair Than an Income Tax?

On a year-by-year basis, a consumption-based tax can appear to be much more regressive than an income tax with the same rate structure. This is because people who have low incomes in any given year on average spend a very high fraction of their incomes—often more than their income—while people with high incomes in a given year save a relatively larger portion of theirs.[13] The temptation might be to conclude that shifting from an income tax to a consumption tax would greatly increase the tax burden on low-income people relative to high-income people.

However, looking at a snapshot of income-saving patterns for a single year of data significantly overstates the regressivity of the consumption tax compared to an income tax. First of all, in any given year some people with temporarily low income have maintained a level of spending corresponding to their usual income. Conversely, some people who had an exceptionally good income-earning year might not expect their good fortune to continue and therefore keep their spending well below their income, saving up for the years of relatively bad fortune. In both cases, one year's income is not a good measure of how well off those people are, and the fact that the consumption-income ratio varies widely across persons, being high for the temporarily low-income people and low for the temporarily high-income people overstates how much more regressive a consumption tax is relative to an income tax.

Second, most people have a natural life-cycle pattern of earning and saving. In the early years of working life, family expenses are pressing and income relatively low, so savings are minimal or even negative, as families borrow to finance consumption. In the later working years, incomes have grown to the point where many families begin to save for their retirement and higher education for their children. In retirement, the pattern reverses again, as people live off their accumulated savings, spending more than they earn. Looking across people of different ages, low-income people (young and old) would appear to do little (or none or even negative) saving, and high-income people would seem to be relatively big savers. That picture would be misleading because—leaving aside for a moment bequests, inheritances, other gifts, and government transfers—over a lifetime people cannot spend more than they earn, and over a lifetime people end up spending all of what they earn.[14] Thus, from a lifetime perspective it doesn't make a huge difference whether the tax base is income or consumption: it all adds up the same. Big savers age 45 to 65, who might appear to be getting off easy under a consumption tax because they consume relatively little of their annual income, will eventually pay more tax when they take their trip around the world and otherwise live the high life when they retire. A single-rate tax on consumption and a single-rate tax on labor income both end up being single-rate levies on lifetime resources. Similarly, over a lifetime, a consumption tax with graduated rates could in principle achieve about the same degree of progressivity as a graduated income tax. One is not inherently more progressive than the other. Rather, the degree of progressivity depends on the kind of tax rates that we impose, which is in principle a separate issue.

Many economists would also argue that, again ignoring bequests and inheritances, a consumption tax is more horizontally equitable than a comprehensive income tax on both labor earnings and the return to capital. This is because when comparing families with equal lifetime incomes, a consumption tax avoids imposing a tax penalty on those who are relatively frugal. Over a lifetime, it levies the same present value of taxation regardless of a family's saving propensity. In contrast, under an income tax savers pay more tax than nonsavers because the return to their saving triggers an additional tax liability that does not arise under a consumption tax.

However, a consumption tax that does not include bequests or inheritances in the tax base will lower the average tax rate over a lifetime on those families that pass on wealth to their heirs. Evidence suggests that people who have higher lifetime incomes tend to save a larger fraction of their incomes over their whole lives and correspondingly devote a larger share of their lifetime resources to bequests than do other people. This turns a flat-rate consumption tax into a somewhat regressive tax on lifetime resources. For this reason, some economists who favor a consumption tax do so only if a bequest is treated (that is, taxed) as if it were an act of consumption by the bequeathor. A tax on bequests, however, might be viewed as a double tax on deferring consumption, as a tax is levied both when the bequest is made and then again when the heirs consume it. If people leave bequests because they value the consumption of their heirs, then this would reduce the incentive to save for bequests in much the same way as an income tax does. We consider these issues in more detail when we discuss the estate tax in chapter 8.[15]

Fairness and the Transition to a Consumption Tax

As we discuss in chapter 3, whenever the tax system changes, some people are bound to lose in the transition, and others are bound to gain. The bigger the tax change, the bigger the likely size of the windfall gains and losses. Replacing the current tax system with any kind of consumption tax is surely a massive change, and potentially large windfall gains and losses would occur in the transition.

The most important distributional issue in the transition to a consumption tax is the treatment of preexisting wealth. The transition to a new tax system could mean either a major windfall or a substantial loss for the owners of wealth, depending on how the change is implemented and in what form the wealth is held.

As mentioned above, the two ways to remove taxation's impact on the incentive to save are a wage tax and a consumption tax. If we were to replace our income tax with a wage tax, not only could wealth owners earn interest, dividends, and capital gains tax-free, but their wealth could (as under the income tax) be spent tax-free as well. This change would clearly provide a big gain to holders of existing wealth, who otherwise would have had to pay tax on the returns to that wealth. It is a windfall gain because these people gain financially from the new tax rules, even if they don't do any extra new saving at all.

On the other hand, adopting a pure consumption tax could impose a large burden on owners of existing wealth. Suppose that we adopted a 20 percent consumption tax and it caused the prices of all goods and services to rise by 20 percent. The purchasing power of labor income would decline by 20 percent relative to a situation with no taxes, just as it would under a wage tax of the same rate. The difference is that under a consumption tax, the purchasing power of all existing wealth also falls by 20 percent. For example, suppose you had built up a substantial savings account before the imposition of the new consumption tax. When you withdraw money from the account and spend it, it would be taxed at the full 20 percent rate by a consumption tax but not taxed at all by a wage tax.

Setting aside for a moment temporary inflexibilities in contracts for wages, bonds, and so forth (we address these later), whether the overall level of prices changes or not does not materially affect this story.[16] Even if prices do not rise at all, moving to a consumption tax would cause the purchasing power of both wages and existing wealth to decline by an average of 20 percent relative to a situation with no taxes. Nominal wages would be forced down because firms would be earning 20 percent less, after taxes, from the output produced by workers. The nominal value of existing capital assets—in the form of, for example, share prices—which constitute much of old wealth, would also decline because the output they produce provides 20 percent less in after-tax revenues.

Whether or not prices go up, we would be eliminating our current income tax if we adopted the consumption tax, and the offsetting effect this produces needs to be considered. For wages, the offset would be roughly one-for-one: the elimination of income taxes on wages would compensate for the new burden of consumption taxes on wage earners. Different wage earners might gain or lose depending on how the progressivity of the tax burden on wages changes, but this is a separate issue.

The future benefits from eliminating income taxes on capital, however, are unlikely to cancel out the immediate one-time tax on existing wealth from instituting a consumption tax. Eliminating double taxation of all future dividends and capital gains would provide a counterbalancing gain to corporate shares, as would forgiving the tax on all previously accumulated capital gains.[17] But eliminating the income tax also imposes a loss on owners of capital assets because firms would no longer be able to take depreciation deductions on previously purchased capital assets to offset taxes on the output they produce. All new investment goods, by contrast, could be purchased tax-free or deducted from the business tax base immediately, which would offset the taxes owed on the future returns to those new assets. As a result, the demand for existing assets would fall sharply relative to the demand for new assets, reducing the value of existing wealth. The net impact on the value of existing wealth from a switch to a consumption tax depends on many factors and is hard to predict.[18] All things considered, however, the most likely scenario is that owners of existing wealth would take a one-time hit in the switch from the income tax to a consumption tax. This transitional loss would be offset, over the long run, to the extent that under the new tax regime wealth owners receive higher after-tax returns on that wealth.

The more transition relief that is provided to existing assets in the switch to any consumption tax, the more it becomes like a wage tax. For example, allowing businesses to continue taking depreciation deductions for past investments would greatly reduce the revenue raised from holders of preexisting wealth. Taxes on labor compensation would have to pick up the slack. A similar result occurs in the transition to a personal consumption tax if individuals are allowed to deduct some or all of their existing wealth in the same way as they could deduct new saving. To the extent they can, their tax base is less than their consumption done after the imposition of the tax. A similar outcome results from incremental changes in the income tax that exempt more and more of the return to saving from taxation without imposing any transitional burden on preexisting wealth. In sum, whether moving toward consumption taxation provides a windfall gain or loss to existing wealth holders depends crucially on the transition provisions that are adopted.

What characterizes the owners of wealth who will be affected most by these transitional gains or losses? They are, on average, very wealthy; for example, the richest 1 percent of the population owns approximately one-third of the nation's private wealth.[19] They are also, on average, elderly; in 1998 the mean net worth of households headed by someone age 65 or over was 60 percent higher than it was for households headed by someone under age 65.[20] If Social Security benefits are indexed to compensate for any price change, as they probably would be, then the impact is concentrated on the better-off portion of the elderly.

Whether it is "fair" to hit wealth holders, elderly or not, with an unexpected burden is an equity issue about which economic analysis cannot be decisive. The fact that moving to a consumption tax with no transition relief places a burden on the wealthy is probably appealing to many people, especially because the wealthy could benefit greatly in the future from the removal of tax on returns to saving. But experience suggests that wealth owners and their representatives—such as corporations—would be sure to push very hard for transition relief, and the political system is likely to accommodate them. Indeed, an article in *Fortune* magazine predicts that "Were Washington to disallow deductions [for depreciation on existing capital], every CEO-laden corporate jet in America would commence strafing Capitol Hill."[21] The other major group hit especially hard by the transitional burden, retirees with significant wealth outside of Social Security, would also likely see their interests defended by strong lobbying, a powerful voting bloc, and general public sympathy, so some kind of transitional relief could be expected here as well.

Because many important prices are temporarily inflexible, the transition to a consumption tax can also lead to a variety of other, often capricious redistributions. Depending on whether the Federal Reserve allows a price change, all sorts of redistributions can occur surrounding contracts written in fixed nominal terms, such as bonds, mortgages, and long-term wage contracts. For example, if the adoption of a consumption tax is accompanied by an increase in consumer prices, bondholders suffer the same one-time loss as stockholders because the real value of their bonds declines. On the other hand, if prices do not rise, the change to a consumption tax will not hurt bondholders because firms are legally obligated to pay them the full nominal value of their bonds. In this case, the owners of businesses who borrowed from those bondholders are hit hard because they cannot pass through the cost of lost depreciation deductions to the bondholders. Some of these firms might be forced into bankruptcy or layoffs, hurting the employees as well.

One other notable issue of transitional fairness concerns government transfer payments that are not automatically indexed for price changes, such as food stamps and welfare. If a consumption tax is accompanied by a price increase, and transfer payments are not increased in value to keep real benefits constant, the tax change levies an extra burden on the poor.

Economic Reasons for Switching to a Consumption Tax

What would be the long-term economic impact of switching to a consumption tax? The most talked-about potential benefits arise from increasing the incentive to save and invest. A less publicized but perhaps more important benefit is that a consumption tax could make it easier to "level the playing field" among different types of investment. Finally, the shifting of tax burdens that occurs in the transition to a new system could have important economic effects.

Switching to a consumption tax would remove any negative impact of the tax system on the incentive to save and invest. Thus, a consumption tax involves one less distorted decision than an income tax. By itself, this is a step toward a more efficient tax system because individuals' choices between current and future consumption will more closely reflect the merits of the alternatives rather than the influence of the tax system. However, it is not necessarily true that this makes a consumption tax more economically efficient overall than an income tax; the tax that alters the smallest number of relative prices is not necessarily the most efficient. In theory, a reform that removes the tax distortion to saving decisions while raising the same revenue should increase saving and capital accumulation, which many economists argue would be beneficial. By providing workers better machines and tools to work with, increased capital accumulation could improve productivity and long-run living standards.

As shown in chapter 4, however, the magnitude of any increase in saving that would arise from improved incentives is highly uncertain. This is a crucially important question on which the available evidence is simply not very good. In recent history, the periods with the highest incentives to save coincided paradoxically with the *lowest* rates of saving. This might have occurred for many different reasons, each with different policy implications, and it is difficult to distinguish empirically among these reasons. Nonetheless, the best guess of most economists is that private saving is probably not very responsive to the after-tax rate of return, so that switching to a consumption tax would be unlikely to increase the quantity of saving much. Because we can find more direct ways to increase national saving (for example, by reducing the budget deficit), the likely but not guaranteed prospect of a somewhat higher saving rate does not appear to be, by itself, a reason to undertake a wholesale transformation of the tax system.

A second possible benefit of a consumption tax is that achieving "neutrality" or "uniformity" in the tax treatment of various types of investment would be made easier. Under the current income tax, different types of investment are effectively taxed at varying rates. For example, corporate business investments are taxed more heavily than noncorporate business investments, which are in turn taxed more heavily than investments in owner-occupied housing. Investments in certain types of capital equipment or in certain lines of business are capriciously favored relative to others by depreciation schedules that are more front-loaded, or accelerated, than true economic depreciation. Business endeavors that can be packaged into assets that appreciate in value are more attractive than those that pay their returns in the form of dividends or interest because of the preferential treatment of capital gains. Inflation can introduce arbitrary variation in tax rates. All of these deviations from "neutrality" are economically harmful because they attract investment into the tax-favored investments even though their social return is not higher than the social return to the investments that are not tax-favored.

A consumption tax would eliminate all of these distortions to the choice among different types of investment. It would transform the effective marginal tax rate on the returns to all investment to a single uniform rate—zero. Of course, in principle an income tax could also be made more neutral, taxing the returns to investment at a uniform but positive rate. Thus, to some extent, this is a separate issue from the choice between an income tax and a consumption tax: it's a matter of having a "clean base." But this particular aspect of "cleanliness" is much easier to achieve in a consumption tax than in an income tax. Some of the existing distortions are hard to avoid in an income tax because capital income is difficult to measure accurately. For example, measuring economic depreciation exactly right is impossible, so some distortions will inevitably be caused here by favoring investments in assets whose depreciation for tax purposes exceeds true depreciation. Similarly, including all capital gains in taxable income as they accrue is probably infeasible, so appreciating assets will be favored. It is theoretically possible to adjust the measurement of capital income for inflation, but in practice doing so would be complicated and inevitably imperfect. Because a consumption tax eliminates the need to address any of these issues, it can achieve this aspect of uniformity in a simple way.

The transition to a consumption tax can also have significant economic consequences. For example, from an efficiency point of view, placing a surprise, one-time tax on holders of existing wealth, as moving to a consumption tax could, is not unattractive. Raising revenue from the returns to *past* investments has no effect on the incentive to invest, to work, or to do anything else. Shifting tax burdens onto the elderly—whose work and saving decisions are nearly finished—also avoids costly disincentives. Moreover, because the elderly have a relatively high propensity to consume, transferring some of the tax burden onto them and away from others could give a boost to national saving. This last effect is likely to be offset, however, by the fact that the wealthy as a whole have a much higher propensity to save than everyone else, and placing an extra burden on them through a consumption tax might reduce their contribution to national saving.[22] As we see in the next chapter, models that attempt to work out the economic impact of switching to a consumption tax suggest that, all things considered, a very large portion of any economic gain from the switch comes from replacing other, distorting, taxes with this one-time tax on already accumulated wealth.

We have been discussing the potential economic benefit that could occur because switching to a consumption tax might impose a transitional tax on preexisting wealth. But we must consider whether people will really believe that this is a "one-time only" strategy. If a surprise one-time tax on wealth is so economically efficient if we do it "just this one time," politicians might well be tempted to try it again some time in the future. If doing it once increases people's estimates of the probability that it will happen again, then the "surprise" tax on wealth creates a disincentive to accumulate wealth.

As we have emphasized, we now have a messy hybrid between an income tax and a consumption tax. This is a mixed blessing for the case for switching entirely to a consumption tax. To the extent that saving already receives consumption tax treatment due to pensions, IRAs, and the like, the potential increase in saving and corresponding economic benefits that could arise from going all the way to a consumption tax are apparently reduced. This should not be overstated, however. Although a large share of capital income is already sheltered from taxation, a large share of the capital income that would arise from *additional* saving, which matters for decisions about how much to save, is still taxed. This is largely because pensions, IRAs, and similar plans shelter saving only up to some limit. For anyone whose saving is at or above those limits, the marginal incentive to save is still distorted by tax. On the positive side, this means that switching entirely to a consumption tax would still improve incentives substantially for the people who do most of the saving—and at a lower cost in terms of lost revenue (which must be recouped somehow) than if we were starting from a pure income tax. But it also means that the capital income that remains unsheltered from the current tax disproportionately goes to high-income people, which heavily influences the distributional impact of such a reform.

Simplification and Enforcement Aspects of a Consumption Tax

Even with all the compromises that we make in our current system, calculating and reporting capital income can be a complex and burdensome process. These compromises, in turn, create opportunities to achieve tax savings in complicated and socially unproductive ways, such as devising schemes to rearrange financial and business transactions. In principle, measuring consumption accurately is simpler than measuring even a compromised version of income, mainly because the need for measuring capital income can be completely avoided. But in practice, a consumption tax could end up being just as, or even more, difficult to administer and comply with than the current income tax. The simplicity and enforceability of moving to a consumption tax depend crucially on which approach is chosen and how it is operated. These issues are addressed fully in chapter 7.

Here, too, transitional issues are critically important. Moving cold turkey to a consumption tax like a VAT or flat tax could immediately make the taxpaying process simpler. But the pleadings of those likely to suffer windfall losses will be difficult to resist, so a switch to a consumption tax is likely to offer various forms of transition relief. Special transitional provisions can be exceedingly complex because they require the simultaneous operation of parallel tax systems, at least for a while. The real choice is not between the current system and a clean consumption tax but between the current system and a new tax encumbered by as yet unspecified rules for how to get from here to there, which can be unaesthetic at best and complicated and loophole-ridden at worst.

One other transitional issue has important implications for evaluating a new system. Depending on how it is implemented, the switch to a consumption tax can lead to enormous incentives to postpone or speed up transactions around the date of switchover. Firms will postpone investment until the expensing rules are in place, and under some plans, individuals will rush to consume as much as possible before the implementation date. This could cost a great deal of revenue and raises a very delicate problem of minimizing the short-run disruption at the time of transition.

A Clean Tax Base

A third element of proposals for fundamental tax reform is to eliminate many or all of the features that provide special treatment of particular types of consumption or investment. The aim is variously described as "flattening" or "broadening" the tax base, "leveling the playing field," or making the tax system more "neutral." We refer to this aspect of flatness as a *clean* tax base. (At least the connotation of *clean* is less ambiguous than that of *flat*.)

One important source of messiness in the tax base has to do with compromises or peculiarities about the taxation of capital income, such as the failure to index capital income for inflation and the double taxation of corporate income. These can be important sources of inefficiency, inequity, and complexity. As discussed above, a consumption tax could sweep away many of these problems. Chapter 8 addresses specific options for making the taxation of capital income more neutral while retaining an income tax.

This section focuses on a second source of messiness in the tax base—preferences for particular types of expenditures or activities that are deemed worthy of special treatment. Important examples are housing, health care, charity, taxation and borrowing by state and local governments, and education. Although we concentrate here on a few important examples, the current personal and corporate income taxes feature scores of other deviations from a clean-base system, from incentives to invest in low-income housing to tax breaks for the production of ethanol.[23] Each needs to be evaluated on its own merits.

Some ambitious proposals for overhauling the tax system, such as the Hall-Rabushka flat tax, would eliminate *all* preferences of this sort. Other proposals eliminate some but not all of these features. In contrast, recent U.S. policy changes are moving the tax system closer to a consumption base and flatter rates, but at the same time they are rapidly *increasing* the variety and generosity of deductions, exclusions, and credits. Any attempt to remove the most cherished and politically entrenched of these tax goodies would undoubtedly engender a fierce political fight. Were we to move to a consumption tax that features a personal tax return, such as the flat tax, it could easily end up retaining many current preferences or even adding new ones. And even though consumption taxes that have no personal tax returns, such as a retail sales tax or VAT, could no longer contain the preferences in their current form, similar ones could be reintroduced by exempting purchases of preferred items.

Throughout this book, we have discussed a host of reasons why special preferences in the tax base can be a problem. Every preference is a penalty for someone else because it requires tax rates to be higher than otherwise. Tax deductions are also a regressive way to subsidize activities: people with larger incomes receive bigger subsidies from deductions because on average they engage more in the deductible activities and have higher marginal tax rates. Those who don't itemize get no benefit at all from the deductions. Except in special cases, tax preferences are inefficient because they create an incentive to engage "too much" in the lightly taxed activity and too little in other activities, relative to what the free market would dictate. And, finally, they are a big reason that our tax code is so complicated.

For all of these reasons, the burden of proof should rest on those who defend deviations from a clean tax base. There are two main acceptable lines of defense. First, allowing certain deductions can make the tax system fairer if by so doing the tax base provides a more accurate measurement of well-being. Second, a tax preference can improve economic efficiency if it corrects a significant market failure—that is, a situation where the incentives in the market do not lead to an economically efficient outcome by themselves. An example would be an externality, which occurs when an activity generates important benefits or costs for others that are not reflected in the incentives faced by the individual undertaking the action. Even if a significant market failure is identified, the tax preference must be the best alternative for dealing with it. As discussed in chapter 4, there is a third potential defense for deviating from a "clean" or "uniform" tax base: taxing goods for which supply or demand is relatively insensitive to price at relatively higher rates could conceivably reduce the economic costs of taxation. But for reasons discussed in that chapter, this is generally impractical as a guide for policy, so we focus mainly on the first two defenses. As specific exceptions to a clean base are examined, each of them is evaluated in light of these criteria.

Even if some preferences meet these criteria, one powerful argument for maintaining a clean base is that the political system is incapable of distinguishing legitimate arguments from illegitimate ones and often succumbs to the political clout of powerful pleaders. Once any preference is allowed, we may begin to slide down the slippery slope to more preferences.

Housing and the Mortgage Interest Deduction

Owner-occupied housing is favored by our tax system in a number of ways. For example, the double taxation of corporate income makes housing investments more attractive by comparison, and capital gains are untaxed on most home sales. But the deduction for home mortgage interest payments is the most visible and traditionally the most politically sacred aspect of the tax treatment of housing. Notably, its "sacredness" is now being challenged, for it is swept away in some of the more ambitious tax reform proposals. When push comes to shove, however, there would undoubtedly be an all-out fight to retain it.

The home mortgage interest deduction is an expensive one, costing $64 billion in revenues in fiscal year 2002. It requires personal tax rates to be about 7.5 percent (not 7.5 percentage *points*) higher than they otherwise could be.[24] So a lot is at stake in this debate. What are the issues?

First of all, let's consider whether there is any good economic reason to favor housing over other types of consumption or investment. To answer yes to this question requires demonstrating that an owner-occupied house provides important benefits to people other than the residents themselves; that the residents themselves take pleasure in ownership is an inadequate argument. Although undoubtedly neighbors prefer to gaze out their window at a well-kept, rather than a ramshackle, house, and owner-occupiers arguably maintain their houses better than the combination of renters and landlords, these benefits are certainly quite localized and probably fairly small. Sometimes vague appeals are made to the role of homeownership in maintaining a strong democracy, but these arguments are not convincing. Remember that to the extent that the tax system attracts investment into housing, it diverts funds from other business investments, which lowers the productivity of workers and the wages that businesses can profitably pay them. Why isn't broad stock ownership a healthy aspect of democracy? Preferential treatment of housing, in general, is difficult to justify on economic grounds.[25]

Some evidence shows that homeowners are more likely to engage in home maintenance, especially gardening. Homeowners are also more apt to join organizations and socialize with their neighbors compared to renters. In addition, homeowners are more likely to be politically informed and active than renters. All of these activities may create positive externalities. The clear correlation between homeownership and these behaviors may not be indicative of a causal relationship, however, and could instead arise from personal characteristics that make people more likely to be homeowners and also make them join more clubs, be more conscientious gardeners, and so on. [26]

In the specific case of the home mortgage interest deduction, there is a second possible rationale: it is needed to correctly measure the tax base in a comprehensive income tax. After all, to achieve a comprehensive measure of income, interest payments ought to be deductible, just as interest receipts are taxable. The catch to this argument is that, under a comprehensive income tax, the rental value of owner-occupied housing, net of depreciation and maintenance expenses, should also be subject to tax. To be sure, most homeowners don't think of the rental value of their home as income in the same way that they think of their salary and their dividend receipts. But the failure to include the services provided by housing in the tax base, in conjunction with the deductibility of mortgage interest, adds up to a big preference for residential housing.

Consider a family that is trying to decide whether to buy a $300,000 house or instead to buy a more modest $200,000 house and invest the extra $100,000 in the stock market. Suppose further that the annual rent for such houses would be 10 percent of their value and that stocks provide an annual pretax return of 10 percent, so that each would be an equally attractive investment in the absence of taxes. Buying the more expensive house will certainly make the family better off; they'll have nicer living quarters, more rooms, a better view, and so on. How much better off they are per year is approximated by the rental value of the extra housing, or $10,000 per year. Investing the $100,000 in stocks, on the other hand, will yield considerably less than $10,000 per year because of the taxes that would be due on the investment return.

The preferential tax treatment could tip the scales in favor of investing in the more expensive house. As a result, in some cases nonhousing investments are passed up in favor of more expensive homes even though, taxes aside, the return to these investments equals or exceeds the value of the housing services; from a social point of view, this is wasteful. Allowing the deductibility of mortgage interest exacerbates this problem because it enables homeowners to use tax-deductible debt to finance an investment for which the return, the rental value of the housing, is untaxed. In addition, families and individuals who, for one reason or another, prefer to rent housing, end up being penalized. Because the net rental income of landlords is taxed, rental housing does not get the same preferential tax treatment afforded to owner-occupied housing. This generates an additional source of inefficiency. Not only is there an excessive amount of housing, but some households are induced to own housing when, taxes aside, they would find it more attractive to rent housing.

The tax system also makes housing an especially attractive investment for households that do not have the liquid funds to take advantage of tax-advantaged savings vehicles such as IRAs and assets that promise to have capital gains because they can borrow against their housing, deduct the interest, and put the proceeds into a tax-preferred saving instrument. Rules attempt to prevent this, but they are almost impossible to enforce because of the difficulty of establishing the purpose of any particular mortgage balance. This kind of *tax arbitrage* is also wasteful, as it reduces revenues and causes extra complications without creating any new saving or investment.

Even if we wanted to, there is no clean and easy way to put owner-occupied housing on a level playing field with other investments. The mortgage interest deduction would be perfectly appropriate if, in addition, all homeowners were required to estimate the rental value of their housing, subtract depreciation and maintenance expenses, and report the difference as taxable income. But taxing the net rental value of housing would be complicated and imprecise. Moreover, it would undoubtedly be resisted strenuously by the public, so it is probably not a practical option. It is not inconceivable, however, as several European countries attempt to do this, albeit in a very rough fashion.[27]

A simpler approach to reducing the tax preference for housing (that is, the penalty for everything else) would be to eliminate the deduction for home mortgage interest; Canada and Germany are two countries that take this approach.[28] This would certainly make mortgage-financed housing less attractive, reducing the inefficient bias toward housing investment. But this is not a flawless option because it would eliminate the bias only for taxpayers who must borrow to finance their houses. For those who are wealthy enough (or who have wealthy-enough relatives) to pay cash, the cost of housing would still be the forgone, after-tax, return on an alternative investment. This would create an inequitable and still inefficient situation: it would cost mortgage holders the pretax rate of interest to own housing because interest is not deductible, but for wealthy individuals who need not borrow the cost would be the lower after-tax interest rate.

Thus, under an income tax, the treatment of home mortgage interest is problematic because the ideal measurement of the tax base dictates such a deduction but also requires the practically difficult step of including as taxable income the rental value of the housing itself. No such dilemma arises under a consumption tax. Although under some proposed variants of the Hall-Rabushka flat tax the deduction for mortgage interest is retained, it is completely incongruous in such a consumption tax because other interest payments are not deductible and all forms of capital income are untaxed. Indeed, the problem of tax arbitrage created by a mortgage interest deduction would be much worse in a consumption tax compared to an income tax. Homeowners would find it attractive to be as "mortgaged up" as possible, deducting the mortgage interest and simultaneously earning unlimited amounts of tax-free return from other investments. The only limit to how much you could reduce your taxes would be how much mortgage borrowing you wanted to take on. This situation would be wasteful and unfair, and it would exacerbate rather than reduce the bias toward housing investment.

The problem of measuring the rental value of owner-occupied housing can also be easily avoided under a consumption tax. A house's purchase price reflects the value of the future flow of consumption services, so taxing the purchase price effectively "prepays" the tax on that consumption. A consumption tax that treats purchasing housing just like other purchases and does not allow mortgage interest deductions would be a clean and simple way of eliminating the existing bias toward housing. Deviating from either of these prescriptions, however, could make the bias as bad or worse than it is now.

Tax preferences for owner-occupied housing are often defended on the grounds that their elimination would lead to unfair transitional effects. For example, homeowners are understandably concerned about what eliminating the mortgage interest deduction would do to house prices. By itself, eliminating the home mortgage deduction makes it more expensive to buy a house for anyone who relies on mortgage financing and could expect to itemize deductions. This would tend to reduce the demand for housing, which in turn would cause housing prices to drop. The greatest decline in demand would be for the high-priced homes that itemizers in high tax brackets generally desire, so that eliminating the tax preference for housing should shift demand from more to less expensive homes.

If, however, tax reform leads to lower interest rates, the hit to housing prices could be eased. Lower interest rates would make house buying less expensive, which would help support demand and prices. But how pretax interest rates would change is unclear and depends on whether eliminating the deduction is part of a switch to a consumption tax or a plank of income tax reform. One reason moving to a consumption tax should put downward pressure on interest rates is that a consumption tax removes tax on lenders' interest income and eliminates the deductibility of borrowers' interest payments; as a result, lenders should be willing to accept a lower pretax interest rate, and borrowers will be less willing to tolerate a high pretax interest rate. Many other factors are at work in the switch to a consumption tax that would tend to offset this effect, however. For example, because a consumption tax removes tax on the normal return to investment, firms would probably increase their demand for loanable funds, which would push up interest rates. Removing the tax preference for debt over equity would also tend to push up interest rates. In an analysis that takes many of the relevant factors into account, Martin Feldstein of Harvard University has concluded that interest rates are more likely to go up than down if the current income tax were replaced with a consumption tax.[29]

All things considered, the overall transitional impact of tax reforms on homeowners is subject to much uncertainty. Experience in the United States and other countries casts doubt on predictions of large impacts on either housing prices or the extent of homeownership. After all, dire predictions for the housing market were made about the Tax Reform Act of 1986, which made the deductibility of mortgage interest less valuable by lowering marginal tax rates, but it has been difficult to discern any negative effects on housing prices from that reform.[30] Canada has no deduction for mortgage interest at all but has about the same homeownership rate as the United States.[31] William Gale of the Brookings Institution points out that mortgage interest subsidies have been reduced dramatically in the United Kingdom since the mid-1970s, yet homeownership rates, mortgage debt, and housing as a share of the capital stock actually grew faster than in the United States.[32] Gale argues that a fundamental reform that eliminates all tax preferences for housing and moves to a consumption tax could, though, have a fairly large impact, with real house prices falling by about 7 to 10 percent in the short run and from 2 to 6 percent in the long run.

Health Care

Health care is a second area where our tax code provides very favorable treatment, and it will undoubtedly be a major source of contention in any reform effort that attempts to change it. The most important preference in this area is the exclusion from tax of employer contributions to employee medical insurance plans. In 2002, this treatment cost an estimated $99 billion in revenues, requiring personal tax rates to be 11.5 percent (not percentage points) higher than otherwise. In addition, an itemized deduction for large out-of-pocket medical care expenditures (those that exceed 7.5 percent of adjusted gross income) costs about $6 billion in revenues.[33]

Does health care merit special treatment? The most important issue is that health insurance is plagued by serious market failures arising from imperfect information.[34] First, a problem of *adverse selection* arises in an open market for health insurance. Because individuals know more about their health risks and status than insurers do, the insurance company charges a premium based on the average level of risk for a particular population and in some cases a perfunctory medical examination. Some healthier, lower-risk people will find this price unattractive and leave the market, which increases the average risk level of people left in the insurance pool. This in turn pushes up premiums, driving out even more low-risk people, and a vicious cycle ensues. As a result, many people end up without insurance, even though the insurance could be both valuable to the buyer and profitable for the insurance company in the absence of this problem. The system of employer-provided insurance helps mitigate the adverse selection problem, since employees work for firms for reasons generally unrelated to health risks, so that an insurance provider has reason to expect that any firm's employees are a mix of high-risk and low-risk people. Nevertheless, adverse selection is a serious problem for people who are not covered by employer-provided insurance and are charged high premium rates. It is also arguably responsible for the complete absence of a market for long-term contracts for health insurance that would be fully portable across jobs and would not skyrocket in price if you develop a chronic illness *after* purchasing it. All in all, the tax preference for employer-provided health care serves to offset the adverse selection problem that would otherwise plague this market.

A second market failure associated with health insurance is known as *moral hazard*. This means that because health insurance changes the incentives faced by insured people, they may change their behavior in a way that drives up expenditures on health care. For instance, since most people with insurance face a low or zero out-of-pocket price for additional medical services, they may consume extra medical services for which the true social costs (which are higher than their out-of-pocket costs) exceeds the benefits.

Special treatment of health care might also be justified by equity objectives. The itemized deduction for medical expenditures is consistent with horizontal equity concerns; people who experience large, unavoidable, out-of-pocket medical costs are deemed to have a lower ability to pay. A desire to redistribute resources to the poor in the form of health care might be motivated by vertical equity concerns. In some cases, voters may prefer redistribution for a specific meritorious (in their eyes) purpose such as health care over redistribution that can be used for any purpose, meritorious or not. Moreover, low-income uninsured people often end up getting care anyway—for example, through uncompensated care from a public or charitable hospital. This creates a kind of moral hazard problem by reducing the incentive to buy insurance. While such care does help the poor who receive it, both the benefits and the costs are distributed in a capricious fashion. For instance, whether a particular uninsured individual has access to uncompensated care is largely a matter of luck, and the costs may be borne through higher insurance premiums for certain people or perhaps lower compensation for health-care providers who happen to be willing to work in certain areas. Arguably, a more systematic government policy could provide a fairer and more efficient way of helping the poor than uncompensated care.

Although solid rationales can be found for some form of government intervention in the market for health care, the current tax treatment of health insurance is poorly designed for addressing these problems and may even make some of them worse. To the extent that helping low-income people afford health insurance is the goal, we now go about achieving that goal backward. The tax exclusion of employer-provided health insurance provides no help to people whose incomes are too low to pay taxes, and it provides very large amounts of help to those high-income people who have high marginal tax rates.

The exclusion is also inefficient because it provides an incentive not only to buy health insurance in the first place (which may be desirable) but also to buy the most expensive health insurance possible (which is not). Consider an employee who faces a 50 percent marginal tax rate, which is not unrealistic when federal and state income taxes are combined with employer and employee Social Security tax rates. If an employer wants to give that worker $50 more in net-of-tax compensation, the firm would pay only $50 to grant that compensation in the form of a better health insurance policy but $100 to provide compensation in the form of a higher cash salary. This creates a strong incentive for employers to offer, and employees to prefer, much more generous health benefits than otherwise, which exacerbates the moral hazard problem considerably, leading to some wasteful expenditures on medical care.

For these reasons, eliminating or capping the exclusion from tax of employer-provided medical benefits is often a feature of proposals for health reform as well as tax reform. Many economists believe that if we want to help people afford health insurance, providing a voucher or credit of a fixed amount would be much more sensible than having a tax exclusion. This would give an equal dollar amount of subsidy to everyone and would eliminate the incentive to buy expensive policies. Either capping the exclusion or offering a credit would certainly not solve all the problems in the health-care market. For instance, this voucher plan does little to address the adverse selection problem, and special care would need to be taken in designing such a voucher plan to avoid weakening the incentive for employers to provide group insurance plans, or that problem could become even worse. But a carefully designed voucher or tax-credit program for health insurance still has many advantages over the current tax exclusion.

Although the itemized deduction for extraordinary medical expenditures can be justified as an appropriate adjustment for ability-to-pay, it too creates an incentive to avoid economizing on health-care expenditures, and it adds some complication to the tax system. Some advantages would be gained by rolling all of the tax system's health-care assistance into a single coherent policy instead of having numerous different provisions that sometimes duplicate each other.

Many proposals for fundamental tax reform would eliminate preferences for health-care and insurance expenditures altogether. This is one reason that they can apparently feature such a low single rate of tax. Such a change would be politically difficult, and moreover, the plans typically do not provide anything else that would help address health-care problems in a more rational fashion as a replacement. During the 2000 presidential campaign, George W. Bush advocated the introduction of tax credits for low-income people to purchase health insurance but did not propose any changes to the existing exclusion for employer-provided insurance.[35]

Charitable Contributions

Under current law, charitable contributions to qualifying organizations are deductible from taxable income for those who itemize deductions. Let's subject to our two-tiered test this provision, which is in effect a penalty on those who are not charitably inclined. First, are charitable contributions an indication that the contributing family is less well off than their income would suggest? Some would argue yes—that people who make charitable contributions are sacrificing some of their own well-being for moral purposes. However, these are voluntary contributions. The contributors must be getting some satisfaction from the act of giving, otherwise they would not have done so. Perhaps they are motivated by the "warm glow" they feel when they help others. So their level of well-being is really no different than that of people with equal incomes who don't give to charity. If that is the case, we cannot invoke an ability-to-pay justification.

Test number two is whether there is something inherent about charity that justifies subsidies to encourage charitable giving. In this case, the answer is arguably yes, as charitable contributions involve positive externalities. Charitable contributions provide benefits to people who do not make contributions themselves. For example, many noncontributors might feel better knowing that charities provide food and shelter for homeless families. But in these cases, people have an incentive to free ride on the contributions of others; economists call such a situation a public goods problem. Charitable giving still occurs because some people are motivated by the satisfaction they receive from giving, but because of free-riding, an inefficiently low amount of giving is done. To the extent this occurs, an extra incentive from the tax code may lead to a higher level of charitable activity that makes everyone better off. Of course, another approach would be for the government to provide the public goods directly, instead of relying on private contributions. However, some things that are arguably public goods would tend to be underprovided by the combination of government and unsubsidized charity. For example, the U.S. government could not contribute directly to religious institutions because of the constitutionally mandated separation of church and state, and some public goods that are valued only by a minority of the population might not be provided by a majority-rule government. Some argue, in addition, that private charitable contributions are a more efficient and less intrusive way of financing public goods such as aid to the poor than is government intervention. In an age of government cutbacks, this argument becomes more relevant.

The charitable contribution deduction is not without its costs, however. In 2002, it reduced income tax revenues by about $39 billion. It adds to complexity and recordkeeping requirements. A broad array of activities qualify as "charity," so there's no guarantee that the gifts will go to areas that really deserve to be subsidized by the tax system. For example, only a small portion of subsidized giving goes to help the poor; much of it goes to higher education and cultural institutions, which may or may not deserve subsidy. Contributions can also be difficult to monitor, so unfortunately some inequity arises from cheating. Finally, evidence suggests that the deduction has only a moderate impact on the amount of giving, so some of the revenue loss serves as a reward to giving that would have occurred anyway. For example, the Tax Reform Act of 1986 significantly reduced the incentive for high-income people to give to charity by sharply reducing their marginal tax rates. High-income people may have reduced the share of their income devoted to charity as a result, but not by very much.[36]

On balance, some form of incentive for charity may be justified. Even so, justifying why the rate of subsidy should be tied to the donor's tax rate and be zero for taxpayers who do not itemize or who have incomes below the filing threshold is difficult. This is the pattern of subsidy that the deduction for giving creates. More appropriate might be a fixed credit per dollar donated rather than a deduction, so that we are subsidizing all of our charitable contributions at the same rate and not subsidizing more heavily the contributions of affluent taxpayers.[37]

State and Local Government Taxes and Bonds

Two important preferences in our tax code have to do with state and local governments. The itemized deduction for tax payments (other than retail sales tax) to state and local governments costs the federal government about $69 billion in revenues. The exclusion from federal income tax of interest on state and local government bonds costs an estimated $30 billion.[38] Are these features justifiable?

One potential rationale for the deductibility of state and local taxes is that families that have the same income but live in high-tax states and municipalities have less ability to pay and therefore should pay fewer federal taxes than families who live in low-tax places. The flaw in this argument is that people who live in high-tax states presumably benefit from a higher level of public expenditures. Why should someone who chooses to live in a low-tax state and make do with fewer government services be penalized for that choice? Of course, the relationship between state and local taxes and the benefits from public services is certainly not one-to-one. So the ability-to-pay argument against deductibility has some merit, although it is limited.

Another problem with the deduction is that it provides an inefficient subsidy to state and local spending. The cost to (itemizing) taxpayers of a dollar of such spending is less than a dollar because part of the cost is shifted to taxpayers in other states. On the margin, this may encourage state and local governments to undertake projects that would not meet taxpayer approval in the absence of the tax incentive and that use up resources that would be more efficiently used for other purposes. Moreover, because it is linked to itemized deductions, this subsidy is larger for governments who have relatively more high-income (and therefore high-tax-rate, itemizing) residents.

Such a subsidy for state and local expenditures might be desirable if those expenditures provide benefits that spread beyond the state's or municipality's borders. In this case, some expenditures that are worthwhile from the country's perspective might not be enacted by a state or local government. This argument certainly does not apply for many expenditures, such as garbage collection or municipal swimming pools. It could arguably apply to primary education on the grounds that it builds an "educated citizenry," which benefits all Americans. This argument has some intuitive appeal but is hard to prove. Even granting that argument, it applies only to a subset of what state and local governments do, and it does not justify the general deductibility of state and local taxes. Nor does it justify effectively giving a larger subsidy to more affluent communities where the residents have higher tax rates.

On balance, if tax reform results in the elimination of deductions for state and local taxes, this would not be a major loss. Although these deductions have some merit as an adjustment for ability to pay and perhaps as an encouragement of certain worthy public expenditures, it also involves significant inefficiency, unfairness, and complexity.[39]

Some of these same arguments apply to the exclusion of interest on state and local bonds. In this case, there is no ability-to-pay rationale because the decision to buy the bonds is entirely voluntary. The main effect of the interest exclusion is to subsidize debt-financed expenditures in the states and municipalities because it enables these governments to borrow money at a lower interest rate than otherwise. High-tax-rate investors are willing to accept the lower interest rates because they pay no tax on the interest; the increased demand by investors drives up the prices of these bonds or, in other words, pushes the yields on these bonds down near the after-tax rate of interest offered on similar, but taxable, bonds.

Not all of the benefits of the interest exclusion go to state and local governments, however. If all potential buyers of these bonds had the same tax rate—say, 20 percent—the interest rates on the bonds would end up being about 20 percent lower than on other bonds, so the purchasers would gain little or no benefit. Their *implicit* tax would equal the *explicit* tax on other investments. But in a system of graduated rates, to sell all the bonds that state and local governments want to issue, the rate of interest must be high enough to attract not only those taxpayers with the highest tax rate—currently 35 percent—but also many investors with lower tax rates. This means that taxpayers in the top tax brackets benefit because they can invest at a higher after-tax rate of return than otherwise.

Given that the case for subsidizing state and local expenditures is shaky, the interest exclusion seems hard to justify. Because a substantial portion of the subsidy represents a windfall to very high-income people, it is even harder to justify. An alternative to both the exclusion of bond interest and the deductibility of tax payments that would avoid these problems would be for the federal government to provide direct subsidies to these governments for the intended class of expenditures. This idea has always been resisted by states and municipalities, largely due to their fear that once the tax preference becomes a straightforward appropriation, it could more easily go onto the budget chopping block. This is a good example of how the tax system can sustain implicit subsidies that would not survive as equivalent stand-alone programs.

The Standard Deduction and Rough Justice

To this point, we have addressed the most important itemized deductions. Recall, though, that only about one-third of all taxpayers deduct these expenses and that these are predominantly affluent families. This is because all taxpayers are offered the option of bypassing the itemizing process and instead receiving a *standard deduction*, which varies only by marital status. In 2003, the standard deduction amounted to $9,500 for a married couple filing jointly and $4,750 for a single taxpayer.

The standard deduction makes sense because it would not be cost-efficient for the IRS to have to monitor and occasionally audit the deductions claimed by the 85 million or so taxpayers who do not now itemize, not to mention the cost in time and expense of these taxpayers having to keep track of their expenses. By having a standard deduction, however, the tax system loses its ability to finely differentiate among taxpayers with differing abilities to pay. As it stands now, two otherwise identical families, both with $30,000 of income and both taking the standard deduction, owe the same tax even though one family has incurred $5,000 in medical expenses and the other hasn't. Although in principle the tax system allows extraordinary medical expenses to reduce income subject to tax, in practice we settle for "rough justice" by differentiating tax liability only when relatively large sums of money are involved.

If some or all itemized deductions end up being retained, a larger standard deduction could still simplify taxpaying for many people by cutting down on the number of itemizers. This could save substantial administrative and compliance costs. It would mean settling for even more rough justice, but the trade-off might be worth it. One simplifying change that would cost no revenue would be to couple a reduction or elimination of personal exemption allowances for the adults in a family with a corresponding increase in the standard deduction. Similarly, if some itemized deductions are retained in a flat tax, the family allowance could be treated as a large standard deduction.

Conclusion

This chapter has addressed the policy issues that arise in contemplating any major tax reform. As with most contentious policy choices, the contemplated changes often require a balancing among the desirable characteristics of a tax system. The next two chapters examine specific proposals for overhauling the tax system. All of these proposals involve some combination of the three elements discussed in this chapter—a single rate (or at least low marginal rates), a consumption base, and a clean base. Each of these three elements of tax reform is conceptually and practically distinct from the others, so that a reform could achieve any or all to varying degrees.

What Are the Alternatives?

This chapter and the next examine specific proposals for improving the tax system. Options for replacing the current system entirely with a tax based on consumption—including the retail sales tax, the value added tax (VAT), the "flat tax," and the personal consumption tax—are addressed in this chapter. Each of these proposals would represent a truly sweeping change in the way we tax ourselves, and they have recently attracted much more attention than in previous rounds of soul-searching about reform.

First, we explain how each of these four varieties of consumption taxation works, and why they are all close relatives in spite of different appearances. Second, to make the discussion more concrete, the chapter examines the tax rates that would have to be levied to make up for the revenue lost from the income tax. With this as background, we can then move on to how to evaluate the consumption tax approaches and how they stack up to the current system. Since each of the four approaches to consumption taxation can achieve the same basic economic goal—removing taxation's negative impact on the reward for saving—a choice among them must depend on other factors. As is so often the case with issues as complex as this one, the devil is in the details. Deciding which approach is best depends crucially on administrative factors—simplicity and enforceability—and the ease with which the tax base can be adjusted for ability to pay. This chapter shows that the VAT and flat tax emerge as superior to the other choices for simplification and enforcement reasons. Moreover, if you are concerned at all about the tax burdens placed on low-income people, the flat tax, perhaps modified to include progressive rates, appears to be the best choice among consumption taxes. Finally, we consider estimates of the distributional and economic effects of some specific proposals to start the tax system over from scratch.

How the Consumption Tax Plans Work

Since the four consumption tax approaches appear on the surface to be quite different, their essential similarity is often completely misunderstood. Moreover, each of these basic alternatives could be adopted with either a clean or a messy base and with a single rate or with measures to make it more progressive. Specific proposals in the political arena vary greatly on these latter details.

How a Retail Sales Tax Works

The most familiar type of consumption tax is the retail sales tax (RST), now levied by all but five states and by many cities and counties at rates that range in most cases from 4 to 6 percent. Billy Tauzin, a congressman from Louisiana, has been touting the RST as a replacement for personal and corporate income taxes, as did some of the candidates in the 1996 and 2000 Republican presidential primaries.[1] A well-financed lobbying campaign has been trying to drum up support for this idea.

The retail sales tax is a tax remitted by businesses on all sales to consumers. Thus, it excludes from tax all goods and services sold to other businesses for use as an input to what they produce. As discussed later, this is one area where, in practice, the retail sales tax often runs into trouble.

A pure, clean-base, single-rate retail sales tax would tax *all* sales of both goods and services to consumers. It would be a completely "impersonal" tax in the sense that the rate of tax would not be adjusted to account for any characteristic of the consumer, such as income, marital status, number of dependents, or personal tastes. In practice, most states exempt certain items, such as food and medicine, in an attempt to exempt "necessities" and ease the burden on the poor. Many items, particularly certain services, are also exempt in practice because they are difficult to tax. Some states even charge different sales tax rates on different items or allow certain customers, such as the elderly or the poor, to apply for refunds.[2] If production inputs are successfully excluded from tax and the broadest possible array of goods and services is taxed, the aggregate tax base is the total value of final sales to consumers (that is, aggregate consumption). Recall from chapter 3 that, administrative and compliance issues aside, who writes the checks and which side of a transaction bears legal liability for a tax on a given base do not ultimately matter for either the economic ramifications or for who bears the burden of the tax. This point is critical to keep in mind when investigating some other tax systems that, judging from their mechanics, look to be very different from a retail sales tax but in fact are close relatives.

How a Value Added Tax Works

One close relative to the sales tax is the value added tax, widely known by its acronym, *VAT* (generally pronounced to rhyme with *flat*). The VAT has been a staple of European tax systems since the late 1960s and is now levied in almost every industrialized country in the world and over 120 countries worldwide.[3] As Sijbren Cnossen of Erasmus University in Rotterdam has remarked, "The nearly universal introduction of the value added tax should be considered the most important event in the evolution of tax structure in the last half of the twentieth century."[4] Most countries that adopted a VAT used the revenues to replace either retail sales taxes or general business taxes that they had decided were deeply flawed.

In the aggregate, the VAT features exactly the same base as the retail sales tax—total final sales from businesses to consumers. The difference is entirely in the mechanics of how the money is remitted from the private sector to the government. Although the retail sales tax collects money all at the retail stage, the VAT collects money in pieces, firm by firm, as businesses sell to consumers along the production and distribution chain. The tax base for a firm under a VAT is simple—total sales revenue minus the cost of purchased inputs, where the definition of purchased inputs does *not* include payments to labor but does include purchases of material inputs and capital goods. So unlike the income tax, investment in machinery, factories, and other capital goods is expensed (deducted immediately) under a VAT instead of being deducted over several years through depreciation allowances. If investment goods were depreciated rather than being immediately deductible by the firms that purchase them, the aggregate tax base would be consumption plus net investment: in other words, it would be a form of income tax instead of a consumption tax.[5]

A simple example can help show why the tax base for a VAT is equal to final sales of goods and services to consumers, just as it is for a retail sales tax. Say you go to a bakery and buy a loaf of bread for $2. Under a retail sales tax, the tax base is simply $2 (assuming, of course, food isn't exempt). To illustrate the VAT, let's greatly simplify the process of making bread into just two steps. First, suppose there is a farmer who grows wheat, grinds it into flour, and sells it to the baker for $1. Then the baker turns the flour into dough, bakes it into bread, and sells it to you for $2. The value added by the baker is $1—the sale price of the bread minus the cost of the flour. Under the VAT, the tax base is $1 for the farmer and $1 for the baker, adding up to a total of $2, the same tax base as under the retail sales tax. The example could be complicated by adding the cost of other ingredients, an oven, a tractor and seeds for the farmer, a separate flour company, and so on, but the net result would turn out to be identical: the tax base would still be $2.

On the surface, the retail sales tax might appear to be a tax paid by consumers, and the VAT a tax paid by businesses. But again, the only difference is how the remittance of the tax base to the government is divided up among various parts of the transaction, which ultimately can't make any difference for who bears the burden of the tax or its economic effects. And don't forget that "business" can't bear the burden: only people can. What's more, if you've ever been to Europe or Canada, you know that a VAT need not even look different from a retail sales tax to the consumers. The VAT (in Canada it's called the *goods and services tax*, or GST) generally appears right on top of the sales price whenever you buy something. For instance, if the country has a 10 percent VAT, your cash register receipt will show the before-tax sales price and then tack on the 10 percent VAT, just like it does with a retail sales tax in the United States.[6] Some advocates of a national retail sales tax have argued that it would somehow be more inherently "visible" to the consumer than a VAT, but they are mistaken.

There are a couple of different ways that a VAT can be implemented. Under the rarely used *subtraction method*, the VAT is administered like a corporation income tax. Every year (or quarter), a firm's accountants report to the government the total amount of sales, subtract the total cost of purchased inputs, and pay tax on the difference.[7]

Virtually every country that has a VAT uses a second approach, known as the *credit-invoice* method. Under this approach, the VAT is administered more like a sales tax; tax is charged on each individual transaction. With a 10 percent VAT, every sale a firm makes incurs a 10 percent VAT, as does every purchase it makes from other firms.[8] An "invoice," which records the amount of tax charged, is required for each transaction. Periodically (often monthly), the business remits to the government the amount of VAT due on its sales, less the amount of VAT that was due on its own purchases. In other words, it gets "credit" for the amount of tax that was remitted by the businesses it buys from.

Under this approach, the net amount of tax remitted by each firm to the government is identical to the tax that would be remitted under the subtraction method, but there's more of a paper trail. If a business is audited, it must have invoices to back up the credits it claims: it needs to prove that the VAT has been remitted on its purchases. Thus, firms have an incentive to purchase goods and services from tax-law-abiding suppliers; otherwise, they may get no credit for their expenditures.

Another mechanical feature of a VAT that is often misunderstood involves the treatment of imports and exports. Most countries "rebate" VAT on exported goods; in other words, the VAT is not levied on the value of goods sold to other countries. Imported goods, on the other hand, are subject to the VAT by the country into which they are imported because imports are not treated as deductible inputs. Some observers in the United States have envied this aspect of the VAT, viewing it as an ingenious export promotion scheme; they are, though, simply confused. As explained in detail in chapter 4, no VAT nor any other tax system can so simply give us any kind of "edge" in international competition.[9]

Finally, like the retail sales tax, the VAT is often much messier in practice than it is in theory. For example, many countries levy preferential or zero rates on certain "necessary" or hard-to-tax goods and services, exempt some kinds of businesses from the tax net altogether, and levy special high rates on luxury goods.[10]

If a VAT is equivalent to a retail sales tax, except that more businesses are involved in the collection process, why go through all the extra trouble? There must be some reason because just about every country that ever had a sales tax has abandoned it in favor of the VAT. In a nutshell, the answer is that the retail sales tax suffers from important administrative and enforcement problems that are greatly magnified as the rate gets higher, while the VAT minimizes these problems in clever ways. Most tax experts believe that a retail sales tax large enough to replace our personal and corporate income taxes would be unadministrable but that a VAT of that size could be run (and *has* been run) fairly smoothly. Later in this chapter, when we discuss the simplicity and enforceability aspects of consumption taxes, we explain why.

How the Hall-Rabushka Flat Tax Works

The VAT is seldom mentioned in the popular media in the United States, and in recent years no national political figure has supported it. Nevertheless, it is important to understand how a VAT works because the "flat tax" that has gained so much attention lately *is* essentially a VAT. What is this "flat tax"?

The original flat tax was developed in 1981 by economist Robert E. Hall and political scientist Alvin Rabushka, both of Stanford University. It was laid out in their 1983 book *Low Tax, Simple Tax, Flat Tax* (renamed *The Flat Tax* in its 1995 edition), which has come to be known as the flat tax bible. Hall and Rabushka first attracted attention by claiming that flat tax returns could fit on a postcard. For most of its short life, the flat tax had a devoted but small band of supporters. It formed the basis of a few proposals introduced in Congress during the years leading up to the Tax Reform Act of 1986, but the proposals soon fell from serious consideration. But the flat tax really hit the public consciousness after the Republicans took control of Congress in the 1994 elections. The House majority leader at the time, Richard Armey (R-TX), and Senator Richard Shelby (R-AL) introduced legislation based on the Hall-Rabushka plan in Congress in 1995, and flat tax stories soon proliferated in the popular media. Steve Forbes then made it the centerpiece of his bid for the 1996 (and 2000) Republican presidential nomination. Numerous other politicians have now proposed plans that have at least one element of flatness discussed in chapter 6—a single rate, a consumption base, or a clean base. But the innovative design of the Hall-Rabushka plan, which involves all three elements of "flatness," has earned it the right to be called *the* flat tax.

Readers vaguely familiar with the flat tax may be surprised that we lump it together with the retail sales tax and the VAT. The flat tax looks a lot more like the current income tax system than either of the other two, mostly because along with a tax remitted by businesses it imposes a separate tax on individuals, who must annually file returns, albeit simple ones. Recall that under either a sales tax or a VAT, individuals are completely outside the tax system and need never fill out and send in personal tax returns.

Although the flat tax looks superficially like our existing income tax, it is fundamentally different. It is a reconfigured VAT or, in other words, a reconfigured sales tax. Under the flat tax, businesses pay tax on their total sales, minus purchases of material inputs and investment goods (which are deducted immediately), just like a VAT—with only one main difference. Unlike a VAT, the flat tax also allows firms to deduct payments of wages and salaries (but not fringe benefits) to their workers. Now comes the key innovation of the flat tax. Although, unlike a VAT, wages and salaries are deductible by employers, these same wages and salaries are then taxed separately, at the same rate as the business tax, at the personal level. Thus the flat tax simply takes payments to employees out of the business tax base and makes them part of the employees' tax base. This is where the discussion of "tax incidence" back in chapter 3 leads to a truly surprising insight. Which side of a transaction is technically subject to the tax—in this case, the employer or the employee—ultimately makes no difference, so a Hall-Rabushka flat tax with a single rate and no exemptions is no different than a VAT or a comprehensive sales tax.

That the flat tax is a consumption tax (in sheep's or wolves' clothing, depending on your point of view) is not widely understood. For example, none other than recently retired House Ways and Means chair Bill Archer, who favors a consumption tax, rejects the flat tax, saying, "In my common sense, if your wages are going to be taxed before you get them, that's an income tax."[11] Widely accepted economic theory makes clear that whether a tax on the flow of labor is remitted by the employer or the employee makes no fundamental difference to the impact of the tax, regardless of what one calls it.

If a flat tax is just a VAT in disguise, why go through the extra trouble of having employees fill out returns and pay tax on their wages and salaries? The main reason is that this scheme allows some adjustment of individual tax liabilities according to ability to pay. The individual wage portion of most flat tax proposals features a large family allowance, similar to but larger than today's standard deduction, as well as personal exemptions. Thus, people with low wage and salary income are exempt from tax, at least at the personal level. As illustrated in the last chapter, the ratio of personal tax to labor income gradually increases from zero for families with labor income at or below the exemption, up to close to the uniform flat rate for high-income families. This means that the flat tax is more progressive than a value added tax. Having a standard deduction and personal exemptions is a much simpler and more efficient method of introducing progressivity than would be possible under either a sales tax or a VAT.

Although the Hall-Rabushka flat tax is quite similar to a VAT, it differs critically from the existing personal income tax. As in the current system, pension contributions would be deductible by businesses, and benefits paid would be included in the recipients' taxable income. Just two kinds of payments would be reported on the personal tax return: (1) wages and salaries and (2) pension receipts. That's it. All of the other components of what we are used to being part of taxable income—interest, dividends, capital gains, rents, royalties, and so on—would be completely exempt from tax at the personal level.[12] All of the familiar deductions and credits would also be eliminated, including the deduction for mortgage interest payments, charitable contributions, state and local taxes, and medical expenses.

The business portion of the flat tax is radically different from the current corporation income tax. For one thing, all businesses, not just corporations, would remit this tax. So instead of sole proprietorships and partnerships reporting their income on Form 1040 as they do now, this income would be subject to a separate business tax. One implication of this is that noncorporate business losses could not offset wage and salary income.

The business tax base would also be quite different than it is now, especially in three key ways. First, in keeping with the consumption tax concept, capital expenditures would be deducted immediately when made instead of generating deductions as they depreciate. (On enactment of a flat tax, all remaining depreciation deductions for past investments would be disallowed unless special transition rules were introduced.) Second, interest payments (and other financial outflows) would no longer be deductible, nor would interest receipts (and financial inflows) be subject to tax.[13] In the absence of transition rules, deductions for interest payments due on past borrowing would also be disallowed. Third, employer contributions to Social Security, health insurance, and other nonpension benefits would no longer be deductible by businesses, nor would tax payments to state and local governments. All would therefore be subject to the flat rate of tax.

The essence of what distinguishes the Hall-Rabushka flat tax from all other plans is the way it defines the tax base, dividing a VAT into a business component and a wage component. Many of its details could be changed, while retaining its essential character. For example, certain itemized deductions could be allowed under the wage tax. The base could even be subject to graduated rates. A flat tax with deductions and multiples rates may sound like a contradiction in terms, but such a system arguably retains many of the advantages of the idea but can deliver a more progressive and finely tuned distribution of that burden.

On the other hand, many reform proposals that have been labeled "flat" involve a fundamentally different tax base. For example, in the 1996 Republican presidential primaries, Phil Gramm and Pat Buchanan proposed "flat taxes" that included interest, capital gains, and other capital income in the personal tax base and did not change the taxation of business income in the ways described above. These plans are not consumption taxes but rather income taxes. To keep things straight, whenever we refer to *flat tax* in this chapter, we are talking about taxes with a consumption tax base, as in the original Hall-Rabushka proposal.

How a Personal Consumption Tax Works

A fourth approach to consumption taxation goes by a number of different names, such as the *savings-exempt tax*, the *consumed income tax*, or the *personal consumption tax*. In this alternative, consumption is measured person by person. No, it doesn't require each household to keep track of everything it buys.[14] Instead, it makes use of the fact that consumption equals income minus saving and requires taxpayers to calculate not only income but also net saving.

A personal consumption tax includes all income in the individual tax base—wages and salaries, net interest receipts, dividends, and capital gains realizations, and so forth—and allows an unlimited deduction for all net new savings. Think of this as an unlimited, unrestricted traditional individual retirement account (IRA) that allows for the deduction of net additions to savings accounts, investments in stocks, bonds, mutual funds, life insurance, and other assets. Unlike IRAs, there would be no annual limit on deductions, nor would there be any penalties for withdrawals before retirement, although like IRAs, withdrawals from the accounts would be taxable at the taxpayer's marginal rate. All new borrowing must be subtracted from saving because borrowing is simply "dissaving." For example, if you were to borrow $10,000 and then put that money into a bank account, your net saving wouldn't have increased at all, so such a transaction shouldn't be allowed to affect your tax liability. Under a personal consumption tax, the borrowing would exactly offset the addition to the bank account, so no deduction would be allowed.

Although sketches and blueprints of personal consumption taxes have been around for a while, the one fleshed-out version is the USA tax, where the USA stands for unlimited savings allowance.[15] In 1995, a bill to replace the current personal and corporate income taxes with the USA tax was put forward by former Georgia senator Sam Nunn and Senator Pete Domenici of New Mexico. It featured a personal exemption and standard deduction similar in size to today's system, plus a graduated three-rate structure. The USA tax base allowed a deduction for charitable giving and mortgage interest and excluded interest on state and local bonds. The USA tax also included a business tax akin to a VAT, although a VAT is not a necessary component of a personal consumption tax.

The USA tax excluded certain types of borrowing, such as a home mortgage, from the calculation of net saving. Moreover, elaborate transition rules were devised. These rules allowed a certain amount of past savings to be withdrawn without being counted as "dissaving," and they also allowed businesses to continue taking depreciation deductions on past investments. Both this treatment of borrowing and the transition rules would create opportunities for complex avoidance schemes, which we address later. Although the USA tax has largely dropped off of the radar screen in recent years, the continued expansion of IRAs and other tax-preferred saving vehicles in the current tax code could move us closer to this kind of tax.

At What Rate?

Consumption tax advocates often advertise rates that look low compared to the current income tax. Unfortunately, at the advertised rates the government would collect less revenue than the current system and in some cases a lot less. Of course, this can make any tax system look attractive indeed. This section focuses on the rates that would be required for the consumption tax alternatives to raise the same amount of revenue as the current corporate and personal tax system—so-called *revenue-neutral* rates.

Any discussion of tax rates needs to be clear about how the tax rate is calculated, since equivalent taxes can appear quite different if the tax rate is defined differently. Rates of sales tax or VAT are often quoted as a percentage of the price of a good excluding the tax—that is, on a *tax-exclusive basis*. Income tax rates, personal consumption tax rates, and flat tax rates are all generally quoted as a percentage of the tax base including the tax—that is, on a *tax-inclusive basis*. So, for example, if $20 of retail sales tax is charged on a good that costs $100 exclusive of the tax (so that you pay a total of $120, including tax, at the cash register), we'll say the rate is 20 percent. But an equivalent flat tax rate would be reported as 16.67 (= 100*(20/120)) percent.

If any one of the four consumption tax proposals was somehow able to tax all personal consumption expenditures in the United States with a single rate and no exemptions whatsoever, the revenue-neutral rate in 2001 would have to have been about 16.4 percent (tax-exclusive) or

14.1 percent (tax-inclusive).[16] In practice, however, a higher rate would be needed to make it be revenue-neutral. First of all, many types of consumption are difficult to tax and almost certainly would not be included in the tax base. Moreover, there will always be some evasion. As already discussed, several hundred billion dollars of taxable income now goes unreported. Although reducing evasion might be possible under an alternative system, undoubtedly a significant amount will persist. Finally, some consumption tax proposals purposely have exemptions from the base in an effort to ease the tax burden on those with low incomes; these exemptions must lead to higher rates of tax on what is not exempt.

How high would the rate have to go in practice? First, consider the retail sales tax. The revenue-neutral tax rate depends heavily on how extensive the tax base is. Among the states, it is common to exempt medical expenditures (including insurance), food for home consumption, clothing, the imputed rental value of housing, religious and charitable activities, and most services. If the federal sales tax base were to look like that of the average state, replacing the personal and corporate income taxes in 2001 would require a tax-exclusive rate of about 26.9 percent.[17] Emulating the states with the very broadest sales tax bases could lower the rate to perhaps 18.8 percent.[18] At that level of coverage, the sales tax would fully tax food, which is the most expensive exemption, comprising nearly a quarter of potential sales tax revenue.[19]

Both of these figures are gross underestimates for a *clean* national sales tax rate, however, because a great deal of state sales tax revenue comes from purchases of business inputs, which are supposed to be exempt from a retail sales tax. One recent study[20] estimated that on average only 59 percent of state sales tax revenues came from final purchases by resident consumers; almost all of the rest represented taxation of business inputs. Taxing business inputs with a retail sales tax is economically harmful and becomes much more so as the tax rate gets higher. If business inputs were to be completely eliminated from the base and the base was that of a typical state, the national rate would almost certainly have to be at least 30 percent and would possibly approach 40 percent.

This is a far cry from the rates that advocates have been quoting, such as the 1997 proposal by Congressmen Dan Schaefer (R-CO) and Billy Tauzin (R-LA) for a 15 percent sales tax, which they claim would produce enough revenue to replace not only personal and corporate income taxes but also excise taxes and the estate tax. To ease the burden on low-income people, the plan would rebate to all households the sales tax liability on an amount of consumption equal to the poverty threshold. The 15 percent rate is misleadingly low for many different reasons. First of all, unlike the standard practice for sales taxes, they report the rate on a tax-*inclusive* basis. Moreover, they would impose sales tax not only on personal consumption expenditures but also on government purchases (which implies a very large reduction in real government spending), and they assume that the national sales tax base would essentially include all consumption, with no avoidance, evasion, or special exemptions, except for education. William Gale of the Brookings Institution calculates that if government purchases and transfer payments were adjusted to keep their real value constant in the face of sales-tax-induced price increases, and 30 percent of the tax base were eroded by avoidance, evasion, and exemptions, the tax rate required for the Schaefer-Tauzin plan would be 37.4 percent (tax-inclusive), or *59.8* percent on a tax-exclusive basis![21]

In principle, because the VAT base is the same as the retail sales tax base, the same calculations for estimating the revenue-neutral rate should apply. In practice, the VAT does a much better job of avoiding the taxation of business inputs and probably generates considerably less evasion. Still, many types of consumption would be difficult, if not impossible, to tax under either a sales tax or a VAT. Just two among many examples are the imputed rental value of the existing housing stock and the value of financial services that are paid for through lower interest rates rather than fees. Estimates done by the Congressional Budget Office suggest that a comprehensive VAT, which provided no special treatment for purchases of food or housing, could successfully tax about 81 percent of personal consumption expenditures. A base of this size implies that a rate of about 20.2 percent (tax-exclusive) would be required to replace federal revenue from the individual and corporate income tax systems in 2001.[22] This calculation, however, does not include any measures to provide relief to the poor or to provide preferential treatment to certain types of consumption (which are common in most real-world VATs) and involves a significant reduction in the real purchasing power of government transfer payments. As with the retail sales tax, addressing any of these issues could push the revenue-neutral VAT rate dramatically higher.

A flat tax requires a higher rate than a VAT because the family allowances in the flat tax reduce the tax base significantly and because the flat tax exempts a large amount of wealth—for example, owner-occupied housing—from the transitional tax on preexisting wealth. On the other hand, the labor income of government employees would be taxed under the flat tax but not necessarily under a VAT.

In their book on the flat tax, Hall and Rabushka propose a tax-inclusive rate of 19 percent on individuals and businesses and set the exempt level of income for a family of four at $25,500 for 1995.[23] They present a calculation suggesting this plan would have raised as much revenue as the current tax system at that time. As they admit, their calculation is "back-of-the-envelope" and assumes no evasion; it also involves a few small errors.[24] Using a methodology based on actual tax returns, the U.S. Treasury Department has calculated more reliable estimates for a number of related but slightly different flat tax proposals. They estimate that the Armey-Shelby version, which has a $31,400 exemption for a family of four in 1996 and would eliminate the EITC and estate and gift taxes, would require a rate of 20.8 percent to be revenue-neutral; the same plan could achieve a 17 percent rate if the allowance for a family of four were reduced to $15,000.[25] Adding back in some itemized deductions or changing the tax base in other ways could raise the revenue-neutral rate for a flat tax significantly. For instance, allowing deductibility of home mortgage interest and charitable deductions would push the revenue-neutral rate on the July 1995 Armey-Shelby plan from 20.8 percent to about 22.7 percent.[26]

Due to the recently enacted tax cuts, the rate necessary to replace revenues under fully phased-in versions of current law would generally be a bit lower than noted above. It is also possible that if tax reform were to induce greater economic growth, the revenue-neutral rates on any of these plans could *eventually* be somewhat lower than the ones we have discussed. However, setting the rates lower than what would be necessary to replace current revenues makes it less likely that this eventuality will ever occur, due to the negative economic effects of budget deficits in the interim. Spending cuts, on the other hand, could allow the deficit-neutral level of rates to be lower right away. The Armey-Shelby flat tax plan was explicitly packaged as a tax cut, and thus it was unapologetically short of being revenue-neutral: unspecified spending cuts were promised to offset some of the cost. The appropriate level of spending, however, is a separate issue from tax reform, and the reduced rates that spending cuts allow could make any tax system, including the existing one, look more attractive.

Simplicity and Enforceability of the Consumption Tax Plans

Now that what rate of tax we're talking about has been established, an evaluation of the consumption tax plans can begin. Some important practical questions must be reviewed first: how simple or complicated is each approach, and how easy is it to enforce? The answers to these questions turn out to be crucial for determining which approach to consumption taxation is the best, and they are also an important factor in deciding whether any of them would be better than the existing system or a reformed income tax.

Administrative Problems of a Retail Sales Tax Compared to a VAT

On the surface, the retail sales tax seems like a fairly simple and straightforward way to raise money, and to the average citizen, it probably appears to work reasonably well. But as mentioned before, virtually every developed country that ever had a national retail sales tax has by now replaced it with a VAT. One important reason is that serious administrative problems arise with the retail sales tax that most average Americans never hear about. These problems are not too glaring when rates are low, as they are in most states (usually in the 4 to 6 percent range). But at the 30 percent (or higher) rate that would be required to replace U.S. personal and corporate income taxation, these problems would be serious indeed.

Our current state retail sales taxes appear to be simpler and relatively less costly to administer than our income tax system. Recent studies suggest that the total cost of enforcing and complying with current state retail sales taxes is between 2.4 percent and 4.8 percent of revenues raised.[27] This is lower than the 10 percent we estimated for the current income tax system, but it is not necessarily a reliable indicator of what the costs would be like for a national retail sales tax because current administrative costs do not give a flavor of the kinds of problems that could be created at high rates.

The first problem with the retail sales tax is the taxation of business inputs. An RST is supposed to tax only the final purchases of consumers and not the purchases of businesses. If businesses pay sales taxes when they purchase their inputs and then again when they sell their outputs, a problem of *cascading* develops. Goods that require more intermediate steps in production and distribution end up being taxed more heavily. This distorts incentives in the economy, leading to inefficient changes in the types of goods that get produced and consumed and in the way that businesses are organized. Most states try to avoid this problem by giving businesses a registration number to present when purchasing goods from other firms, exempting them from sales tax liability. But this procedure works very poorly in practice, as evidenced by the high percentage of RST revenues that apparently come from business purchases. This is not an important problem at low rates of tax but would be serious if rates were approaching 30 percent or more, as they would if a national RST were added on top of the state taxes.

Another problem with the retail sales tax is that at high tax rates, it becomes difficult to enforce because it collects all the money from what is, for compliance purposes, the weakest link in the production and distribution chain—retail. Consumers have no incentive to make sure retailers are paying their sales tax, and retailers have no incentive to pay aside from the threat of audit. Consumers have the incentive to inappropriately acquire business registration numbers to avoid the sales tax. A 1994 study by the Florida Department of Revenue estimated that 5 percent of tax-free business purchases involved abuse or misuse of business exemption certificates, and it recounts how "paper" businesses are created solely as a means of obtaining business exemption certificates and avoiding taxes on purchases intended for personal use.[28] Florida has a sales tax rate of 6 percent, and the magnitude of this problem for a rate five times higher can only be imagined.

In contrast, under a standard credit-invoice-style VAT, firms have an incentive to make sure that any other firm they are buying from has paid its VAT so that they can claim credit for it on their tax returns. A retailer that evades a 10 percent RST costs the government tax revenue equal to the full 10 percent of the final value of the good or service. In the case of evasion by a retailer, the VAT puts at risk, at most, only the revenue from the portion of the final value of the good or service produced at the given firm, which in the case of a retailer is a fairly small percentage. For a firm at an intermediate point in the production and distribution chain, failure to file a return or collect VAT on sales actually *increases* VAT revenue because the credit for taxes paid at earlier stages is lost. Although evasion of current state RSTs may not appear that serious, the problem would be much worse at higher rates. As a leading expert on VAT has put it, "At 5 percent, the incentive to evade tax is probably not worth the penalties of prosecution; at 10 percent, evasion is more attractive, and at 15–20 percent, it becomes extremely tempting."[29] The expert did not even characterize the problems that would occur with a rate of 30 percent or more.

Just as with an income tax, all sorts of difficult issues of interpretation arise under the sales tax. The difference is that unless you run a retail sales business, most people never hear about these problems. Whenever some commodities are exempt from tax, where the line is drawn is important. Consider the problem if expenditures on food but not on restaurant meals are exempt. What is the appropriate tax treatment of salad bars in grocery stores or fast-food restaurants where the customer may eat in or take out? These sorts of problems become much more troublesome as the rate rises.

Worst of all, no historical precedent is available to reassure us that these problems are manageable in a retail sales tax. Undoubtedly for the reasons discussed above, only six countries have operated retail sales taxes at rates over 10 percent. Five of them have since switched to a VAT, and the sixth is very likely about to switch as well.[30] Based on a review of worldwide practice, Vito Tanzi, the former director of the Fiscal Analysis Division of the International Monetary Fund, concludes that 10 percent is probably the maximum rate feasible for a retail sales tax.[31] We believe that because of compliance and enforcement problems, replacing the income tax with a retail sales tax would be unwise, especially given that a VAT can achieve the same goals while avoiding most of these problems.

Just How Simple and Easy to Enforce Is a VAT?

The VAT clearly has many administrative advantages over a retail sales tax, but how does it compare to the current system? Replacing the income tax with a comprehensive, single-rate VAT *could* provide an enormous amount of simplification. Individual income tax returns could be completely eliminated, and business tax returns could be significantly simplified, requiring little more information than is now collected in the normal course of business. Complex depreciation deductions would be eliminated. It would also be easier to enforce than the combined personal and corporate income tax codes.

A few studies have estimated the enforcement and compliance costs of adopting a VAT in the United States. Several studies suggest that a broad-based, single-rate VAT could involve considerably lower enforcement and compliance costs than the current income tax in the United States.[32] For instance, a CBO study concluded that the combined administrative and compliance costs of raising $150 billion in 1988 from a relatively clean European-style VAT would be between $4 and $7 billion, or between 2.7 and 4.7 percent of revenues collected. They note that these costs would be "largely independent" of the amount of revenue raised. This suggests that the cost-revenue ratio for a trillion-dollar VAT could be substantially lower than the 10 percent of revenue we estimate for the current U.S. income tax system, but to an unknown degree. Before jumping to this conclusion, however, several points should be noted.

First, a portion of the apparent compliance cost saving of replacing the income tax with a VAT stems from the elimination of individual tax returns. Much of this saving would disappear if the states do not abolish their own personal income tax systems. Because most of the information required to calculate income is currently used for both federal and state income tax purposes, eliminating only the federal return requirement would not spare most individuals of the need to file returns and keep track of the requisite information.

Second, the cost estimates done by the CBO and others presume that firms with turnover (that is, gross revenue from sales) less than a certain amount will be exempt from VAT liability. In a VAT, *exemption* means that the firm is completely outside the tax system. It does not remit tax to the government on its sales, nor is it allowed to take a credit for VAT paid on its purchases from suppliers. Exemptions for retailers cost the government revenue on the final slice of a product's value. But exempting a firm in the middle of the production and distribution chain can *increase* revenues because neither the exempt firm nor the next firm in the chain can take a credit for taxes paid at earlier stages in the chain. So overall, exempting small firms is unlikely to cost the government much revenue. It does involve some economic costs, however. It can distort firms' decisions about size and organizational form, and it can tax different types of goods more heavily or lightly depending on how many firms in the production and distribution chain are exempt and where in the chain these firms are located. The conventional wisdom among VAT experts is that the administrative and compliance cost savings from exempting firms with revenues below some moderate threshold outweighs the efficiency cost of this approach. For this reason, most countries that operate a VAT do exempt firms with turnover below a certain threshold—for example, below about $75,000 in the United Kingdom.[33] In any event, the hidden efficiency cost arising from exemption of small firms offsets some of the administrative and compliance cost saving from switching to a VAT.

The fact that the cost estimates presume that many small businesses would be exempt also makes the comparison with the current income tax somewhat unfair. Recall that under either an income tax or a VAT, small business is the most costly sector to tax as judged by the cost-to-revenue ratio. So exempting small business from tax would achieve considerable simplification under the income tax, too. To put it another way, part of the calculated compliance and administrative cost savings from adopting a VAT comes from dropping hard-to-tax entities out of the tax system, which has nothing inherently to do with a VAT. Moreover, some of the simplification benefit of eliminating the existing tax reflects elimination of complicated features that are not essential to the corporate income tax—such as the corporate alternative minimum tax. The possibility of simplifying the existing personal and corporate codes are addressed in more detail in the next chapter.

Finally, the VAT poses some tricky administrative issues, such as how to tax financial transactions. Recall that the VAT base applies only to the cash flow from the firm's real operations—sales revenue minus the cost of inputs—but does not depend on the financial operations of a firm. For example, in a VAT interest receipts are not part of taxable income, and interest payments are not deductible. But for a financial institution, the financial operations are the real purpose of the business, and the pricing of the services offered is often implicit in the interest charges and payments. Thus, by placing net interest receipts outside of the tax base, we may be seriously mismeasuring the true value added of a financial firm or of a nonfinancial firm with financial operations. To be sure, taxing financial services can be problematic in an income tax, so it is not obvious that things would be any worse under a VAT. But some unique problems do arise under a consumption tax like the VAT. For example, procedures would have to be developed to deal with installment sales of automobiles because a car dealer would have the incentive to characterize the payment as (untaxed) interest, while a consumer would be indifferent as to how the payment is labeled.[34]

Although these problems with a VAT are difficult, we also have three decades of experience in other countries, particularly in Europe, on which to draw. In contrast to the retail sales tax, VATs at the rate necessary to replace the U.S. income tax are not out of the range of historical experience. The standard rate that is applied to most goods and services is 20 percent or more in several European countries. Although 11.6 percent—the ratio of federal personal and corporate income tax receipts to gross domestic product in the United States—is higher than what is collected by nearly any other country, it is not higher by much. The nations with the largest VATs as a percentage of GDP are Israel (11.7 percent) and Iceland (10.3 percent). Among the largest European countries, France raises 7.7 percent of GDP with its VAT, Germany raises 7.0 percent, and the United Kingdom raises 6.8 percent.[35]

The fact that VATs have been around a while, at levels comparable to what the United States would need to replace the income tax, is both the good news and the bad news for advocates. It is good news because we would not be stepping into unknown territory, as would be the case with a retail sales tax. It is bad news because the experience from other countries is not encouraging about the possibility of realizing the simplification potential of a VAT. For the most part, the European countries do not levy the kind of broad-base, uniform-rate VAT we have been discussing or perhaps fantasizing about. Instead, the European VATs have multiple rates and numerous exemptions, features that require difficult-to-make distinctions, invite abuse, and call for close monitoring.

The scant quantitative evidence that exists suggests that, warts and all, the European countries' VATs are no less costly to collect than their income taxes. A careful study of the British tax system of 1986 to 1987 concluded that the ratio of collection cost to revenue raised was only slightly lower for the VAT compared to the personal income tax— 4.7 percent for the VAT (1 percent for administration, 3.7 percent for tax-payer costs) and 4.9 percent for the personal income tax (1.5 percent for administration, 3.4 percent for taxpayer costs).[36] A study of the Swedish tax system suggests that its VAT is *more* expensive to operate than its income tax, costing 3.1 percent of revenue to collect compared to 2.7 percent for the income tax, prompting the author of the study to remark that "the VAT is evidently not the simple tax it has been marketed as."[37] Undoubtedly, in both these cases the failure of the VAT to display a collection-cost advantage reflects both that actual VATs are more complex than ideal VATs and also apparently that European income taxes are less costly than the U.S. income tax to collect.

Nor do enforcement problems disappear under a VAT, in spite of the self-enforcement feature of the invoice-credit method of administration. Estimates of evasion range from 2 to 4 percent of potential revenues in the United Kingdom to as much as 40 percent in Italy.[38] A VAT requires a strong enforcement system to monitor such things as unregistered businesses, exaggerated refund claims, unrecorded cash purchases, underreported sales, and false export claims.

All in all, a VAT *potentially* represents a major simplification compared to our current income tax. But the failure of European VATs to be as simple as the drawing-board version of a VAT suggests caution when comparing the messy real world to an ideal. More practically, this lack of simplicity is a warning that if the United States were to adopt a VAT, it would be well advised to keep it simple and in particular to levy a uniform rate on all goods and services.

Simplicity and Enforceability of a Flat Tax

As shown above, the Hall-Rabushka flat tax adds an extra step to the VAT by taking wages and salaries out of the business tax base and requiring individuals to fill out their own returns on which they report that income. This extra step makes a big difference in the ease with which tax burdens can be adjusted according to ability to pay. It also adds some degree of extra compliance costs and enforcement problems. Nevertheless, advocates argue that if the personal tax base is kept relatively clean and simple, the flat tax would not be much more difficult to administer or comply with than a VAT. In that case, like a VAT, the flat tax would have the *potential* to greatly reduce the costs of compliance and enforcement relative to the current income tax, but it could also end up quite messy, as with many real-world VATs.

Unlike the VAT, however, the flat tax is a relatively new concept, no country has ever actually adopted a flat tax, and in fact, no flat tax proposal has ever been written out in enough legal detail that it could actually be implemented.[39] For that reason, there is greater uncertainty surrounding it. Since the flat tax first garnered significant attention in the mid-1990s, academic tax experts have begun to put some serious thought into the administrative and enforcement problems that it might introduce.[40] They point out that some of the problems that arise in the existing income tax would remain, some would be eliminated, and some new problems would be introduced. The consensus of this literature is that on balance, the flat tax would very likely be simpler and easier to enforce and administer than the current income tax but that the difference is a lot smaller than initially indicated by Hall and Rabushka.

The flat tax would suffer from some of the same problems as a VAT, such as the incentive for businesses to redefine "sales to consumers" as nontaxable interest received from consumers. Many of the potential problems with the flat tax, however, arise from differences in the way the flat tax and VATs are implemented. First of all, taxing labor compensation separately at the individual level (with an exemption level and possibly at different rates) necessitates a deduction-based rather than credit-invoice-based tax system. The Hall-Rabushka flat tax proposal thus features what is essentially a subtraction-method VAT (with labor costs deductible) at the business level. A subtraction-method VAT lacks some of the enforcement advantages of a credit-invoice VAT, which is why almost all countries use the latter method. Since a fixed tax rate can no longer be charged on each transaction, it becomes harder to monitor whether tax is paid on each transaction. A subtraction-method VAT also makes exempting small businesses somewhat more difficult. Neither the Hall-Rabushka flat tax blueprint nor the Armey-Shelby version mentions a small-business exemption. In its absence, the substantial cost savings of being able to ignore the hardest-to-tax sector are lost.

In principle, implementing a flat tax would be possible where purchases by business could be deducted only if evidence could be provided that business tax had been paid by the seller of the input. This would not be as easy or effective as the credit-invoice method, but it would improve the enforcement properties of the tax and make it less costly to exempt small businesses.[41] Neither the Hall-Rabushka proposal nor its descendants take this approach, however. Failure to do this means that deductions from the business tax base are not necessarily offset by an inclusion in the tax base elsewhere, which opens up a wide variety of troubling avoidance opportunities. For example, an owner of a small business could sell personal property to the business at a vastly inflated price, generating an arbitrarily large deduction and corresponding tax cut for the business but no tax liability at all for the individual. Similarly, just prior to implementation of the tax, two businesses could sell their entire capital stocks to each other and then buy them right back immediately after implementation, producing deductions for each business that enable them to avoid the transition tax on preexisting wealth. David Weisbach of the University of Chicago Law School has identified a broad array of such problems, many that involve similar principles but that sometimes take advantage of sophisticated financial techniques or difficult-to-monitor international transactions. Some of these avoidance opportunities can in principle be eliminated under a flat tax: for example, disallowing deductions in cases where no flat tax had been paid on the input would fix many of them. But this and other potential fixes would require detailed legal rules and enforcement that would make any flat tax that could actually be implemented less simple than it would appear at first glance and less simple than a VAT.

What about the trademark postcard-size tax form? Contrary to what Hall and Rabushka claim, flat tax business returns would probably not be able to fit on postcards. Doing so would require combining many different items into single entries, making it difficult for the IRS to verify the results. In any event, the postcard would merely summarize what could be millions of transactions, understating the difficulty of monitoring the tax return. Still, some aspects of the flat business tax make it simpler and easier to enforce than a corporate income tax, in part because of the replacement of depreciation deductions with expensing and the fact that financial transactions generally have no tax consequences. The flat business tax would also have the advantage of eliminating many of the complicated special provisions in the current corporate code, although some of this could be accomplished within the context of the income tax as well.

At the personal level, the flat tax is obviously more complicated than a VAT because a VAT eliminates personal returns altogether. But it is vastly simpler and easier to enforce than the current income tax system. Since only wage and pension income need be reported, all of the complications associated with measuring and reporting personal capital income are eliminated. The Hall-Rabushka claim that personal returns could be made to fit on postcards may indeed be feasible. With a single rate, moreover, withholding could also be much more accurate, making the process that much simpler. Workers whose wages are subject to information reporting and withholding would have high compliance rates, as under the current system, although the self-employed would continue to pose an administrative and compliance problem. For example, the knotty issue of whether a car is for business or personal purposes looms just as large and possibly even larger. A clean flat tax also eliminates most opportunities for tax arbitrage, a major source of complex avoidance schemes discussed earlier. Ways to "game the system," some of which are noted above, would surely still exist, but with sufficient attention to design and implementation, such opportunities could be greatly reduced relative to the current system.

It is difficult to come up with a precise estimate of the compliance and enforcement costs associated with a flat tax, especially because no other country has ever operated such a system. If it were kept clean and care were taken to address some of the implementation issues identified above, the total cost could surely be much lower than our estimate of $110 billion per year for the current system.

The simplification promise of the flat tax depends on a lot of big "ifs." What starts as a very simple plan could end up becoming a mess as it winds its way through the political process. For instance, allowing lots of itemized deductions would make the personal system more complicated, and retaining home mortgage interest deductions, in particular, would create arbitrage problems. Transition rules could make things even more complicated than the current system in the short run. Some flat tax advocates have also proposed eliminating withholding of taxes on wages, which would undoubtedly cause major enforcement problems.[42] And simplifying the federal code would only help taxpayers to the extent that the states followed suit. It's also worth noting that some of the simplification, such as eliminating itemized deductions, could be achieved while retaining the existing income tax structure. Nonetheless, the potential simplicity of the flat tax approach to progressive consumption taxation cannot be denied.

The Personal Consumption Tax: Complexity and Enforcement Problems

Unlike the other kinds of consumption tax discussed so far, the personal consumption tax would complicate tax matters for many individuals. Some of the difficult compromises made by the current income tax, such as including capital gains in taxable income only on realization, are handled easily by a personal consumption tax. For example, if accrued capital gains are left unrealized, they constitute both income and saving, so they have no tax consequences. The tax affairs of the average taxpayer, however, for whom the conceptual measurement difficulties of capital income are now of little concern, would be complicated by the addition to the tax base of borrowing and savings account withdrawals. Even credit-card borrowing could have tax consequences.

For those families with extensive and complicated capital income flows, calculating taxable income can be simplified to the extent that assets are kept within the IRA-type accounts. Some features of the new requirement to keep track of net saving will be complex, however, and aspects of personal financial affairs that currently have no tax implications would have some under a personal consumption tax. Note that although a personal consumption tax is akin to having an unlimited, unrestricted standard IRA, IRA participation is a voluntary decision taken to reduce tax liability. Under a personal consumption tax, all taxpayers would be required to measure and report their net savings, which is significantly more difficult than reporting limited deposits to an IRA account and reporting withdrawals only during retirement.

A whole host of new enforcement issues and complex avoidance schemes arise under a personal consumption tax. For example, while taxpayers would have the incentive to report all the deductions for new saving to which they are entitled, they would have an incentive not to report withdrawals or borrowing. The Treasury Department's 1984 study of this issue concluded that compliance with a personal consumption tax would require "a more extensive system of information reporting and monitoring than does an income tax," including "a comprehensive inventory of all existing wealth upon enactment of the tax, registration of private borrowing, and a far-reaching system of exchange controls to facilitate policing of foreign transactions."[43] Martin Ginsburg of Georgetown Law Center took a close look at life under the USA tax and concluded that the plan was fundamentally flawed. He noted numerous ways that high-income taxpayers could manipulate the definition of net saving to avoid taxes, leading to bizarre situations in which "municipal bonds pay interest in even years only, executive compensation and the yield on at least one class of each corporation's stock is paid only in odd years, and the rich with borrowed money buy raw land or works of art they admire but may not keep forever."[44] Some of these problems are caused by transition rules, deductions, and compromises that are unique to the USA tax, but others are hard to avoid in any personal consumption tax of this type.

All in all, the complications caused by a personal consumption tax outweigh the potential simplifications along some dimensions. If we undertake a massive overhaul of our tax system, with all the associated transition costs, we don't want to end up with a system that is no less complicated than the current system. This is particularly true given that many of the same goals of the personal consumption tax could be achieved by the flat tax.

Distributional Effects of the Consumption Tax Alternatives

Of course, simplicity and enforceability are not the only criteria for choosing a tax system, nor are they necessarily the most important. Most everyone also has a strong and abiding interest in the distributional consequences of tax reform: which plans will make *your* tax bill larger or smaller, and more generally, how will the burdens be shared by people with different abilities to carry the load?

Distributional Consequences of a Retail Sales Tax or VAT

We have argued that, although a retail sales tax and a VAT have essentially the same economic and distributional effects, the VAT has important administrative advantages. In what follows, therefore, we mainly refer to the effects of a VAT, although the same basic results also hold for an equivalent national retail sales tax.

In chapter 6 we argued that, over a lifetime, a single-rate VAT would exact from individuals a burden that is approximately proportional to their lifetime incomes. It would be regressive to the extent that inheritances and bequests escape tax and to the extent that transfers are not indexed to keep up with any price increase the tax causes. Given this presumption, a complex analysis is not needed to reach the conclusion that, compared to an income tax with a generous level of tax-free income, graduated rates, and an earned income credit for the working poor, a VAT would substantially increase the burden on low-income households. For example, someone who spends an entire lifetime at the poverty level would remit no income taxes under the current system because tax-exempt levels are currently set above the poverty line. In fact, if such a person were poor in spite of working, he or she would currently receive a refund because of the earned income tax credit. In stark contrast, a 17 percent VAT would impose a tax burden equal to approximately 17 percent of that person's lifetime income. Similar reasoning suggests the tax burden on high-income households will fall greatly if the graduated income tax is replaced by a flat-rate VAT. Both low- and middle-income people would be likely to pick up the slack through higher tax burdens.

The $64,000 policy question then boils down to this: do the potential gains from simplification and stimulation of economic growth justify a tax burden redistribution of this magnitude? Economic analysis by itself cannot provide a decisive answer to this question because it involves evaluating a policy that makes some people better off and others worse off. Even with the possibility that the economy could grow faster and eventually compensate people who initially suffer increased tax burdens, such an evaluation inescapably involves value judgments that must ultimately be resolved by our political system. We suspect, though, that most Americans do not favor such a dramatic shift in the tax burden and that for this reason they would not support the VAT as a replacement for the income tax.

Can the VAT be saved by somehow dampening its redistributional consequences? The answer is yes, but at significant cost in terms of simplicity and economic efficiency. One way to soften the regressivity of a switch to a VAT is to abandon tax-rate uniformity and instead to impose a zero tax rate on those commodities that figure more heavily in the expenditures of poorer families, such as food, shelter, and health care. The European experience with the VAT, however, shows that multiple-rate VAT systems are significantly more complex and therefore more expensive to administer. Preferential taxation of necessities also sharply reduces revenues, requiring an even higher tax rate on other goods. Most important, because in aggregate most purchases of the preferentially taxed commodities are made by middle- and high-income families, this is a very poorly targeted way to increase the progressivity of the VAT. Finally, it also causes significant economic distortions, creating an inefficient incentive to consume more of the goods and services that are untaxed and less of the ones that are taxed. Because tax rates well above 25 percent would probably be required for a VAT with exempt commodities, the distortion to incentives would be nontrivial.

Alternatively, we could impose a uniform-rate VAT simultaneously with a large increase in income maintenance programs designed to offset the impact of the VAT on lower-income households or with a new universal tax credit or rebate paid to all individuals and families. The former approach would probably be unpopular, especially considering current public opinion about welfare. A rebate or credit would require that a whole new administrative apparatus be set up in addition to the one needed to run the VAT. Tracking low-income people to ensure that they received rebates could prove difficult, as the IRS has relatively little experience dealing with this population, as evidenced by pervasive fraudulent claims for the EITC.[45]

Distributional Consequences of a Flat Tax

None of the alternatives mentioned for the VAT addresses the vertical equity issue as easily as a flat tax, whose genesis was exactly as a scheme to administer a VAT with an effective method for achieving some progressivity. The tax-exempt level of labor income in the flat tax makes it equivalent to a VAT plus a limited (and nonrefundable) credit for labor income set at the flat rate.[46]

How would a flat tax distribute the burden of taxes relative to the current system? First, as illustrated in chapter 6, replacing the current graduated rate structure with a single rate unambiguously shifts the tax burden dramatically away from those with the highest incomes and toward others. If the EITC and child credits are eliminated, the negative impact on the poor is particularly large. Second, the flat tax would exempt from tax the returns to postponing consumption that are not already exempt under the current system. As indicated in chapter 6, this also mainly benefits upper-income people, which necessarily comes at the expense of everyone else in a revenue-neutral reform. These two effects are offset to some extent by the transitional tax on preexisting wealth (unless this is removed by transitional relief) and by eliminating various deductions and exclusions, both of which can be expected to be somewhat progressive.

Analyses that put all of these effects together for a few specific flat-tax proposals were conducted by the U.S. Treasury Department's Office of Tax Analysis in 1995 and 1996. Their projections were done on an annual basis rather than the theoretically preferable but difficult-to-implement lifetime basis. The estimates depend on a number of assumptions about tax incidence. In particular, the Treasury's analysis assumes that both the existing corporate income tax and the new business tax are borne by individuals in proportion to their capital income, that the existing individual income tax is borne by those households that remit the tax, and that all taxes on labor compensation are borne by workers.

These assumptions are by no means uncontroversial, but they provide a reasonable starting point for assessing the distributional impact of a change to a flat tax.[47] Certainly the analysis is better than one that considers only the individual wage portion of the flat tax. By ignoring the business tax and (implicit, because of the loss of deductibility at the business level) new taxes on employer contributions for Social Security and fringe benefits, such examples can give a misleading impression of the true impact on tax burdens. In addition, to make an appropriate comparison, the Treasury analysis adjusts the rates or exemptions in the flat-tax proposals so that they would raise the same revenue as the taxes they would replace, as they stood in 1996.

Table 7.1 illustrates the Treasury's estimates of the initial percentage change in after-tax income that would be caused at different points in

Table 7.1

Treasury estimates of the distributional impact of replacing the 1996 income tax with a flat tax: Percentage change in after-tax incomes

Family income		Percentage change in after-tax income		
		(1)	(2)	(3)
Percentile rank	Income range (thousands of 2003 dollars)	20.8% flat tax, $36,800 exemption, no EITC	17% flat tax, $17,600 exemption, no EITC	22.9% flat tax, $40,700 exemption, keep EITC
Lowest quintile	0–19	−6.8	−7.7	−1.0
Second quintile	19–35	−5.4	−7.2	−1.2
Middle quintile	35–57	−2.9	−4.7	−1.8
Fourth quintile	57–93	−2.4	−3.8	−2.2
Next 10 percent	93–128	−2.7	−2.9	−3.0
Next 5 percent	128–170	−1.8	−1.0	−2.4
Next 4 percent	170–409	1.2	3.2	0.9
Top 1 percent	over 409	11.7	14.7	10.8

Source: U.S. Department of the Treasury, Office of Tax Analysis (1995, 1996).

Notes: Each flat-tax plan above was estimated by the Treasury to raise the same revenue as the taxes it replaced in 1996, assuming no induced economic growth. Assumes that the burden of labor taxes falls on workers and the burden of business taxes falls on recepients of capital income generally. Exemption levels are for a married couple with two children and are converted from their values in the original analysis to 2003 dollars. The 17 percent and 20.8 percent flat-tax options assume repeal of estate and gift taxes.

the income distribution if the 1996 personal and corporate income taxes (and in the first two cases, the estate tax) were replaced by each of three different flat tax proposals. Income is here defined broadly to approximate as closely as possible economic income. Alternative 1 is the July 1995 version of the Armey-Shelby plan, which would provide a family of four with an exempt level of $36,800 (all exemptions are converted here to 2003 dollars) and would eliminate both the EITC as well as estate and gift taxes, requiring a rate of 20.8 percent. Alternative 2 is the same plan but with a $17,600 exemption for a family of four and a 17 percent rate. Alternative 3 has a $40,700 exemption with a 22.9 percent rate and keeps the EITC and estate and gift taxes. Note that in all three cases the exemptions are lower for single individuals and smaller families, as in the current system.

The Treasury analysis suggests that each of the three plans causes a stark shifting of the tax burden away from those with very high incomes and onto everyone else. Under all three flat taxes, tax burdens drop sharply for those in the top 1 percent of the income distribution, drop moderately for those in the next highest 4 percent, and go up for all other income groups. Thus, all groups outside of the top 5 percent would see their after-tax incomes decline. Under the first two alternatives, the largest percentage declines occur among the poorest families. For example, people in the bottom fifth of the income distribution, with incomes below $19,000, would see their after-tax incomes decline by 6.8 percent under the first flat tax alternative. Much of this is due to the elimination of the refundable EITC. The 22.9 percent flat tax of alternative 3 is noticeably more progressive than the other two options because it retains the EITC and has a larger family allowance. Under this alternative, the decline in after-tax income for most people ranges from 1 to 3 percent. It is certainly possible to design a flat tax where the income loss for most people is modest, as long as the exemption level is kept large and the EITC or some close substitute is retained. Such a plan would, however, require a rate higher than is usually advertised—in this case, about 23 percent.

Since these estimates were done, personal income tax rates have been reduced and made somewhat less progressive (see chapter 3). Replacing the fully phased-in version of current law would thus require a somewhat lower tax rate, and the distributional impact of the change would be slightly less dramatic. But it is not clear how meaningful this is, since the projected path of spending and taxes generates large deficits and for that reason may be unsustainable.

Some aspects of these distributional estimates are debatable. For example, some economists argue that assuming that the burden of the business portion of the flat tax is proportional to capital income may understate burdens imposed on upper-income households and overstate them for everyone else.[48] As noted in chapter 6, relative to the current income tax, the flat tax would exempt the return to saving and any compensation for inflation. But both approaches would treat similarly other components of capital income, such as rewards to entrepreneurship, innovation, and risk taking. The problem is not mismeasurement of the overall burden of taxes on capital income that remain under the flat tax: this is just the revenue from the flat business tax, which is fairly straightforward to estimate. Rather, the argument is that the kinds of capital income that are treated similarly under consumption and income taxes probably constitute a disproportionately large share of capital income at the upper end of the income distribution. It is impossible to observe exactly what portion of capital income represents a reward for what, but a number of economists have attempted to infer the likely impact of this consideration using information on the types of assets owned by people at different points in the income distribution. Some find this makes only a small difference to the estimated distributional effects.[49] Bill Gentry of Williams College and R. Glenn Hubbard of Columbia University find a larger effect, but it still is not nearly large enough to undo the fact that there is a large tax cut for high-income people and a tax increase for everyone else under these plans.[50] This conclusion is hard to avoid given the much less controversial effects of replacing multiple graduated rates with a single rate.

These distributional estimates also ignore any improvements to the economy that might arise from tax reform. Some economists' estimates of the likely size of the boost will be discussed below. In anticipation of that discussion, note that table 7.1 illustrates, to a rough approximation, how much economic growth would have to increase someone's income to make up for any initial change in tax burden.

In weighing the impact of a flat tax on different peoples' levels of well-being, we shouldn't forget the benefits of having a much simpler tax. As discussed above, these benefits could be substantial for a flat tax, which has the *potential* to save a significant fraction of the estimated $110 billion in annual compliance costs of the current system. For most of the people who would pay higher taxes under a revenue-neutral flat tax, however, the income tax is already fairly simple, so the simpler flat tax will deliver little or no direct offset. Most of the direct gains from simplification would go to people with higher incomes because they're typically the ones with the complicated tax affairs. This doesn't diminish the fact that increased simplicity is valuable; other things being equal, all that time and effort devoted to tax affairs is a waste that doesn't do anybody any good. But it also means that the gains from simplicity don't much change the overall distributional impact of a switch to a flat tax.

It is also worth remembering that special transition rules, which would be likely to accompany any reform that is enacted, could have a major influence on the distributional effects of a flat tax. In particular, transitional relief for depreciation deductions on existing capital would greatly reduce the revenues available from the business tax, forcing tax-rate increases and therefore tax burdens to rise on wage earners, which would make the flat tax considerably less progressive.

What if you like the flat tax but don't think that a single low rate with an exempt level of labor income provides enough progressivity for your tastes? Moreover, you are willing to sacrifice the extra efficiency cost of higher marginal tax rates to achieve that progressivity. Then you should consider a "graduated flat tax," which may sound as self-contradictory as jumbo shrimp. Such a tax, known as the X-*tax*, has been developed and championed by David Bradford of Princeton University.[51] The X-tax business and personal tax bases are the same as the flat tax, but the X-tax sets the business tax rate and the top personal rate on labor income at a higher level (say, 35 percent) and imposes lower, graduated rates on labor income in addition to a tax-exempt level. The point of introducing graduated tax rates on labor income is to roughly replicate the overall degree of progressivity of the current system, although for reasons detailed in chapter 6, this would likely require rates that were *more* graduated than in the current system. The X-tax retains many of the efficiency and simplification advantages of a flat-rate consumption tax, while raising revenue in a more progressive way. Because it is more progressive, it does not achieve the incentive advantages of a lower marginal rate of tax. However, if no transition relief is provided, this is offset to some extent because the higher business tax rate means that the efficient one-time "surprise" transitional tax on preexisting wealth accounts for a larger share of revenues, which reduces how much we must rely on distorting taxes. The X-tax has not as yet garnered as much attention as the flat tax itself, undoubtedly because it does not have the easy-to-understand attraction of a single low rate.

Another fairness issue is lurking here that might end up being even more decisive in the political fate of these plans than their effect on the actual distribution to tax burden. This is the *perceived* fairness of the reforms. Americans are accustomed to an individual tax base that includes not only wages and salaries but also interest, dividends, and capital gains. With this frame of reference, we suspect that many people will think the personal tax base of the flat tax just doesn't smell right and will therefore fail the "sniff test" they apply to determine what's fair and what isn't. That one family with $50,000 in dividends and interest remits no personal tax while another family with $50,000 in wages does will just not fly for many Americans. This is true in spite of the economic arguments that, because of the changes in the business tax, the flat tax is no better or worse than a retail sales tax. This state of affairs is a bit ironic because the flat tax is supposed to be a more progressive alternative to the RST or VAT. Nevertheless, its political prospects may founder because, although it in some ways looks like our current system, in other possibly critical dimensions it does not at all look like what people are accustomed to.

Distributional Consequences of a Personal Consumption Tax

Supporters of the personal consumption tax approach prefer it to a sales tax or VAT in part because it can more easily accommodate a graduated rate structure and therefore can be made to achieve a more progressive distribution of the tax burden. The USA tax has been explicitly designed to replicate the progressivity of the current income tax and, although we can't predict how close it would come to this goal, it's probably not too far off. But as just discussed, a Hall-Rabushka flat tax base could also support a graduated rate structure that would make it comparably progressive on a lifetime basis. Given the much greater complexity of the personal consumption tax base, this X-tax modification of the flat tax seems like a far preferable option if further progressivity of tax burdens is desired. Moreover, whatever the perception problems associated with the flat tax, there appears to be little public enthusiasm for a reform like the personal consumption tax that could make the taxpaying process more complicated.

Economic Effects of Consumption Tax Plans

Chapter 4 considers all of the major channels through which the tax system affects how well the economy performs. The proposals discussed in this chapter affect many of these channels. Each would remove taxation's negative impact on the incentive to save; more saving would lead to a larger capital stock, which in turn would make U.S. workers more productive and improve our long-run standard of living. They would eliminate capricious variation in tax rates on different types of investment, leading to a more efficient allocation of our capital stock and risk-bearing. All of the consumption tax plans also promise to clean up the tax base to some degree, removing distortions among different types of consumption. To the extent that the consumption taxes shift tax burdens onto existing wealth and the elderly, they also provide an economic boost. The retail sales tax, VAT, and flat tax lower marginal tax rates by scaling back progressivity, which would reduce the tax system's drag on incentives to achieve success through hard work, initiative, innovation, and risk-taking.

At the outset, the economic effects of tax *reform* (such as switching to a consumption base, cleaning the tax base, and changing the rate structure) must be distinguished from the economic effects of tax *cuts*. Tax cuts raise issues regarding the economic effects of budget deficits and the appropriate level of government spending that have nothing inherently to do with tax reform. We address the economics of tax cuts in detail in chapter 4, and in the rest of the discussion here, focus on the economics of tax reforms that are designed to raise the same revenue as the taxes they replace.

The potential economic benefits of switching to a consumption tax are real, but how large would these benefits be? Ideally, we would want to quantify the impacts of each of the elements of the proposals and then see how the economic impacts add up in various packages. But, as shown in chapter 4, the evidence on each of these effects is uncertain. In many cases, the best evidence suggests only a moderate effect.

Despite the uncertainty, bounds can be put on the kind of economic benefit that can be reasonably expected. Clearly, promises of miraculously higher growth rates forever are unjustified by the existing evidence. For instance, while some have claimed that switching to a flat-rate consumption tax could double our long-term rate of economic growth indefinitely,[52] this result is totally unsupported by the evidence, and no serious economist is making such claims. In fact, switching to a consumption tax is unlikely to increase permanently our rate of growth at all. Rather, even if the tax change were successful at raising saving, growth would increase only for a while as we added to the economy's level of capital intensity, moving us to a level of income permanently higher than we would otherwise achieve. The effect on growth rates reaches a limit because eventually a higher level of saving will be needed just to maintain that greater degree of capital intensity. Those factors that could arguably induce a persistent increase in growth rates, such as investment in R&D or human capital, are either left untouched or made relatively less attractive by a flat tax and so are unlikely to noticeably increase.

Putting aside such overly optimistic estimates, how can we get a sense of the size of economic benefits we can expect from reform proposals? One approach is to make an educated guess, considering all the types of evidence we discussed in chapter 4. Robert Hall and Alvin Rabushka, the inventors of the flat tax and therefore hardly disinterested observers, take this approach and claim their plan would increase real incomes by a total of 6 percent after seven years. As they point out,

this is a significant improvement: "By 2002 [seven years after the hypothetical enactment date], it would mean each American will have an
income of about $1,900 higher, in 1995 dollars, as a consequence of tax
reform."[53] Although this claim seems to imply (without evidence) that
the benefits of such economic growth would be shared equally, overall
growth of this magnitude is plausible.

A careful reading of the evidence presented in chapter 4, however,
could easily suggest an even more modest economic impact. Based on
historical experience, many important areas of economic behavior,
especially saving rates and hours worked, appear to be unresponsive to
moderate changes in incentives. A stronger economic response cannot
be ruled out, though, because some areas of economic behavior that
might be responsive to incentives, such as entrepreneurial effort, are
hard to measure. But there's no compelling evidence either way on
these latter issues.

Some economists have taken a more ambitious approach to gauging
the potential economic benefits of reform. They have put together
stylized models of the economy that can be used to simulate the effects
of adopting a new tax system. Although these models produce precise
answers, these should not be taken to be anything more than what they
are, which is just a more sophisticated kind of educated guess subject to
a wide margin for error. The results of any such modeling exercise
depend heavily on the assumptions that are made about the responsiveness of economic behaviors, such as saving and labor supply, to
incentives. And these assumptions can be derived only from a review
of the same uncertain historical evidence that we've discussed in this
book. Moreover, both the tax system and economic behavior are
incredibly complicated, so any feasible model must leave out potentially important aspects of the problem and must rely on potentially
restrictive simplifying assumptions. Nonetheless, the models are still
useful because they help us work out in a systematic way the implications of reasonable assumptions regarding the evidence and how the
economy works. It is difficult to see how everything fits together in any
other way.

Perhaps the most useful exercise to date along these lines is a paper
by economists David Altig, Alan Auerbach, Laurence Kotlikoff, Kent
Smetters, and Jan Walliser.[54] They construct a detailed model of the
economy and use it to analyze the effects of switching to several different possible replacements for the 1996 U.S. personal and corporate
income taxes. The model incorporates behavioral responses of labor

supply, saving, and capital accumulation to taxation based on a reasonable interpretation of typical results from the empirical research literature on these topics. The model includes multiple different generations and, within each generation, people with varying amounts of lifetime labor income, and offers predictions about the distributional impacts of tax changes both within and across generations.

The study estimates the long-run change in per-capita national income from each of several tax reforms. For example, switching to a single-rate income tax that eliminates all deductions and exemptions is estimated to increase per-capita income by 4.4 percent. Replacing the current system with a single-rate consumption tax, such as a retail sales tax or VAT, would increase long-run per-capita income by more than twice as much—9.4 percent. A flat tax is estimated to increase long-run per-capita income by 4.5 percent.

The smaller estimated economic impact of a flat tax relative to a VAT arises both because the flat tax is more progressive (and thus features higher distorting marginal tax rates) and because unlike a VAT it is assumed to exempt housing, which accounts for about half of the capital stock, from the efficient transitional tax on preexisting wealth. This requires higher tax rates on the remaining tax base. The importance of the transitional tax to any potential economic gains is further illustrated by their estimate that a flat tax with transition relief, allowing continued deductions for depreciation on old capital, would increase per-capita income by only 1.9 percent in the long run. Finally, perhaps somewhat surprisingly, they estimate that replacing the current system with an X-tax, involving rates on labor income that are about as progressive as the current system (and which does not offer transition relief), would produce *larger* economic gains than would the less progressive flat tax. Per-capita income is estimated to increase by 6.4 percent in the long run under the X-tax. This result occurs because the higher business tax rate in the X-tax (which is set equal to the top rate on labor income) means that the transitional tax on existing capital is larger so that the tax on other things can be smaller.

To this point, we've been focusing on projected increases in income or output, but this is not a good measure of how much better off people might be as a result of a tax change. For example, the higher output is achieved in part through a higher saving rate, which means that some consumption today must be sacrificed. Similarly, some of the increased output occurs because people are projected to work a greater number of hours. Working longer hours obviously has a cost in terms of lost leisure, so the increased output is an overestimate of the net benefit. *Welfare* is the economists' term for a dollar measure of well-being that takes these factors into account. In these stylized models, increases in welfare from tax reform are considerably smaller than increases in output.

Table 7.2 summarizes the estimated welfare gains and losses implied by the Altig et al. model for people of different generations and different levels of lifetime labor earnings. Changes in welfare are reported as a percentage of remaining lifetime potential earnings.[55] When interpreting the results, it is worth noting that while the model captures many essential features of the economy and the current tax code, it does not include the EITC or child credit, and it does not take into account the fact that under the current system, low- and middle-income people shelter a much larger share of their capital income in tax-preferred pensions and retirement accounts than do upper-income people. This may cause it to somewhat overstate the benefits of reform for low- and middle-income people.[56]

Among those age 55 when the reform is enacted, the poor lose under the proportional income and consumption tax plans, but otherwise everyone at this age is predicted to experience at least modest gains. The analysis suggests that the gains from lower tax rates on capital income apparently outweigh any losses imposed by transitional taxes on preexisting wealth or higher tax rates on remaining labor income for most people in this particular age group.

For younger generations, represented by those age 21 at the time of enactment, the proportional income and consumption taxes tend to significantly hurt low- and moderate-income people and benefit upper-income people, which is not surprising given the elimination of progressive rates and exemptions. Among people who are young at the date of enactment, the flat tax improves the welfare of the highest- and lowest-income people by about 1 percent and reduces the welfare of those in the middle class by a similar proportion. For future generations, people at all income levels are predicted to roughly break even or gain slightly under the flat tax. Adding transition relief to the flat tax, though, causes most young and future middle-income people to be worse off than under current law: only the highest-income people are better off in the long run. Finally, under the X-tax, all categories of people shown in the table gain on average. The welfare gains to future generations range from 1 to 2 percent, with the largest gains going to low-income people. Even here, however, there are some losers, not

Table 7.2
Estimated percentage change in remaining lifetime welfare under various tax reform proposals

Age and percentile of lifetime labor income distribution	Proportional income tax	Proportional consumption tax	Flat tax	Flat tax with transition relief	X-tax
Future generations					
Top 2 percent	3.0	4.5	1.5	1.0	1.0
70th–80th percentile	0.5	2.0	0.0	−1.5	1.0
40th–50th percentile	−0.5	1.0	0.0	−1.5	1.0
10th–20th percentile	−1.5	−1.0	0.5	−1.0	1.5
Bottom 2 percent	−6.0	−4.5	1.5	0.0	2.0
Age 21 at date of enactment					
Top 2 percent	3.0	3.0	1.0	1.0	0.0
70th–80th percentile	0.0	1.0	−1.0	−2.0	0.0
40th–50th percentile	−1.0	−0.5	−1.0	−2.0	0.0
10th–20th percentile	−3.0	−2.0	−0.5	−1.0	0.5
Bottom 2 percent	−6.5	−6.0	1.0	−0.5	1.0
Age 55 at date of enactment					
Top 2 percent	3.0	2.0	0.5	3.5	1.0
70th–80th percentile	2.0	1.0	1.0	2.0	0.5
40th–50th percentile	1.0	0.5	1.0	2.0	0.5
10th–20th percentile	0.5	−0.5	1.0	2.0	0.5
Bottom 2 percent	−1.5	−2.0	2.5	1.0	0.5

Source: Altig, Auerbach, Kotlikoff, Smetters, and Walliser (2001).
Notes: Depicts percentage change in remaining potential lifetime earnings that would leave someone as well off as they would be under the tax reform. "Future generations" are represented by those born 25 years after enactment of the reform. Percentage changes are rounded to the nearest 0.5.

shown in the table. All but the poorest of the oldest generations at the time the X-tax is adopted face welfare reductions in the vicinity of 2 percent, due to the large transitional tax on preexisting wealth.

The bottom line of this analysis is that, even after taking into account the positive effects of tax reform on the economy, there will be both winners and losers. Although the specific numbers are subject to plenty of uncertainty, the analysis probably provides a reasonable estimate of who the winners and losers are likely to be under each reform option and roughly what order of magnitude of gains and losses to expect. The results are not far from what most reputable models come up with.[57]

In addition to the uncertainty regarding the magnitude of behavioral responses to taxes, a number of modeling issues can make a difference. For example, Eric Engen of the American Enterprise Institute and William Gale of the Brookings Institution have shown that after taking into account that a large portion of saving in the United States is done for precautionary reasons, which is relatively insensitive to incentives, the impact of tax reform on saving and capital accumulation is very small.[58] On the other hand, a number of changes could be made to the modeling that could increase the positive economic impact relative to what Altig et al. found. For instance, their model does not address the positive effects of making the tax treatment of different types of investment more neutral. Nor does it address the potential effects of tax reform on innovation and technological development, an important issue about which there is little or no good evidence. In addition, incorporating international considerations could strengthen the positive economic impact of tax reform somewhat—for example, because increases in domestic saving are more valuable if they can take advantage of good investment opportunities overseas.[59] Overall, given the state of evidence on these considerations, they do not provide a compelling reason to think that the estimates shown in table 7.2 are way off the mark, but they do add to the degree of uncertainty.

No one will be surprised to learn that a lot of disagreement still exists among economists about the potential economic benefits of tax reform. In our judgment, the kinds of tax reforms discussed here would likely yield important economic improvements—but these would not be nearly large enough to provide a free lunch. For instance, dramatically cutting tax rates on high-income people will still impose significant costs on other people. Economists pride themselves on emphasizing the ubiquity of trade-offs, and we believe that tax reform is no exception to this rule. As we have stressed, economic reasoning is an essential input to an informed opinion of the likely effects, but the evidence is highly imperfect, so there's still plenty of uncertainty. In such an environment, *someone* can always be found with a model that says that the economic benefits will be tremendous and maybe there's a free lunch after all, but for reasons detailed throughout the book, a skeptical attitude toward such claims is appropriate.

Conclusion

Where does our discussion of alternatives to the income tax leave us? A national retail sales tax is an unproven alternative, which is likely to be administratively infeasible at the rates necessary to replace the federal income tax. The VAT is a proven alternative that accomplishes the same economic goals. But either tax entails a radical shift in tax burden from affluent to poor and middle-class families, and for this reason either is likely to be unacceptable to most Americans, although this is a value judgment rather than a matter of economics. The personal consumption tax complicates rather than simplifies the personal tax system and is unacceptable on these grounds. So the flat tax (or its more progressive version, the X-tax) is the most attractive of the consumption tax alternatives to the income tax.

We are not faced, however, with an either-or choice between the flat tax and the tax system we have now, warts and all. On the contrary, many tax experts favor substantial reform, but reform that stays within the basic framework of the current system. Indeed, in the history of U.S. taxation, abolishing the whole tax system and starting over from scratch is unprecedented, but incremental changes happen all the time and are the stuff of political battles every day. The next chapter discusses the prospects and problems of changes to the way we tax ourselves that start from the system we have now.

8   Starting from Here

In his 1986 book *Untangling the Income Tax*, David Bradford relates the old story of a tourist who asks a native of Ireland for the best route to Dublin. The Irishman responds: "If I was you, I wouldn't start from here."[1] The analogy to tax reform is apt in more ways than one. Bradford means to illustrate his point that, having himself gained the familiarity of a native in the strange territory of comprehensive income measurement, his advice to a visitor thinking about tax reform would be to start somewhere else. He argues that because economic income is so difficult to measure, any tax system based on income will inevitably be something of a mess. In his view, completely untangling the tax system would require switching to a consumption tax.

Ironically, Bradford's story also illustrates that we have no choice but to start from where we are. Any reform effort will have to begin from the fact of the income tax we've already got. Our income tax evolved into its present state over the course of a century, forged by political compromise in a democratic system, the inevitable influence of special interests, and the government's responses to efforts by taxpayers to devise ever more sophisticated ways of avoiding taxes. The structure that has already been built up over time has important implications for who would win and who would lose from any reform, for how well any reform would work, and for the likelihood of any particular reform actually happening. Historically, policy changes that are as ambitious as eliminating the income tax and starting over from scratch have been extremely rare.

Whether completely replacing the income tax would be a good idea is a fascinating and important question. But significant, if not radical, changes to the tax system are being debated and enacted all the time. Most of these changes focus mainly on reducing or increasing revenue, but often they also have major impacts on the design of the system. The purpose of this chapter is to discuss and evaluate some possible changes in the way we tax ourselves that start from the system we have now. Constructing a tax system that is simpler, fairer, and better for the economy than what we have now is certainly possible to do without throwing out the whole current system. At the same time, many of the tax changes that have been at the top of the political agenda recently, while perhaps falling short of the label "fundamental tax reform," still involve very large stakes in terms of effects on the economy and government revenues, impact on the distribution of tax burdens, and influence on the complexity of the tax system. Changes that stay within the general framework of the current system, whether or not they deserve to be called *reforms*, are the subject of this chapter.

Integration: Eliminating the Double Taxation of Corporate Income

Economists have long considered the double taxation of corporate income to be an important problem with the U.S. income tax system, but until recently, it received little attention in the political arena. This changed to some extent in 2003, when a Bush administration proposal pushed it to the top of the domestic policy agenda. For both these reasons, we first consider this option for reforming the income tax.

Chapter 4 discusses the distortions that arise because corporation income can be taxed twice under our current tax system—first by the corporation tax and then again when the income is received by share-holders in the form of dividends or, to a lesser extent, capital gains. This tax treatment puts an inefficient penalty on business activity carried out in corporate form, and it distorts corporate financial structure toward debt finance. It also makes investment in corporate stock particularly unattractive relative to nonbusiness investments such as owner-occupied housing, causing too much high-priced housing to be built at the expense of more productive corporate investments.

The argument for eliminating the double taxation of corporate income is largely one of economic efficiency and not fairness, although it is often sold politically as an issue of fairness. The sound economic argument is that uneven taxation of different forms of investment causes investment to be allocated in a less productive manner than it could be. But uneven treatment is not necessarily unfair because putting savings into corporate equities is a voluntary choice. To the extent that the return to corporate stocks is taxed more heavily than other assets, demand for corporate stocks declines, and their prices go down until they offer a similar expected rate of return (after adjusting for risk) as other assets. The double taxation arguably caused horizontal inequity for people who owned stocks at the time it was originally instituted because they suffered a capital loss. But most people who own stocks today have not been penalized relative to other asset owners because they were largely compensated for the higher tax burden by paying a lower price for the stocks. As we discuss in chapter 6, a horizontal equity argument can be made for removing taxes on the return to saving in general, but there's nothing special about the double taxation of corporate income in this regard.

For similar reasons, if double taxation of corporate income is removed, some of the benefits will be dissipated into a windfall gain for current shareholders, as demand for stocks should rise in anticipation of their more favorable tax treatment, pushing up their prices and generating an immediate capital gain. There is no clear reason to think that such a windfall is in any way "deserved." The immediate rise in share prices also mitigates the degree to which the after-tax incentive to save rises, thus limiting any long-term economic gains. Taxpayers will still have improved incentives to channel saving toward more productive uses, though (reflected in increased demand for corporate stocks relative to other assets), and that's the best argument for addressing the problem.

At first blush, the obvious solution to the problem of double taxation is to simply eliminate the corporate income tax altogether. The obvious solution is not the right one. Just eliminating the corporation income tax would create formidable new problems, mainly because a large fraction of corporate income goes untaxed at the individual level. Recall that accrued capital gains are not taxed until they are realized, are not taxed at all if held until death and passed on to heirs, and even when realized are taxed at preferential rates. With no corporate income tax at all, taxpayers would have a strong (and inefficient) incentive to keep as much income in corporations as possible, deferring or perhaps eliminating taxation on that income altogether. Individuals would have a great incentive to incorporate themselves and devise schemes to "pay" themselves in ways that escape personal taxation, such as providing company cars, apartments, and so on. As a practical matter, an income tax system such as ours requires some form of corporate tax to serve as a backstop to the personal taxation of capital, and possibly labor, income. At the very least, it is needed to serve as a way to withhold individual tax liability for shareholders. As we have noted before, collecting tax at the business level is often more effective and less costly than collecting it at the personal level.

For these reasons, most proposals for eliminating the double taxation of corporate income involve some form of tax relief at the personal level for dividends and sometimes capital gains, on which corporate income tax has already been paid. This is known as *integration* of the corporate and personal tax systems. Indeed, many countries have already adopted such an approach. The most common policy is to grant taxable individual shareholders a credit against personal tax liability for a portion of the corporate tax attributable to the dividends they receive.

In early 2003, the Bush administration proposed a plan to do away with the double taxation of corporate income. As originally formulated, the Bush plan would allow individuals to exclude from adjusted gross income (AGI) any dividends that came from profits on which corporate income tax had been paid. The plan would also effectively exclude from AGI any capital gains that arose from new retained corporate earnings on which corporate tax had been paid. Currently, when an individual sells stock shares, the capital gain is calculated as the dollar proceeds from the sale of the stock, minus the amount that the shareholder originally paid (known as "basis") for that same stock. Under the proposal, each year shareholders would be allowed to add an amount to the basis of their stocks corresponding to their share of the corporation's profits that were taxed under the corporate income tax in that year and then reinvested in the firm, which would absolve those gains from personal taxation. Excluding *all* corporate capital gains and dividends from taxation at the personal level would be simpler than the Bush proposal, but it would suffer from two serious problems. First, a nontrivial portion of corporate income would be taxed at very low or zero effective rates, due to corporate tax sheltering. Limiting dividend and capital gains relief to cases where corporate tax was paid, moreover, has the beneficial effect of reducing (but not eliminating) the incentive to undertake corporate income tax avoidance and evasion. Second, a complete exclusion would provide a large windfall to shareholders by exempting capital gains on corporate stock that accrued *before* the plan was enacted. This would come on top of the windfall to shareholders already noted above. Such windfalls are highly inefficient because they do nothing to improve incentives and require raising other taxes that *do* harm incentives to make up the lost revenues. This is one reason that just lowering the capital gains tax rate is a poor substitute for a corporate tax integration plan.[2]

The Congressional Budget Office estimated the 10-year cost of this proposal, not including interest costs, to be $388 billion.[3] The larger deficits caused by the plan could be expected to reduce the amount of capital that is accumulated and owned by Americans, offsetting the improved incentives for the accumulation and allocation of capital caused by the tax cut. So it is not clear whether the net economic effect of the proposal would even be positive. As for the distributional effects, approximately half of all corporate stock outside of tax-preferred retirement accounts is owned by the wealthiest 1 percent of households, and approximately 85 percent is owned by the wealthiest 10 percent.[4] So the share of immediate benefits from any plan to cut personal tax rates on dividends and corporate capital gains across the board would be concentrated in a roughly similar fashion.[5] To the extent that the rest of the population owns stocks, they are held mostly in retirement accounts, which would receive no direct benefit from the plan.

The plan that Congress eventually enacted in May of 2003 was substantially different than the original Bush proposal. It reduced the top tax rate on *all* capital gains (not just those on corporate stock), as well as all dividends, to 15 percent. This did indeed reduce the extent of double taxation of corporate income. But since the capital gains tax cut applied to past as well as future accumulations of gains, a substantial portion of its revenue cost represented windfall gains related to past decisions and so had no incentive effects. There was no provision to limit tax relief at the personal level to cases where tax was actually paid at the corporate level, so there was no reduction in incentives for corporate tax sheltering. To reduce the advertised cost of the dividend and capital gains provisions to $148 billion, they were scheduled to "sunset" in 2009.[6] An Urban-Brookings Tax Policy Center analysis estimated that if the dividend and capital gains provisions were eventually made permanent, which seems politically likely, the cost would be $313 billion over 2003 to 2013, nearly as large as the original proposal.[7]

It would certainly be possible to design a plan that removes the inefficient tax treatment of corporate investment *without* the revenue or distributional effects described above. In a 1992 report that had been requested by the first President Bush, the U.S. Treasury put forward a proposal for a *comprehensive business income tax* (CBIT).[8] The CBIT plan offered the same treatment of dividends as the George W. Bush's 2003 proposal and included a provision for capital gains similar to that in the 2003 Bush plan as an option. But the CBIT would also eliminate interest deductions from the corporate tax, would exclude corporate bond interest from taxation at the personal level, and would apply to almost all businesses, not just corporations. The change in the treatment of corporate interest, in particular, would raise revenue because some interest income that currently escapes taxation at any level would now be taxed at the corporate level. As a result, the Treasury estimated that the plan as a whole (including the provision for capital gains) could reduce the corporate tax rate by three percentage points and still be roughly revenue-neutral. In addition to avoiding budget deficit problems, the CBIT would eliminate any tax preference for debt finance relative to equity finance of corporations because the returns to both would be taxed once at the same corporate rate under the CBIT.

This CBIT proposal would move the tax system closer to something like the Hall-Rabushka flat tax or the X-tax. It would still be a type of income tax, however, because business investment would continue to be depreciated rather than expensed. In this way, the normal return to corporate investment would be taxed, albeit only at the firm level.

Another option would be the "tax capital income once" plan put forward by Len Burman of the Urban Institute. This would combine the 2003 Bush administration plan for addressing double taxation with a provision to *fully* tax at the personal level any capital gains realizations that are not currently double taxed, including gains on corporate shares that do not arise directly from reinvested profits, and gains on noncorporate assets such as real estate. These sorts of capital gains are now taxed at much lower effective rates than other income. This proposal would move the tax system closer to a uniform comprehensive tax on all income and would reduce the tax-sheltering opportunities that arise from the possibility of relabeling ordinary income as capital gains. Moreover, Burman estimates that it would increase revenues while making the system slightly more progressive.[9]

Corporate Welfare and Corporate Tax Shelters

The Bush proposal of 2003 focused attention on the *double* taxation of corporate income that can occur under the U.S. income tax structure. Ironically, at the same time the public spotlight was directed toward cases of egregious corporate tax avoidance, tax evasion, and preferential tax treatment, all of which suggest that some corporate income is not double taxed, single taxed, or even taxed at all. We turn to these issues next.

One frequent rhetorical target of politicians is *corporate welfare*. Although everyone claims to be against corporate welfare, not everyone defines it the same way. Defining it as "programs and subsidies that primarily benefit profitable corporations," a Stop Corporate Welfare Coalition of organizations drawn from all across the political spectrum could come up with only 12 programs that cost slightly more than $11 billion over five years. A *Time* magazine exposé in 1998 put the bill for federal corporate welfare at $125 billion per year, a small part of which represented tax breaks.[10]

We must tread carefully in addressing corporate welfare delivered via the income tax system because much corporate-source income is taxed relatively heavily. Certainly some provisions in the tax code, however, provide preferences for investments done by certain types of corporations or businesses. The most obvious example is the generous depreciation deductions granted to oil, gas, and mining operations. Other industries that tend to be favored include rental housing, real estate, insurance, and financial services. The libertarian Cato Institute argues that targeted tax breaks are not corporate welfare because allowing corporations to keep more of their own earnings is not a form of welfare. Even the Cato Institute admits, though, "that while targeted tax breaks are not welfare, they are bad policy and should be eliminated."[11]

As with double taxation of corporate income, the main problem with these types of preferences once they are in place is inefficiency, not unfairness. For example, the preference for oil drilling has caused investment funds to flow into that line of business at the expense of other, more productive investments. The uneven playing field that results prevents the country's resources from going toward their most efficient use.

Whether it makes sense to eliminate these preferences in the name of equity is less clear-cut. People who owned oil-drilling operations when the preference was instituted certainly profited handsomely. By now, however, the value of any tax preference is probably reflected in the price that people pay to buy shares in such a business, so that people who have recently bought into oil-drilling operations probably have gained little or nothing from the special depreciation allowances. They would, however, lose if the preference were removed. In any event, getting rid of these preferences would likely enhance the efficiency of our tax system.

Most recently, corporate tax shelters have grabbed the headlines from corporate welfare, implying that rich corporations were dodging

their tax obligations at the same time they were deceiving their shareholders about their financial health and prospects. But the headlines
don't capture the subtleties of this topic. First of all, there is no consensus on how to even define *tax shelter*. Some would apply the term to a
broad range of activities that help taxpayers to either avoid or evade
taxes, while others would limit the term to transactions that have
no purpose but to reduce taxes and that technically violate the law.
Avoidance opportunities often arise from the difficulty of measuring
true economic income and the resulting compromises that the tax code
makes in defining income. As discussed in chapter 5, tax avoidance
often involves principles such as tax arbitrage (taking advantage of
differences in tax rates applied to different entities or different types
of income or deductions) and deferral of taxes (made possible, for
example, by taxation of capital gains on realization or reinvestment of
profits earned by an offshore subsidiary in a low-tax country). These
activities may be combined with efforts to improperly recharacterize
income or payments into forms that receive favorable tax treatment (for
example, converting ordinary income into capital gains or labeling
nondeductible repayments of debt principal as deductible interest payments) or to create fictional losses, many of which cross over the line
into tax evasion. Efforts of this sort can be embedded in a series of complicated transactions that are difficult to monitor. Some of these activities are perfectly legal and some are not, and in many cases it is unclear
whether they are legal or not. Tax shelters often capitalize on ambiguities in the law or in complicated situations that were not foreseen by
drafters of the law. These are usually resolved eventually by the IRS,
the courts, or Congress but can produce significant tax savings in the
meantime.

Regardless of their legality, all of these efforts can be economically
wasteful. While they often make sense from the individual corporation's perspective, they are inefficient from a societal perspective. They
use up real resources (including the time and effort of the lawyers,
accountants, and investment bankers who devise the shelters) that
could have otherwise been devoted to some socially productive purpose, they divert resources toward particular types of investments or
other activities that help facilitate such avoidance behavior, and they
require tax rates to be higher than they otherwise would have to be to
raise a given amount of revenue.

No good evidence is available on how much corporate income
escapes taxation through shelters. There is broad agreement that tax

shelters were an especially important problem between 1981 and 1986. They were curtailed significantly by a combination of the Tax Reform Act of 1986 and lower inflation (which reduced the effectiveness of shelters that rely on deductions of high nominal interest payments that largely reflected inflation). Many have argued that tax shelters have been a growing problem again in recent years, but this is difficult to verify conclusively. Aside from the lack of agreement on a definition, tax shelters are by their nature difficult to detect and highly secretive, both to avoid arousing the suspicion of the IRS and to hide the details of their operation so that tax shelter promoters can continue to collect fees for explaining them. Some have pointed to an apparent increase since the early 1990s in the gap between corporate profits reported to shareholders and corporate taxable income reported to the IRS as evidence of the proliferation of tax shelters. But much of this gap can be explained by legitimate differences in accounting and reporting rules for the two different income concepts, and publicly available data cannot definitively establish what is responsible for the portion of the gap that cannot be explained in this way.[12]

What evidence we do have on tax shelters is largely anecdotal, but some of these anecdotes are striking. For example, the Joint Tax Committee recently issued a 2,700-page report largely devoted to explaining the tax shelters used by the Enron Corporation. Eleven specific shelters that could be identified were estimated to have reduced Enron's U.S. tax liability by a total of $257 million, while at the same time increasing the profits Enron reported to its shareholders by $651 million between 1995 and 2001.[13] Still, the potential size of the problem needs to be kept in perspective. The corporate income tax continues to raise a great deal of revenue—$180 billion in 2002. The widely cited $10 billion figure for the annual amount of revenue lost to corporate tax shelters—based on the educated guess of Joseph Bankman of Stanford Law School, an expert in the field and advocate of cracking down on shelters—amounts to just 6 percent of corporate tax revenues.[14]

What can be done about corporate tax shelters? Some have argued that switching to a consumption tax like the flat tax or the X-tax would greatly reduce the problem because it would feature fewer compromises and inconsistencies in the definition of the tax base than would an income tax. This argument undoubtedly has merit, but recall from our discussion in chapter 7 that academic tax lawyers have already started to find inconsistencies in the flat tax that could be exploited.

Practicing tax lawyers and other professionals will, after all, invest their time and talents in finding loopholes only once a new law is in place.

Moving part of the way toward a consumption tax (for example, by accelerating depreciation deductions and otherwise reducing the effective tax rate on capital income) while retaining provisions that make sense only in an income tax (such as deductibility of interest payments) would *exacerbate* the inconsistencies in the current system and would tend to *expand* opportunities for tax sheltering. While switching wholesale to a consumption tax would make the tax rate on the ordinary return to saving and investment zero, an inconsistent combination of consumption and income tax features could create effective tax rates that are effectively *less* than zero on some investments and greater than zero on others. For that reason, a piecemeal approach might increase rather than diminish the inefficiency and complexity of the tax system.

In the context of the current income tax, addressing tax shelters is to some extent an issue of enforcement. Expanding efforts by the IRS to uncover tax shelter activities, clarify their legality, and impose penalties for abusive behavior could all reduce sheltering activity. The IRS is faced with a particularly difficult job here, though, as the people who devise tax shelters are highly compensated and highly skilled and seem able to come up with ever more ingenious—indeed, diabolical— methods of sheltering corporate income from tax. In 2003, the IRS implemented a regulation creating a list of specific tax-shelter-related transactions that corporations must now disclose to the IRS if the transactions exceed a certain value. This is intended to make it easier for the IRS to monitor such transactions. It is unclear how effective this regulation will be by itself, especially given the problems the IRS is having in keeping up with its existing workload, discussed in chapter 5.

Another set of suggestions would exploit the fact that managers of corporations have an incentive to maximize *book income*, the measure of corporate profits reported in financial statements to shareholders, to boost share prices. Therefore, many tax shelters attempt to reduce taxable income while leaving reported book income unchanged or even increasing it. Some have argued that requiring corporations to report to the public more detailed and informative numbers regarding their taxable income and tax payments might reduce the incentive to engage in tax shelters and to artificially inflate reported book income. This could have benefits not only for the tax system but also for the efficiency of financial markets. A large gap between profits reported to shareholders and profits reported to the IRS might be taken as a signal that the company was misleading investors about its true profits. This signal would have been a good one in the case of Enron, for example. On the other hand, shareholders' desire for accurate information may be swamped by their desire for low taxes, so whether or how much this would help is not clear. Better information disclosure could make tax shelters more transparent to the public, which might lead to greater pressure to address them. Another proposal recommends revising corporate tax forms to require a more informative accounting of the reasons for differences between book income and taxable income.[15] This would presumably allow the IRS to identify and investigate potential tax shelters more easily and to target its resources more effectively. It could also be used to strengthen the effectiveness of the public-disclosure measures mentioned above.

Inflation Indexing

The U.S. income tax ignores inflation in the measurement of capital income. In some cases, this leads to an overstatement of income and finds taxable income where no real income exists. In other cases, it understates income by overstating deductions. It does all this capriciously and in a way that leads to inefficient patterns of saving and investment. In chapter 4, we explain why failure to exclude the portion of capital income or deductions that represents compensation for inflation can greatly increase the effective tax rate applied to the real portion of that income or deduction, which exacerbates the distortion of incentives. In chapter 6, we discuss why it is difficult to fix this in an income tax and why no such problem arises in a consumption tax.

At the current low rate of inflation, the problems caused by this mismeasurement are not large because nominal returns to capital largely reflect real rather than inflationary gains. If we could be sure inflation would go no higher, fixing this problem in the income tax would probably not be worth the complications that would be involved. If inflation approaches double digits, mismeasurement gets to be a serious problem—big enough that the Treasury Department included in its 1984 tax reform proposal a comprehensive scheme to *index* the measurement of capital income for inflation. This is by no means an easy task and would surely complicate the taxpaying process. The Treasury proposed to allow taxpayers to calculate taxable capital gains using a purchase price that reflects the inflation that has occurred since the purchase of the asset. In addition, the proposal allowed firms to inflation-index the "basis" of depreciable assets, to allow firms the option of using indexed first-in, first-out inventory accounting rules, and to index interest receipts and payments (other than payments on mortgages) by excluding a given fraction that depends on the previous year's inflation rate.[16] Even then, the adjustments for inflation would in most cases be only rough approximations. Primarily because of its complexity, the indexing scheme did not survive the legislative process and was not part of the Tax Reform Act of 1986.[17]

Making the entire income tax system inflation-neutral is clearly a tall order. Nonetheless, a number of countries, mostly those that have experienced very high inflation rates, have to some extent indexed their income tax systems. Partially indexing the tax system leads to its own problems. For example, consider the consequences if only capital gains were indexed, by allowing the seller of appreciated assets to increase the buying price used to calculate taxable gains by the rise in the average price level since the asset was purchased. This would certainly improve the measurement of real capital gains; however, this would make investments in assets that yield capital gains even more attractive than they already are relative to other investments. Moreover, in high-inflation environments it would give a tremendous tax-induced advantage to debt-financed purchases of capital assets. The presumably high nominal interest rates on borrowing would remain completely deductible, even though most of the nominal interest rate represented an inflation premium, while any nominal capital gains would go tax-free. This is the recipe for a classic tax shelter: borrow, deduct the interest, and purchase a tax-preferred asset. The economic cost of this scenario is that investment would be drawn away from other outlets that, taxes aside, yield a higher return to their investors. Another cost would be additional complication, not only because the process of indexing itself is complicated but also because it would encourage extra financial transactions (such as borrowing money to buy appreciating assets) for the sole purpose of reducing one's taxes.

Finally, note that mismeasurement of the real value of capital income and deductions due to inflation is completely separate from the issue of *bracket creep* caused by inflation. That phenomenon arises when the real value of tax brackets, exemption levels, and all other dollar figures are eroded over time as the price level rises. For example, as noted in chapter 2, in tax year 2002, a married couple with two children paid no income tax until their income reached $38,150. If the standard deduction, exemption, and credit amounts stayed the same, as prices rise that $38,150 would correspond to a lower and lower real income, and more and more families would find, by dint of inflation alone, that they had gone from nontaxable to taxable status. Other families would move from one tax bracket to the next. The problem of bracket creep has been almost entirely eliminated from the U.S. income tax system since 1984; now all dollar figures for brackets, personal exemptions, standard deductions, and similar features are automatically increased by the rate of inflation.[18] It threatens to return as a major problem soon, however, because the alternative minimum tax is not indexed for inflation. In any event, the problem that capital income is mismeasured where there is inflation remains even though bracket creep has been mostly eliminated. Indeed, this problem would exist even under a single-rate tax system where bracket creep is not an issue because that system has no brackets at all.

Capital Gains

The treatment of capital gains is one of the most controversial and publicly debated issues about the income tax, with Republicans generally wanting to reduce rates on capital gains as much as possible and Democrats wanting to keep them near rates on other income. It is a particularly divisive issue because realized capital gains are highly concentrated among high-income individuals. In 1999, for example, 73 percent of gains were received by households whose adjusted gross income (AGI) exceeded $200,000, and capital gains constituted 28 percent of the AGI of these taxpayers.[19] Because of this concentration, preferential tax treatment of capital gains is the archetypical example of "trickle-down economics," where the immediate benefits go to a small group of highly affluent people, and the extent of longer-term, more widely distributed benefits is hotly disputed.

According to the economist's definition of income—consumption plus the change in wealth—increases in the value of capital assets are certainly income. When a stock you own increases in value from $1,000 to $1,100, you are $100 wealthier just as you would be if you won $100 in the lottery or got paid $100 for overtime work.[20] By this logic, all of capital gains should be included in taxable income as they accrue with no preferences.

Implementing this definition is not simple. For many capital assets, obtaining a market value that can be verified by the IRS or even be known to the owner is extremely difficult. It's no problem for highly liquid securities such as shares of companies traded on the NASDAQ or the New York Stock Exchange. But it is a real problem for closely held businesses, real estate, and other assets such as paintings. From an administrative standpoint, requiring taxpayers to value all their capital assets each year (so that they could report as income the increase in value) and having the IRS monitor these reports would be very cumbersome.

Rather than requiring taxpayers to annually value all their capital assets and include the change in value as income, capital gains are taxed only on *realization*, which usually means when the asset is sold.[21] One implication of postponing the taxation of the gain until the time of sale, rather than when the asset appreciated, is that it confers on the taxpayer the time value of money: paying the bill later rather than sooner is always better. In one sense, the IRS offers the asset holder an interest-free loan that is equal to the tax due at the time the asset appreciates and that begins when the gain is made until the time the asset is sold. This loan is more valuable the higher interest rates are and the longer an asset is held. Taxing capital gains at the time of sale rather than at the time of accrual provides an incentive to hold on to appreciated assets longer than otherwise, a phenomenon known as the *lock-in effect*. The lock-in effect is greatly exacerbated because of another feature of current law that is discussed further below: there is no tax at all on capital gains if the asset is not sold during the holder's lifetime.

This combination—the deferral of tax until sale and the eventuality that all the gain will be forgiven from tax—makes potentially appreciating assets much more attractive than assets (like taxable bonds) that pay out their return in a taxable form. This provides a purely tax-related advantage to investments (such as real estate) that more easily can provide returns to their investors in the form of appreciation. This was a key element of the rash of tax shelter investments of the early 1980s, which involved purchases of appreciating assets coupled with loans offering fully deductible interest.

Tax preferences accorded to capital gains also create a tremendous incentive to repackage ordinary income into capital gains. People who buy fixer-upper houses take advantage of this feature because their time and effort is not taxed as labor income. Instead, they are reflected in a higher sale price for the house and hardly taxed at all due to generous rules about capital gains on owner-occupied housing. Other sophisticated taxpayers make use of stock options or "collapsible" corporations to convert labor compensation into capital gains. Some lawyers speculate that, before the Tax Reform Act of 1986 when the capital gains tax rate preference was especially large (a 30 percentage-point difference for top-bracket taxpayers), about half of all the transactional complexity of the tax law was due to this feature of the law.[22]

The 1986 tax reform virtually eliminated the rate differential on capital gains, although the advantages of deferral and tax exemption at death remained. The rate differential has since crept back up, as taxpayers in the 35 percent tax bracket for ordinary income now pay no more than 15 percent on their realized capital gains.

For all the problems caused by preferential taxation, taxing capital gains realizations like other income poses its own problems, particularly given other features of the current tax code. For one thing, in inflationary periods much capital appreciation represents not a real increase in income but only a catching up to higher prices. Second, the income that generates capital gains on corporate shares is already taxed to some extent by the corporate income tax. Third, given the realization-based tax system, imposing higher rates of tax will inevitably provide some deterrent to efficient sales of capital assets— the lock-in effect already discussed. Fourth, allowing full deductibility of capital losses is not feasible because investors with diversified portfolios could "cherry-pick" their assets, selling only those with losses and holding those with gains and thereby consistently generating losses for tax purposes.[23] But the current asymmetrical treatment of losses and gains makes the private investor's prospects look less attractive: she pays a share to the government if the investment turns out well but gets little help if it turns out badly. Such treatment can inefficiently deter risky investments.

A corporate integration plan, such as the 2003 Bush administration proposal, the CBIT, or Len Burman's "tax capital income once" plan, all discussed earlier in this chapter, could help solve some of these problems. These plans would all eliminate double taxation of capital gains on corporate shares. They would also eliminate the lock-in effect associated with capital gains arising from corporate profits reinvested after enactment of the plan. This is because such gains would no longer be taxed when realized at the personal level and the income underlying the gain would be taxed at the corporate level as it accrues. The Burman plan would additionally reduce the undertaxation (relative to a comprehensive income tax) of other sorts of capital gains.

Lock-in effects and tax avoidance could be further reduced by addressing the exclusion from tax of capital gains that are held until death. For income tax purposes, the taxable capital gain is calculated as the difference between the proceeds from selling an asset and the basis of that asset, where the basis is generally the amount the individual originally paid to buy the asset. Under current law, heirs are able to *step up* the basis of inherited assets to the value at the date of the donor's death so that any unrealized capital gains accumulated to that point escape income taxation forever. This provides an effective avenue for avoiding income taxes. In fact, the income arising from unrealized capital gains can effectively be consumed during the lifetime of the asset's owner without the owner ever paying tax on it, and the owner can even reduce other taxes in the process. For example, someone could hold an appreciated asset until his or her death and thus never pay tax on the gains, borrow through a home equity loan and use the proceeds to consume, and deduct the interest payments on the loan from the income tax. When the heir sells the asset (with no tax) after the asset owner's death, he or she can use the appreciated asset to pay off the debt.

One reform option would tax unrealized capital gains at death, which would greatly reduce the lock-in effect and avoidance opportunities. Another option would require heirs to carry over the donor's basis on inherited assets, so capital gains that had accumulated prior to the donor's death would eventually be taxed whenever the heirs sell the assets. As a result of the 2001 tax act, a limited form of *carryover basis* is scheduled to apply for wealthy people in conjunction with the scheduled (temporary) elimination of the estate tax in 2010. Under the new law, the amount that could be added to the basis of all assets bequeathed to heirs by a married couple would effectively be limited to a total of $5.6 million.[24] Any excess of unrealized capital gains beyond that amount would eventually be taxed if the heirs sell the assets. Legislators adopted this provision because they recognized that the estate tax currently puts at least some brake on the attractiveness of avoiding income taxes by holding appreciated assets until death and were concerned that this variety of tax avoidance would otherwise expand greatly if and when the estate tax is repealed. A similar carryover-basis plan, but without the exemption, was passed as part of the 1976 tax bill to take effect one year hence. Its implementation was subsequently delayed, and then it was later repealed before it ever took effect, partly because of concerns about the administrative burden of requiring that records of the purchase price of assets that were bequeathed be kept across generations. This legislative history creates some doubt about whether the plan enacted in 2001 will survive to actually be implemented.

As discussed earlier in this chapter, indexing the income tax for inflation could limit inadvertent overtaxation of capital gains but would be difficult to implement. However, indexing capital gains but not other capital income or deductions is flawed. Taxing capital gains at a rate that is below the rate levied on other income is often defended as a means of reducing the lock-in effect, encouraging risk-taking, and reducing double taxation. But applying differential rates on different types of income leads to all the problems mentioned above. It is a blunt instrument for attacking double taxation because there are many appreciating assets besides corporate stock.

For all these reasons, the tax treatment of capital gains under an income tax involves a conceptually unsatisfying compromise between the desire to tax all income uniformly to minimize distortions and complexity and the difficulty of implementing a truly uniform regime. Whatever uneasy compromise is reached, one caveat about changes in capital gains taxation applies. Expanding the preferential treatment of existing accrued capital gains provides no incentive to buy new stock or new real estate; instead, it just provides a windfall gain related to past decisions. Any new preferences should, if feasible, be restricted to new gains.

Savings Incentives in the Income Tax

As we have emphasized throughout the book, the U.S. federal income tax is in fact an awkward hybrid of income and consumption taxes. This is partly because a variety of provisions—including IRAs, Keogh plans, 401(k) and 403(b) pension plans, and numerous other tax-preferred pension plans and saving accounts—to various degrees of effectiveness eliminate the tax on the return to savings. In recent years, these kinds of plans have been expanded considerably. Their popularity partly reflects a growing enthusiasm for consumption taxation, perhaps combined with a skeptical appraisal of the likelihood of fundamental tax reform, so that tax-preferred savings accounts are seen as a feasible way to move toward consumption taxation. However, for reasons we discuss below, most recent proposals to expand these sorts of accounts would be highly imperfect substitutes for a revenue-neutral switch to a consistently designed consumption tax.

These plans have three essential features. First, the ordinary return on contributions to such plans is exempt from tax as it would be under a consumption tax. In most cases, this is accomplished by excluding employer and employee contributions from tax, allowing interest, dividends, and other returns on the assets in the account to accumulate tax-free, and then taxing withdrawals from the accounts. In some cases, such as Roth IRAs, contributions cannot be deducted from taxable income, but no tax is charged on either the assets' returns or on withdrawals, which also effectively exempts the return to saving from tax. Second, maximum limits are imposed in various ways on the amount of contributions that can receive favorable tax treatment. For example, in 2003 annual individual contributions to IRAs are limited to $3,000 for those under age 50 and $3,500 for those age 50 and over, with the respective limits scheduled to rise to $5,000 and $6,000 by 2008. Combined employer-employee contributions to 401(k) and 403(b) plans are limited to $40,000 per employee (indexed for inflation after 2002), and the employee portion of the contribution is limited to $12,000 (or $14,000 for those over age 50) in 2003, rising to $15,000 and $20,000, respectively, by 2006. Third, in some cases, eligibility is limited to people with incomes below a certain level. For example, eligibility for conventional IRAs is phased out for married couples with AGI between $60,000 and $70,000 in 2003 (rising to $80,000 to $100,000 in 2007), unless neither spouse has access to an employer-provided pension plan. Eligibility for Roth IRAs is phased out for married couples with AGI between $150,000 and $160,000.

Advocates of tax-preferred saving plans argue that they provide many people with the opportunity to attain the economic advantages of a consumption tax—no tax on the return to saving—but that they do so in a "limited" way that, compared to abandoning completely all taxation of returns to saving, costs less government revenue and restricts the size of the windfall going to very high-income people with large amounts of capital income. But a big problem arises with this argument. In some cases, this compromise between income and consumption taxation essentially provides the worst of both worlds—losing revenue without actually affecting the incentive to save or increasing saving.

Consider the implications of contribution limits—for example, the current $3,000 limit on contributions to IRAs for those under age 50. This limit makes no difference to taxpayers who would not in any event want or be able to contribute as much as $3,000 in a year, so for them an IRA could provide an incentive to save more than they otherwise would. For those taxpayers who would otherwise save more than that, however, and don't mind subjecting their funds to a penalty for early withdrawal, the IRA deduction is a nice gift, but *at the margin* it will have absolutely no influence on how much they save. If you're trying to decide whether to save $5,000 or $6,000, the IRA program is immaterial because you've already maxed out on your contribution. Thus, the IRA provides a reward for saving you would have done anyway rather than an inducement to do more saving. In fact, because the tax reduction you obtain from it adds to your disposable income, having an IRA should therefore *increase* your consumption, which reduces rather than increases national saving. Moreover, reducing taxes without improving incentives is inefficient because it means we have to forgo some other equal tax reduction that would have improved incentives. This is a major reason why, in the Tax Reform Act of 1986, eligibility for deductible IRAs was restricted mainly to people with incomes low enough that they would have been unlikely to save more than the contribution limits anyway.

The other key problem is that while IRAs and other tax-favored saving plans are intended to encourage saving, they actually subsidize deposits into an account, and making a deposit is not at all the same as saving. As a result, people can use IRAs and pensions to reduce their taxes without doing any saving at all, as long as they have assets outside of these accounts or an ability to borrow. To see how this works, consider an individual who over the years has saved up $12,000, which is now invested in stocks and bonds. If she takes $3,000 of this and deposits it into an IRA account, she gets the tax benefits even though her saving has not increased or decreased; it's just been moved from one account to another. Of course, if she deposits $3,000 every year into an IRA account and does no more new saving, after four years she will have transferred all of her wealth into the IRA account. At that time, she may face the decision that the IRA is designed to alter: to get any further tax benefit, she might have to do some new saving. But even then, she could avoid actually doing any net saving by increasing her borrowing by the same amount that that she contributes to her account (or equivalently, reducing the rate at which she pays back an outstanding loan). The taxpayer makes money on this strategy as long as the interest on the loan is deductible from tax, as it would be on a home mortgage, for example.

Our current savings incentives in general subsidize deposits rather than saving because deposits are a lot easier to measure. Accurately measuring saving would require at a minimum every taxpayer keeping track of all additions to assets, subtracting out all withdrawals, and recording and reporting to the IRS all borrowing. As discussed earlier, this procedure would substantially complicate the tax system.

Some basic facts about utilization of IRAs and pensions can help illustrate the nature and extent of the problem. In 1996, when the IRA contribution limit was $2,000, about two-thirds of people who contributed to an IRA contributed the maximum amount.[25] For most IRA participants, therefore, the IRA probably provided a windfall rather than an incentive to save.[26] Moreover, the vast majority of people *eligible* to contribute to a deductible IRA simply didn't contribute anything. In 1996, only 6 percent of households eligible to contribute to tax-deductible IRAs actually did so.[27]

The story for pensions is a bit more complicated. In 1998, about 47 percent of all workers actively participated in tax-deferred pension plans, with 36 percent of workers participating in a defined-contribution plan such as a 401(k), and 11 percent of workers participating in a defined-benefit plan only (see chapter 2 for an explanation of the different types of pensions).[28] Defined-benefit plans have essentially no impact on individuals' incentive to save at the margin because individual workers have no control over how much is saved in these plans on their behalf. Most participants in defined-contribution plans do have the opportunity to increase their tax-deductible contributions, so that these plans do increase the incentive to save (or at least to contribute to the account). For example, a study by the General Accounting Office found that only about 6 percent of defined-contribution pension plan participants were constrained by a legal contribution limit, and an additional 4 percent were constrained by a lower limit imposed by their employers; the other 90 percent could have contributed more but did not.[29]

The bottom line, then, is that between IRAs and defined-contribution pension plans, most people probably have the opportunity to do additional saving that receives consumption tax treatment, although apparently many do not take advantage of this opportunity. On the other hand, a substantial number of people who actually participate in IRA and pension plans are making the maximum allowable contribution, and these tend to be upper-income people who account for most of saving done in the United States. For these people, the special tax treatment applied to such plans generally provides a windfall rather than an incentive to save.

Some economists maintain that retirement saving accounts provide an important institutional commitment device that helps people overcome their natural tendency not to do the retirement saving that they ultimately know is good for them. Traditional economic models assume that people are forward-looking, well informed, and fully rational with regard to their saving (and all other) behavior. But increasingly well-documented evidence shows that many people suffer from problems like temptation to spend cash in hand today, have a poor understanding of basic principles of financial planning, and put little thought into saving decisions. For example, recent research suggests that employee decisions regarding pension saving often follow the "path of least resistance," accepting whatever the default plan provided by the employer is. By contrast, a model of fully rational saving behavior would tend to predict that employees would take advantage of options provided by these plans to finely tailor the amount and kind of saving they do to match their tastes, circumstances, and incentives. This suggests that institutions like employer-provided pensions may have important impacts on saving independent of their effects on incentives.[30] Thus, tax preferences that create an incentive for employers to operate such plans might increase saving. But switching all the way to a consumption tax could conceivably weaken the employer-provided pension system, as the tax advantage to setting up such plans with an employer would disappear. As a result, this theory suggests that such a reform might actually reduce saving.

Many economists now take seriously the idea that certain people are unable to commit to save as much as they "should" and that the problem is particularly severe for low- and moderate-income people, as both the pressures to spend today and the consequences of undersaving are the worst for this group. Moreover, low- and moderate-income workers are also much less likely to be enrolled in a pension plan and thus do not benefit from private pensions' role as a commitment device. This could support a case for going beyond removing distortions and perhaps subsidizing saving among low-income people, as well as creating institutions that do a better job of getting low- and moderate-income people in the habit of saving. The 2001 tax act took a step in this direction by enacting a temporary 50 percent credit for contributions to IRAs by low-income people.[31]

In 2003, the Bush administration floated a proposal that would dramatically expand opportunities for tax-favored saving by increasing contribution limits and eliminating or weakening income limits for eligibility.[32] Increasing contribution limits reduces the number of people who are constrained by contribution limits, and for those people the plans might now provide an incentive to do additional saving rather than serving *solely* as a windfall. On the other hand, it would increase the size of the windfall going to those who remain above the limits. Extending eligibility for contribution-limited saving accounts like IRAs to higher-income people might improve incentives to save for some of them, but for many it would just provide an opportunity to shift assets from taxable to tax-free accounts. The vast majority of people, who are already contributing less than the limits, would be unaffected, and most of the benefits of the changes would go to upper-income people. On the positive side, consolidating existing saving accounts, making the rules simpler and more uniform, and eliminating phase-outs of eligibility would simplify the taxpaying process and rationalize what saving incentives now exist.

While expanding tax-deferred saving accounts is sometimes promoted as a step in the direction of a consumption tax, this approach is in fact fundamentally different from switching to a consumption tax. As explained in chapter 6, moving to a consumption tax would impose a tax on preexisting wealth as it is consumed, and much of the economic benefit of such a reform comes from that transitional tax. In contrast, expanding tax-deferred saving accounts enables people to avoid taxes on the returns to their preexisting assets by moving those assets into the accounts, without imposing any transitional burden. As such, this approach is more like adopting a wage tax. Moreover, this approach retains elements of the income tax that are inconsistent with a consumption tax, such as deductibility of interest, which exacerbates inefficient tax-sheltering opportunities and continues to subsidize immediate consumption relative to saving.

All in all, the array of tax-preferred saving plans is an inefficient way to reduce the disincentives to save under an income tax. If people are presumed to systematically undersave—and this is by no means obvious—then other policies, such as providing refundable credits for low-income savers and expanding their participation in pension plans, are worth considering. Finally, if private pensions are the key to more saving, the tax incentive for employers may be the most important incentive of all. The fact that, under a consumption tax system, employer-provided pensions might be cut back suggests that private saving might actually decline.

The Estate Tax

Estate taxation serves purposes similar to income taxation, and the arguments for and against each are closely related. The modern estate tax was enacted just three years after the income tax, in 1916, but until recently received little attention in the political arena. However, while thus far talk of abolishing the income tax has been just that, talk, a law that eventually abolishes the estate tax has already been passed. The 2001 tax legislation has scheduled a gradual increase in the estate tax exemption and a reduction in rates through 2009, eliminates the tax in 2010, and then restores the tax to its pre-2001 condition in 2011. This bizarre situation guarantees that the issue will be revisited in the near future.

Why have an estate tax? The main argument made by proponents of the estate tax is that it is an important component of a progressive tax system. In 1998, only the richest 2 percent of decedents in the United States paid federal estate tax. Since then, the exemption has been raised from $625,000 to $1 million in 2002, and it is scheduled to rise in gradual steps to $3.5 million by 2009. So as time goes by, the estate tax will apply to a thinner and thinner slice of only the very wealthiest segment of society. In 2000, estates over $5 million, which represented the richest 0.1 percent of decedents in the United States, accounted for 51 percent of all estate and gift tax revenues. Given the recent dramatic rise in wealth and incomes at the top of the distribution documented in chapter 3, the amount of revenue that would be raised by a tax imposed only on the wealthiest could be expected to grow significantly in the future. Thus, the exemption can be raised considerably without losing much revenue.

Above the exempt level, high rates apply, ranging from 41 to 49 percent in 2002, although unlimited deductions are allowed for gifts to a spouse or to charity. A married couple can effectively leave twice the amount of the exemption to heirs tax-free by making full use of the exemptions at the death of each spouse. These features make the estate tax by far the most progressive component of the tax system.

In 2001, the estate tax collected $28 billion in revenues for the federal government (and approximately $4 billion for the states).[33] Although this represents a small portion of federal revenues, at about 1.4 percent in 2001, it represents a nontrivial portion of the tax burden placed on upper-income people. For instance, taxpayers with adjusted gross income above $200,000 represented roughly the top 2 percent of income earners, and the personal income tax raised $369 billion in revenue from them in 2001. Estate tax liability was equal to about 7.6 percent of that.[34]

The cases for and against a progressive tax system are addressed in chapter 3. But if the goal of the estate tax is to achieve progressivity, this

raises the question of why an estate tax is preferable to levying somewhat higher income tax rates on upper-income people. For instance, in
2000, if we had eliminated the estate tax and increased the marginal tax
rate in the top bracket of the income tax by 3 percentage points, we
would have raised about the same revenue and achieved very roughly
the same distributional effects over the course of peoples' lifetimes.[35]

One argument for using an estate tax as a supplement to income
taxation is that our income tax fails to tax a considerable portion of income, which may make it difficult to achieve the degree of vertical and
horizontal equity that society might desire. For instance, estimates by
economists James Poterba of MIT and Scott Weisbenner of the Federal
Reserve Board of Governors suggest that 42 percent of the value of
estates over $5 million represents unrealized capital gains, income that
would never be taxed by the personal income tax.[36] Taxing estates is
also an administratively convenient way of raising tax revenue from
the very wealthy. Even in the absence of taxes, estates are required to
go through a detailed legal process that reveals much information
about the decedent's economic resources that would be difficult to
obtain in any other way.

Horizontal equity arguments are invoked by both supporters and
opponents of the estate tax. Supporters of the estate tax contend that
people who receive very large inheritances start off unfairly with a big
unearned advantage in life. Opponents of the tax focus on the donor
rather than the donee, questioning whether people who prefer to
"spend" their money on their children via bequests should be penalized relative to people who prefer to spend their money while they are
alive. Between two people who earn the same incomes over their lives,
the one who saves more of it will face a higher estate tax burden (if they
are sufficiently wealthy to face the tax, that is).

The estate tax is also defended on the grounds that it creates a strong
incentive for the wealthy to give to charity, both during life and at
death. Because charitable bequests are fully deductible from the estate
tax, someone who faces a 49 percent marginal estate tax rate can leave
$1 to charity while sacrificing only 51 cents of bequests to heirs. Thus,
the estate tax effectively cuts the relative price of a charitable bequest in
half for the wealthiest members of society. The estate tax also increases
the incentive to give to charity during life, since anything given to charity while alive is not left over at death to be included in the taxable estate. In 2000, $16 billion of charitable bequests were reported on estate
tax returns, and $55 billion of charitable donations were reported on the

income tax returns of the top 2 percent of income earners.[37] Most empirical research done on this topic suggests that charitable giving can be expected to decline if the estate tax is repealed. For example, over the twentieth century, as the marginal tax rate on the typical estate tax return increased, the share of the value of estates that was left to charity also increased significantly.[38] Although this correlation could conceivably have been caused by other influences on charitable behavior that changed over time, research that controls for these influences and takes advantage of the fact that estate tax and inheritance tax rates changed in different ways over time across different real wealth levels and different states also finds that charitable bequests respond strongly to incentives and that repeal of the estate tax is likely to reduce charitable giving.[39]

The estate tax reduces the incentive to save for those whose saving is at least partly motivated by the desire to leave a large bequest. After all, the most straightforward way for taxpayers to avoid estate tax liability is to consume all of their wealth while alive. Wojciech Kopczuk of Columbia University and one of us have found evidence that aggregate reported estates in the United States were somewhat smaller than would be predicted based on other variables during periods when federal marginal estate tax rates were relatively high. However, this result could reflect increased tax avoidance as well as reduced wealth accumulation in high-tax periods.[40]

The estate tax's disincentive effect on saving may be fairly small for several reasons. To the extent that bequests are unintentional, a tax on them is a relatively efficient way to raise revenue. While some bequests undoubtedly occur because people desire to provide a gift to their heirs, bequests also occur because people accumulate enough wealth to ensure that they do not outlive their resources, and some of these people die early. In those cases, people may put relatively little value on what happens to the wealth after their death. If so, taxing that wealth after death would be economically efficient, as it would have little effect on peoples' behavior. And to the extent that the estate tax reduces inheritances received by heirs, it *increases* their need to do saving on their own.[41]

The other main economic argument against the estate tax is the same argument that can be made against any progressive tax—that it reduces the incentive to do any of the things that make people better off, including working hard, taking risks, or starting a business. The estate tax could plausibly have an important impact on these kinds of decisions among the very wealthy (or those who think they have a realistic prospect of becoming very wealthy), given the high marginal tax rates it imposes. For example, a person of advanced age who has already achieved a comfortable level of wealth may be motivated to continue working by the prospect of leaving a bequest, and a high tax rate on such bequests could affect that decision. With the estate tax in particular, there is little evidence one way or the other on this question. There is evidence that large inheritances *reduce* the labor supply of the heirs that receive them, however.[42]

Public discussion of the estate tax has focused heavily on the extent to which it forces sales of farms and other small businesses to pay the tax. This concern, however, has been greatly exaggerated. In 1998, only 6 percent of taxable estates reported having farm assets, and the value of these assets represented 2.4 percent of the aggregate value of taxable estates. Business assets aside from publicly traded stock accounted for about 10 percent of the value of taxable estates, but much of this represented businesses that were not in any way "small."[43] The value of small businesses and farms included in a taxable estate are eligible to receive discounts that can reduce the value of their taxable estate by up to $770,000. In addition, the tax need not be paid in one lump sum at death. Taxes on businesses and farms can be paid in installments over a 14-year period after death, and a standard element of estate planning is to purchase a life insurance policy sufficient to pay the estate tax liability so that the payments are spread out over many years before death as well. Given this, the impact of the tax need not be much different from that of any other progressive tax for which payment would be spread in smaller installments over many years, such as the income tax. Nor is there any compelling ethical or economic reason to provide preferential treatment to someone who has a farm or small business relative to someone with equal wealth who just happened to accumulate it in some other form. Nevertheless, the image of someone having to sell the family farm or business because of taxes serves as a particularly vivid symbol of how a highly progressive estate tax could impact the well-being and incentives to create wealth of the people affected.

The estate tax is not a popular tax. According to a 2003 poll done by National Public Radio, 57 percent of Americans think it should be eliminated. Part of this opposition undoubtedly reflects a visceral dislike of associating the unhappy event of death with the unhappy event of paying taxes. But there is another reason for its unpopularity. A large number of people who support abolition of the estate tax are apparently under the erroneous impression that it applies to people who are not particularly wealthy. In the NPR poll, 39 percent of respondents said that they opposed the estate tax because "it might affect YOU someday," and 49 percent of those who favored elimination of the tax said they thought "most families have to pay the federal estate tax when someone dies." Thus, some combination of wild optimism and misunderstanding of how the tax works appears to play a role in opposition to the estate tax.[44]

Simplifying the Income Tax

Just about everyone claims to favor a simpler tax system, but ever since the arguably simplifying Tax Reform Act of 1986 was enacted, almost every single subsequent substantial change to the tax code (and there have been scores of them) has made things more complicated. Many features in the current income tax cause a great deal of complication but are by no means inherent aspects of an income tax. In this section, we discuss a number of specific things that could be done to make the income tax system considerably simpler.

The alternative minimum taxes (AMTs) in the personal and corporate codes have to come at the top of any list of options for simplifying the tax system. The personal AMT is discussed in chapter 2. It is a complicated tax and has little justification on policy grounds. Because of a combination of the 2001 tax cut pushing regular tax liabilities below AMT liabilities and the failure to index the AMT exemption for inflation, the personal AMT is poised to become an enormous problem that affects over a third of taxpayers by 2010. At the corporate level, the AMT requires many businesses to do a tremendous amount of extra accounting, often without even knowing whether they will be subject to it. The corporate AMT raised only $3 billion of revenue in 1999, yet many corporations cite this as one of the most complicated and burdensome aspects of the taxpaying process.[45] The AMT is also in many cases inefficient because it mismeasures income and in some cases can force companies with real economic losses to pay tax.

Eliminating both the corporate and personal AMTs would dramatically simplify the taxpaying process and reduce compliance burdens. The stumbling block in practice is that eliminating the personal AMT, in particular, would cost a large amount of revenue—close to $1 trillion over the next 10 years. Of course, the revenue losses from eliminating the AMT could be offset by a small upward adjustment in the ordinary tax rates that apply over income ranges where many people would otherwise face the AMT. In the long run, this would give us a simpler tax system than we would otherwise end up with, and it would on average have little net impact on the tax liabilities faced by people in each income class. However, since hardly any of the people who will eventually be impacted by the AMT are currently aware of its existence, such a plan could easily be portrayed as a "tax increase" by politicians who would prefer to see further cuts in government revenues.

The personal and corporate AMT provisions were originally adopted by Congress in an effort to increase the *perception* of fairness by limiting the ability of taxpayers to take "too much" advantage of the various deductions, exclusions, and exemptions that the legislators themselves had incorporated into the tax code. While a more rational solution would be to eliminate any deductions, exclusions, or exemptions that are viewed as unjustified, the more likely outcome is that many politicians will cling to the AMT to avoid the embarrassing spectacle of a small number of upper-income people and apparently profitable corporations paying little or no income tax in a particular year. Thus, although one could easily design a revenue-neutral plan to eliminate the personal and corporate AMTs, and although such a plan would be a commonsense compromise simplification that in principle should appeal to people of all political stripes, the AMT will likely end up becoming a contentious political football instead. Still, at some point there must be a limit to how much unnecessary complexity politicians are willing to impose on the middle class for the sake of scoring political points. Eventually, some kind of compromise will have to be reached, and a reasonable one would probably involve a substantial increase in exemption levels for the AMT and indexing the exemption for inflation. But such a plan will require recouping a great deal of lost revenue, or else budget deficits will get much larger.

Other complicating features of the personal code that in most cases serve little purpose are the large number of phase-outs of various exemptions, deductions, and credits. In most cases, these have essentially the same effect as raising marginal tax rates in certain income ranges. But they have the political advantage that they don't *look* like higher tax rates and the practical disadvantage that they require taxpayers to go through extra forms and much more complicated calculations.[46] As a result of the 2001 tax act, phase-outs of itemized deductions and personal exemptions are scheduled to be eliminated between 2006 and 2010. Many other such phase-outs remain, however, for a myriad of deductions and credits. While some may have a legitimate, if debatable, purpose (such as the income limits on eligibility for saving accounts discussed above), many do not and could easily be replaced by adjusting the regular tax rate schedule.

A third aspect of the income tax code that causes largely needless complication is the duplication of features that serve the same purpose. For example, numerous different tax credits, deductions, and special accounts are designed to subsidize higher education expenditures, and a multitude of others to promote retirement saving. The same goals can be achieved while consolidating the programs. Similarly, the EITC, child credit, and personal exemption all serve similar purposes but have different rules (for instance, each imposes a different definition of an "eligible dependent child") and require different calculations. These could be consolidated into a single feature that accomplishes essentially the same objectives and does so much more simply.

A change that would considerably simplify the taxpaying process would be to eliminate some of the itemized deductions, credits, and exclusions that currently clutter the tax form and often require taxpayers to pore through complex instructions and to undertake considerable recordkeeping and documentation. The revenues from paring these features could then be used to lower marginal tax rates. Unlike some of the other simplifications suggested above, this would have other real consequences as well, both pro and con, some of which (itemized deductions) are discussed in chapter 6. As noted there, much simplification could also be achieved through the more modest step of a large increase in the standard deduction, which would reduce the number of itemizers.

Another reform that would greatly simplify tax planning and the ability of taxpayers to understand the law would be to eliminate the practice of gradually *phasing in*, *phasing out*, and *sunsetting* changes in the tax law over time. This practice reached disturbing dimensions in the 2001 tax act, the most egregious example being the provision to sunset all of its provisions in 2011, returning the tax law to how it had been before 2001. The 2003 tax similarly made copious use of sunset provisions. These gimmicks arise largely from politicians' desire to squeeze a tax bill into some predetermined overall revenue cost over the budget horizon, now set at 10 years, while still ultimately getting all the tax cuts they want. This strategy relies on the unwillingness of future legislators to allow the scheduled expiration of tax cuts due to the risk of being accused of supporting tax increases. One downside is that tax policy becomes much less transparent to the public: it becomes hard for voters to tell by how much, in what way, and for whom taxes are really being changed. In addition, these gimmicks create uncertainty that makes long-term planning difficult and may require extra efforts to plan for various possible contingencies that would otherwise be unnecessary. Scaling back this practice may require changes in congressional budget rules, but it will ultimately depend on the willingness of voters to punish such behavior.

Technological Improvements and the Promise of a Return-Free System

Modernization of IRS operations promises continual, although gradual, improvement in the tax-filing process. The most notable recent innovation is electronic filing. In 2002, about 47 million returns were filed electronically, which represented 36 percent of individual taxpayers. That included 33 million computer-prepared returns filed by paid tax preparers, 9 million computer-prepared returns submitted over the Internet by taxpayers themselves, and 4 million TeleFile returns (which allows qualified taxpayers to file Form 1040EZ using a toll-free number and a touch-tone telephone).[47] The IRS believes that electronic filing reduces errors, speeds processing time, and provides better security for private information; for taxpayers, refunds can arrive in half the time compared to paper filing. The emergence of software such as TurboTax has also made the tax-filing process easier for many people at a low cost, eliminating much of the need for reading complicated tax instructions and going through calculations and worksheets for those who use it.

Although electronic filing simplifies and expedites the filing process for those who make use of it, as a simplification, it pales in comparison to the postcard-size return of the flat tax. But in the income tax systems of the United Kingdom and Japan, the ultimate simplification has been achieved for a large share of taxpayers—no filing at all. They manage this by having a very simple tax base for most taxpayers and a sophisticated system of employer withholding (called PAYE, or *pay as you earn*, in the United Kingdom) that ensures that at year-end, exactly the appropriate amount of tax has been withheld by employers—no refund and no tax due. This can work because interest and dividend income is taxed at the source of payment at a fixed rate that applies to the vast majority of taxpayers, because there is an individual-based rather than family-based system (which makes it easier to get withholding of tax liabilities exactly right for two-earner couples), and because there is a limited range of itemized deductions. Withholding can accurately reflect itemized deductions if they are implemented in certain ways. For instance, in the United Kingdom, the tax saving from deductibility of mortgage interest at a flat 15 percent rate is applied directly at the bank level. Similarly, charitable contributions can be made through tax-exempt payroll deductions administered by the employer. Although the United Kingdom has in recent years started to move away from the return-free approach, its system clearly demonstrates the potential for operating an income tax system where most people don't have to file a return.

In fact, 36 countries use some form of no-return system for at least some of their taxpayers. Almost all of these countries use some form of exact withholding as in the United Kingdom, but Denmark and Sweden achieve it with a *tax agency reconciliation* (TAR) system. Under a TAR system, taxpayers provide basic information to the tax authority, which then calculates tax liability based on this information and what is provided to it from employers and other institutions. Taxpayers have a chance to review (and contest) these calculations, after which refunds or additional tax payments may be needed.

The U.S. Treasury tax proposals of 1984 contained an exact withholding scheme, called the *return-free system*, which was to be available for more than half of all taxpayers. It was never enacted, though, because the system was never simplified enough to make it feasible. Note that establishing a return-free system for many taxpayers accomplishes what might be called "populist simplification," because it completely eliminates the hassle of tax filing for a large number of voters. But it does not address the difficult issues of complexity that would continue to affect businesses and many high-income households. For example, neither system could handle business income or some of the itemized deductions or credits in our current system, and thus a significant fraction of taxpayers for whom these are relevant would still have to file.[48]

Putting It All Together: Ideas for Fundamental Income Tax Reform

In recent years, public discussion of fundamental tax reform has been practically monopolized by proposals for flat taxes and sales taxes. In contrast, politicians who support more progressive taxation have been reluctant to put forward any bold ideas for fixing the income tax. A rare exception was a plan put forward in 1995 (and revised in 1998) by Congressman Richard Gephardt (D-MO) that would retain the graduated income tax but would take the approach of the Tax Reform Act of 1986 (which he helped get started) much further, eliminating many deductions, exclusions, and saving incentives in exchange for substantially lower marginal rates. However, Gephardt seems to have distanced himself from this proposal. For instance, no mention of tax reform appeared on the Web site for his presidential campaign as of mid-2003.

Meanwhile, the actual policy being enacted has been relentlessly incremental and complicating. As the tax system becomes ever more of a mess, the potential gains from a thoroughgoing reform must become more apparent. In this environment, alternatives for building a better income tax might be expected to reemerge on the political landscape.[49]

Just about any income tax reform plan combines some set of the changes discussed above. To consider just one example of a plan that would put many of these ideas together, consider a proposal put forward by William Gale of the Brookings Institution in 1997. He suggests that all itemized deductions should be converted to 15 percent tax credits and would use the revenue raised thereby to cut the top marginal tax rate. The plan would also replace the primary taxpayer's personal exemption with a larger standard deduction, repeal various phase-outs of deductions and exemptions, and eliminate the personal and corporate AMTs. Many sector-specific subsidies in the corporate income tax would be eliminated to make the system more neutral toward different types of investment. As a simplification measure, Gale also suggests replacing depreciation deductions with an immediate deduction equal to the "present value" of future deductions—that is, their equivalent value in today's terms after taking into account the fact that deductions in the future are worth less than today because of the forgone opportunity to earn interest. To this list could be added some form of integration of personal and corporate income taxes, as well as all of the other simplification measures mentioned above. Such a reform plan could easily be designed to raise the same revenue as the current system and achieve the same distribution of tax burdens, but it would be both simpler and more economically efficient.[50]

A Hybrid Approach: Combining a VAT with Income Taxation

We close our discussion of tax reform options with a plan that has been embraced by no politician that we know of, for reasons that we outline below. It recognizes that the either-or policy choice between income and consumption taxation is false and embraces a "third way" that features an income tax and a consumption tax like a VAT. This third way is in reality the world norm, as nearly all other countries levy both kinds of taxes.

Introducing a value added tax would allow us to reduce both personal and corporate income tax rates substantially and perhaps even exempt most people from personal income taxation altogether.[51] Michael Graetz of Yale Law School has been the most vocal advocate of this approach in recent years.[52] He proposes adopting a broad-based VAT with a single rate of approximately 15 percent. The resulting revenue would be used to replace the standard deduction, personal exemption, and various credits of the current personal income tax with a standard deduction of $100,000 (or $50,000 for singles) and to lower the corporate and personal income tax rates to 25 percent. The large standard deduction would exempt over 80 percent of current filers from the personal income taxation altogether and would cause most remaining taxpayers to eschew itemized deductions. In 1992, a similar plan, albeit with a smaller VAT and smaller standard deductions, formed the essence of a proposal floated by the outgoing Bush (the elder) administration's Treasury Department.[53]

A plan of this nature would give the United States lower income tax rates than almost any industrialized country.[54] The shift would offer many of the economic advantages ascribed to the VAT, although the simplification gains would be mitigated due to having to maintain the administrative infrastructure of the income tax system. This is an excellent example of "populist simplification" because by raising the income threshold for filing, it relieves millions of taxpayers of any obligation to file a tax return, and at the same time it induces many others who still file to pass up itemizing their deductions. On the other hand, this plan retains the income tax infrastructure for just those people (and corporations) for whom the tax is most complicated. Although it would greatly reduce the number of income tax returns, it would not reduce by much the number of complex returns. The reduction in the aggregate cost of compliance would be proportionately much smaller than the reduction in the number of filers.

While using a VAT to finance a large increase in the standard deduction could be done in a way that has little net impact on tax burdens faced by most of the middle class, it would dramatically increase tax burdens on low-income people who already pay no income tax and in fact often receive large refundable credit payments. So this approach at first glance seems like a particularly bad compromise, combining the most unsatisfactory elements of each kind of tax—the regressive shift in the distribution of taxes caused by a VAT for low-income people as well as the complications and inefficiencies of the income tax for high-income people.

Graetz argues that these defects can be fixed. For the low end of the income distribution, he suggests that measures to restore progressivity could be implemented by offering a rebate or credit tied to the level of reported labor earnings for the Social Security payroll tax. Given the way the payroll tax is currently administered, such a provision would have to be based on individual rather than family labor income, but this could conceivably be changed. Even if it could, the payroll tax would not be helpful for administering tax relief to nonworking low-income people. To replicate the degree of progressivity of the current system, the refundable tax relief paid out in this manner would have to be very large as it would need to replace features like the EITC and child credits and also to offset the new burden imposed by the VAT. Graetz estimates that the 15 percent VAT and 25 percent income tax rates would be sufficient to finance enough of this sort of relief to on average render low-income people no worse off, and raise the same revenue as under the current system.

At the upper end of the income distribution, the efficiency and simplicity of the income tax could be improved through revenue-neutral versions of many of the measures discussed earlier in this chapter, including integration to eliminate double taxation of corporate income. Although all of the inherent structural as well as some of the man-made inefficiencies of the income tax would remain, they would be considerably less costly because of the lower rates of tax.

Unlike proposals such as the flat tax, the X-tax, and the personal consumption tax, the hybrid VAT/income tax approach has the distinct advantage of relying on two taxes that have actually been implemented successfully before in the real world. Because essentially all other countries now operate both types of tax, a great deal of experience has been built up regarding how to make them work. Under this approach, the VAT could operate using the credit-invoice method, which is important for its administrative and enforcement advantages. In addition, compared to adopting a consumption tax laden with politically likely transition relief for preexisting capital, the VAT/income tax hybrid would avoid granting an enormous and inefficient windfall to the wealthy. On the other hand, this approach has the disadvantage relative to the consumption tax plans of still exposing the people who account for most capital accumulation to some of the messiness and distortions to saving and investment decisions caused by the income tax.

Professor Graetz emphasizes one other potential advantage of the VAT/income tax hybrid—that it would greatly reduce political pressures to adopt deductions, exclusions, and credits that clutter up the tax base because the tax would contain no "personal" element for most taxpayers. Given the proliferation of various forms of preferential treatment such as exemptions in real-world VATs, we probably should not be overly optimistic about this claim. It is at least plausible, however, that convincing the middle class to give up itemized deductions, a major obstacle to many fundamental reform plans, might be easier if at the same time they were offered freedom from filing income tax returns altogether.

Although this proposal has many attractive features, no politician has embraced it. One reason, we suspect, is that in the current environment no politician could endorse something that could possibly be characterized in a 30-second TV spot as a "new tax." If the number of tax systems is the principal indicator of simplicity, efficiency, and fairness, this plan rates a low score because it adds one to the number. But the number of separate taxes is by no means a sensible criterion by which to judge a tax system. To be sure, fixed costs are associated with each separate kind of tax, but these additional costs are likely to be small relative to the other potential simplification and economic advantages of a VAT plus a scaled-back income tax system like that described here. Another problem is that some conservatives apparently fear VATs because they believe they are somehow responsible for the higher levels of government spending in Europe relative to the United States: the VAT is *too* efficient for those who believe that big government is a more important problem than an inefficient tax system. It is not clear that there is any truth to this: certainly other influences, such as culture, must dominate in determining the size of countries' governments. Finally, questions remain unanswered about how well tax relief for the poor could be administered through the payroll tax and whether such a policy would be perceived differently by the public than equivalent features in the income tax, particularly since they would have to be much larger to offset the VAT liability.

Conclusion

The reform options discussed so far represent only a subset of the possible alternatives, and the political process may eventually focus on other possibilities. Any alternative, though, can be classified according to what it does to the rate structure, how clean the tax base is, and how much it relies on an income or consumption base.

Where does this leave the intelligent citizen who is convinced that the income tax system needs fixing but is unsure about what should be done? One option is to pull the tax system out "by its roots," as Representative Archer has called for, and replace it with a clean-base, single-rate system based on consumption rather than income. We have argued that a national retail sales tax is not administrable at the usual standards of equity and intrusiveness we should expect of a tax system. Its close cousin, the value added tax, is administrable, but because without other policy changes it would starkly shift the burden of tax from affluent families to everyone else, we suspect that it will be rejected by a majority of Americans. That leaves the flat tax and X-tax (or "graduated flat tax") as the best consumption tax options. But these plans are untested, often still entail a regressive change in the distribution of tax burdens, and could produce large windfall gains and losses; moreover, the critical but potentially complex details about how to get from here to there are still to be fleshed out. Aside from the substantive issues of equity, efficiency, and simplicity, we sense that they will fail a simple "sniff test" of Americans accustomed to a personal tax on all income, who will find that a tax that appears to be on labor income only just doesn't smell right. The recent National Public Radio poll confirms our suspicion. According to this poll, most Americans think it's fair that families with higher charity, medical expenses, or mortgage interest pay less tax than otherwise similar families, but a majority of Americans think it is not fair that taxes should be lower if a family receives more of its income in the form of investment income rather than labor income.[55]

Contemplating this sort of change is not for the meek. We are reminded of a sketch from the old British television series *Monty Python's Flying Circus*. In the sketch, an accountant comes to a job-change counselor, complaining of his boring job and inquiring about the career possibilities of being a lion tamer. Once the counselor makes abundantly clear how ferocious a lion is (the accountant had thought it to be a more domesticated sort of animal), the accountant decides to settle for pursuing opportunities in banking.

Can the income tax be fixed enough so as to be worthy of saving? The base can certainly be thoroughly cleaned, eliminating substantial complexity and inefficiency. By so doing the tax rates can be lowered, which reduces the cost of those bugs that remain. And remain they will, because any system based on income contains inherent difficulties that have no simple solution.

Many people's views about tax policy can be boiled down to one question: under which system will I pay the least? If you've read this far, however, the odds are that your interest in tax policy goes beyond which plan offers you and your family the best deal to which tax policy is best for the country.

Coming to a reasoned judgment about tax policy requires clarifying your own values about fairness, sifting through some subtle conceptual issues, and, perhaps hardest of all, evaluating conflicting claims about the economic impact of tax alternatives. This is particularly difficult because the public debate about tax reform is dominated by advocates whose purpose is not to educate but rather to persuade. In this book, we have attempted to explain clearly the conceptual issues and have presented what is known and what is not known about economic impacts. You must supply your own value judgments.

In this environment, a citizen must learn how to ask the right questions. To help you do that, we offer a voter's guide to tax policy choices to keep by your television as the issue is debated, in the same way that newspapers offer viewers' guides to the Super Bowl or the Academy Awards. But unlike the Academy Awards, in this election you have a vote.

Tax Cuts versus Tax Reform

Tax cuts are politically popular partly because advocates can plausibly claim that most, or even all, taxpayers come out ahead. But that claim is highly misleading because the revenue shortfall they cause will certainly have further repercussions. Either some kinds of expenditures will be cut, or the deficit will grow, requiring higher tax or fewer government services or both at some point in the future. This caveat applies both to making tax cuts in the context of the current tax system and to evaluating a radically different kind of tax system that will raise much less revenue.

Tax Cuts as a Trojan Horse

For many advocates of tax cuts, the real objective is not the tax system but rather the size of government, and tax cuts are really a tactical weapon in the battle to downsize government. The idea is to lower taxes and hope that politicians' (and voters') fear of deficits and dislike of tax increases will force expenditures below what they would otherwise be. Because the ultimate objective is to limit spending initiatives, this is a good idea only if the benefits of the spending that is cut or forestalled fall short of their cost. So the real issue is not the tax system, but the proper size and scope of government.

The appropriate response to a tax-cut-as-Trojan Horse policy proposal is to inquire about the rest of the plan. Exactly what spending programs do tax cut advocates want cut back or eliminated? Is it farm subsidies or the Head Start program? What proposed programs do they wish would never see the light of day? Is it prescription drug subsidies or homeland-security enhancements? Only when the whole strategy is known can an informed judgment about its wisdom be made.

The Devil Is in the Details

After eight decades, the U.S. income tax system has grown encrusted and Byzantine. In comparison, a two-page sketch of a replacement is bound to look breathtakingly simple. But be warned that, in taxation, the devil is in the details.

All tax systems have gray areas that require rules and regulations. All tax systems require an enforcement agency to see that the tax burden is shared equitably and not unfairly shouldered by those who feel morally obligated to pay taxes or have no opportunity to avoid them. All tax systems will be subject to the same political pressures that have contributed to the current system's problems. Finally, a tax plan that includes transition rules or other aspects "to be fleshed out later" will later turn out to be a lot more complicated than it appears.

The Tax System Can't Encourage Everything

In defending a tax break, politicians always point out how it will encourage or reward some laudable activity, such as housing, charity, or saving. Every time you hear the word *encourage*, remember that the break, by virtue of the higher tax rates it requires, discourages all other endeavors. Every time you hear the word *reward*, remember that it penalizes other activities.

It might make sense to implement social or economic policy through the tax code in some cases, but these must clear a high hurdle. Tax preferences in the tax code are too easily hidden from plain view, leading to what is in effect a hidden industrial or distributional policy.

Fairness Is a Slippery Concept but an Important One

No politician, and certainly no economist, has the one true answer to what is fair. This is an ethical judgment that each person must make. It is also an issue that cannot be avoided in deciding how to raise a trillion dollars in taxes. Nearly a century ago, the then dean of American public finance, Edwin R. A. Seligman of Columbia University, remarked that "the history of modern taxation is the history of . . . class antagonisms." These days, *class* is a four-letter word, used derisively to attack another political party's concern about the distributional implications of tax policy, as in "That's class warfare!" But this issue should not be dismissed with a slogan. Using less inflammatory language, the *distribution* of incomes—and not just total income—matters. We may disagree about how to trade off total income against the distribution of total income—and in the end this involves values as well as economics—but because policy implicitly makes this trade-off, we must face up to it and not only by name calling and allusions to Karl Marx.

Be Skeptical of Claims of Economic Nirvana

High tax rates can certainly stifle initiative, and wrong-headed taxes can waste resources. To some degree, these problems can be reduced by tax reform. But another part is an unavoidable consequence of the desire for an equitable distribution of tax burden. The terms of this trade-off between justice and prosperity are uncertain.

The unresolvable differences about what is fair could be put aside if we could move to a tax system that is so good for the economy that everyone ends up better off. But don't hold your breath. Vague promises of an economic nirvana are just that. Neither tax reform nor tax cuts will double the growth rate forever. Tax reform can, though, deliver long-term economic gains that are worth pursuing.

Tax policy can help the economy in the short term if it can increase demand and thereby reduce excess capacity. But so can spending increases. It is not a coincidence that liberal economists tend to think that the best countercyclical policy is either tax cuts for low-income households or social spending directed to the same folks and that conservative economists generally think that the best stimulus is a tax cut designed to stimulate saving and investment and maybe just investment in the stock market. The underlying and generally unspoken concern is that these alternative stimulus plans benefit different people and have different implications for the long-term level of government spending. These things matter, to be sure, but they have nothing to do with which is the best short-term economic stimulus.

The truth is that these days most economists are not very enamored of any kind of short-term fiscal policy—whether tax credits targeted to the poor, tax cuts aimed at the affluent, or expenditure increases.

The Tax System Can Be Improved

From a tactical point of view, much can be gained from having Congress clearly separate the distinct aspects of tax reform we have discussed in the book and debate which aspects are not desirable rather than consider what, if any, steps toward reform should be taken. Recall the plight of Hercules, who, as penance for having killed his wife and children in a fit of madness, was given 12 tasks of immense difficulty. The fifth of these tasks was one of the most daunting of all—to clean, in one day, 30 years of accumulated manure left by thousands of cattle in the stables of Augeas. (The analogy to the tax system is, we fear, obvious.) Hercules did not attempt to clean out the stables one shovelful at a time. Instead, Hercules diverted the rivers Alpheus and Peneus through the stables, ridding them of their filth at once. There is much to clean in the tax system, and contemplating a Herculean approach is an appropriate way to begin the great debate about tax reform.

But the best should not become the enemy of the good. If fundamental reform is not to be, then the debate ought to continue because the tax system is too important for us to neglect.

The U.S. tax system can be made simpler. It can be made fairer. It can be made more conducive to economic growth. Some changes can accomplish all three, but in most cases difficult choices among these objectives must be made. We hope this book will help to clarify those choices and guide us toward the best way to tax ourselves.

Notes

Preface

1. We began the foreword of the first edition of this book with this quote, but learned afterward that it isn't entirely clear that Einstein ever uttered it. It is widely cited, though, and even if it is apocryphal, it illustrates the popular view that the income tax system can defeat even the brightest among us.

Chapter 1

1. Bartlett (2003).

2. Burman (2003a, p. 1c).

3. Survey evidence on the share of the population that wants a smaller government is mixed and depends heavily on how the question is asked. In a March 2003 poll by National Public Radio, Kaiser Family Foundation, and Harvard's Kennedy School of Government, 48 percent of respondents said they "would rather have lower taxes even though there would be fewer services," and 44 percent said they "would rather have more services even if it costs more in taxes." On the other hand, 80 percent of respondents said that "maintaining spending levels on domestic programs such as education, health care, and Social Security" was "more important than lowering your taxes."

4. IRS, Statistics of Income Division, *Statistics of Income Bulletin* (Winter 2002–2003, p. 153).

5. Blumenthal and Slemrod (1992, p. 189).

6. Blumenthal and Slemrod (1992, p. 185).

7. In 2001, 55.4 percent of all individual tax returns bore the signature of a paid preparer. Many of those who use a professional preparer have simple returns, as suggested by the fact that 9.6 percent of those who filed a Form 1040EZ and 13.4 percent of those who filed a Form 1040A used a preparer (IRS, Statistics of Income Division, *Statistics of Income Bulletin*, Winter 2002–2003, pp. 153, 194). Presumably, many of these taxpayers use a preparer not because their returns are complex but because they hope to speed up their tax refund.

8. OMB (2003, p. 242) (accessed June 16, 2003).

9. IRS (2003b, tables 10, 25).

10. See chapter 5.

11. See chapter 5 and General Accounting Office (2003).

12. OMB (2003, p. 242) (accessed June 16, 2003).

13. National Public Radio, Kaiser Family Foundation, and Kennedy School of Government (2003).

14. Gray (1995, p. 18).

15. Rieschick (1997, p. 1661).

16. We defer to chapter 7 the question of whether a 17 percent rate is high enough to raise as much revenue as is now collected by the income tax.

17. Lugar (1995, p. 3).

18. Hall and Rabushka (1995, p. vii).

19. Hall and Rabushka (1995, p. vii).

20. Hall and Rabushka (1995, pp. vii, 52).

21. Birnbaum and Murray (1987, p. 52); Steuerle (1992, p. 94).

22. Slemrod (1995b, p. 134).

23. Donmoyer (1998a, 1998b).

24. McIntyre (1995, p. 1).

25. Survey evidence on all of these questions is discussed in more detail in chapter 3.

Chapter 2

1. State and local revenues exclude grants-in-aid from the federal government, to avoid counting the same tax revenues twice. Certain nontax revenues, such as fees and fines, are included at the federal, state, and local levels. The U.S. Bureau of Economic Analysis (BEA) substantially revised its methods of accounting for national income and its components, including taxes, in 1999. See Moulton, Parker, and Seskin (1999) for a detailed explanation of these changes. The largest change relevant to taxes was that employer and employee contributions to pension plans for government employees are no longer classified as taxes. The numbers reported throughout chapter 2 reflect all of these accounting changes except for one. BEA reclassified estate and gift taxes as capital transfers rather than taxes, but we continue to count them as taxes.

2. U.S. Bureau of Economic Analysis (2003, table 3.6).

3. The 30 OECD member nations, listed in descending order by their 1999 tax-to-GDP ratios, are Sweden, Denmark, Finland, France, Belgium, Austria, Italy, Norway, Netherlands, Luxembourg, Czech Republic, Hungary, Germany, Greece, Iceland, United Kingdom, Canada, Slovak Republic, Poland, Spain, New Zealand, Switzerland, Portugal, Ireland, Turkey, Australia, United States, Japan, Korea, and Mexico. Mexico and the Czech Republic joined the OECD in 1994 and 1995, respectively. Since then, Korea, Hungary, Poland, and the Slovak Republic have joined the OECD. Revenue totals in the United States for a given year are a few percentage points smaller under the OECD

definition used in table 2.2 compared to the BEA definition used in table 2.1 (this is not apparent because of the tax cuts between 1999 and 2001). The OECD calculations exclude certain nontax revenues, such as fees and fines.

4. The Supreme Court decision barring income taxation was in *Pollock v. Farmers Loan and Trust Company*, 158 U.S. 601 (1895). Its ruling was based on the clause in article I, section 9, of the Constitution, which states: "No capitation, or other direct, tax shall be laid, unless in proportion to the census or enumeration herein before directed to be taken."

5. Histories of the U.S. personal income tax are provided in Brownlee (1989), Goode (1976), Pechman (1987), and Witte (1985).

6. Goode (1976) discusses the history of deductions and exclusions in the personal income tax base. Later additions include the standard deduction (1941), the deduction for medical expenses (1942), and the deduction for child and dependent care expenses (1954), which was later turned into a tax credit.

7. Historical information presented in this section on the number of tax returns filed is from U.S. Bureau of the Census (1975).

8. In March, 2003, the Congressional Budget Office projected income tax revenues (assuming no change in tax law) of $924 billion and GDP of $11,309 billion for fiscal 2004 (CBO 2003a). In May, the Joint Committee on Taxation (2003c) estimated that the 2003 tax cut would reduce individual income tax revenues by $106.8 billion in fiscal 2004. So individual income taxes would be $[(924 - 106.8)/11309] \times 100 = 7.2$ percent of GDP. The last fiscal year where individual income taxes were below 7.2 percent of GDP was 1965, based on OMB (2003, "Historical Tables").

9. As Thorndike (2002) relates, in 1909 the specific issue was stock watering, which caused the public to innocently invest in corporations that were too thinly capitalized. Stock watering, however, merely illustrated a broader problem of a general lack of information. As George Wickersham, President Taft's attorney-general-to-be, stated on the eve of Taft's inauguration, this lack of information fostered "the misrepresentation or concealment of material facts in soliciting financial aid for the corporation." The new corporate tax and its publicity provision would, according to its supporters, solve this problem by revealing the critical information investors needed to make informed decisions. See also Kornhauser (2002). At the beginning of the twenty-first century, concerns about the informativeness of financial reports have reemerged in the wake of the Enron and WorldCom scandals, prompting some to call for public disclosure of corporate tax-return information. For a discussion of these proposals, see Lenter, Shackelford, and Slemrod (2003).

10. Brownlee (1989, p. 1615) notes the special Civil War tax on corporations. Pechman (1987, p. 135) discusses the constitutional questions surrounding the 1909 corporate income tax.

11. U.S. Bureau of Economic Analysis (2003, tables 1.1, 1.16). "Pretax profits" are based on BEA's line item for "profits before tax" (table 1.16, line 10), which is a measure of the net profits of all businesses treated as corporations by BEA, using federal income tax measures of depreciation and inventory valuation.

12. U.S. Bureau of Economic Analysis (2003, tables 1.1, 1.16). "Net interest payments by corporations" comes from line 17 of table 1.16. Steuerle (1992, p. 28) discusses this issue in more detail.

13. See, for example, the interchange between Kies (1999) and Sullivan (2000, 2003).

14. Rates below 50 percent were reduced by 10 percent in each of 1982 and 1983 and by an additional 5 percent in 1984. Tax rates in 1984 equaled (90 percent × 90 percent × 95 percent =) 76.95 percent of their 1981 levels, so the total tax cut was 23.05 percent.

15. See Kiefer et al. (2002) and Joint Committee on Taxation (2003b) for detailed descriptions of EGTRRA 2001.

16. See Shapiro and Slemrod (2003a, 2003b) for evidence regarding how successful the tax rebate program was in stimulating the economy.

17. Estimates made in 2001 by the Joint Committee on Taxation and reported in Gale and Potter (2002, p. 139).

18. In 2002, the Job Creation and Worker Assistance Act included two temporary corporate tax cuts. Depreciation deductions for corporations were made more generous on a temporary basis through 2004, and corporations were allowed to use business losses in 2001 and 2002 to get a refund on tax payments made as long as five years before (there is normally a two-year limit).

19. See Joint Committee on Taxation (2003e) for a summary of the provisions of JGTRRA. Other provisions included an increase in the alternative minimum tax exemption for 2003 and 2004 and some temporary increases in the portion of depreciation on new investments that firms can deduct immediately (described in the corporate income tax section below). The estimates of the costs of extending the sunsetting provisions come from Gale and Orszag (2003). The direct revenue cost of extending the expiring tax provisions is 2.4 percent of GDP, and the interest costs are 0.6 percent of GDP. CBO (2003b) estimates that without extending the expiring provisions, federal revenues would be 20.6 percent of GDP in 2013.

20. Economists refer to this as the Haig-Simons definition of income, after Robert M. Haig and Henry C. Simons, who helped develop it.

21. Campbell and Parisi (2002, p. 23).

22. A provision placing limitations on certain itemized deductions for high-income taxpayers, discussed later in the chapter, effectively raises the top marginal tax rates on both capital gains and ordinary income slightly above the rates listed in the text. This is because above the threshold where the limitation begins, each additional dollar of AGI causes a fraction of itemized deductions to be lost. The 2001 act would gradually phase out this provision between 2006 and 2010.

23. See note 41 below.

24. Inflation is as measured by the Consumer Price Index for All Urban Consumers (CPI-U), as reported in the *Economic Report of the President* (2003).

25. The $261 billion of interest in AGI includes $199 billion counted directly as interest (from Campbell and Parisi, 2002, p. 23), plus $62 billion of interest income from mutual funds that are lumped in with dividends on the tax form (Gale, 2002).

26. The excluded dividend figure comes from Park (2002). The estimate of $102 billion in dividends that are included in AGI in section B of table 2.3 is calculated as follows. Dividends reported as AGI on tax forms were $147 billion (Campbell and Parisi, 2002, p. 23). From this, we subtract the $62 billion that was actually interest payments from mutual funds and add back in $17 billion of dividends on personal trusts (from Gale 2002).

27. The rental value of owner-occupied housing reported here is the value after subtracting out depreciation but before subtracting out interest payments, since these interest payments are subtracted out later as an itemized deduction.

28. Nominal and real capital gains accruing to households and nonprofit institutions are derived from Board of Governors of the Federal Reserve System (2003a, table R.100). Capital gains net of losses in AGI are reported in U.S. Bureau of Economic Analysis (2003, table 8.28). We estimate the amount of capital gains realizations that are fully taxable under the personal income tax by taking this figure and subtracting an estimate of the exclusion equivalent of taxing capital gains at lower rates than ordinary income since 1991. The exclusion equivalent is calculated as the revenue loss from preferential tax rates on long-term gains, divided by revenues raised on long-term gains plus the revenue loss from preferential rates, all multiplied by realized long-term gains in AGI. The revenue loss from preferential rates comes from the tax-expenditure budget in OMB, *Budget of the U.S. Government* (various years), while long-term gain realizations and revenues are from U.S. Department of the Treasury, Office of Tax Analysis (2002). C-corporation income subject to tax comes from IRS, Statistics of Income Division, *Statistics of Income Bulletin* (various issues). We calculate reinvested C-corporation profits by subtracting dividend payments by C corporations from C-corporation income subject to tax. C-corporation dividend payments are reported in articles in the *Survey of Current Business* (various issues) by Thae S. Park (see Park, 2002, for example). In those articles, C-corporation dividends equal total dividends in personal income, less the BEA's measure of S-corporation dividends (which are reported in the line for "other personal income exempt or excluded from adjusted gross income"). Data on capital gains realizations reported in AGI are not available yet for 2001. We assume they are half of the 2000 level, based on a preliminary estimate in CBO (2002b). C-corporation income subject to tax less dividends is not yet available for 2000 or 2001, so we assume it bears the same relationship to the BEA's measure of "corporate profits with inventory valuation and capital consumption adjustments" in 2000 and 2001 as it did in 1999. Throughout, adjustments for inflation are based on the CPI-U. Based on all of this, we estimate that between 1985 and 2001, nominal capital gains accruals were $20.56 trillion, and nominal capital gains realizations fully taxed under the personal income tax were $3.18 trillion. In constant 2002 dollars, the portion of capital gains accruals that did not represent compensation for inflation totaled $9.59 trillion, capital gain realizations fully taxable under the personal income tax totaled $3.88 trillion, and taxable retained earnings of C corporations totaled $7.17 trillion.

29. Authors' calculations based on data in Campbell and Parisi (2002).

30. The graduated tax system ensures that, ignoring phase-outs as in the earned income tax credit, a taxpayer's marginal tax rate is always larger than his or her average tax rate.

31. Above an AGI threshold ($209,250 for a joint return in 2003), 2 percent of the value of exemptions is phased out for every additional $2,500 of AGI. Similarly, itemized deductions are reduced in value by 3 percent of the amount by which AGI exceeds $139,500 (as of 2003) until only 20 percent of itemized deductions are left. For example, consider a family of four in the 33 percent tax bracket with $250,000 in AGI. Earning one more dollar of income causes them to lose 3 cents of itemized deductions and 9.8 cents worth of personal exemptions. At a 33 percent tax rate, this increases their tax bill by 4.2 cents, in effect increasing the family's marginal rate by 4.2 percentage points to 37.2 percent.

32. Note, however, that Social Security benefits are related to taxes paid in during the working years and the ratio of benefits received to income also declines with income. The system as a whole is probably mildly progressive, less so than otherwise because on average lower-income individuals live fewer years after retirement collecting benefits.

33. Campbell and Parisi (2002, pp. 33–36).

34. OMB (2003, "Historical Tables": table 8.5; 2003, "Analytical Perspectives": table 6.3). In fiscal year 2004, the EITC is estimated to involve direct outlays of $31.4 billion and revenue reductions of $5.1 billion. Outlays for "food and nutrition assistance" (including programs like food stamps and WIC) are estimated at $37.9 billion, and outlays for "family and other support assistance" are $25.8 billion.

35. Parameters for 2003 for the EITC, as well as for all other inflation-adjusted components of the tax code, are reported in IRS (2002c).

36. A phase-out of the AMT exemption effectively raises the AMT tax rate by a fourth over certain ranges (above $150,000 for a joint return).

37. The 1.3 million figure comes from Campbell and Parisi (2002). The National Taxpayer Advocate (2002) estimates that in 1998, 6.4 million returns required an AMT calculation, 4.4 million submitted the AMT form with the IRS, and 1 million returns had AMT liability.

38. Urban-Brookings Tax Policy Center (2003b, table 5.32).

39. Moreover, because of the AMT, the benefit of the 2001 tax cut is much lower than it would have been for many people. For example, in 2010 the AMT will eliminate 42 percent of the benefits of the 2001 tax cut for those with AGI between $75,000 and $100,000 and 71 percent for those in the $100,000 to $200,000 range. By contrast, the AMT only takes away 8 percent of the tax cut given to millionaires, on average. See Burman, Gale, Rohaly, and Harris (2002). These figures do not reflect the (probably small) impact of the 2003 act.

40. AMT revenues for 2000 are from Campbell and Parisi (2002, p. 34). The 10-year revenue cost of repealing the AMT is from the Urban-Brookings Tax Policy Center (2003b, table 5.31). It includes the effects of the 2003 tax act but assumes that the act is allowed to sunset. Note that the dividend and capital gains tax cut has little impact on the cost of repealing the AMT because the AMT includes a provision to retain the benefits of those tax preferences in the calculation of AMT tax liability.

41. Data for partnerships and nonfarm sole proprietorships are from IRS, Statistics of Income Division, *Statistics of Income Bulletin* (Fall 2002, "Selected Historical and Other Data"). Nonfarm sole proprietorship data are from table 10 entries "number of nonfarm businesses" and "net income (less deficit)." Partnership data are from table 11 entries "total number of active partnerships" and "net income (less deficit)." Data for corporations are from IRS, Statistics of Income Division, *Corporation Income Tax Returns 1999* (published October 2002). Data for all corporations are from table 2, entries for "number of returns, total" and "net income (less deficit)." Data for S corporations are from table 14, entries for "number of returns, total" and "net income (less deficit)." Numbers of businesses and incomes of C corporations are calculated by subtracting S-corporation data from data for all corporations.

42. The benefits of low rates in the lower brackets are phased out in certain income ranges, effectively leading to higher marginal tax rates in those ranges.

43. Even this procedure is imperfect as it makes no allowance for whether the firm's combine was in better or worse condition than the ones for sale on the market.

44. Depreciation rules are explained in detail in IRS (2002a).

45. The foreign tax credit is available to all businesses, not only to C corporations, but we discuss it here because C corporations claim the great majority (nearly 90 percent) of total foreign tax credits. There is also a similar foreign tax credit provision for the personal income tax.

46. The current rules for the research and experimentation tax credit, along with a 2003 proposal by the Bush administration to make it permanent, are described in Joint Committee on Taxation (2003a, pp. 241–254).

47. In an attempt to combat tax shelters, the Tax Reform Act of 1986 introduced a restriction on the deductibility of losses from "passive" investments—that is, investments in which the taxpayer does not materially participate.

48. Mitrusi and Poterba (2000).

49. IRS, Statistics of Income Division, *Statistics of Income Bulletin* (Fall 2002, "Selected Historical and Other Data," table 17).

50. See Kiefer et al. (2002) for details on the phase-out of the estate tax.

Chapter 3

1. Whitney (1990) describes the protesting and rioting over the U.K. poll tax. Smith (1991) offers an analysis of its failure.

2. McHardy (1992, p. xxiv). Accounts of the peasant revolt of 1381 are also given in McKissack (1959) and Powell (1894).

3. Fisher (1996, p. 37).

4. Curl (2003, p. A4).

5. Stevenson and Stolberg (2003, p. A18).

6. Although in this illustration we use income as the tax base and measure of well-being, the definitions would apply to any alternative measure of well-being.

7. A tax system can be progressive over some income ranges and not others. Similarly, when comparing two tax systems, one might be more progressive over some income ranges and not over others.

8. Clinton (1992, pp. 644–645).

9. Safire (1995, p. A19). Safire advocated an income tax with fewer deductions, a large exempt level of income, a rate of 25 percent on income above the exempt level but less than $150,000, and a rate of 30 percent on income above $150,000.

10. Hall and Rabushka (1995, p. 26). Political advocates of the flat tax as well as Hall and Rabushka advocate a large exempt level of income, which would add some progressivity. But they oppose having multiple tax rates, which almost certainly means that their systems would impose less of a tax burden on high-income families than the current income tax. These issues are discussed in more detail in chapter 7.

11. Higgins (1995, p. A11).

12. Vos Savant (1994, p. 12), quoted in Miller (2000, p. 529).

13. Davies (1995, p. A11).

14. Of course, the "fair" pricing of ordinary goods and services is facilitated by the voluntary nature of the transaction: if the price is too high, the consumer need not buy the product. The benefit principle suggests that fairness would require replicating what someone would be willing to pay if the transaction were voluntary *and* the person could be excluded from benefiting if he or she did not pay.

15. In the *Wealth of Nations*, Adam Smith stated his first principle of taxation: "The subjects of every state ought to contribute towards the support of the government, as nearly as possible, in proportion to their respective abilities; that is, in proportion to the revenue they enjoy under the protection of the state. The expense of government to the individuals of a great nation, is like the expense of management to the joint tenants of a great estate, who are all obliged to contribute in proportion to their respective interests in the estate." *Wealth of Nations* was originally published in 1776; the quote is from pp. 777–778 of the 1937 edition.

16. Gates and Collins (2003). Murphy and Nagel (2002) provide a spirited and controversial treatment of similar arguments.

17. See, for example, Nozick (1977).

18. A similar argument is an important element of Rawls's (1971) theory of justice. Varian (1980) provides a formal economic argument along these lines.

19. Krugman (2001, p. 36).

20. Simons (1938, p. 24).

21. CBO (2003c, table B-1c). The measure of income used here is CBO's "adjusted pretax comprehensive household income." According to CBO, "that measure includes all cash income (both taxable and tax-exempt), taxes paid by businesses (which are imputed to individuals on the basis of assumptions about incidence), employee contributions to 401(k) retirement plans, and the value of income received in kind from various sources (including employer-paid health insurance premiums, Medicare and Medicaid benefits, and food stamps, among others)" (CBO, 2003c, p. 3). Cash income includes wages, salaries, self-employment income, personal rents, interest, dividends, realized capital gains, employer contributions to Social Security, and government cash-transfer payments. To adjust for differences in well-being caused by differing household sizes, household income is adjusted in the CBO analysis by dividing household income by the square root of the number of people in the household. The CBO arranges quintiles to contain an equal number of people, not households.

22. The minimum "adjusted" income needed to qualify for the top 1 percent (that is, the minimum income for a single person or the minimum income divided by the square root of the number of people in the household for a larger household) was $257,100 in 2000 (CBO, 2003c, table B-1c). The CBO analysis divides the income of a four-person household by two (that is, the square root of four), which implicitly assumes that such a household requires twice as much income as a single person to achieve the same standard of living for each of its members. Thus, the minimum income to qualify for the top 1 percent for a four-person household in the CBO analysis was $257,100 × 2 = $514,200.

23. Johnston (2003b).

24. All numbers in the paragraph are from Kennickell (2003, tables 1, 5, 6, and 10). Kennickell's analysis is based on data from the Survey of Consumer Finances (SCF).

He also finds that the share of wealth held by the richest 1 percent rose from 30 percent to 33 percent between 1989 and 2001 but cautions that the difference is within the reasonable statistical margin for error for the SCF. The recent stock market slide has apparently had an effect on the wealth of the richest Americans. According to the *Forbes* reports (2002), the average wealth of the richest 400 fell from $3.057 billion to $2.148 billion between 2000 and 2002, and the number of billionaires fell from 301 to 205. As indicated in the text, however, both of these figures were still dramatically higher in 2002 than they were in 1989.

25. These results come from a study by Gottschalk reported in Mishel, Bernstein, and Schmitt (1997), also referenced in Sawhill and McMurrer (1996). For his study, Gottschalk used data from the Panel Study of Income Dynamics, which follows a random sample of households over time. A similar study by the Treasury Department using income tax return data between 1979 and 1988 suggested a bit more mobility, but it suffered from a number of problems. It considered only taxpayers who had filed a tax return in every year between 1979 and 1988, thereby omitting the vast majority of poor people. Moreover, in the Treasury study, the average age of people in the lowest quintile in 1979 was just 21 so that much of the apparent income mobility was due to the natural increase in earnings over a lifetime. See Nasar (1992) for a discussion of the Treasury study. A recent study by Krueger and Perri (2002) found, using data from the Consumer Expenditure Survey, that *consumption* inequality increased significantly less than income inequality between 1972 and 1998. Consumption depends partly on expected lifetime income and not just on current income. Thus, the pattern they found would be consistent with a situation where temporary fluctuations in incomes became greater over time but where the inequality of lifetime incomes did not increase much. However, they note that their result appears to be driven largely by improved access to credit among low- and moderate-income people, which enabled those people to smooth consumption during years with income fluctuations. For this reason, their result may say nothing about what happened to long-term incomes (on which they have no direct evidence) but rather might have resulted from changes in financial markets. In addition, their study does not provide information on what happened in the top 1 percent of the income distribution because of a negligible number of such people in their sample.

26. This claim is based on tabulations of 1994 and 1995 individual tax returns provided to us by the Office of Tax Analysis, United States Treasury. For 1995, the top 1 percent of earners received 14.8 percent of expanded adjusted gross income. For taxpayers in the age class 45 to 54, the top 1 percent received 15.3 percent of income, and for those in the age class 55 to 64, the fraction was 18.2 percent. Income was less concentrated for those age classes below age 45.

27. More generally, *why* incomes are unequal plays a role in the arguments about what, if anything, the tax system ought to do about it. For example, if the predominant factor is luck, then the disincentive effects of a progressive tax system are less worrisome, and taxes arguably provide some social insurance against bad outcomes. If, alternatively, a principal source of inequality is variations in the willingness to work hard, then the case for highly progressive taxes is less compelling. In this case, hard-working people pay more tax than "leisure lovers" of the same ability, and the tax system differentially taxes people according to tastes rather than according to ability to pay. In fact, both luck (including the inheritance of money and other advantages) and hard work are factors in determining incomes.

28. Cited in Bowman (2003, p. 16).

29. National Public Radio, Kaiser Family Foundation, and Kennedy School of Government (2003).

30. National Public Radio, Kaiser Family Foundation, and Kennedy School of Government (2003).

31. McKee and Gerbing (1989), cited in Roberts, Hite, and Bradley (1994).

32. Associated Press poll, March 26–30, 1999, cited in Associated Press (1999).

33. See, for example, Fox News Opinion Dynamics Poll, January 14–15, 2003 (in Blanton 2003) and National Public Radio, Kaiser Family Foundation, and Kennedy School of Government (2003). Evidence on public opinion regarding the estate tax is discussed in more detail in chapter 8.

34. Bowman (2003, p. 17).

35. A later survey by Roberts, Hite, and Bradley (1994) examined people's understandings of concepts such as "marginal," "average," "proportional," and "progressive" as applied to taxes and found that even when these concepts are defined for respondents, they often become confused or give inconsistent responses.

36. To be precise, individual taxpayers pay the difference between tax liability and withheld taxes *plus* estimated tax payments.

37. The importance of mobility in escaping the burden of taxes was recognized by the group of tax scholars popularly known as The Who, who wrote in their song "Goin' Mobile": "Watch the police and tax man miss me, I'm mobile."

38. With heavily advertised goods like Coke and Pepsi, even if all consumers could not distinguish them in a blind taste test, many still might strongly prefer to buy one or the other. This example presumes that consumers think the two products are identical and choose solely on the basis of price.

39. See table 2.1.

40. As Martin Feldstein (1994) of Harvard University has argued, although there is certainly foreign investment over short periods, over the long term a country's investment is limited by its own citizens' saving. If this is true, the link between domestic savings and domestic investment is restored.

41. See, for example, Feldstein and Horioka (1980).

42. Gravelle and Smetters (2001) and Baldwin and Krugman (2002) provide compelling theoretical and empirical support for the notion that much of the burden of corporate income taxes falls on domestic owners of capital.

43. Bastiat (1964, p. 1).

44. Urban-Brookings Tax Policy Center (2003b, table 5.18, May 23) and Cronin (1999). In the Treasury analysis, the burdens of excise taxes and customs duties are allocated to labor, capital, and consumption in a rather complicated fashion described in Cronin (1999). Since these taxes represent a small portion of federal revenues (4.7 percent in 2002), these assumptions make little difference to the estimated distribution of overall federal taxes.

45. To get from AGI to family economic income, the Treasury adds an estimate of unreported and underreported income and the AGI of nonfilers; subtracts realized capital gains and adds accrued capital gains based on retained earnings of corporations and estimates of accruing gains on other assets; adds various forms of excluded income including pension and retirement account contributions, employer-provided fringe

benefits, real capital income accruing in pensions, retirement accounts, and life insurance, imputed rent on owner-occupied housing, and government cash-transfer payments; adds and subtracts a few other miscellaneous items; and adjusts everything for inflation to convert figures into real income. See Cronin (1999) for further details, including the derivation of the 67 percent figure cited in the text.

46. See Kasten, Sammartino, and Toder (1994).

47. Based on the same methodology as outlined in Cronin (1999), the Urban-Brookings Tax Policy Center estimated that the pre-EGTRRA estate tax would contribute approximately 2.1 percent to the average tax rate (expressed relative to AGI) on the highest-income 1 percent of taxpayers in 2010.

48. For example, in January 2003, Bush said regarding his tax cut proposal: "Let me just give you the facts, that under this plan a family of four with an income of $40,000 will receive a 96 percent reduction in federal income taxes." See Stevenson and Stolberg (2003).

49. CBO (2003c, table B-1a). See note 21 above for the definition of income used by CBO for this analysis.

50. Donmoyer (1997, p. 1305).

51. Compare horizontal equity to the concept introduced earlier of vertical equity, which concerns the appropriate relation of tax burden of families at *different* levels of well-being.

52. At present the federal government doesn't levy a special tax on movies. But in 1990 it did impose a new "luxury" tax of 10 percent of the purchase price over $10,000 for furs and jewelry, over $30,000 for autos, over $100,000 for boats, and over $250,000 for airplanes. The luxury tax on everything but automobiles was repealed in 1993.

53. For this reason, the deduction for medical expenses is limited to "involuntary" expenses and specifically excludes such things as elective cosmetic surgery.

54. The interest rate spread between tax-exempt and taxable bonds is, however, significantly less than the top individual marginal tax rate, so that top-bracket investors can indeed receive a strictly higher after-tax rate of return by investing in those securities. In fact, if the interest payments on the borrowing were deductible, borrowing to buy tax-exempt bonds could be highly lucrative at the expense of the U.S. Treasury. Complicated tracing rules exist to prevent this practice, but the rules are complex and difficult to enforce.

55. Note that an application of the benefit principle might suggest that larger families should have *higher* tax liabilities, reflecting the fact that many tax-funded benefits, like public education, increase with family size. This argument is made by Kaplow (1999).

56. CBO (1997).

57. Carasso and Steuerle (2002).

58. Another way to reduce these horizontal inequities is to make the rate structure less progressive, but this comes at the expense of what many people view as a desirable degree of vertical equity.

59. One reason for abandoning the earlier system of taxing each spouse separately was that spouses in community property states could claim to earn half of family income, thus lowering the couple's total taxes. Many states adopted community property laws, apparently so their residents could receive this benefit.

Chapter 4

1. Murray (1996).

2. Bush (2003).

3. Hall and Rabushka (1995, p. 89).

4. Gale (1995, p. 22). Note that Gale refers here to the gain in welfare, not income. In other words, the gain is net of costs of forgone leisure, forgone current consumption, and the like. See chapter 7 for more discussion of this issue.

5. Board of Governors of the Federal Reserve System (2003b).

6. Krugman (2001, pp. 27–28).

7. Parker (1999). Additional evidence comes from Nicholas Souleles (2002) of the University of Pennsylvania. He finds that consumers responded to the 1981 Reagan tax cuts, which were gradually phased in over several years, by increasing their consumption only gradually as their after-tax incomes increased rather than by changing their consumption immediately in response to the anticipated future increase in after-tax income and then just keeping it at that level. Browning and Crossley (2001) provide a more comprehensive review of the evidence on consumption smoothing.

8. See Shapiro and Slemrod (1995) for analysis of survey data on the 1992 withholding change.

9. See Shapiro and Slemrod (2003a, 2003b) for details of how taxpayers behaved on receiving the 2001 tax rebates.

10. Stevenson (2002, p. A1).

11. Hubbard (2001, p. 653).

12. Gale and Orszag (2002).

13. Laubach (2003).

14. Gale and Orszag (2002) and Laubach (2003).

15. Dow Jones Newswire (2003). The Council of Economic Advisers' estimate was initially misreported, and its correct estimate is noted in a "Corrections and Amplifications" note attached to the article.

16. Andrews (2003, p. A1).

17. This judgment applies to deficits created (or surpluses reduced) by reducing taxes collected, holding constant government expenditure on consumption. It may not apply to increasing government-funded investment in infrastructure or education, which provide current and future benefits.

18. See Becker and Mulligan (1998) for an expression of this point of view.

19. Firestone (2003).

20. Friedman (2003, p. A10).

21. Sanger (2002).

22. For opposing views on the evidence about whether tax cuts automatically lead to lower government spending, see Calomiris and Hassett (2002) and Gale and Potter (2002).

23. In 1999, 27.7 percent of the value of Medicaid payments was made on the behalf of people age 65 and over, and 43.0 percent was made for disabled people. Centers for Medicare and Medicaid Services (2002).

24. See Diamond and Orszag (2002) for a description of the proposals put forward by the Social Security commission appointed by George W. Bush, along with a discussion of their impacts on the federal budget and national saving.

25. See Slemrod (1995c).

26. For the rest of this chapter, we refer to taxes other than lump-sum, or poll, taxes.

27. Compensation of employees was 71.6 percent of national income in 2000. *Economic Report of the President* (2002, table B-28).

28. This argument applies even more directly when the base broadening refers to eliminating the deductibility of state and local income taxes. This may allow a lowering of the federal tax rate, but it does not permit an overall reduction in the combined rate of tax from local, state, and federal levels.

29. As discussed earlier, this is but one example where our country's (and every other country's) national income statistics will incorrectly measure the economic cost of tax disincentives. The statistics will record the $200 decrease due to lost labor income, but since the value of leisure is not included in national income, they ignore the $150 worth of extra leisure that Roger enjoys when taxed. It should take only a moment's reflection to convince yourself that national income measured without considering the value of leisure does not accurately reflect national prosperity. If it did, then a law forcing everyone to work, regardless of whether they wanted to or not, would make us better off.

30. It also depends on how sensitive labor demand is to changes in the cost of hiring workers. To the extent that hiring is not cost sensitive, taxes on labor income increase the equilibrium pretax wage rate, offsetting the decline in labor supply.

31. Only responsiveness due to the substitution effect of taxes is relevant to this argument. The change in behavior due to the income effect is inevitable regardless of how a given amount of revenue is raised, and so it is not relevant to the economic cost of alternative ways of raising that revenue.

32. Killingsworth (1983) and Heckman (1993) provide surveys of this literature.

33. Costa (2000) provides evidence on the number of hours worked in a day and the wages for men and women of different income levels between the 1890s and 1991. She finds that the average workday shortened over time as wages increased, which is consistent with an income effect outweighing the substitution effect. Costa also finds that early in the period low-wage workers worked the longest days, that by 1973 workers at all wage levels worked similar hours, and that by 1991 high-wage workers worked the longest hours, although the differences were still small. This would be consistent with a growing substitution effect and a shrinking income effect over time. Fullerton (1999) presents historical statistics on labor-force participation.

34. Eissa (1995, 1996). In an earlier study, Eissa found that wives of very high-income husbands increased their hours of work significantly after 1986 but that this group's labor supply is too small to have had a major impact on overall national income.

35. See Ziliak and Kniesner (1999) and Moffitt and Wilhelm (2000).

36. Lindbeck (1993).

37. Bell and Freeman (2000).

38. How the *demand* for labor by businesses depends on the wage they must pay workers is also relevant to the impact of taxes on labor income. Even if the supply of labor were quite responsive to the after-tax wage, if firms wanted to hire a given amount of labor regardless of the cost, then taxes would not cause much decrease in hours worked or much inefficiency in the labor market. The most extensive study of this issue is Hamermesh (1993).

39. Triest (1990).

40. Technically, these taxes eliminate the tax on the "normal" return to saving and investment and do exact a burden on above-normal returns. We discuss this issue in more detail in chapter 6.

41. See Gravelle (1994) for details. The real after-tax rate of return is based on the yield on Baa corporate bonds. A fixed premium for holding equity of 2.67 percentage points is added in all years. This is based on an assumption of a 4 percent premium for holding equity, multiplied by the typical share of corporate investments financed by equity, which Gravelle puts at two-thirds. The tax rate used is a measure of the average marginal individual tax rate on interest income. We revise and update her series as follows. For all years, we estimate the expected inflation rate based on the one-year ahead forecast of CPI inflation from the Livingston survey of economic forecasters, now conducted by the Federal Reserve Bank of Philadelphia (see <http://www.phil.frb.org/files/liv/datai.html>). The nominal yield on Baa bonds is taken from the Economic Report of the President. The saving rate is determined based on data from U.S. Bureau of Economic Analysis, *National Income and Product Accounts of the United States,* based on Gravelle's definitions. Net private saving is defined as gross private saving (which includes both personal saving and retained corporate earnings) minus capital consumption allowances. Disposable income is defined as gross national product minus capital consumption allowances and total federal, state, and local government receipts. The dollar-weighted average marginal tax rate on interest income from 1960 through 1999 is taken from the National Bureau of Economic Research Web site (<http://www.nber.org/~taxsim/mrates/mrates2.html>). Because data on the tax rate is not available after 1999, we assume that this tax rate is the same in 2000 through 2002 as it was in 1999.

42. See Gale and Sabelhaus (1999) for a discussion of this issue.

43. For a review of these studies, see Bernheim (2002) and Elmendorf (1996). Ironically, one influential study suggesting that saving has a low responsiveness to incentives was authored by Robert E. Hall, who is also one of the designers of the flat tax, which reduces the tax on saving. See Hall (1988). One recent exception to the consensus on a low responsiveness of saving to incentives is a paper by Mulligan (2002). He calculates a measure of the after-tax rate of return to capital based on aggregate business profits and rents in the United States, less aggregate tax payments on capital income, all divided by an estimated value of the capital stock. Using aggregate time-series data for the United States spanning most of the twentieth century, he finds in some specifications that the rate of growth of consumption is strongly positively related to this measure of the after-tax rate of return to capital. Mulligan argues that in a life-cycle model of consumption behavior, this would be consistent with a strong behavioral response of consumption and saving to incentives. However, it appears that his results are driven largely by the fact that both

consumption and business profits decline during recessions and rise during recoveries, which probably reflects the influence of a third factor (business cycles) for which he does not control. In addition, the life-cycle model suggests that when the incentive to save increases, consumption will instantaneously drop, and only after that will the rate of growth of consumption increase. Studies by Mulligan and others that take this approach do not account for this initial drop. Finally, Mulligan's measure of the after-tax rate of return to capital produces a roughly similar pattern of changes in the incentive to save after 1960 as we illustrate in figure 4.6 (see Mulligan 2002, figure 3).

44. Chirinko, Fazzari, and Meyer (1999).

45. OMB (2003, "Analytical Perspectives," table 6-1).

46. Mackie (2002, p. 310).

47. Compared to taxation of commodities, deviating from uniform taxation of investment on efficiency grounds—say, by favoring machinery over structures or manufacturing over agriculture—is much harder to justify. See Slemrod (1990) for a nontechnical review of optimal tax theory.

48. Mackie (2002, pp. 309–311) provides evidence of wide variation in effective income tax rates on the returns to different industries and different types of productive capital assets.

49. The most sophisticated study of this issue to date is by Leonard Burman, currently of the Urban Institute, and William Randolph of the U.S. Department of the Treasury (1994). It examines the effects of differences in state capital gains tax rates on capital gains realizations by individual taxpayers. They conclude that the long-run responsiveness of capital gains realizations to changes in marginal tax rates is probably low but that a wide confidence interval exists around their estimate.

50. See Poterba (1989) for a discussion of this issue.

51. See Burman (1999) for an excellent review of the issues and evidence about capital gains taxes.

52. Hall and Rabushka (1995, p. 87) make this case. Hubbard (1998) and Gentry and Hubbard (2000a) review the implications of capital market imperfections that prevent entrepreneurs from obtaining external financing.

53. Carroll, Holtz-Eakin, Rider, and Rosen (1998).

54. Gentry and Hubbard (2000b).

55. For an expansion of this view, see Krugman (1994) or Slemrod (1992).

56. Hines (1999) and Wilson (1999) offer good summaries of the issues relating to taxation of multinational companies and tax competition. Rodrik (1997) and Baldwin and Krugman (2002) also offer interesting perspectives and evidence.

57. See Slemrod (1995a) for a discussion of tax policy toward foreign direct investment and its relationship to trade policy.

58. Rodrik (1997, p. 64).

59. Kornblut and Blanton (2003).

60. Some policies, such as the minimum wage, can in principle lead to involuntary unemployment even when the economy is operating normally. We leave these aside here to

focus on tax policy issues. Because taxes reduce after-tax wages, they also can cause people who would be willing to work at the pretax wage to voluntarily decline employment at the after-tax wage.

61. See Davies and Whalley (1991) for a review of this issue.

62. We focus on the subject of tax evasion in chapter 5.

63. Burman, Clausing, and O'Hare (1994).

64. Authors' calculations based on IRS, Statistics of Income Division, *Corporation Income Tax Returns* (various years).

65. See Feenberg and Poterba (1993). The figures they reported were biased because they failed to account for changes in the definition of adjusted gross income. The text cites the corrected numbers presented in Slemrod (1996a).

66. See Feldstein (1995b), Auten and Carroll (1999), and Gruber and Saez (2002) for analyses of the high-income response to changes in marginal tax rates during the 1980s. Slemrod (1998) provides a detailed overview of the issues involved in these types of studies.

67. Sherwin Rosen of the University of Chicago discussed this phenomenon in a 1981 article. A 1995 book written by Robert Frank of Cornell University and Philip Cook of Duke University, *The Winner-Take-All Society*, documents many examples of it in the U.S. economy in recent years.

68. See Moffitt and Wilhelm (2000).

69. Feldstein and Feenberg (1996).

70. Whether tax increases on the rich are a bad idea depends on a person's views about the benefit of a more equal distribution of well-being. But regardless of how one judges this benefit, progressivity is less desirable as the economic cost of high taxes increases, which depends on the magnitude of the behavioral response they cause. In the extreme, consider the case of a "high-income Laffer curve," in which a higher top bracket rate causes enough response as to *lower* the amount of tax collected on those affluent families. In this case, no one is better off, certainly not the high-income families that face the higher tax rate, and not anyone else, as there is no extra revenue to use to lower anyone else's tax burden or to increase social expenditures.

71. Fastis (1992) and Peers and Tannenbaum (1992).

72. Goolsbee (2000).

73. *Economic Report of the President* (1996, p. 92).

74. See Parcell (1996).

75. Piketty and Saez (2003). We focus on income excluding capital gains both because capital gains tax rates changed in different ways than tax rates on ordinary income over time and because capital gains realizations fluctuate a great deal, mainly for reasons (such as stock market valuations) that are unrelated to taxpayers' responses to incentives created by the tax code. In any event, using a measure that includes capital gains yields the same general patterns and in particular yields an even larger increase in incomes of the top 1 percent between 1980 and 2000. See Piketty and Saez (2003) for more details.

76. Goolsbee (1999) provides a formal analysis of how incomes at the top of the distribution responded to five major tax reforms between 1924 and 1966, finding mixed results.

77. There are other factors unrelated to taxes that can help explain some of the historical pattern of the share of income going to the top 1 percent. For example, pretax wage inequality declined sharply during the 1940s, and much of this is probably explained by the massive increase in the number of relatively high-paying manufacturing jobs for low-skill workers that developed during and after World War II. And as we have mentioned before, there are many good nontax explanations for the well-documented steady increase in pretax wage inequality during the 1970s, 1980s, and 1990s. Goldin and Margo (1992) discuss the decline in wage inequality during the 1940s. Katz and Murphy (1992) examine nontax causes of increasing wage inequality during the 1970s and 1980s.

78. Steuerle (1992, p. 186).

79. Each year for many years, former Senator Bob Packwood (R-OR) asked the Joint Committee on Taxation to prepare an analysis of a 100 percent marginal tax rate applied to income over $100,000 or $200,000. Senator Packwood was not considering such a proposal but wanted to illustrate that the official government procedures would overestimate the amount of revenue a confiscating tax rate would generate. The JCT responded reasonably to this request, calculating the revenue that would be raised if there were no behavioral responses but adding that "if the 100 percent tax rate were to be in effect for a substantial period of time . . . then in our judgment there would be a substantial reduction in income-producing activity in the economy and, thus, a significant reduction in tax receipts to the federal government." This episode is discussed in written testimony of the staff of the Joint Committee on Taxation (1995).

80. VandeHei and Weisman (2003).

81. Crippen (2002).

82. See Auerbach (1996) for a discussion of the pros and cons of dynamic revenue estimation.

83. CBO (2003b).

84. CBO (2003b, p. 27, n. 15). Auerbach (2002) performs a dynamic analysis of the 2001 tax cut that presents results over the very long run. He finds that the long-run effect on economic output is negative unless large portions of the tax cuts are offset by reductions in government spending.

85. One heroic, although now dated, attempt to measure the total welfare cost of all taxes—federal, state, and local—came up with a range of estimates from 13 to 24 cents per dollar of revenue. See Ballard, Shoven, and Whalley (1985).

Chapter 5

1. Tritch (1998, p. 104).

2. Garcia (2002). The General Accounting Office publishes similar results annually. According to Rossotti (2002, p. 6), results improved markedly in recent years, and by the end of 2002, 84 percent of tax law questions and 90 percent of tax account questions were answered accurately.

3. *Internal Revenue Code 2002* (2002); *Federal Tax Regulations 2002* (2002).

4. The 7.3 million number is our estimate, based on 12,186 pages with approximately 600 words per page.

5. The IRS budget for fiscal year 2002 is from OMB (2003, p. 242). Collections (net of refunds) for all taxes administered by the IRS totaled $1.733 trillion in fiscal year 2002 (IRS 2003b, table 1). This includes not only the federal individual and corporate income taxes but also employment and general retirement taxes, unemployment insurance, estate and gift taxes, and excise taxes.

6. The 3 billion total and 27-hour average come from Blumenthal and Slemrod (1992).

7. The average expenditure on professional help for all taxpayers was $66 in 1989 dollars, or $98 in 2003 dollars. Because about 48 percent of all taxpayers used professional preparers at that time (IRS, Statistics of Income Division, *Statistics of Income Bulletin*, Winter 2002–2003, pp. 153, 194), the average for those who use preparers was $204 in 2003 dollars.

8. See Slemrod (1996b) for more details of this estimate and those that follow.

9. IRS *Statistics of Income Bulletin*, Winter 2002–2003, p. 193.

10. Slemrod (1997). In 1996, the average Fortune 500 company spent $3.9 million (or $4.6 million in 2003 dollars) to comply with corporate income tax laws at the federal, state, and local levels of government. About 75 percent of this amount was spent on complying with federal tax laws.

11. Slemrod (1997). In 1996, the average large company (defined as among the largest 1,700) spent $1.9 million, which comes to a total of $3.2 billion, or $3.8 billion in 2003 dollars.

12. Slemrod and Blumenthal (1996).

13. See, for example, Slemrod and Blumenthal (1996), Hall (1995, table 2), and Sandford (1995).

14. The Blumenthal/Slemrod study asked about compliance with the personal income tax and did not specify how businesses taxed under the personal code should be treated. It appears that self-employed people (sole proprietors) generally reported the costs of compliance for their businesses. Owners of partnerships and S corporations probably reported only a small fraction of the costs. Although income from these latter types of firms is taxed under the personal code, most of the difficult parts of the taxpaying process, such as calculating depreciation allowances, are performed on a separate business tax form.

15. Slemrod and Venkatesh (2002). The $22 billion figure is for the federal income tax only.

16. This assumes that combined personal and corporate income tax revenues are $1.055 trillion, based on the estimate for fiscal year 2003 in CBO (2003a).

17. This study relies on a flawed Arthur D. Little (1988) estimate of the total hours spent by business for tax compliance. For why it is flawed, see Slemrod (1996b). Moreover, it uses very high estimates of the cost per hour for both individuals and businesses, arbitrarily based on an average of the IRS budget per employee hour and the total revenues of a large accounting firm per employee hour.

18. Herman (1995, p. A1).

19. Gephardt (1995).

20. IRS *Statistics of Income Bulletin*, Winter 2002–2003, p. 153.

21. IRS *Statistics of Income Bulletin*, Winter 2002–2003, p. 153.

22. Blumenthal and Slemrod (1992, table 1).

23. Goolsbee (forthcoming).

24. Studies have examined the compliance cost of income taxation in other countries, but differences in methodology make comparisons tenuous. That being said, a careful study of the United Kingdom's tax system provided an estimate of 4.7 cents on the dollar of collection cost. See Sandford (1995). One reason for the lower cost is the special nature of the British individual income tax system, under which most taxpayers need not even fill out and file a return.

25. We consider here what makes any given tax structure complex, but continuous change in the tax system is itself complex, as time and effort are needed for taxpayers to learn and adjust to the new environment. This raises a classic problem of policy reform: should the movement to a better policy be put off because of the costs of getting there?

26. As the British experience discussed in chapter 3 suggests, a poll tax would likely also be difficult to enforce if it is widely perceived to be unfair.

27. The British are, however, moving away from this system. Starting in April of 1996, 9 million residents with more than a modicum of income from rents, dividends, interest, or capital gains were required to file an eight-page tax return, plus related schedules. See Johnston (1996).

28. On the other hand, delivering subsidies to low-income families through the tax code means that they can no longer be exempted from filing returns. It also postpones the receipt of the tax credit to when the return is filed, unless the subsidy can be integrated into the employer withholding system. Currently, employers are allowed to make a limited portion of refundable EITC payments available to eligible workers throughout the year through their withholding systems.

29. In 2001, 34 percent of all personal returns itemized, according to the IRS *Statistics of Income Bulletin*, Winter 2002–2003, pp. 153, 155.

30. There is no reason that the tax system could not provide a subsidy that is a constant rate for all taxpayers. If this is desired, it should be a refundable credit rather than an itemized deduction.

31. Sullivan (2001) reports that PAC contributions to Ways and Means Committee members during the 2000 election cycle totaled $38.7 million. The Center for Responsive Politics (at <http://www.crp.org>) reports that PAC contributions to all winners of House races in the 2000 election cycle totaled $168.5 million. Both figures are based on Federal Election Commission data compiled by the Center for Responsive Politics. There are 41 members of the Ways and Means Committee, and 435 members of the House.

32. Strict limitations constrain what members of Congress can accept from lobbyists. For example, members of Congress can still accept a dinner invitation but cannot accept payment for meals or gifts totaling more than $100 from any one source per year.

33. The Joint Committee on Taxation (2003f) analysis of tax complexity for the Jobs and Growth Tax Relief Reconciliation Act of 2003 can be found in the *Congressional Record*, May 22, 2003.

34. Moore (1987, p. 1167).

35. Joint Committee on Taxation (2001, vol. 2, pp. 79–91).

36. In some ways, the existence of the corporate income tax is just such a policy. It acts as a backstop to the personal income tax, to keep income earned through corporations from escaping tax entirely. We address this issue in chapter 8.

37. A notable exception is the Social Security payroll tax, where benefits do depend on the amount of tax "contributions" made, although the relationship between contributions and benefits is far from one-for-one.

38. Landler (2002); Usborne (2002).

39. Crenshaw (2002).

40. Donmoyer (2002).

41. The dependent exemption episode is chronicled in Lewin (1991) and Szilagyi (1990). The child-care credit underwent a similar reform with similar results. Beginning in tax year 1989, taxpayers who wanted to claim a child-care credit had to report the name of the care provider plus the provider's Social Security number or employer identification number. As in the dependent exemption case, the results were immediate and striking. The number of taxpayers claiming child-care credits dropped from 8.7 million in 1988 to 6 million in 1989, reversing a nine-year trend of annual increases; the dollar amount claimed fell from $3.7 billion to $2.4 billion. Even more incredible, the number of taxpayers reporting self-employment income from child-care services rose from 261,000 in 1988 to 431,000 in 1989, a 65 percent increase. The combination of the decrease in child-care credits taken and increase in income reported by self-employed child-care providers resulted in a $1.5 billion increase in tax revenues. See O'Neil and Lanese (1993).

42. IRS (2002b). The principal purpose of the National Research Program is to gather information that enables the IRS to come up with a formula, based on the information provided on tax returns, for determining which returns are cost-effective to audit. This was also the purpose of the TCMP. IRS (2002b) notes that in the years since 1988, the last time the TCMP was done, the percentage of IRS audits that find no evasion has increased substantially. This probably suggests that the formula used to select returns for audit is growing less effective at identifying the returns most likely to involve tax evasion, perhaps because it is based on outdated data.

43. See IRS (1996). Revenue for the federal personal and corporate income taxes was $1,018 billion in 2002 (see table 2.1). If 18 percent of true tax liability were lost to evasion, then true tax liability was $1,018 billion/$(1 - 0.18) = $1,241 billion, so revenue lost to evasion was $1,241 billion – $1,018 billion = $223 billion.

44. Based on the latest data available, for 2000, taxable income in the personal income tax was $4,544 billion, and income subject to tax by the corporate income tax was $760 billion. Income tax after credits was $204 billion for the corporate income tax and $980 billion for the personal income tax. The combined average tax rate was thus $(204 + 980)/(760 + 4544) = 22$ percent. See IRS, Statistics of Income Division, *Statistics of Income Bulletin*, Winter 2002–2003, pp. 154–156, 169.

45. The General Accounting Office (1997, n. 1) notes that the IRS tax gap estimate for 1992 did not include unreported income from illegal sources, such as illegal gambling, drug trafficking, and prostitution. Other hard-to-uncover evasion, such as unreported income from tips and moonlighting, was estimated on the basis of special studies.

46. Reported in Roth, Scholz, and Witte (1989, p. 51) and based on evidence from the 1979 Taxpayer Compliance Measurement Program.

47. Roth, Scholz, and Witte (1989, p. 55).

48. Alm (1985).

49. IRS (2003b, table 10).

50. See IRS, *Internal Revenue Service Data Book* (various years).

51. IRS (2003b, table 10).

52. IRS (2003b, table 10).

53. IRS (2003b, table 25).

54. The 82 percent figure is the amount withheld by employers divided by net (of refund) collections for 2001 from IRS (2003b, table 1).

55. IRS, Statistics of Income Division, *Individual Income Tax Returns* (1999, tables 1.4, 3.3).

56. Steuerle (1986, p. 27).

57. Bruno Frey of the University of Zurich has argued that heavy-handed enforcement can even backfire to reduce compliance. He stresses the difference between what he calls intrinsic and extrinsic motivation. With *intrinsic motivation,* taxpayers pay because they admire "civic virtue." With *extrinsic motivation,* they do so because they fear punishment. Frey argues that increasing extrinsic motivation—say, with more punitive enforcement policies—"crowds out" intrinsic motivation by making people feel that they pay taxes because they have to rather than because they want to. He argues that where the relationship between the individual and the tax authority is seen as involving an implicit contract sustained by trust, individuals will comply due to high "tax morale." To sustain citizens' commitment to the contract and therefore their morale, the tax authority must act respectfully toward citizens and protect the honest from the free rider. It does this, he argues, by giving taxpayers the benefit of the doubt when it finds a mistake, by sanctioning small violations more mildly, and by sanctioning large and basic violations more heavily. For a detailed account of this argument, see Frey and Jegen (2001).

58. Burnham (1989), Payne (1993), and testimony from the 1997 congressional hearings on the IRS, collected at <http://www.unclefed.com/TxprBoR/1997/>, provide abundant anecdotes of arguably abusive practices.

59. NBC/*Wall Street Journal* poll conducted in October 1997, cited in Bowman (2003, p. 58).

60. The argument against the shift in the burden of proof is laid out nicely in Wolfman (1998).

61. Roper/ASW poll cited in Bowman (2003, p. 58).

62. ABC News (2002).

63. General Accounting Office (2003).

64. IRS (1997, table 11); IRS (2003b, table 10); the Transactional Records Access Clearinghouse (TRAC) Web site at <http://trac.syr.edu/tracirs/newfindings/current/>.

65. IRS data cited in Johnston (2003a).

66. The Transactional Records Access Clearinghouse (TRAC) Web site at <http://trac. syr.edu/tracirs/newfindings/current/>.

67. Rossotti (2002, p. 16).

68. Johnston (2003a), based on IRS data.

69. OMB (2003, p. 242).

70. This argument is presented in Yitzhaki (1974).

71. Sheffrin and Triest (1992) offer a literature review as well as some new evidence on this subject.

72. Hessing, Elffers, Robben, and Webley (1992, p. 298).

Chapter 6

1. Deductions, dividends, and capital gains as a percentage of adjusted gross income in each income class are calculated based on data from tax returns filed in 2000 in Campbell and Parisi (2002). Dividends reported in the tax return data are adjusted to remove the average fraction that actually represents interest from mutual funds, reported in Gale (2002). We assume that the percentage applies at the midpoint of each income class and linearly interpolate the percentage between each midpoint. The family is assumed to claim the earned income tax credit and two child credits, when eligible, but no other credits. Itemized deductions disallowed by the alternative minimum tax at each AGI level are estimated in the same manner as for total deductions. We take these disallowed itemized deductions into account to calculate AMT liability but assume that the family has no other AMT preference items. The revenue-neutral single tax rate comes from the Urban-Brookings Tax Policy Center tax calculator, which estimates that in 2003, income tax liability will be $776 billion and taxable income will be $4.52 trillion (this includes the effects of the tax cut enacted in May 2003). The 17.2 percent rate comes from (776/4520).

2. The $4,900 is approximately $1,018 billion in personal and corporate income taxes raised in 2002 (from table 2.1), divided by a population of 209 million people age 18 or over in 2002.

3. If the consumption tax is administered as a retail sales tax, the tax described here would be considered a 25 percent tax on the value of purchases excluding tax.

4. This is net worth of households and nonprofit organizations. Board of Governors of the Federal Reserve System (2003a, table B.100).

5. Warren (1996) offers a more detailed treatment of the following discussion.

6. Mehra and Prescott (2003) discuss the historical difference between returns on risky and relatively risk-free assets. They note, for instance, that between 1889 and 2000, the average pretax real annual rate of return on corporate stocks was about 8 percent, compared to 1.1 percent for relatively risk-free short-term government bonds. On the other hand, Jagannathan, McGrattan, and Scherbina (2001) present evidence that over the past three decades, the risk-free rate of return has increased substantially and the difference between the return on stocks and bonds has declined. Moreover, the historically high ratio of stock prices to earnings in recent years, which persists even after the recent stock market decline, suggests that the future premium for bearing risk will be much lower than it was historically, unless future corporate earnings performance is much better than it was historically.

7. See Domar and Musgrave (1944). An example can help illustrate. Suppose that you've got $100 (after taxes) to save and there's a 20 percent income tax. You have a choice of investing in the risky asset described above or a risk-free asset paying 10 percent for sure. Consider first a situation where we only tax the risk-free portion (10 percent) of the return on each asset. Suppose that in this situation, you would put half your portfolio into each asset. If the risky investment turns out well, you get ($50 × 1.1) + ($50 × 1.4) − .2(10) = $123 after taxes. If it turns out badly, you get ($50 × 1.1) + ($50 × 0.9) − .2(10) = $98 after taxes.

Now suppose that the government instead imposes a 20 percent income tax on the entire return, not just the risk-free portion. You can exactly replicate the earlier outcome by just increasing the share of your portfolio invested in the risky asset by a factor of $1/(1 - t)$, where t is the tax rate. In this example, it means investing 62.5 percent of the portfolio in the risky asset and 37.5 percent in the risk-free asset. With that portfolio, with good luck you get ($37.5 × 1.1) + ($62.5 × 1.4) − .2[($37.5 × .1) + ($62.5 × .4)] = $123 after taxes. With bad luck, you get ($37.5 × 1.1) + ($62.5 × 0.9) − .2[($37.5 × .1) − ($62.5 × .1)] = $98 after taxes. So you indeed have the opportunity to achieve *exactly* the same outcome as you would if the government only imposed a tax at the same rate on the risk-free portion of the return. Therefore, you must be at least as well off. The level of risk you face is the same, the after-tax return you receive is the same, and the amount you get to consume in each state of the world is the same. In this sense, a proportional income tax taxes only the risk-free return and exempts compensation for risk from tax.

This example assumes that there is some way for everyone to change their portfolios in this way at the same time and ignores the implications of the fact that government revenues become more uncertain because they fluctuate with the aggregate return to investment. Louis Kaplow (1994) of Harvard University has shown that both of these issues are taken care of if the government trades risky assets to individuals in exchange for the risk-free assets that the individuals want to get rid of. In that case, the outcome of the income tax for individuals, the government, and the economy as a whole would be exactly identical to a tax on only the risk-free return. However, it is unclear how realistic this is.

8. For instance, the Hall-Rabushka flat tax proposal places limitations on the deductibility of business losses.

9. In this context, it is interesting to note that recently Norway, Sweden, and Denmark have adopted a *dual income tax* system, under which all capital income (including corporation income) is taxed at a low flat rate, while labor income is taxed with graduated rates that exceed the capital income tax rate. The system requires somewhat arbitrary and often complicated rules about how to identify the labor and capital income of small, closely held businesses. For more details, see Sørenson (1998) and Cnossen (1997).

10. Gordon, Kalambokidis, and Slemrod (2003). See Gordon and Slemrod (1988) for a similar analysis conducted for tax year 1983. The 15 percent of revenues figure is calculated based on 1995 total personal income tax revenue of $588.4 billion, and total corporate income tax after credits of $156.4 billion. See IRS, Statistics of Income Division, *IRS Statistics of Income Bulletin*, Fall 2002, pp. 254, 267.

11. Note that if the consumption tax were levied on the price exclusive of tax, it would have to be set at a 25 percent rate to be equivalent to a 20 percent tax on wage and salary income. Also note that when considering the transition from an income tax to either a consumption or wage tax, the consumption tax places a burden on preexisting wealth, and the wage tax does not. The consumption tax also taxes "supernormal returns" while the wage tax does not. These factors allow the consumption tax to impose lower tax rates than the wage tax and yet raise the same revenue, in which case the consumption tax has *less* of a negative impact on the incentive to work than does an equal-revenue wage tax.

12. This may not be true for people who are already fairly old when the consumption or wage tax is adopted because their saving won't benefit from many years of higher after-tax returns. This matters, however, only in the transition to a consumption tax. Once it is in place, a consumption tax that raises the same revenue as an income tax need not provide a greater disincentive to working.

13. See Sabelhaus (1993) for an examination of consumption and saving rates by income level.

14. The precise statement is that the present discounted value of consumption must equal the present discounted value of labor earnings and inherited wealth.

15. See Dynan, Skinner, and Zeldes (2000) for evidence that high-income people save a larger share of their lifetime incomes. Aaron and Galper (1985) present an argument for accompanying a consumption tax with a tax on bequests.

16. Whether in fact consumer prices would rise in the event of tax reform depends on the monetary policy set by the Federal Reserve Board.

17. Whether eliminating the tax on dividends would increase the value of corporate stock depends on whether these taxes have been capitalized (negatively) into the value of shares or whether firms can find ways to distribute funds to shareholders in ways that avoid the dividend tax—say, through share repurchases. This is a controversial topic among economists, although the evidence points to at least some capitalization. See Bradford (1981) or Auerbach (1979) for discussion of this issue.

18. Indeed, Lyon and Merrill (2001) show that under certain conditions the value of existing assets could actually *increase* if we were to switch to a consumption tax.

19. Kennickell (2003), based on the 2001 Survey of Consumer Finances.

20. Wolff (2000, table 12).

21. Richman (1995, pp. 36, 44), quoted in Pearlman (1996, p. 416).

22. Fullerton and Rogers (1996) argue that a wage tax could increase saving by more than a consumption tax because it leaves more wealth in the hands of the very wealthy, who have a much higher propensity to save than everyone else.

23. We mention ethanol here because, for a few weeks every four years, the tax preference for ethanol attracts a lot of attention because ethanol is an alternative fuel made from corn and the caucuses in the corn state of Iowa are the first major event of the U.S. presidential election process. Under current law, the federal excise tax on gasoline is reduced for ethanol-blended fuel or, alternatively, refiners can claim an income tax credit per gallon of ethanol used to produce ethanol-blended gasoline.

24. OMB (2003, "Analytical Perspectives," table 6.1). Personal income tax revenues were $858 billion in fiscal year 2002 (OMB, 2003, "Historical Tables," table 2.1). This latter figure is used to calculate the increase in personal income tax rates necessary to finance deductions and exclusions throughout the rest of this chapter.

25. The best argument may be that a federal tax preference offsets a bias against housing due to the heavy reliance of local governments on property taxes. Many economists argue, however, that property taxes on housing act not as a disincentive to purchase housing but rather as the price for obtaining local public services, predominantly elementary and secondary education. To the extent that local property taxes are a user

charge for public services, they do not act as a disincentive to purchase housing, and the argument for offsetting preferences in the federal income tax does not apply.

26. This evidence is discussed in Glaeser and Shapiro (2002). Note, though, that Glaeser and Shapiro conclude that, whatever the spillover benefits of homeownership, the effect of the home mortgage interest deduction on the homeownership rate is minimal.

27. Messere (1993, p. 234) notes that 12 European countries tax the imputed rental value of owner-occupied houses. These countries generally estimate the rent by applying a low, fixed percentage rate to an estimate of the value of the home.

28. Messere (1993, p. 234).

29. See Feldstein (1995a) and Hall and Rabushka (1995, pp. 94–95).

30. Poterba (1990) finds that single-family housing starts showed similar patterns in the United States and Canada after 1986, despite the fact that Canada did not have a tax reform that made owner-occupied housing less attractive. Moreover, in the 1970s and 1980s, movements in the real price of single-family homes in the United States were only partially consistent with tax-induced changes in the cost of housing.

31. Canada's homeownership rate for 1992 was 63 percent, compared to 64 percent for the United States. See Bartlett (1995), who draws on data from the International Housing Association and the OECD.

32. See Gale (2001) and Bruce and Holtz-Eakin (2001) for more details.

33. OMB (2003, "Analytical Perspectives," table 6.1).

34. See Glied and Remler (2002) for a more detailed discussion of the economic issues involved in health insurance.

35. The Hall-Rabushka flat tax would actually penalize employer-provided health insurance in some cases. The cost of health insurance premiums would be included in the business tax base and taxed at the single rate; that is, unlike wages and salaries, it would not be deductible from the business tax base. For workers with wages below the large tax-exempt level, their employers would find it cheaper to provide them cash wages instead of health benefits. These workers do not remit any tax regardless of the form of compensation, but only in the case of cash wages is it deductible to the employer. To the extent that this reduces employer-provided health insurance coverage, it could greatly worsen adverse selection problems. Any fundamental tax reform proposal that could actually get enacted would likely fix this problem, but it means that a higher tax rate than that advertised by Hall and Rabushka would be required.

36. The revenue cost of the charitable contribution deduction in the personal income tax is for fiscal year 2002 and is taken from OMB (2003, "Analytical Perspectives," table 6.1). See Auten, Cilke, and Randolph (1992) and Bakija (1999) for time-series evidence on the effect of tax incentives on charitable contributions. Randolph (1995) and Bakija (1999) perform econometric analyses examining how charitable contributions of individuals responded to changes in marginal tax rates over the 1980s. Both conclude that, in the long run, giving is only moderately sensitive to tax incentives, although the *timing* of giving is very sensitive.

37. If a uniform rate of subsidy is desired, it could in theory be administered not through the tax system but by direct government grants to qualifying charitable organizations. Many resist this idea as inappropriate government intrusiveness; others fear it because

once the rate of subsidy is decoupled from marginal income tax rates, it could be arbitrarily reduced when budget-cutting fever breaks out.

38. OMB (2003, "Analytical Perspectives," table 6.1). Both figures are for fiscal year 2002.

39. In its current form, the deductions for state and local taxes also encourage subfederal governments to use income and property taxes, which are deductible, instead of sales taxes, which since 1986 are not deductible. The federal tax bias against sales taxes has not, though, resulted in a post-1986 movement away from sales taxes. On the contrary, if anything, the trend has been *toward* greater reliance by states on sales taxes.

Chapter 7

1. Senator Richard Lugar (1995) advocated a national retail sales tax in the 1996 Republican presidential primaries. Alan Keyes (2000) advocated a similar plan in the 2000 Republican presidential primaries.

2. Due and Mikesell (1994, pp. 52–54) catalog numerous examples of states that charge different rates for different goods, such as preferential lower rates on automobile purchases. They also discuss (pp. 80–84) refund programs for the elderly and the poor, which are generally administered through personal income tax forms.

3. Ebrill, Keen, Bodin, and Summers (2001, p. xi).

4. Cnossen (1998, p. 399).

5. If sales of investment goods were taxable under the VAT but were not deductible at all for the firms that purchased them, then the tax base would include *gross* investment, making the base broader than an income tax. Alternatively, if investment goods were deducted gradually as they depreciated, this would turn the VAT into an income tax. Immediate expensing of capital goods or the equivalent, exemption of sales of investment goods from tax, is necessary to make the VAT a true consumption tax.

6. A VAT may be levied either on the price inclusive of the tax or the price before-tax, as with a retail sales tax. A tax that raises a given amount of revenue will have a lower rate if levied on the after-tax price than on the before-tax price, but the two are equivalent. For example, a 10 percent tax on the before-tax price is equal to a 9.09 percent tax on the after-tax price. According to Tait (1988, p. 8), Finland and Sweden are the only countries that have persistently charged the VAT on the after-tax price.

7. As of 2001, the only national VAT implemented using the subtraction method is that of Japan. See Ebrill et al. (2001, p. 20).

8. As noted above, a credit-invoice method VAT need not necessarily visibly charge the tax as a percentage of the before-tax price, but nearly every country that has one does.

9. Indeed, Desai and Hines (2002) find evidence that, other things equal, the more countries make use of the VAT, the *less* foreign trade they have.

10. An invoice-credit type of VAT makes a distinction between *exemption* and *zero-rating*. Exemption generally applies to small firms and is explained in the section on simplicity and enforceability of a VAT. Zero-rating in a VAT means that credits are allowed for purchased inputs, although sales are not taxed. When applied to sales to consumers or sales out of the country, this method frees the entire final purchase price of the good from taxation. In general, zero-rating is used either for goods accorded preferential treatment, such as food, or for exports.

11. Rieschick (1997, p. 1661).

12. As in the current system, pension contributions would be deductible by businesses, and benefits paid out would be included in the recipients' taxable income.

13. Financial institutions may be subject to special tax rules.

14. Laurence Kotlikoff of Boston University has proposed using an electronic debit card system that would automatically record consumers' transactions and calculate their tax liability. A brief description is offered in Kotlikoff (1995, p. 17). This would share many of the administrative difficulties associated with a retail sales tax that are discussed later in this chapter. It would also require either that all transactions use this electronic payment method or that individuals keep records of and voluntarily report all cash transactions. Banning all other means of payment, including cash, would probably be necessary, rendering it impractical.

15. See Christian and Schutzer (1995) for a description of the USA tax proposal.

16. In 2001, federal corporate and personal income taxes raised $1,145 billion. Personal consumption expenditures in 2001 were $6,987 billion. *Economic Report of the President* (2003, tables B-16 and B-82). Note that for this calculation, no adjustment is made to government transfers, so that their real purchasing power would decline.

17. We calculate the 26.9 percent figure as follows. According to Due and Mikesell (1994, pp. 21–22), the average state's retail sales tax base is equal to 49 percent of personal income. Personal income for 2001 was $8,685 billion. See U.S. Bureau of Economic Analysis, *National Income and Product Accounts of the United States* (2003, table 2.1). This suggests a sales tax base of $4,256 billion for 2001 if the United States adopted a base typical of the states. Raising revenue of $1,145 billion (see previous note) would thus require a 26.9 percent tax-exclusive rate.

18. According to Due and Mikesell (1994), leaving aside Hawaii, the five states with the broadest sales tax coverage are Arizona, Arkansas, New Mexico, South Dakota, and Wyoming. These five have a sales tax base equal to 70 percent of personal income. This implies a national sales tax base of $6,080 billion in 2001 and a tax-exclusive rate of 18.8 percent. Hawaii is an outlier, with a retail sales tax base equal to 126 percent of personal income, which must imply heavy taxation of business inputs.

19. Of the five states listed with broad sales tax coverage, all but Arizona fully subject food to sales tax. Due and Mikesell (1994, p. 75) estimate that a food exemption costs a state between 20 and 25 percent of sales tax revenue.

20. Ring (1989, table 1). For the five states with broad coverage mentioned in the previous note, Ring estimated consumer purchases represented only 45 percent of retail sales tax revenues. Due and Mikesell (1994, pp. 72–73) note that other studies are consistent with this finding. For instance, a 1979 Texas survey estimated that 58 percent of RST revenues came from business purchases, and a study of Iowa by KPMG Peat Marwick found that 39 percent of RST revenues came from business purchases (Peat, Marwick, Mitchell, and Company, 1982).

21. See Gale (1999) for more details about this calculation, which applies to 1995.

22. CBO (1992, table 8) estimated that the broadest possible VAT base for 1988 would be $2,823 billion or $2,682 billion assuming a 95 percent compliance rate. Personal consumption expenditures (PCE) in 1988 were $3,296 billion, so the VAT base would be 81.4 percent of PCE (*Economic Report of the President*, 1995, table B-1). Multiplying this by PCE for 2001 of $6,987 billion implies a tax base of $5,680 billion. Replacing income

taxation would take $1,145 billion, suggesting that a rate of 20.2 percent (1145/5680) would be required for revenue neutrality. The CBO uses this tax base to estimate the amount of revenue that could be raised by the adoption of a 5 percent VAT on top of the existing tax structure and adjusts its revenue estimates downward significantly to reflect reduced revenues from other taxes. This last adjustment is not relevant to the rate required for a VAT that would provide a revenue-neutral replacement for the personal and corporate income taxes.

23. Hall and Rabushka (1995) propose a personal allowance of $16,500 for a married couple filing jointly, $9,500 for a single filer, and $14,000 for a single head of household. In addition, there would be an exemption of $4,500 per dependent for 1995. Exemptions in the Armey-Shelby and Forbes plans follow a similar pattern.

24. Hall and Rabushka (1995, table 3.1) estimate the revenues raised by their flat tax by starting from GDP for 1993 and subtracting out items from the National Income and Product Accounts that would be excluded from their tax base. One item they subtract out is "income included in GDP but not in the tax base," which in the appendix they note is imputed rent from owner-occupied homes. They copied the number from the wrong table in the *Economic Report of the President*, however, and as a result measure it in 1987 dollars rather than 1993 dollars. A second error is that when they subtract out "wages, salaries, and pensions," they subtract out only wages and salaries and forget to count pension contributions, even though they are deductible from the flat tax base. Finally, all of their tax-base data is for calendar year 1993, but the revenues they say they need to replace are from fiscal year 1993. Since the federal fiscal year starts three months before the calendar year, this underestimates the amount of revenue they need to raise. All of these factors would cause them to underestimate the revenue-neutral tax rate. On the other hand, they correctly note that they probably overestimated the aggregate revenue cost of their family allowances.

25. U.S. Department of Treasury, Office of Tax Analysis (1996).

26. Sullivan (1996, p. 490). Gale (1996, p. 721) comes up with a similar estimate. There is no one rate to examine for a graduated personal consumption tax. The USA tax, however, features personal rates of 19, 27, and 40 percent, plus an 11 percent business tax. These rates are certainly in the ballpark of revenue neutrality, although this has not been checked as carefully as the other systems.

27. Due and Mikesell (1994) report that, for a sample of eight states from 1991 to 1993, the administrative cost as a percentage of revenue ranged from 0.41 to 1.0. Over a much larger sample of states from 1979 to 1981, the average ratio was 0.73 percent. A study by Peat Marwick, Mitchell, and Company (1982) of seven states concluded that private compliance costs ranged from 2.0 to 3.75 percent of revenue. A more recent survey in *Tax Administrator News* ("Vendor Collection," 1993) reported an overall average compliance cost of 3.18 percent. This puts the range of enforcement and private compliance costs at 2.4 to 4.8 percent of revenue raised.

28. Florida Department of Revenue, *Examination of Resale Abuse/Misuse: Summary of Findings*, June 1994.

29. Tait (1988, p. 18).

30. Tait (1988, p. 18) notes that Iceland, Norway, South Africa, Sweden, and Zimbabwe all at one time had retail sales taxes with rates over 10 percent. Sweden and Norway switched to VATs many years ago, Iceland switched to a VAT in 1990, and South Africa switched in 1991. In 1996, Slovenia's new tax administration levied a national retail sales

tax of 20 percent, but it was replaced with a VAT in 1999. In Zimbabwe as of 2003, the government was planning to replace its sales tax with a VAT and had introduced a bill, although it was still being debated. A number of countries have had other types of sales taxes, such as wholesale sales taxes or turnover taxes on the gross sales revenues of manufacturing firms, with rates higher than 10 percent, but most of these have switched to VATs as well. For example, Australia replaced its wholesale sales tax with a VAT in 2000.

31. Tanzi (1995, pp. 50–51).

32. See the U.S. Department of Treasury (1984), CBO (1992), and the General Accounting Office (1993), all ably surveyed in Cnossen (1994).

33. Issues surrounding the tax-exempt threshold for the VAT and the levels for various countries are discussed in Ebrill et al. (2001, pp. 113–124).

34. Bradford (1996) discusses how income and consumption taxes treat financial services, argues that important problems arise under either type of tax, and discusses some options for addressing the problems.

35. Cnossen (1998); OECD (2001). All OECD data are for 1999.

36. The corporation income tax was the lowest of the three at 2.7 percent of revenue, comprised of 0.5 percent administration and 2.2 percent compliance costs. See Godwin (1995, p. 75).

37. The income tax cost consisted of 1 percent for administrative cost and 1.7 percent for taxpayer cost. For VAT, it was 0.6 percent for administrative cost and 2.5 percent for taxpayer cost. See Malmer (1995, p. 258).

38. Tait (1988, p. 304).

39. Both Russia and Hong Kong now operate flat-rate *income* taxes but do not use the Hall-Rabushka consumption tax base.

40. See Feld (1995), Weisbach (2000), Calegari (1998), and Pearlman (1998).

41. McLure (1993, pp. 349–350) discusses using this approach in conjunction with an exemption for small businesses.

42. Representative Armey's original flat tax proposal, introduced in 1994 as H.R. 4585, proposed to eliminate withholding and replace it with monthly payments. This proposal was eliminated from Armey's later flat tax proposal, H.R. 1040. See <http://www. theapologiaproject.org/reforms.html>.

43. U.S. Department of Treasury (1984, vol. 1, p. 203).

44. See Ginsburg (1995, p. 21). Another lawyer, Clifton Fleming, Jr. (1995) disagrees, concluding that the USA tax would be simpler than the current system but nevertheless "significantly intricate."

45. See Gillis, Mieszkowski, and Zodrow (1996) for a discussion of these issues.

46. To see this equivalence, assume that a (tax-inclusive) 20 percent VAT imposes a burden that is proportional to labor income. Granting a nonrefundable $5,000 per family credit with the VAT is equivalent to imposing a 20 percent tax on labor income in excess of $25,000.

47. Assuming the burden falls on individuals or families according to their consumption would make the change in tax burdens caused by adopting the flat tax look more

regressive. See Mieszkowski and Palumbo (2002), who provide evidence on this, as well as a review of the literature on distributional effects of fundamental tax reform.

48. See, in particular, Bradford (1998) and Gentry and Hubbard (1997).

49. See Cronin, Nunns, and Toder (1996) and Dunbar and Pogue (1998).

50. See Gentry and Hubbard (1997).

51. See, for example, Bradford (1986).

52. This is the claim made in the Kemp Commission report on tax reform. See National Commission on Economic Growth and Tax Reform (1996).

53. Hall and Rabushka (1995, p. 89).

54. See Altig et al. (2001).

55. Lifetime potential earnings are calculated as remaining available hours (including both leisure and work hours) multiplied by the individual's wage rate.

56. The Altig et al. (2001) model does account for the fact that much capital income is excluded from taxation under the current system by applying a lower tax rate to capital income than to labor income. But it assumes the same capital income tax rate applies to all households. Only labor income is subject to progressive rates under the current system in their model. On the other hand, as noted above, a disproportionately large share of the capital incomes of high-income people may represent "supernormal" returns that are still taxed under the consumption tax plans, and the Altig et al. paper does not account for this either.

57. Gravelle (2002) provides an excellent review of this literature and explains why results vary across models.

58. Engen and Gale (1996).

59. Ballard (2002) addresses the various ways in which international considerations could affect the economic case for fundamental tax reform. He concludes that international considerations likely increase the potential economic benefits of reform but not by very much.

Chapter 8

1. Bradford (1986, p. 312).

2. Note that while proposals for fundamental reform like the flat tax would exclude *all* capital gains and dividends from tax at the personal level, they would (possibly) offset the resulting windfall gain to shareholders with an efficient revenue-raising windfall loss arising from the elimination of depreciation deductions on old capital.

3. CBO (2003a, 2003b).

4. Wolff (2000, table 6). Data is for 1998 and comes from the Federal Reserve's Survey of Consumer Finances. Note that these figures include both directly owned stock and mutual funds held outside of retirement accounts such as pensions and IRAs. Some of the mutual fund total includes bonds.

5. The Urban-Brookings Tax Policy Center estimated that 46 percent of the dollar value of the initial Bush administration dividend and capital gain proposal would have gone to

people in the top 1 percent of the income distribution, and 80 percent would go to people in the top 10 percent. Urban-Brookings Tax Policy Center (2003a, table 5.7, January 27).

6. The $148 billion revenue cost estimate comes from Joint Committee on Taxation (2003c).

7. Gale and Orszag (2003). They estimate that the cost of eliminating the sunset provision for the dividend and capital gains tax cut would be $165 billion over 2003 to 2013, and we add this to the JCT estimate of $148 billion that assumes the sunset is allowed to take place.

8. See U.S. Department of the Treasury (1992).

9. Burman (2003b).

10. Barlett and Steele (1998).

11. Cato Institute (2003).

12. Manzon and Plesko (2002) examine recent evidence on differences between book income and taxable income and argue that not much can be learned from this given problems with the available data.

13. Joint Committee on Taxation (2003d).

14. Tax Analysts (2000).

15. See Mills and Plesko (2003) for an example of such a proposal. Lenter, Shackelford, and Slemrod (2003) discuss the pros and cons of greater public disclosure of corporate tax return information.

16. See Halperin and Steuerle (1988) for an insightful discussion of the issues concerning indexing of capital income taxation for inflation.

17. Another reason for its demise was the exception made for home mortgage interest, which would have continued to be fully deductible. This provision would have exacerbated the tax bias toward owner-occupied housing and opened up tax arbitrage opportunities tied to home equity loans.

18. Other examples of indexing in the current system include the thresholds for phasing in and phasing out the EITC and the thresholds for itemized deduction and personal exemption phase-outs. The parameters of the alternative minimum tax are not, however, indexed.

19. IRS, Statistics of Income Division, *Individual Income Tax Returns* (1999, table 1.4).

20. For this example, we ignore inflation, and therefore the issue just discussed—that some of the increase in the stock price (the part that just keeps up with price level increases) does not represent income at all.

21. For example, if you bought a share of Pfizer stock at $100, you would owe no tax until you sold it. If you sold it five years later at $300, $200 of capital gains would be taxable in the year of sale, even if the $200 increase all occurred in the first year that you held the stock.

22. This problem was eloquently stated by the economics Nobel-laureate William Vickrey (1977): "It cannot be too strongly emphasized that there is no way in which capital gains can be distinguished from other forms of income without creating a host of arbitrary and

capricious distortions, which on the one hand will place a heavy burden on the administration of the tax, and on the other will lead to a whole complex of unnatural practices designed to convert what might ordinarily appear as ordinary income fully taxable into the capital gains eligible for various kinds of special favor. . . . There is no reason to suppose that the types of capital formation that might be promoted through special favors to capital gains will have any special advantage over others, and every reason to suppose that the distortions introduced by this form of investment promotion will materially detract from the advantages that might be secured."

23. Indeed, allowing capital losses to be fully deductible against other income would provide an incentive to purposely hold portfolios with negatively correlated (when one goes up in price, the other goes down) assets, so that there are always assets to be sold with losses that can be offset against other income.

24. This is the sum of the $3 million step-up in basis for gifts of appreciated assets to a surviving spouse and the $1.3 million step-up allowed on gifts of assets to other heirs by each spouse.

25. Copeland (2002, p. 9), based on tabulations from the Survey of Income and Program Participation.

26. Some of those IRA contributors might have been members of a family where at least one spouse was not contributing at the limit, and a few might have been people who otherwise would have saved less than $2,000 but were induced by the IRA to save enough more to get to $2,000.

27. Smith (2002, p. 549).

28. General Accounting Office (2001, p. 4), based on the 1998 Survey of Consumer Finances. Some of the 36 percent of workers participating in defined-contribution plans also participated in defined-benefit plans. "All workers" includes both full-time and part-time workers, as well as very young and very old workers who have low participation rates.

29. General Accounting Office (2001, p. 15). The data included information on 1,831 defined contribution pension participants provided by a New York law firm that administers pension plans. Joulfaian and Richardson (2001) find that in 1996, 4.5 percent of tax-filing workers who contributed to defined-contribution plans were constrained by the then-current $9,500 individual limit on contributions.

30. Choi, Laibson, Madrian, and Metrick (2001) and Bernartzi and Thaler (2004) discuss evidence on the effects of default options in employer-provided pensions. Bernheim (2002) discusses theory and evidence for behavioral models of saving more generally.

31. However, the plan is not effectively designed for achieving its intended purpose, as the credit is nonrefundable and therefore few people can benefit. In addition, the program suffers from the problem, discussed above, that it subsidizes deposits into an account rather than saving.

32. Under this proposal, all retirement-based IRAs would be replaced with *retirement savings accounts* (RSAs), which would work like Roth IRAs except that the annual individual contribution limit would be raised to $7,500, eligibility would be extended to people of all income levels, and withdrawals could be made penalty-free only after age 58 or in cases of death or disability. Second, new *lifetime saving accounts* (LSAs) would be introduced. These would be identical to and in addition to RSAs, except that withdrawals could be

made penalty-free for any purpose. Third, the plan would create *employee retirement saving accounts* (ESRAs), which would replace seven different types of defined contribution plans available under current law with a single plan similar to current 401(k)s. Compared to current defined-contribution plans, ESRAs would also have looser "nondiscrimination" rules, which place limits on differences in the generosity of pension plans that can be offered to employees of different income levels within a firm. U.S. Department of the Treasury (2003) describes the administration's proposal, and Burman, Gale, and Orszag (2003) provide a critique.

33. See table 2.1.

34. IRS, Statistics of Income Division, *Statistics of Income Bulletin*, Winter 2002–2003, p. 146.

35. In 2000, $952 billion of taxable income was in the 39.6 percent tax bracket, which applied only to people in the top 2 percent of the income distribution (Campbell and Parisi, 2003, p. 9). Federal estate tax revenue was $28.1 billion in 2000 (U.S. Bureau of Economic Analysis, *National Income and Product Accounts of the United States*, table 8.29). Replacing estate tax revenue with the income tax would thus require increasing the top marginal income tax rate by 2.95 percentage points.

36. Poterba and Weisbenner (2001, p. 440) estimate, based on the 1998 Survey of Consumer Finances, that expected decedents in 1998 with estates above $5 million would have $21.3 billion of net worth and that $8.9 billion of that net worth would represent unrealized capital gains. Some portion of these unrealized gains would represent compensation for inflation, and some would be generated by corporate earnings already taxed by the corporation income tax.

37. Johnson and Mikow (2002) and Campbell and Parisi (2002).

38. Kopczuk and Slemrod (2003, figure 7.2), based on data from IRS, Statistics of Income Division (various years).

39. See Bakija, Gale, and Slemrod (2003) for evidence on the impact of estate and inheritance taxes on charitable bequests. Joulfaian (2001) and Auten and Joulfaian (1996) find evidence that giving during life is sensitive to estate tax rates.

40. See Kopczuk and Slemrod (2001). Holtz-Eakin and Marples (2001) find evidence that people who are born in states with larger inheritance and estate taxes tend to accumulate somewhat less wealth by the time they are old. Their data, however (from the Health and Retirement Survey, a random sample of about 8,000 elderly households), contain hardly any very rich people, so it is not clear whether this result extends to the people who would be affected by repeal of the estate tax.

41. Gale and Perozek (2001) discuss the theory of how estate tax repeal might affect saving.

42. Holtz-Eakin, Joulfaian, and Rosen (1993).

43. Gale and Slemrod (2001, p. 214), based on data from Johnson and Mikow (2002).

44. National Public Radio, Kaiser Family Foundation, and Kennedy School of Government (2003). The 39 percent figure is the product of the 57 percent who say they favor eliminating the estate tax, and the 69 percent of those people who agree that "it might affect YOU someday" is one of the reasons they favor eliminating it. Overall, 52 percent of respondents supported keeping the estate tax if the exemption were raised to $5 million.

45. IRS, Statistics of Income Division, *Statistics of Income Bulletin*, Fall 2002, table 13.

46. This is not by any means the only aspect of income tax design that has the effect of reducing the *perceived* tax burden. Krishna and Slemrod (2003) discuss how many income tax features take advantage of what psychologists and marketing experts know about how the perception of a given choice is affected by how it is framed.

47. IRS (2003a).

48. For an excellent discussion of how no-return systems work around the world, see Gale and Holtzblatt (1997).

49. See Gephardt (1995) and Kirchheimer (1995) for descriptions of Gephardt's original plan.

50. Gale (1997). Since 1997, eliminating the AMT has become much more expensive, so the plan would have to be modified to address this.

51. It would *not* be a good idea, however, to simply replace our corporate income tax with a VAT while retaining a personal income tax. As noted earlier, the corporate income tax is an important "backstop" to the personal income tax for taxing capital income. Replacing it entirely with a VAT would create many inefficient and complicating avoidance opportunities that involve the sheltering of personal income in businesses.

52. This discussion is based on the proposal in Graetz (2002). See also Graetz (1999) for arguments in favor of this general approach.

53. Brady (1992).

54. Even though the income tax rates could be much lower, the tax disincentive to earning income depends on (approximately) the *sum* of the income tax and VAT rates, so that the switch would not necessarily reduce these disincentives. The tax disincentive to saving would be substantially reduced, though, since the VAT does not create such a disincentive.

55. National Public Radio, Kaiser Family Foundation, and Harvard Kennedy School of Government (2003). For each of several items, the poll asked, "When two families have the same income, do you think it is fair that one family pays less tax because they . . . ?" When the sentence was completed with "give more to charity than the other family," 62 percent said it was fair. When it was completed with "have more medical expenses than the other family," 71 percent said it was fair. When completed with "have a home mortgage while the other family does not," 55 percent said it was fair. And when completed with "receive more of their income from investments than the other family," 42 percent said it was fair, and 52 percent said it was unfair.

References

Aaron, Henry J., and Harvey Galper. 1985. *Assessing Tax Reform.* Washington, DC: Brookings Institution.

ABC News. 2002. *Evaluating the IRS.* ABC News Poll, April 10–14.

Alm, James. 1985. "The Welfare Cost of the Underground Economy." *Economic Inquiry* 23, no. 2 (April): 243–263.

Altig, David, Alan J. Auerbach, Laurence J. Kotlikoff, Kent A. Smetters, and Jan Walliser. 2001. "Simulating Fundamental Tax Reform in the United States." *American Economic Review* 91, no. 3 (June): 574–595.

Andrews, Edmund L. 2003. "Greenspan Throws Cold Water on Bush Arguments for Tax Cut." *New York Times,* February 12, A1.

Armey, Richard, and Richard Shelby. 1995. *The Freedom and Fairness Restoration Act: A Comprehensive Plan to Shrink the Government and Grow the Economy.* Washington, DC, July.

Arthur D. Little, Inc. 1988. *Development of Methodology for Estimating the Taxpayer Paperwork Burden.* Final Report to the Department of the Treasury, Internal Revenue Service, Washington, DC, June.

Associated Press. 1999. "Most Americans Think Taxes Are Too Complicated, New Poll Finds." *St. Louis Post-Dispatch,* April 4, A3.

Auerbach, Alan J. 1979. "Wealth Maximization and the Cost of Capital." *Quarterly Journal of Economics* 93, no. 3 (August): 433–446.

———. 1996. "Dynamic Revenue Estimation." *Journal of Economic Perspectives* 10, no. 1 (Winter): 141–157.

———. 2002. "The Bush Tax Cut and National Saving." *National Tax Journal* 55, no. 3 (September): 387–407.

Auten, Gerald, and Robert Carroll. 1999. "The Effect of Income Taxes on Household Income." *Review of Economics and Statistics* 81, no. 4 (November): 681–693.

Auten, Gerald, James Cilke, and William Randolph. 1992. "The Effects of Tax Reform on Charitable Contributions." *National Tax Journal* 45, no. 3 (September): 267–290.

Auten, Gerald, and David Joulfaian. 1996. "Charitable Contributions and Intergenerational Transfers." *Journal of Public Economics* 59, no. 1 (January): 55–68.

Bakija, Jon M. 1999. "Consistent Estimation of Transitory and Permanent Price and Income Elasticities: The Case of Charitable Giving." Working paper. Williamstown, MA: Williams College.

Bakija, Jon M., William Gale, and Joel Slemrod. 2003. "Charitable Bequests and Taxes on Inheritances and Estates: Aggregate Evidence from across States and Time." *American Economic Review* 93, no. 2 (May): 366–370.

Bakija, Jon M., and C. Eugene Steuerle. 1991. "Individual Income Taxation since 1948." *National Tax Journal* 44, no. 4, pt. 2 (December): 451–485.

Baldwin, Richard, and Paul Krugman. 2002. "Agglomeration, Integration, and Tax Harmonization." NBER Working Paper No. w9290. Cambridge, MA: National Bureau of Economic Research, October. <http://www.nber.org/papers/w9290> (accessed June 10, 2003).

Ballard, Charles. 2002. "International Aspects of Fundamental Tax Reform." In *United States Tax Reform in the 21st Century*, edited by George R. Zodrow and Peter Mieszkowski (pp. 109–139). Cambridge: Cambridge University Press.

Ballard, Charles L., John B. Shoven, and John Whalley. 1985. "The Total Welfare Cost of the United States Tax System: A General Equilibrium Approach." *National Tax Journal* 38, no. 2 (June): 125–140.

Barlett, Donald L., and James B. Steele. 1998. "Corporate Welfare." *Time* 152, no. 19 (November 9): 36–39.

Bartlett, Bruce. 1995. "Will the Flat Tax KO Housing?" *Wall Street Journal*, August 2, A10.

———. 2003. "Changing Tax Systems," *Town Hall on the Web*, February 4. <http://www.townhall.com/columnists/brucebartlett/printbb20030204.shtml> (accessed June 10, 2003).

Bastiat, Frédéric. 1964. *Selected Essays on Political Economy*. 1850. Reprint. Irvington-on-Hudson, NY: Foundation for Economic Education.

Becker, Gary, and Casey Mulligan. 1998. "Deadweight Costs and the Size of Government." NBER Working Paper No. w6789. Cambridge, MA: National Bureau of Economic Research, November. <http://papers.nber.org/papers/W6789> (accessed June 10, 2003).

Bell, Linda A., and Richard Freeman. 2000. "The Incentive for Working Hard: Explaining Hours Worked Differences in the U.S. and Germany." NBER Working Paper No. 8051. Cambridge, MA: National Bureau of Economic Research.

Bernartzi, Shlomo, and Richard Thaler. 2004. "Save More Tomorrow: Using Behavioral Economics to Increase Employee Saving." *Journal of Political Economy* 112, no. 1 (February): S164–S187.

Bernheim, B. Douglas. 2002. "Taxation and Saving." In *Handbook of Public Economics*, vol. 3, edited by Alan J. Auerbach and Martin Feldstein (pp. 1173–1249). Amsterdam: Elsevier Science B.V.

Birnbaum, Jeffrey H., and Alan S. Murray. 1987. *Showdown at Gucci Gulch*. New York: Random House.

Blanton, Dana. 2003. "Poll: Economy beyond Tweaking—Needs Big Jolt." *Fox News on the Web*, January 16. <http://www.foxnews.com/story/0,2933,75733,00.html> (accessed June 16, 2003).

Blumenthal, Marsha, and Joel Slemrod. 1992. "The Compliance Cost of the U.S. Individual Income Tax System: A Second Look after Tax Reform." *National Tax Journal* 45, no. 2 (June): 185–202.

Board of Governors of the Federal Reserve System. 2003a. *Flow of Funds Accounts of the United States: Annual Flows and Outstandings.* Washington, DC, March. <http://www.federalreserve.gov/releases/z1/current/data.htm> (accessed June 5, 2003).

————. 2003b. *Open Market Operations.* Washington, DC, June 3. <http://www.federalreserve.gov/fomc/fundsrate.htm> (accessed June 17, 2003).

Bowman, Karlyn. 2003. "Public Opinion on Taxes." *AEI Studies in Public Opinion.* Washington, DC, American Enterprise Institute for Pubic Policy Research, April 25. <http://www.aei.org/publication16838> (accessed June 10, 2003).

Bradford, David F. 1981. "The Incidence and Allocation Effects of a Tax on Corporate Distributions." *Journal of Public Economics* 15, no. 1 (February): 1–22.

————. 1986. *Untangling the Income Tax.* Cambridge, MA: Harvard University Press.

————. 1996. "Treatment of Financial Services under Income and Consumption Taxes." In *Economic Effects of Fundamental Tax Reform,* edited by Henry J. Aaron and William G. Gale (pp. 437–464). Washington, DC: Brookings Institution Press.

————. 1998. "Review of Taxing Ourselves (1st ed.)." *Regulation* 21, no. 1 (Winter): 70–72.

Brady, Nicholas. 1992. Speech given at Columbia University Graduate School of Business, New York, December 10.

Browning, Martin, and Thomas F. Crossley. 2001. "The Life-Cycle Model of Consumption and Saving." *Journal of Economic Perspectives* 15, no. 3 (Summer): 3–22.

Brownlee, W. Elliot. 1989. "Taxation for a Strong and Virtuous Republic: A Bicentennial Retrospective." *Tax Notes* 45, no. 13 (December 25): 1613–1621.

Bruce, Donald, and Douglas Holtz-Eakin. 2001. "Will a Consumption Tax Kill the Housing Market?" In *Transition Costs of Fundamental Tax Reform,* edited by Kevin A. Hassett and R. Glenn Hubbard (pp. 96–114). Washington, DC: American Enterprise Institute Press.

Burman, Leonard. 1999. *The Labyrinth of Capital Gains Tax Policy: A Guide for the Perplexed.* Washington, DC: Brookings Institution Press.

————. 2003a. "Fairness: Bush Launches Stealth Attack on the Income Tax—Administration's Proposal Would Poison Roots of Tax." *Charleston Gazette,* February 23, 1C.

————. 2003b. "Taxing Capital Income Once." *Tax Notes* (February 3): 751.

Burman, Leonard E., Kimberly A. Clausing, and John F. O'Hare. 1994. "Tax Reform and Realizations of Capital Gains in 1986." *National Tax Journal* 47, no. 1 (March): 1–18.

Burman, Leonard E., William G. Gale, and Peter R. Orszag. 2003. "The Administration's New Tax-Free Saving Proposals: A Preliminary Analysis." *Tax Notes* (March 3): 1423–1446.

Burman, Leonard E., William G. Gale, Jeff Rohaly, and Benjamin H. Harris. 2002. "The AMT: Out of Control." Urban-Brookings Tax Policy Center, Washington, DC, September 18. <http://www.taxpolicycenter.org/research/Topic.cfm?PubID=310565> (accessed June 5, 2003).

Burman, Leonard E., and William C. Randolph. 1994. "Measuring Permanent Responses to Capital Gains Tax Changes in Panel Data." *American Economic Review* 84, no. 4 (September): 794–809.

Burnham, David. 1989. *A Law unto Itself: Power, Politics, and the IRS.* New York: Random House.

Bush, George W. 2003. *The President's Agenda for Tax Relief.* Washington, DC, April 25. <http://www.whitehouse.gov/news/reports/taxplan.html> (accessed June 17, 2003).

Calegari, Michael. 1998. "Flat Taxes and Effective Tax Planning." *National Tax Journal* 51, no. 4 (December): 689–713.

Calomiris, Charles W., and Kevin A. Hassett. 2002. "Marginal Tax Rate Cuts and the Public Tax Debate." *National Tax Journal* 55, no. 1 (March): 119–131.

Campbell, David, and Michael Parisi. 2002. "Individual Income Tax Returns, 2000." *IRS Statistics of Income Bulletin*, Washington, DC, December. <http://www.irs.gov/taxstats/article/0,,id=97067,00.html> (accessed June 5, 2003).

———. 2003. "Individual Income Tax Rates and Tax Shares, 2000." *IRS Statistics of Income Bulletin*. Washington, DC (Winter 2002–2003): 6–46.

Carasso, Adam, and C. Eugene Steuerle. 2002. "Saying 'I Do' after the 2001 Tax Cuts." *Tax Policy Issues and Option*, no. 4. Washington, DC: Urban-Brookings Tax Policy Center, August 27. <http://www.taxpolicycenter.org/research/Topic.cfm?PubID=310552> (accessed June 16, 2003).

Carroll, Robert, Douglas Holtz-Eakin, Mark Rider, and Harvey S. Rosen. 1998. "Entrepreneurs, Income Taxes, and Investment." NBER Working Paper No. 6374. Cambridge, MA: National Bureau of Economic Research, January <http://papers.nber.org/papers/w6374> (accessed June 10, 2003).

Cato Institute. 2003. *Cato Handbook for Congress: Policy Recommendations for the 107th Congress.* Washington, DC. <http://www.cato.org/pubs/handbook/handbook107.html> (accessed June 17, 2003).

Centers for Medicare and Medicaid Services. 2002. *2002 Data Compendium.* Baltimore. <http://cms.hhs.gov/researchers/pubs/datacompendium/> (accessed June 11, 2003).

Chirinko, Robert S., Steven M. Fazzari, and Andrew P. Meyer. 1999. "How Responsive Is Business Capital Formation to Its User Cost? An Exploration with Micro Data." *Journal of Public Economics* 74, no. 1 (October): 53–80.

Choi, James J., David Laibson, Brigitte Madrian, and Andrew Metrick. 2001. "Defined Contribution Pensions: Plan Rules, Participant Decisions, and the Path of Least Resistance." NBER Working Paper No. 8655. Cambridge, MA: National Bureau of Economic Research, December. <http://www.nber.org/papers/w8655> (accessed June 9, 2003).

Christian, Charles W. 1994. "Voluntary Compliance with the Individual Income Tax: Results from the 1988 TCMP Study." *IRS Research Bulletin, 1993/1994.* Publication 1500, August. Washington, DC: Internal Revenue Service.

Christian, Ernest S., and George J. Schutzer. 1995. "USA Tax System: Description and Explanation of the Unlimited Savings Allowance Income Tax System." *Tax Notes* 66, no. 11 (March 10): 1483–1575.

Clinton, William. 1992. "Acceptance Address: Democratic Nominee for President." Delivered at the Democratic National Convention, New York, July 16. *Vital Speeches of the Day* 58, no. 21 (August 15): 642–645.

Cnossen, Sijbren. 1994. "Administrative and Compliance Costs of the VAT: A Review of the Evidence." Tax Analysts Special Report No. 94, *Tax Notes Today* (June 23): 121–135.

_____. 1997. "Dual Income Taxation: The Nordic Experience." Research Memorandum 9710. Rotterdam: Research Center for Economic Policy, Erasmus University.

_____. 1998. "Global Trends and Issues in Value Added Taxation." *International Tax and Public Finance* 5, no. 3 (July): 399–428.

Congressional Budget Office (CBO). 1992. *Effects of Adopting a Value-Added Tax*. Washington, DC, February.

_____. 1994. "An Economic Analysis of the Revenue Provisions of OBRA-93." Working paper. Washington, DC, January.

_____. 1995. *The Economic and Budget Outlook: An Update*. Washington, DC, August.

_____. 1997. *For Better or for Worse: Marriage and the Federal Income Tax*. Washington, DC, June.

_____. 2001. *Effective Federal Tax Rates, 1979–1997*. Washington, DC, October. <http://www.cbo.gov/showdoc.cfm?index=3089&sequence=0> (accessed June 10, 2003).

_____. 2002a. *Capital Gains Taxes and Federal Revenues*. Washington, DC, October 9. <http://www.cbo.gov/showdoc.cfm?index=3856&sequence=0> (accessed June 5, 2003).

_____. 2002b. *Revenue Projections and the Stock Market*. Washington, DC, December 20. <(http://www.cbo.gov/showdoc.cfm?index=4009&sequence=0)> (accessed June 5, 2003).

_____. 2003a. *An Analysis of the President's Budgetary Proposals for Fiscal Year 2004*. Washington, DC, March. <http://www.cbo.gov/showdoc.cfm?index=4129&sequence=0> (accessed June 5, 2003).

_____. 2003b. *The Budget and Economic Outlook: Fiscal Years 2004–2013*. Washington, DC, January. <http://www.cbo.gov/showdoc.cfm?index=4032&sequence=4> (accessed June 16, 2003).

_____. 2003c. *Effective Federal Tax Rates, 1997 to 2000*. Washington, DC, August. <http://www.cbo.gov/showdoc.cfm?index=4514&sequence=0> (accessed September 30, 2003).

Copeland, Craig. 2002. "IRA Assets and Characteristics of IRA Owners." *Employee Benefit Research Institute Notes* 23, no. 12 (December): 1–9.

Costa, Dora. 2000. "The Wage and the Length of the Work Day: From the 1890s to 1991." *Journal of Labor Economics* 18, no. 1 (January): 156–181.

Crenshaw, Albert B. 2002. "IRS Seeks Credit Card Records in Tax Probe." *Washington Post*, August 30, E01.

Crippen, Daniel. 2002. "Testimony before the House Budget Committee on Federal Budget Estimating," Washington, DC, May 2.

Cronin, Julie-Anne. 1999. "U.S. Treasury Distributional Analysis Methodology." Office of Tax Analysis. Working Paper No. 85. Washington, DC: Department of the Treasury, September. <http://www.ustreas.gov/offices/tax-policy/library/ota85.pdf> (accessed October 1, 2003).

Cronin, Julie-Anne, James Nunns, and Eric J. Toder. 1996. "Distributional Effects of Recent Tax Reform Proposals." Paper presented at the James A. Baker III Institute for Public Policy, Rice University, Second Annual Conference, November 12–13.

Curl, Joseph. 2003. "Bush Refuses to Deny 'Wrong People' Relief; Says Democrats Use Class Warfare on Taxes." *Washington Times,* January 10, A04.

Davies, A. J. 1995. "Only One Name for It: Bureaucratic Theft." *Wall Street Journal,* April 5, A11.

Davies, James, and John Whalley. 1991. "Taxes and Capital Formation: How Important is Human Capital?" In *National Saving and Economic Performance,* edited by Douglas Bernheim and John Shoven (pp. 163–197). Chicago: National Bureau of Economic Research and University of Chicago Press.

Desai, Mihir, and James R. Hines Jr. 2002. "Value-Added Taxes and International Trade: The Evidence." Working Paper. University of Michigan, Ann Arbor.

Diamond, Peter, and Peter R. Orszag. 2002. "An Assessment of the Proposals of the President's Commission to Strengthen Social Security," *Contributions to Economic Analysis & Policy* 1, no. 1, Article 10, Berkeley. <http://www.bepress.com/bejeap/contributions/vol1/iss1/art10> (accessed June 6, 2003).

Domar, Evsey, and Richard Musgrave. 1944. "Proportional Income Taxation and Risk-Taking." *Quarterly Journal of Economics* 58, no. 2 (February): 388–422.

Donmoyer, Ryan J. 1997. "Flat Tax Strategy: The IRS as Poster Boy for Tax Reform." *Tax Notes* 77, no. 12 (December 22): 1305.

_____. 1998a. "In Election Year Gambit, House Votes to Scrap Tax Code." *Tax Notes* 79, no. 12 (June 22): 1534.

_____. 1998b. "With Work Piling Up, Senate Debates Tax Code Termination." *Tax Notes* 80, no. 5 (August 3): 521.

_____. 2002. "IRS Asks Firms for Customer Names. Agency Seeks Credit Cards from Tax Havens." *Seattle Times,* August 30, C2.

Dow Jones Newswire. 2003. "Federal Reserve Economists Tie Deficits to Interest Rates." *Wall Street Journal Online,* April 25.

Due, John F., and John L. Mikesell. 1994. *Sales Taxation: State and Local Structure and Administration.* Washington, DC: Urban Institute Press.

Dunbar, Amy, and Thomas Pogue. 1998. "Estimating Flat Tax Incidence and Yield: A Sensitivity Analysis." *National Tax Journal* 51, no. 2 (June): 303–324.

Dynan, Karen E., Jonathan Skinner, and Stephen P. Zeldes. 2000. "Do the Rich Save More?" NBER Working Paper No. 7906. Cambridge, MA: National Bureau of Economic Research, September. <http://papers.nber.org/papers/W7906> (accessed June 6, 2003).

Ebrill, Liam, Michael Keen, Jean-Paul Bodin, and Victoria Summers. 2001. *The Modern VAT.* Washington, DC: International Monetary Fund.

Economic Report of the President. (Various years). Washington, DC: GPO. <http:// w3. access.gpo.gov/eop/> (accessed June 12, 2003).

Eissa, Nada. 1995. "Taxation and Labor Supply of Married Women: The Tax Reform Act of 1986 as a Natural Experiment." NBER Working Paper No. 5023. Cambridge, MA: National Bureau of Economic Research.

_____. 1996. "Tax Reforms and Labor Supply." In *Tax Policy and the Economy*, vol. 10, edited by James M. Poterba. Cambridge, MA: National Bureau of Economic Research and MIT Press.

Elmendorf, Douglas. 1996. "The Effect of Interest Rate Changes on Household Saving and Consumption: A Survey." Federal Reserve Working Paper No. 27. Washington, DC: Board of Governors of the Federal Reserve System. <http://www.federalreserve.gov/ pubs/feds/1996/199627/199627pap.pdf> (accessed June 6, 2003).

Engen, Eric, and William Gale. 1996. "The Effects of Fundamental Tax Reform on Saving." In *The Economic Effects of Fundamental Tax Reform*, edited by Henry Aaron and William Gale (pp. 83–121). Washington, DC: Brookings Institution Press.

Fastis, Stefan. 1992. "Big Earners Cash in Early to Beat Tax Bite." *San Francisco Chronicle*, December 29, C1.

Federal Tax Regulations 2002. 2002. St. Paul, MN: West.

Feenberg, Daniel R., and James M. Poterba. 1993. "Income Inequality and the Incomes of Very High-Income Taxpayers: Evidence from Tax Returns." In *Tax Policy and the Economy*, vol. 7, edited by James M. Poterba (pp. 145–177). Cambridge, MA: National Bureau of Economic Research and MIT Press.

Feld, Alan. 1995. "Living with the Flat Tax." *National Tax Journal* 48, no. 4 (December): 603–618.

Feldstein, Martin. 1994. "Tax Policy and International Capital Flows." *Weltwirtschaftliches Archiv* 130, no. 4: 675–697.

_____. 1995a. "The Effect of a Consumption Tax on the Rate of Interest." NBER Working Paper No. 5397. Cambridge, MA: National Bureau of Economic Research.

_____. 1995b. "The Effect of Marginal Tax Rates on Taxable Income: A Panel Study of the 1986 Tax Reform Act." *Journal of Political Economy* 103, no. 3 (June): 551–582.

Feldstein, Martin, and Daniel Feenberg. 1996. "The Effect of Increased Tax Rates on Taxable Income and Economic Efficiency: A Preliminary Analysis of the 1993 Tax Rate Increases." In *Tax Policy and the Economy*, vol. 10, edited by James M. Poterba (pp. 89–118). Cambridge, MA: National Bureau of Economic Research and MIT Press.

Feldstein, Martin, and Charles Horioka. 1980. "Domestic Savings and International Capital Flows." *Economic Journal* 90, No. 358 (June): 314–429.

Firestone, David. 2003. "Conservatives Now See Deficit as a Tool to Fight Spending." *New York Times*, February 11, A24.

Fisher, Glenn W. 1996. *The Worst Tax? A History of the Property Tax in America.* Lawrence: University Press of Kansas.

Fleming, J. Clifton, Jr. 1995. "Scoping Out the Uncertain Simplification (Complication?) Effects of VATs, BATs and Consumed Income Taxes." *Florida Tax Review* 2, no. 7: 390–443.

Florida Department of Revenue. 1994. *Examination of Resale Abuse/Misuse: Summary of Findings*. Tallahassee, June.

Forbes. 2002. *The Forbes 400*. New York. <http://www.forbes.com/2002/09/13/rich400land.html> (accessed June 17, 2003).

Frank, Robert H., and Philip J. Cook. 1995. *The Winner-Take-All Society*. New York: Free Press.

Frey, Bruno, and Reto Jegen. 2001. "Motivation Crowding Theory." *Journal of Economic Surveys* 15, no. 5 (December): 589–611.

Friedman, Milton. 2003. "What Every American Wants." *Wall Street Journal*, January 15, A10.

Fullerton, Don, and Diane Lim Rogers. 1996. "Lifetime Effects of Fundamental Tax Reform." In *The Economic Effects of Fundamental Tax Reform*, edited by Henry Aaron and William Gale (pp. 321–352). Washington, DC: Brookings Institution Press.

Fullerton, Howard N., Jr. 1999. "Labor Force Participation: 75 Years of Change, 1950–98 and 1998–2025." *Monthly Labor Review* 122, no. 12 (December): 3–12.

Gale, William G. 1995. "Building a Better Tax System: Can a Consumption Tax Deliver the Goods?" *Brookings Review* 13 (Fall): 18–23.

_____. 1996. "The Kemp Commission and the Future of Tax Reform." *Tax Notes* 70, no. 6 (February 5): 717–729.

_____. 1997. "Tax Reform Is Dead, Long Live Tax Reform." Brookings Policy Brief No. 12. Washington, DC: Brookings Institution, February. <http://www.brook.edu/comm/policybriefs/pb12.htm> (accessed June 10, 2003).

_____. 1999. "The Required Tax Rate in a National Retail Sales Tax." *National Tax Journal* 52, no. 3 (September): 443–457.

_____. 2001. "Commentary on 'Will a Consumption Tax Kill the Housing Market?'" In *Transition Costs of Fundamental Tax Reform*, edited by Kevin A. Hassett and R. Glenn Hubbard (pp. 115–122). Washington, DC: American Enterprise Institute Press.

_____. 2002. "About Half of Dividend Payments Do Not Face Double Taxation." *Tax Notes* 97 (November 11): 839.

_____. 2003. "The President's Tax Proposal: First Impressions." *Tax Notes* 98 (January 13): 265.

Gale, William G., and Janet Holtzblatt. 1997. "On the Possibility of a No-Return System." *National Tax Journal* 50, no. 3 (September): 475–485.

Gale, William G., and Peter Orszag. 2002. "The Economic Effects of Long-Term Fiscal Discipline." Urban-Brookings Tax Policy Center Discussion Paper. Washington, DC: Urban-Brookings Tax Policy Center, December 17. <http://www.brook.edu/dybdocroot/views/papers/gale/20021217.pdf> (accessed June 6, 2003).

_____. 2003. "Sunsets in the Tax Code." *Tax Notes* 99 (June 9): 1553.

Gale, William G., and Maria Perozek. 2001. "Do Estate Taxes Reduce Saving?" In *Rethinking Estate and Gift Taxation*, edited by William G. Gale, James R. Hines Jr., and Joel Slemrod (pp. 216–247). Washington, DC: Brookings Institution Press.

Gale, William G., and Samara R. Potter. 2002. "An Economic Evaluation of the Economic Growth and Tax Relief Reconciliation Act of 2001." *National Tax Journal* 55, no. 1 (March): 133–186.

Gale, William, and John Sabelhaus. 1999. "Perspectives on the Household Saving Rate." *Brookings Papers on Economic Activity* 1: 181–214.

Gale, William G., and Joel Slemrod. 2001. "Death Watch for the Estate Tax?" *Journal of Economic Perspectives* 15, no. 1 (Winter): 205–218.

Garcia, Erica. 2002. "Checking Up on the IRS: MONEY Tested the IRS Agents Who Help You File Your Taxes. They Did Well—Sometimes." *Money* 31 (May): 125.

Gates, William H., Sr., and Chuck Collins. 2003. *Wealth and Our Commonwealth: Why America Should Tax Accumulated Fortunes.* Boston: Beacon Press.

General Accounting Office. 1988. *Tax Administration: IRS' Tax Gap Studies.* Washington, DC: GPO, March.

_____. 1993. *Value-Added Tax: Administrative Costs Vary with Complexity and Number of Businesses.* Study No. GAO/GGD–93–88. Washington, DC: GPO.

_____. 1997. *Taxpayer Compliance: Analyzing the Nature of the Income Tax Gap.* Report Number T-GGD-97.35, Washington, DC, January 9. <http://www.gao.gov> (accessed June 16, 2003).

_____. 2001. *Private Pensions: Issues of Coverage and Increasing Contribution Limits for Defined Contribution Plans.* GAO-01-846, Washington, DC, September. <http://frwebgate.access. gpo.gov/cgi-bin/useftp.cgi?IPaddress=162.140.64.21&filename=d01846.pdf &directory=/diskb/wais/data/gao> (accessed June 11, 2003).

_____. 2003. *IRS Modernization: Continued Progress Necessary for Improving Service to Taxpayers and Ensuring Compliance.* Publication No. GAO-03-796T, Washington, DC. <http://frwebgate.access.gpo.gov/cgi-bin/useftp.cgi?IPaddress=162.140.64.21&filename =d03796t.pdf&directory=/diskb/wais/data/gao> (accessed June 10, 2003).

Gentry, William M., and R. Glenn Hubbard. 1997. "Distributional Implications of Introducing a Broad-Based Consumption Tax." In *Tax Policy and the Economy,* vol. 11, edited by James M. Poterba (pp. 1–47). Cambridge, MA: MIT Press.

_____. 2000a. "Entrepreneurship and Household Saving." NBER Working Paper No. w7894. Cambridge, MA: National Bureau of Economic Research, September. <http://www.nber.org/papers/w7894> (accessed June 10, 2003).

_____. 2000b. "Tax Policy and Entrepreneurial Entry." *American Economic Review* 90, no. 2 (May): 283–287.

Gephardt, Richard. 1995. "A Democratic Plan for America's Economy: Toward a Fairer, Simpler Tax Code." Remarks before the Center for National Policy, Washington, DC, July 6.

Gillis, Malcolm, Peter Mieszkowski, and George R. Zodrow. 1996. "Indirect Consumption Taxes: Common Issues and Differences among the Alternative Approaches." *Tax Law Review* 51 (Summer): 725–784.

Ginsburg, Martin. 1995. "Life under a Personal Consumption Tax: Some Thoughts on Working, Saving, and Consuming in Nunn-Domenici's Tax World." *National Tax Journal* 48, no. 4 (December): 585–602.

Glaeser, Edward L., and Jesse M. Shapiro. 2003. "The Benefits of the Home Mortgage Interest Deduction." In *Tax Policy and the Economy*, vol. 17, edited by James M. Poterba (pp. 37–82). Cambridge, MA: National Bureau of Economic Research and MIT Press.

Glied, Sherry A., and Dahlia K. Remler. 2002. "What Every Public Finance Economist Needs to Know about Health Economics: Recent Advances and Unresolved Questions." *National Tax Journal* 55, no. 4 (December): 771–788.

Godwin, Michael. 1995. "The Compliance Costs of the United Kingdom Tax System." In *Tax Compliance Costs: Measurement and Policy,* edited by Cedric Sandford (pp. 73–100). Bath, UK: Fiscal Publications.

Goldin, Claudia, and Robert A. Margo. 1992. "The Great Compression: The Wage Structure in the United States at Mid-Century." *Quarterly Journal of Economics* 107, no. 1 (February): 1–34.

Goode, Richard. 1976. *The Individual Income Tax.* Washington, DC: Brookings Institution.

Goolsbee, Austan. 1999. "Evidence on the High Income Laffer Curve from Six Decades of Tax Reform." *Brookings Papers on Economic Activity* 2: 1–64.

———. 2000. "What Happens When You Tax the Rich: Evidence from Executive Compensation." *Journal of Political Economy* 108, no. 2 (April): 352–378.

———. (forthcoming). "The Turbo Tax Revolution? Evaluating the Ability of Technology to Solve the Tax Complexity Dilemma." In *The Crisis in Tax Administration*, edited by Henry Aaron and Joel Slemrod. Washington, DC: Brookings Institution Press.

Gordon, Roger H., Laura Kalambokidis, and Joel Slemrod. 2003. "Do We Now Collect Any Revenue from Taxing Capital Income?" NBER Working Paper No. 9477. Cambridge, MA: National Bureau of Economic Research, January. <http://www.nber.org/papers/w9477> (accessed June 6, 2003).

Gordon, Roger H., and Joel Slemrod. 1988. "Do We Collect Any Revenue from Taxing Capital Income?" In *Tax Policy and the Economy*, vol. 2, edited by Lawrence H. Summers (pp. 89–130). Cambridge, MA: National Bureau of Economic Research and MIT Press.

Graetz, Michael J. 1999. *The U.S. Income Tax: What It Is, How It Got That Way, and Where We Go from Here.* New York: Norton.

———. 2002. "100 Million Unnecessary Returns: A Fresh Start for the U.S. Tax System." *Yale Law Journal* 112, no. 2 (November): 261–310.

Gravelle, Jane. 1994. *The Economic Effects of Taxing Capital Income.* Cambridge, MA: MIT Press.

———. 2002. "Behavioral Responses to a Consumption Tax." In *United States Tax Reform in the 21st Century*, edited by George R. Zodrow and Peter Mieszkowski (pp. 25–54). Cambridge: Cambridge University Press.

Gravelle, Jane, and Kent Smetters. 2001. "Who Bears the Burden of the Corporate Tax in The Open Economy?" NBER Working Paper No. 8280. Cambridge, MA: National Bureau of Economic Research, May. <http://www.nber.org/papers/w8280> (accessed June 16, 2003).

Gray, Robert T. 1995. "Blockbuster Tax Reform." *Nation's Business* 83 (April): 18–24.

Gruber, Jonathan, and Emmanuel Saez. 2002. "The Elasticity of Taxable Income: Evidence and Implications." *Journal of Public Economics*, 84 no. 1 (April): 1–32.

Hall, Arthur P. 1995. "Compliance Costs of Alternative Tax Systems: Ways and Means Testimony." *Tax Foundation Special Brief*, Washington, DC, June.

Hall, Robert E. 1988. "Intertemporal Substitution in Consumption." *Journal of Political Economy* 96, no. 2 (April): 339–357.

Hall, Robert E., and Alvin Rabushka. 1983. *Low Tax, Simple Tax, Flat Tax*. New York: McGraw-Hill.

———. 1995. *The Flat Tax* (2d ed.). Stanford, CA: Hoover Institution Press.

Halperin, Daniel, and Eugene Steuerle. 1988. "Indexing the Tax System for Inflation." In *Uneasy Compromise: Problems of a Hybrid Income-Consumption Tax*, edited by Henry J. Aaron, Harvey Galper, and Joseph A. Pechman (pp. 347–380). Washington, DC: Brookings Institution Press.

Hamermesh, Daniel S. 1993. *Labor Demand*. Princeton, NJ: Princeton University Press.

Heckman, James. 1993. "What Has Been Learned about Labor Supply in the United States in the Past Twenty Years?" *American Economic Review* 83, no. 2 (May): 116–121.

Herman, Tom. 1995. "Tax Complexity Weighs Increasingly Heavily on the Economy." *Wall Street Journal*, June 7, A1.

Hessing, Dick J., Hank Elffers, Henry S. J. Robben, and Paul Webley. 1992. "Does Deterrence Deter? Measuring the Effect of Deterrence on Tax Compliance in Field Studies and Experimental Studies." In *Why People Pay Taxes: Tax Compliance and Enforcement*, edited by Joel Slemrod (pp. 291–305). Ann Arbor: University of Michigan Press.

Higgins, Heather Richardson. 1995. "Tax Fairness: Treat All Dollars Equally." *Wall Street Journal*, April 5, A11.

Hines, James R., Jr. 1999. "Lessons from Behavioral Responses to International Taxation." *National Tax Journal* 52, no. 2 (June): 305–322.

Hite, Peggy A., and Michael L. Roberts. 1991. "An Experimental Investigation of Taxpayer Judgments on Rate Structure in the Individual Income Tax System." *Journal of the American Taxation Association* 13, no. 2 (Fall): 47–63.

Holtz-Eakin, Douglas, David Joulfaian, and Harvey S. Rosen. 1993. "The Carnegie Conjecture: Some Empirical Evidence." *Quarterly Journal of Economics* 108, no. 2 (May): 413–435.

Holtz-Eakin, Douglas, and Donald Marples. 2001. "Distortion Costs of Taxing Wealth Accumulation: Income Versus Estate Taxes." NBER Working Paper No. w8261. National Bureau of Economic Research, April. <http://papers.nber.org/papers/w8261> (accessed June 10, 2003).

Hubbard, R. Glenn. 1998. "Capital-Market Imperfections and Investment." *Journal of Economic Literature* 36, no. 1 (March): 193–225.

———. 2001. *Money, the Financial System, and the Economy* (4th ed.). Reading, MA: Addison-Wesley.

Internal Revenue Code 2002. 2002. St. Paul, MN: West.

Internal Revenue Service (IRS). 1996. *Federal Tax Compliance Research: Individual Income Tax Gap Estimates for 1985, 1988, and 1992*. Publication 1415 (Rev. 4–96). Washington, DC: GPO.

———. 1997. *Internal Revenue Service Data Book, Fiscal Year 1996*. Washington, DC. <http://www.irs.gov/taxstats/article/0,,id=97216,00.html> (accessed June 10, 2003).

———. 2002a. *How to Depreciate Property*. IRS Publication 946. Washington, DC. <http://www.irs.gov/pub/irs-pdf/p946.pdf> (accessed June 17, 2003).

———. 2002b. *IRS Sets New Audit Priorities*. IRS News Release FS-2002-12, Washington, DC. <http://www.irs.gov/newsroom/article/0,,id=105695,00.html> (accessed June 10, 2003).

———. 2002c. *Revenue Procedure 2002-70*. Washington, DC. <http://www.irs.gov/pub/irs-drop/rp-02-70.pdf> (accessed June 10, 2003).

———. 2003a. *Individual Income Tax Returns Filed during the 2002 Filing Season (Tax Year 2001)*. Washington, DC. <http://www.irs.gov/taxstats/article/0,,id=96629,00.html> (accessed June 16, 2003).

———. 2003b. *Internal Revenue Service Data Book, Fiscal Year 2002*. Washington, DC. <http://www.irs.gov/pub/irs-soi/02databk.pdf> (accessed June 10, 2003).

———. Statistics of Income Division. Various years. *Corporation Income Tax Returns*. Washington, DC: GPO. <http://www.irs.gov/taxstats/index.html> (accessed June 12, 2003).

———. Statistics of Income Division. Various years. *Individual Income Tax Returns*. Washington, DC: GPO. <http://www.irs.gov/taxstats/index.html> (accessed June 12, 2003).

———. Statistics of Income Division. Various years. *Statistics of Income Bulletin*. Washington, DC: GPO. <http://www.irs.gov/taxstats/index.html> (accessed June 12, 2003).

Jagannathan, Ravi, Ellen R. McGrattan, and Anna Scherbina. 2001. "The Declining U.S. Equity Premium." NBER Working Paper No. w8172. Cambridge, MA: National Bureau of Economic Research, March. <http://www.nber.org/papers/w8172> (accessed June 9, 2003).

Johnson, Barry W., and Jacob M. Mikow. 2002. "Federal Estate Tax Returns, 1998–2000." *Statistics of Income Bulletin* (Spring): 133–186.

Johnston, David Cay. 1996. "British to Adopt American-Style Tax Filing." *New York Times*, February 15, D6.

———. 2003a. "Tax Inquiries Fall as Cheating Increases." *New York Times*, April 14, A16.

———. 2003b. "Top 1% in '01 Lost Income but Also Paid Lower Taxes." *New York Times*, September 27, B1.

Joint Committee on Taxation. 1995. *Written Testimony of the Staff of the Joint Committee on Taxation Regarding the Revenue Estimating Process*. Publication No. JCX-1-95, Washington, DC, January 10. <http://www.house.gov/jct/x-1-95.pdf> (accessed June 12, 2003).

———. 2000. *Overview of Federal Income Tax Provisions Relating to Stock Options*. Publication No. JCX-107-00, Washington, DC, October 10. <http://www.house.gov/jct/x-107-00.pdf> (accessed June 9, 2003).

_____. 2001. *Study of the Overall State of the Federal Tax System and Recommendations for Simplification, Pursuant to Section 8022(3)(B) of the Internal Revenue Code of 1986.* JCS-3-01, Washington, DC, April. <http://www.house.gov/jct/pubs01.html> (accessed June 11, 2003).

_____. 2003a. *Description of Revenue Provisions Contained in the President's Fiscal Year 2004 Budget.* Washington, DC, March. <http://www.house.gov/jct/pubs03.html> (accessed June 9, 2003).

_____. 2003b. *General Explanation of Tax Legislation Enacted in the 107th Congress.* Washington, DC, January 24. <http://www.access.gpo.gov/congress/joint/hjoint01 cp108.html> (accessed June 9, 2003).

_____. 2003c. *The "Jobs and Growth Tax Relief Reconciliation Act of 2003" Estimated Budget Effects of the Conference Agreement for H.R. 2.* JCX-55-03, Washington, DC, May 22. <http://www.house.gov/jct/x-55-03.pdf> (accessed June 16, 2003).

_____. 2003d. *Report of Investigation of Enron Corporation and Related Entities Regarding Federal Tax and Compensation Issues, and Policy Recommendations.* Report No. JCS-3-03, Washington, DC, February. <http://www.gpo.gov/congress/joint/jcs-3-03/vol1/index.html> (accessed June 10, 2003).

_____. 2003e. *Summary of Conference Agreement on H.R. 2, The "Jobs and Growth Tax Relief Reconciliation Act of 2003."* JCX-54-03, Washington, DC, May 22. <http:// www.house.gov/jct/x-54-03.pdf> (accessed June 11, 2003).

_____. 2003f. "Tax Complexity Analysis." *Congressional Record,* May 22, H4699–H4703.

Joulfaian, David. 2001. "Charitable Giving in Life and at Death." In *Rethinking Estate and Gift Taxation,* edited by William G. Gale, James R. Hines Jr., and Joel Slemrod (pp. 350–374). Washington, DC: Brookings Institution Press.

Joulfaian, David, and David Richardson. 2001. "Who Takes Advantage of Tax-Deferred Saving Programs? Evidence from Federal Income Tax Data." *National Tax Journal* 54, no. 3 (September): 669–688.

Kaplow. 1994. "Taxation and Risk Taking: A General Equilibrium Perspective." *National Tax Journal* 47, no. 4 (December): 789–798.

_____. 1999. "Tax Treatment of Families." In *Encyclopedia of Taxation and Tax Policy* (pp. 120–122). Washington, DC: Urban Institute Press.

Kasten, Richard, Frank Sammartino, and Eric Toder. 1994. "Trends in Federal Tax Progressivity, 1980–93." In *Tax Progressivity and Income Inequality,* edited by Joel Slemrod (pp. 9–50). Cambridge: Cambridge University Press.

Katz, Lawrence F., and Kevin M. Murphy. 1992. "Changes in Relative Wages, 1963–1987: Supply and Demand Factors." *Quarterly Journal of Economics* 107, no. 1 (February): 35–78.

Kennickell, Arthur. 2003. "A Rolling Tide: Changes in the Distribution of Wealth in the U.S., 1989–2001." Survey of Consumer Finances Working Paper Series. Board of Governors of the Federal Reserve System, Washington, DC, March. <http://www.federalreserve.gov/pubs/oss/oss2/papers/concentration.2001.6.pdf> (accessed June 11, 2003).

Keyes, Alan. 2000. *Alan Keyes on Tax Reform.* Cambridge, MA: On the Issues. <http://www.issues2000.org/Celeb/Alan_Keyes_Tax_Reform.htm> (accessed June 17, 2003).

Kiefer, Donald, Robert Carroll, Janet Holtzblatt, Allen Lerman, Janet McCubbin, David Richardson, and Jerry Tempalski. 2002. "The Economic Growth and Tax Relief Reconciliation Act of 2001: Overview and Assessment of Effects on Taxpayers." *National Tax Journal* 55, no. 1 (March): 89–117.

Kies, Kenneth. 1999. "Prepared Testimony before the House Committee on Ways and Means on Corporate Tax Shelters," Washington, DC, November 10.

Killingsworth, Mark. 1983. *Labor Supply.* Cambridge: Cambridge University Press.

Kirchheimer, Barbara. 1995. "Gephardt Introduces 10 Percent Tax for Most, Four Brackets for Others." *Tax Notes* 68 (July 10): 135–136.

Kopczuk, Wojciech, and Joel Slemrod. 2001. "The Impact of the Estate Tax on the Wealth Accumulation and Avoidance Behavior of Donors." In *Rethinking Estate and Gift Taxation,* edited by William Gale, James R. Hines Jr., and Joel Slemrod (pp. 299–349). Washington, DC: Brookings Institution Press.

———. 2003. "Tax Impacts on Wealth Accumulation and Transfers of the Rich." In *Death and Dollars: The Role of Gifts and Bequests in America,* edited by Alicia Munnell and Annika Sunden (pp. 213–257). Washington, DC: Brookings Institution Press.

Kornblut, Anne E., and Kimberly Blanton. 2003. "Bush Wants $670B Cut in Taxes over 10 Years: Would Abolish Dividend Levies." *Boston Globe,* January 8, A1.

Kornhauser, Marjorie E. 2002. "More Historical Perspective on Publication of Corporate Returns." *Tax Notes* 96 (July 29): 745.

Kotlikoff, Laurence J. 1995. "Saving and Consumption Taxation: The Federal Retail Sales Tax Example." Paper presented at the Hoover Institution Conference on Frontiers of Tax Reform, Washington, DC, May 11.

Krishna, Aradhna, and Joel Slemrod. 2003. "Behavioral Public Finance: Tax Design as Price Presentation" *International Tax and Public Finance* 10 (March): 189–203.

Krueger, Dirk, and Fabrizio Perri. 2002. "Does Income Inequality Lead to Consumption Inequality? Evidence and Theory." NBER Working Paper No. 9202. Cambridge, MA: National Bureau of Economic Research, September. <http://www.nber.org/papers/w9202> (accessed June 9, 2003).

Krugman, Paul. 1994. *Peddling Prosperity.* New York: Norton.

———. 2001. *Fuzzy Math.* New York: Norton.

Landler, Mark. 2002. "Boris Becker, a Tennis Bad Boy, Faces Prison in German Tax Case." *New York Times,* October 24, A13.

Laubach, Thomas. 2003. "New Evidence on the Interest Rate Effects of Budget Deficits and Debt." Federal Reserve Working Paper. Washington, DC, Board of Governors of the Federal Reserve System, May. <http://www.federalreserve.gov/pubs/feds/2003/200312/200312pap.pdf> (accessed June 11, 2003).

Lenter, David, Douglas Shackelford, and Joel Slemrod. 2003. "Public Disclosure of Corporate Tax Return Information: Accounting, Economics, and Legal Perspectives." *National Tax Journal* 56, no. 4 (December): 803–830.

Lewin, Tamar. 1991. "Data Show Wide Tax Cheating on Child Care, IRS Says." *New York Times,* January 6, 14.

Lindbeck, Assar. 1993. *The Welfare State: Selected Essays of Assar Lindbeck*, vol. 2. Aldershot, UK: Edward Elgar.

Lugar, Richard. 1995. *My Plan to End the Income Tax*. Cato Policy Report. Washington, DC, April 5. <http://www.cato.org/pubs/policy_report/pr-ja-rl.html> (accessed June 17, 2003).

Lyon, Andrew B., and Peter R. Merrill. 2001. "Asset Price Effects of Fundamental Tax Reform." In *Transition Costs of Fundamental Tax Reform*, edited by Kevin A. Hassett and R. Glenn Hubbard (pp. 58–92). Washington, DC: American Enterprise Institute Press.

Mackie, James B. 2002. "Unfinished Business of the 1986 Tax Reform Act: An Effective Tax Rate Analysis of Current Issues in the Taxation of Capital Income." *National Tax Journal* 55, no. 2 (June): 293–337.

Malmer, Hakan. 1995. "The Swedish Tax Reform in 1990–1991 and Tax Compliance Costs in Sweden." In *Tax Compliance Costs: Measurement and Policy*, edited by Cedric Sandford (pp. 226–262). Bath, UK: Fiscal Publications.

Manzon, Gil B., and George A. Plesko. 2002. "The Relation between Financial and Tax Reporting Measures of Income." *New York University Tax Law Review* 55, no. 2 (Winter): 175–214.

McHardy, A. K. 1992. *Clerical Poll-Taxes of the Diocese of Lincoln, 1377–1381*. Woodbridge, Suffolk, UK: Boydell Press.

McIntyre, Robert S. 1995. "Statement Concerning Proposals for a Flat-Rate Consumption Tax before the Joint Economic Committee." Washington, DC, May 17. <http://www.ctj.org/html/tjmjec.htm> (accessed September 30, 2003).

McKee, T. C., and M. D. Gerbing. 1989. "Taxpayer Perceptions of Fairness: The TRA of 1986." Paper presented at the Internal Revenue Service Research Conference, Washington, DC.

McKissack, May. 1959. *The Fourteenth Century, 1307–1399*, vol. 5 of *The Oxford History of England*. Oxford: Clarendon Press.

McLure, Charles E., Jr. 1993. "Economic, Administrative, and Political Factors in Choosing a General Consumption Tax." *National Tax Journal* 46, no. 3 (September): 345–358.

Mehra, Rajnish, and Edward C. Prescott. 2003. "The Equity Premium in Retrospect." NBER Working Paper No. 9525. Cambridge, MA: National Bureau of Economic Research, March. <http://www.nber.org/papers/w9525> (accessed June 9, 2003).

Messere, Ken C. 1993. *Tax Policy in OECD Countries: Choices and Conflicts*. Amsterdam: IBFD Publications.

Mieszkowski, Peter, and Michael Palumbo. 2002. "Distributive Analysis of Fundamental Tax Reform." In *United States Tax Reform in the 21st Century*, edited by George R. Zodrow and Peter Mieszkowski (pp. 140–178). Cambridge: Cambridge University Press.

Miller, John A. 2000. "Equal Taxation: A Commentary." *Hofstra Law Review* 29 (Winter): 529.

Mills, Lillian F., and George A. Plesko. 2003. "Bridging the Reporting Gap: A Proposal for More Informative Reconciling of Book and Tax Income." *National Tax Journal* 56, no. 4 (December): 865–893.

Mishel, Lawrence, Jared Bernstein, and John Schmitt. 1997. *The State of Working America 1996–97*. Armonk, NY: Sharpe.

Mitrusi, Andrew, and James Poterba. 2000. "The Distribution of Income and Payroll Tax Burdens, 1979–1999." NBER Working Paper No. 7707. Cambridge, MA: National Bureau of Economic Research, May. <http://papers.nber.org/papers/W7707> (accessed June 9, 2003).

Moffitt, Robert, and Mark Wilhelm. 2000. "Taxation and the Labor Supply Decisions of the Affluent." In *Does Atlas Shrug? Economic Consequences of Taxing the Rich*, edited by Joel Slemrod (pp. 193–234). Cambridge, MA and New York: Harvard University Press and the Russell Sage Foundation.

Moore, Schuyler M. 1987. "A Proposal to Reduce the Complexity of Tax Regulations." *Tax Notes* 37 (December 14): 1167.

Moulton, Brent R., Robert P. Parker, and Eugene P. Seskin. 1999. "A Preview of the 1999 Comprehensive Revision of the National Income and Product Accounts." *Survey of Current Business* (August): 7–20. <http://www.bea.gov/bea/articles/NATIONAL/NIPA/1999/0899niw.pdf> (accessed June 9, 2003).

Mulligan, Casey B. 2002. "Capital, Interest, and Aggregate Intertemporal Substitution." NBER Working Paper No. 9373. Cambridge, MA: National Bureau of Economic Research, December. <http://www.nber.org/papers/w9373> (accessed June 9, 2003).

Murphy, Liam B., and Thomas Nagel. 2002. *The Myth of Ownership: Taxes and Justice*. Oxford: Oxford University Press.

Murray, Alan. 1996. "GOP Adherents Study Merits of a Flat Tax." *Wall Street Journal*, January 29, A1.

Nasar, Sylvia. 1992. "One Study's Riches, Another Study's Rags." *New York Times*, June 17, D1.

National Commission on Economic Growth and Tax Reform. 1996. *Unleashing America's Potential: A Pro-Growth, Pro-Family Tax System for the 21st Century*. Washington, DC: Author.

National Public Radio, Kaiser Family Foundation, and Kennedy School of Government. 2003. "National Survey of Americans' Views on Taxes," April. <http://www.npr.org/news/specials/polls/taxes2003/index.html> (accessed June 10, 2003).

National Taxpayer Advocate. 2002. *Annual Report to Congress, Fiscal Year 2001*, December 31. <http://www.irs.gov/advocate/article/0,,id=97404,00.html> (accessed June 9, 2003).

Nozick, Robert. 1977. *Anarchy, State, and Utopia*. New York: Basic Books.

Office of Management and Budget (OMB). Various years. *Budget of the United States Government*. Washington, DC: GPO. <http://w3.access.gpo.gov/usbudget.html> (accessed June 12, 2003, June 16, 2003).

O'Neil, Cherie J., and Karen B. Lanese. 1993. "T.I.N. Requirements and the Child Care Credit: Impact on Taxpayer Behavior." Working Paper. Tampa: University of South Florida.

Organisation for Economic Co-operation and Development (OECD). 2001. *Revenue Statistics of Member Countries 1965–2000*. Paris: OECD.

———. 2002. *National Accounts of OECD Countries*. Paris: OECD

_____. 2003. *SourceOECD Statistics*. Paris. <http://www.sourceoecd.org> (accessed June 16, 2003).

Parcell, Ann D. 1996. "Income Shifting in Response to Higher Tax Rates: The Effects of OBRA 93." Paper presented at the Allied Social Science Associations Meetings, San Francisco, January.

Park, Thae S. 2002. "Comparison of BEA Estimates of Personal Income and IRS Estimates of Adjusted Gross Income: New Estimates for 2000 and Revised Estimates for 1999." *Survey of Current Business*. Washington, DC, (November): 13–20. <http://www.bea.gov/bea/an1.htm> (accessed June 9, 2003).

Parker, Jonathan. 1999. "The Reaction of Household Consumption to Predictable Changes in Social Security Taxes." *American Economic Review* 89, no. 4 (September): 959–973.

Payne, James L. 1993. *Costly Returns: The Burdens of the U.S. Tax System*. San Francisco: Institute for Contemporary Studies Press.

Pearlman, Ronald A. 1996. "Transition Issues in Moving to a Consumption Tax: A Tax Lawyer's Perspective." In *The Economic Effects of Fundamental Tax Reform*, edited by Henry Aaron and William Gale (pp. 393–434). Washington, DC: Brookings Institution Press.

_____. 1998. "Fresh from the River Styx: The Achilles Heels of Tax Reform Proposals." *National Tax Journal* 51, no. 3 (September): 569–578.

Peat, Marwick, Mitchell, and Company. 1982. *Report to the American Retail Federation on Costs to Retailers of Sales Use Tax Compliance*. New York.

Pechman, Joseph A. 1987. *Federal Tax Policy* (5th ed.). Washington, DC: Brookings Institution Press.

Peers, Alexandra, and Jeffrey A. Tannenbaum. 1992 "Insiders Race to Exercise Stock Options." *Wall Street Journal*, December 16, C1.

Piketty, Thomas, and Emmanuel Saez. 2003. "Income Inequality in the United States, 1913–1998." *Quarterly Journal of Economics* 118, no. 1 (February): 1–39.

Poterba, James M. 1989. "Capital Gains Tax Policy toward Entrepreneurship." *National Tax Journal* 47, no. 3 (June): 375–389.

_____. 1990. "Taxation and Housing Markets: Preliminary Evidence on the Effects of Recent Tax Reforms." In *Do Taxes Matter? The Impact of the Tax Reform Act of 1986*, edited by Joel Slemrod (pp. 141–160). Cambridge, MA: MIT Press.

Poterba, James M., and Scott Weisbenner. 2001. "The Distributional Burden of Taxing Estates and Unrealized Capital Gains at Death." In *Rethinking Estate and Gift Taxation*, edited by William G. Gale, James R. Hines Jr., and Joel Slemrod (pp. 422–449). Washington, DC: Brookings Institution Press.

Powell, Edgar. 1894. "An Account of the Proceedings in Suffolk during the Peasants' Rising in 1381." *Transactions of the Royal Historical Society* 8: 203–249. London: Longmans, Green.

The President's Agenda for Tax Relief. 2003. Washington, DC, April 25. <http://www.whitehouse.gov/news/reports/taxplan.html> (accessed June 17, 2003).

Randolph, William C. 1995. "Dynamic Income, Progressive Taxes, and the Timing of Charitable Contributions." *Journal of Political Economy* 103, no. 4 (August): 709–738.

Rawls, John. 1971. *A Theory of Justice*. Cambridge, MA: Harvard University Press.

Richman, Louis S. 1995. "The Flat Tax: It's Hot, It's Now, It Could Change the Way You Live." *Fortune* 131, no. 11 (June 12): 36–40.

Rieschick, Jacqueline. 1997. "GOP Lawmakers Step Up Efforts to Turn Tax Code into 'Road Kill.'" *Tax Notes* 76, no. 13 (September 29): 1661–1662.

Ring, Raymond J., Jr. 1989. "The Proportion of Consumers' and Producers' Goods in the General Sales Tax." *National Tax Journal* 42, no. 2 (June): 167–169.

Roberts, Michael L., Peggy A. Hite, and Cassie F. Bradley. 1994. "Understanding Attitudes Toward Progressive Taxation." *Public Opinion Quarterly* 58, no. 2 (Summer): 165–190.

Rodrik, Dani. 1997. *Has Globalization Gone Too Far?* Washington, DC: Institute for International Economics.

Rosen, Sherwin. 1981. "The Economics of Superstars." *American Economic Review* 71, no. 5 (December): 845–858.

Rossotti, Charles O. 2002. *Report to the IRS Oversight Board: Assessment of the IRS and the Tax System*. Washington, DC, September. <http://www.irsoversightboard.treas.gov/documents/commissioner_report.pdf> (accessed June 11, 2003).

Roth, Jeffrey A., John T. Scholz, and Ann Dryden Witte. 1989. *An Agenda for Research*, vol. 1 of *Taxpayer Compliance*. Philadelphia: University of Pennsylvania Press.

Sabelhaus, John. 1993. "What Is the Distributional Burden of Taxing Consumption?" *National Tax Journal* 46, no. 3 (September): 331–343.

Safire, William. 1995. "The 25% Solution." *New York Times*, April 20, A19.

Sandford, Cedric, ed. 1995. *Tax Compliance Costs: Measurement and Policy*. Bath, UK: Fiscal Publications.

Sanger, David E. 2002. "Reversing Course, Bush Signs Bill Raising Farm Subsidies." *New York Times*, May 14, A16.

Sawhill, Isabel V. and Daniel P. McMurrer. 1996. *Economic Mobility in the United States*. Urban Institute, Washington, DC, October. <http://www.urban.org/oppor/opp_031b.html> (accessed June 11, 2003).

Shapiro, Matthew D., and Joel Slemrod. 1995. "Consumer Response to the Timing of Income: Evidence from a Change in Tax Withholding." *American Economic Review* 85, no. 1 (March): 274–283.

_____. 2003a. "Consumer Response to Tax Rebates." *American Economic Review* 93, no. 1 (March): 381–396.

_____. 2003b. "Did the 2001 Tax Rebate Stimulate Spending? Evidence from Taxpayer Surveys." In *Tax Policy and the Economy*, vol. 17, edited by James M. Poterba (pp. 83–109). Cambridge, MA: National Bureau of Economic Research and MIT Press.

Sheffrin, Steven M., and Robert K. Triest. 1992. "Can Brute Deterrence Backfire? Perceptions and Attitudes in Taxpayer Compliance." In *Why People Pay Taxes: Tax Compliance and Enforcement*, edited by Joel Slemrod (pp. 193–218). Ann Arbor: University of Michigan Press.

Simons, Henry. 1938. *Personal Income Taxation*. Chicago: University of Chicago Press.

Slemrod, Joel. 1990. "Optimal Taxation and Optimal Tax Systems." *Journal of Economic Perspectives* 4, no. 1 (Winter): 157–178.

_____. 1992. "What Makes a Nation Prosperous, What Makes It Competitive, and Which Goal Should We Strive For?" *Australian Tax Forum* 9, no. 4 (January): 373–385.

_____. 1995a. "Free Trade Taxation and Protectionist Taxation." *International Tax and Public Finance* 2, no. 4 (November): 471–489. Also appears in *The Taxation of Multinational Corporations*, edited by Joel Slemrod (pp. 133–151). Boston: Kluwer Academic, 1996.

_____. 1995b. "Professional Opinions about Tax Policy: 1994 and 1934." *National Tax Journal* 48, no. 1 (March): 121–147.

_____. 1995c. "What Do Cross-Country Studies Teach about Government Involvement, Prosperity, and Economic Growth?" *Brookings Papers on Economic Activity* 2: 373–431.

_____. 1996a. "High-Income Families and the Tax Changes of the 1980s: The Anatomy of Behavioral Response." In *Empirical Foundations of Household Taxation*, edited by Martin Feldstein and James Poterba (pp. 169–188). Chicago: National Bureau of Economic Research and University of Chicago Press.

_____. 1996b. "Which Is the Simplest Tax System of Them All?" In *The Economic Effects of Fundamental Tax Reform*, edited by Henry Aaron and William Gale (pp. 355–391). Washington, DC: Brookings Institution Press.

_____. 1997. "Measuring Taxpayer Burden and Attitudes for Large Corporations: 1996 and 1992 Survey Results." Office of Tax Policy Research Working Paper 97-1. Ann Arbor: University of Michigan.

_____. 1998. "Methodological Issues in Measuring and Interpreting Taxable Income Elasticities." *National Tax Journal* 51, no. 4 (December): 773–788.

Slemrod, Joel, and Jon Bakija. 2001. "Growing Inequality and Reduced Tax Progressivity." In *Inequality and Tax Policy*, edited by Kevin A. Hassett and R. Glenn Hubbard (pp. 192–234). Washington, DC: American Enterprise Institute Press.

Slemrod, Joel, and Marsha Blumenthal. 1996. "The Income Tax Compliance Cost of Big Business." *Public Finance Quarterly* 24, no. 4 (October): 411–438.

Slemrod, Joel, and Nikki Sorum. 1984. "The Compliance Cost of the U.S. Individual Income Tax System." *National Tax Journal* 37, no. 4 (December): 461–484.

Slemrod, Joel, and Varsha Venkatesh. 2002. "The Income Tax Compliance Cost of Large and Mid-Size Businesses." Report to the Department of the Treasury, Internal Revenue Service, Washington DC, May.

Smith, Adam. 1937 [1776]. *The Wealth of Nations*. New York: Random House.

Smith, Paul. 2002. "Choice Complexity in Retirement Savings Policy." *National Tax Journal* 55, no. 3 (September): 539–554.

Smith, Peter. 1991. "Lessons from the British Poll Tax Disaster." *National Tax Journal* 44, no. 4, pt. 2 (December): 421–436.

Sørensen, Peter Birch. 1998. (ed.) *Tax Policy in the Nordic Countries*. London: Macmillan Press.

Souleles, Nicholas S. 2002. "Consumer Response to the Reagan Tax Cuts." *Journal of Public Economics* 85, no. 1 (July): 99–120.

Steuerle, C. Eugene. 1986. *Who Should Pay for Collecting Taxes? Financing the IRS.* Washington, DC: American Enterprise Institute.

——. 1992. *The Tax Decade: How Taxes Came to Dominate the Public Agenda.* Washington, DC: Urban Institute Press.

Steuerle, C. Eugene, and Jon Bakija. 1994. *Retooling Social Security for the 21st Century.* Washington, DC: Urban Institute Press.

Stevenson, Richard W. 2002. "Bush's Way Clear to Press Agenda for the Economy." *New York Times*, November 11, A1.

Stevenson, Richard W., and Sheryl Gay Stolberg. 2003. "Bush Says His Tax Proposal Will Be Fair for All Incomes." *New York Times*, January 10, A18.

Sullivan, Martin. 1996. "What Rate for the Flat Tax?" *Tax Notes* 70 (January 29): 490.

——. 2000. "News Analysis: Lobbyist's Figures Flawed, Data Indicate Corporate Shortfalls." *Tax Notes* 86 (January 17): 309.

——. 2001. "Money and Ways & Means: Shaw Leads the 'PAC,' Portman Takes None." *Tax Notes* (August 13): 865.

——. 2003. "Economic Analysis: Is the Corporate Tax Withering Away?" *Tax Notes* 98 (February 10): 878.

Szilagyi, John A. 1990. "Where Have All the Dependents Gone?" *Internal Revenue Service Trend Analyses and Related Statistics—1990 Update.* Publication 1500 (August). Washington, DC: Internal Revenue Service.

Tait, Alan A. 1988. *Value Added Tax: International Practice and Problems.* Washington, DC: International Monetary Fund.

Tanzi, Vito. 1995. *Taxation in an Integrating World.* Washington, DC: Brookings Institution Press.

Tax Analysts. 2000. "A Quick Review of Shelter Revenue Estimates." *Insurance Tax Review* 18 (February): 173.

Thorndike, Joe. 2002. "Historical Perspective: Promoting Honesty by Releasing Corporate Tax Returns," *Tax Notes* 96 (July 15): 324–325.

Treubert, Patrice. 2002. "Corporation Income Tax Returns, 1999." *IRS Statistics of Income Bulletin.* Washington, DC, (Summer): 82–106. <http://www.irs.gov/taxstats/article/0,,id=97067,00.html> (accessed June 9, 2003).

Triest, Robert K. 1990. "The Effect of Income Taxation on Labor Supply in the United States." *Journal of Human Resources* 25, no. 3 (summer): 491–516.

——. 1994. "The Efficiency Cost of Increased Progressivity." In *Tax Progressivity and Income Inequality,* edited by Joel Slemrod (pp. 137–169). Cambridge: Cambridge University Press.

Tritch, Teresa. 1998. "Six Mistakes Even the Tax Pros Make." *Money* 27 (March): 104–106.

Urban-Brookings Tax Policy Center. 2003a. Distribution of Administration Dividend Proposal and Alternative Options. Washington, DC. <http://www.taxpolicycenter.org/commentary/admin_dist_dividend.cfm#dividend> (accessed June 17, 2003).

_____. 2003b. *Urban-Brookings Tax Policy Center Microsimulation Model* (version 0503-1). Washington, DC. <http://www.taxpolicycenter.org/commentary/congress/alltables. pdf> (accessed June 17, 2003).

Usborne, David. 2002. "Dennis the Dealmaker Earns a New Nickname: The Artful Tax Dodger." *The Independent* (London), June 6, 3.

U.S. Bureau of the Census. 1975. *Historical Statistics of the United States, Colonial Times to 1970, Bicentennial Edition.* Washington, DC: GPO.

U.S. Bureau of Economic Analysis. Various years. *Survey of Current Business.* Washington, DC: GPO.

_____. 2003. *National Income and Product Accounts of the United States.* Washington, DC: GPO. <http://www.bea.gov/bea/dn/nipaweb/index.asp> (accessed June 9, 2003).

U.S. Bureau of Labor Statistics. 2003. <http://www.bls.gov> (accessed June 16, 2003).

U.S. Department of the Treasury. 1984. *Tax Reform for Fairness, Simplicity and Economic Growth.* Washington, DC: GPO.

_____. 1992. *Report on Integration of the Individual and Corporate Tax Systems.* Washington, DC: GPO. <http://www.ustreas.gov/offices/tax-policy/library/integration-paper/ index.html> (accessed June 16, 2003).

_____. 2003. *General Explanations of the Administration's Fiscal Year 2004 Revenue Proposals,* Washington, DC, February. <http://www.ustreas.gov/offices/tax-policy/library/ bluebk03.pdf> (accessed June 10, 2003).

_____. Office of Tax Analysis. 1995. *A Preliminary Analysis of a Flat Rate Consumption Tax,* Washington, DC, March 7.

_____. Office of Tax Analysis. 1996. "'New' Armey-Shelby Flat Tax Would Still Lose Money, Treasury Finds." *Tax Notes* (January 22): 451–461.

_____. Office of Tax Analysis. 2002. *Long-Term Capital Gains and Taxes Paid on Long-Term Capital Gains, 1977–2000,* Washington, DC. <http://www.ustreas.gov/offices/tax-policy/library/capgain2-2002.pdf> (accessed June 12, 2003).

VandeHei, Jim, and Jonathan Weisman. 2003. "GOP Seeks to Change Score on Tax Cuts; Dynamic Method Can Cut Costs—and Backfire," *Washington Post,* February 6, A35.

Varian, Hal. 1980. "Redistributive Taxation as Social Insurance." *Journal of Public Economics* 14, no. 1 (August): 49–68.

"Vendor Collection of State Sales and Use Tax." 1993. *Tax Administrator News* 57 (August): 88.

Vescey, George. 1994. "Players Weren't the Only Ones Holding Paper Bags." *New York Times,* December 11, S5.

Vickrey, William. 1977. "Design of Taxes to Minimize Evasion." Paper presented at a conference on Tax Losses in Turkey and Preventive Measures, Istanbul, October.

Vos Savant, Marilyn. 1994. "Ask Marilyn." *Newsday* (New York) *Parade Magazine,* April 10, 12.

Warren, Alvin C. 1996. "How Much Capital Income Taxed under an Income Tax Is Exempt under a Cash Flow Tax?" *New York University Tax Law Review* 52 (Fall): 1.

Weisbach, David A. 2000. "Ironing Out the Flat Tax" *Stanford Law Review* 52, no. 3 (February): 599–664.

Whitney, Craig R. 1990. "London's Tax Riot Is Called the Work of a Violent Minority." *New York Times*, April 2, 11.

Wilson, John. 1999. "Theories of Tax Competition." *National Tax Journal* 52, no. 2 (June): 269–304.

Witte, John F. 1985. *The Politics and Development of the Federal Income Tax.* Madison: University of Wisconsin Press.

Wolff, Edward N. 2000. "Recent Trends in Wealth Ownership, 1983–1998." Jerome Levy Economics Institute Working Paper No. 300. Annandale-on-Hudson, NY: Levy Economics Institute of Bard College, April. <http://www.levy.org/docs/wrkpap/papers/300.html> (accessed June 9, 2003).

Wolfman, Bernard. 1998. "Reject Burden of Proof Shift, Urges Tax Prof." *Tax Notes* (February 9): 753–754.

Yitzhaki, Shlomo. 1974. "A Note on 'Income Tax Evasion: A Theoretical Analysis.'" *Journal of Public Economics* 3, no. 2 (May): 201–202.

Ziliak, James P., and Thomas Kniesner. 1999. "Estimating Life Cycle Labor Supply Tax Effects." *Journal of Political Economy* 107, no. 2 (April): 326–359.

Index